Moreton Morrell Site

Strategic Information Management

Books in the series

Strategic Information Management

Challenges and strategies in managing information systems

R. D. Galliers and B. S. H. Baker

BUTTERWORTH
HEINEMANN

To our parents

Tom and Bridie Baker
Will and Kath Galliers

Butterworth-Heinemann
Linacre House, Jordan Hill, Oxford OX2 8DP
225 Wildwood Avenue, Woburn, MA 01801-2041
A division of Reed Educational and Professional Publishing Ltd

A member of the Reed Elsevier plc group

OXFORD   BOSTON   JOHANNESBURG
MELBOURNE   NEW DELHI   SINGAPORE

First published 1994
Reprinted 1995, 1996, 1997, 1998

British Library Cataloguing in Publication Data
Galliers, Robert
   Strategic Information Management:
   Challenges and Strategies in Managing Information Systems -
   (Management Reader Series)
   I. Title   II. Baker, B. S. H.   III. Series
   658.4038

ISBN 0 7506 1731 4

Typeset by Deltatype Ltd, Ellesmere Port, Cheshire
Printed and bound in Great Britain by MPG Books Ltd, Bodmin, Cornwall

Contents

vi *Contents*

8 Sustaining information technology advantage: the role
of structural differences   167
E. K. Clemons and M. C. Row

9 Globalization and information management strategies   193
J. Karimi and B. R. Konsynski

10 Information technology and business process redesign   215
T. H. Davenport and J. E. Short

**Part Three   Some Further Management
Considerations**   241

11 Any way out of the labyrinth for managing
information systems?   247
B. R. Edwards, M. J. Earl and D. F. Feeny

12 Information technology outsourcing: a cross-sectional
analysis   263
L. Loh and N. Venkatraman

13 Organizational factors affecting the success of end-
user computing   282
P. H. Cheney, R. I. Mann and D. L. Amoroso

14 Power, politics and MIS implementation   297
M. L. Markus

15 Information resource management – a cross-cultural
perspective   329
R. I. Tricker

16 Information technology in the 1990s: managing
organizational interdependence   344
J. F. Rockart and J. E. Short

17 Managing information technology evaluation –
techniques and processes   362
L. Willcocks

Author index   383

Subject index   387

Contributors*

D. L. Amoroso, University of Colorado, Colorado Springs, USA (previously undertaking Doctoral research at the University of Georgia, Athens, Georgia, USA)

B. S. H. Baker, Warwick Business School, University of Warwick, Coventry, UK

R. I. Benjamin, Robert Benjamin Consultants, Rochester, New York and Center for Information Systems Research, Sloan School of Management, MIT, USA

J. Blunt, Information Technology Education Services, Waltham, Massachusetts, USA

P. H. Cheney, Department of Information Systems and Decision Sciences, College of Business Administration, University of South Florida, USA

T. D. Clark Jr, Department of Information and Management Sciences, Florida State University, USA

E. K. Clemons, Decision Sciences Department, The Wharton School, University of Pennsylvania, USA

T. H. Davenport, Center for Information Technology and Strategy, Ernst & Young, Boston, Massachusetts, USA

M. J. Earl, London Business School, UK (formerly with Oxford Institute of Information Management, Templeton College, Oxford University)

B. R. Edwards, Brian Edwards & Associates and Oxford Institute of Information Management, Templeton College, Oxford University, UK

D. F. Feeny, Oxford Institute of Information Management, Templeton College, Oxford, University, UK

R. D. Galliers, Warwick Business School, University of Warwick, Coventry, UK (formerly with Curtin University, Western Australia)

J. Karimi, University of Colorado, Denver, Colorado, USA

B. R. Konsynski, Harvard Business School, Boston, Massachusetts, USA

A. L. Lederer, School of Business Administration, Oakland University, Rochester, Michigan, USA

L. Loh, Faculty of Business Administration, National University of Singapore

R. I. Mann, School of Business, Virginia Commonwealth University, Virginia, USA

M. L. Markus, Claremont Graduate School, Claremont, California, USA

---

* Where contributors' institutions have changed since the publication of their article, both their current and previous affilations are listed.

(formerly with the Sloan School of Management, MIT, Cambridge, Massachusetts, USA)

J. F. Rockart, Center for Information Systems Research, Sloan School of Management, MIT, Cambridge, Massachusetts, USA

M. C. Row, Decision Sciences Department, The Wharton School, University of Pennsylvania, USA

V. Sethi, College of Business Administration, University of Oklahoma, USA

J. E. Short, Center for Information Systems Research, Sloan School of Management, MIT, Cambridge, Massachusetts, USA

E. K. Somogyi, The Farringdon Partnership, London, UK (formerly with PA Computers and Telecommunications)

A. R. Sutherland, Corporate Systems Planning, Perth, Western Australia

R. I. Tricker, Hong Kong Business School, University of Hong Kong, Hong Kong

N. Venkatraman, Sloan School of Management, MIT, Cambridge, Massachusetts, USA

L. Willcocks, Oxford Institute of Information Management, Templeton College, Oxford University, UK

Preface

This book has arisen from extensive research into the topics covered and literature referred to by those responsible for providing courses in the area of strategic information management in North American and European universities. It has also arisen from a personal review of the available literature on the part of the Editors in this and related topics, based on our own teaching and consulting experiences, and in the context of recent research[1] into the key issues facing executives in managing their information systems resources (i.e. informational, technical and human resources).

While the book will hopefully be of interest to executives who are tasked with the responsibility of obtaining business benefits from their investments in information technology, and who are concerned with the many complex and inter-related issues associated with managing the information systems resource, its primary audiences are MBA or other Masters level students and senior undergraduate students taking a course in strategic information management or something similar. Students embarking on research in this area should also find the book of particular help in providing a rich source of material reflecting recent thinking on many of the key issues facing executives in information systems management. One thing that should be made clear at the outset, however, is that the book assumes no particular expertise in the technical aspects of information systems. *Management* competence is the watchword!

It is, of course, impossible to cover all the relevant strategic information management issues in all their complexity in a book of readings of this kind. What we have attempted to achieve is to cover some of the more important aspects of the topic, while at the same time providing references to other important works. Similarly, there is bound to be debate as to why a particular paper has been selected for inclusion as opposed to a number of other possible alternatives. However, given the background research that informed the choice, and the fact that we have attempted to refer to some of the other important works in the field in the introduction to each part, we believe that we have covered as much of the ground as is possible in the available space. We hope you agree!

1   See, for example, Clark (1992), Craumer, *et al.* (1992), and Watson and Brancheau (1991).

The book is divided into three parts:

Part One An introductory section which attempts to set the scene for the remainder of the book by charting the progress that has been made in the world of business information systems and setting an agenda for strategic information management both now and into the future.

Part Two A section concerned with the burgeoning interest and literature in the strategic dimension of managing information systems and technology.

Part Three A third and final section which attempts to deal with some of the major management issues that have arisen of late, as well as those which have presented a continuing challenge to managements in organizing themselves in order to obtain value for money from their information technology investment. Examples of the former include such issues as outsourcing information systems services and the global opportunities information technology now provides. Examples of the latter include the organization of the information systems function and enabling, yet controlling, end-user computing.

Each part will now be described in somewhat greater detail so that the range of issues covered becomes more clear.

As indicated above, Part One is entitled *Setting the Scene* and aims to provide a foundation for the remainder of the text. The first chapter, by Elisabeth Somogyi and Bob Galliers, charts our progress in business information systems from the early days of operational data processing systems (such as accounts receivable/payable), through a period when attempts were made to provide executives with regular management control information, and on to the 1980s when the strategic promise afforded by advances in the technology was receiving considerable attention.

An overview of the issues facing senior executives, following in-depth interview research in the USA, is the subject of the second chapter. This is written by Tom Clark. A number of key themes are identified, which are picked up in Parts Two and Three of the book. These include organizational structures for the information systems function, the issue of end-user computing and information systems planning and strategy formation.

Chapter 3, by Bob Benjamin and Jon Blunt, takes us a step further by trying to identify the key issues that we need to face as the decade unfolds and as we approach the millennium. Computing power is growing at a frightening pace. Our ability to utilize this increased power, rather than limitations of the technology itself, is called into question. As a result, the key challenges that we as managers need to address are brought into sharper focus.

Chapter 4 is by Michael Earl. As in Chapter 3, a view of the future is provided, but this time the accent is on placing information technology in context, rather than centre stage. Changed attitudes – on the part of both business executives and information systems professionals alike – are called for if we are to harness the opportunities afforded by the technology and if we are to integrate information systems considerations into our business strategies and on-going management activities.

The first part of the book is brought to a close by a chapter contributed by Bob Galliers and Tony Sutherland. This provides a useful link with Part Two by reviewing the so-called 'stages of growth' concept as it has been applied to planning and managing information systems in organizations. Their use of the McKinsey '7S' model (see, for example, Pascale and Athos, 1981) in this context provides a useful foundation upon whch to build a consideration of the range of information systems management issues, dealt with in Part Three, as well as placing these in the context of the strategic considerations which are the focus of Part Two. All too often, information systems planning approaches do not adequately take into account the current situation with respect to the management and use of information technology in an organization: while the plan may be desirable, it may well not be feasible. The 'stages of growth' concept is useful in providing a means of assessing the current information systems context in any given organization, and thereby assisting in the development of feasible information systems plans and easing implementation issues.

Part Two picks up and expands on the strategic themes introduced in the final chapter of Part One. The first chapter in this part – Chapter 6 – is by Bob Galliers. In it he attempts to summarize much of the literature on the subject of strategic information systems planning, identifying key issues that have to be addressed and debunking some of the mythology that has grown out of the hyperbole that surrounded many of the so-called success stories of strategic information systems about which so much was written in the mid-1980s.

Chapter 7, by Al Lederer and Vijay Sethi, develops the information systems planning theme further and describes results from on-going research in the USA into the problems that still persist in obtaining a successful outcome from all the efforts that are put into the process. Constructive suggestions are made as to how many of these obstacles can be overcome.

Chapter 8 seeks to provide a more balanced perspective on the topic of strategic information systems – systems that are meant to provide the firm with a competitive advantage over its rivals. As indicated above, much of the literature of the mid-1980s – in both the popular press and the academic journals – was characterized by hyperbole. Clemons and Row, while accepting that advantage *may* arise from the application of IT, argue that this advantage can only be *sustainable* if IT is used to leverage differences in the firm's strategic resources. As a result of their analysis, useful advice is proffered as to the identification of opportunities to provide the necessary leverage.

The following chapter, by Jahangir Karimi and Benn Konsynski, develops the strategic theme further by focusing attention on the globalization aspects of a modern information systems strategy. Much of the literature of the 1980s focused attention on overtly aggressive competitive stances utilizing information technology. This chapter looks at coordination and partnership across organizational boundaries. It argues for a coherent strategy for alignment between a developing information technology architecture and an evolving global business strategy.

Part Two is brought to a close by a chapter on business process redesign (or business re-engineering) by Thomas Davenport and James Short – a subject close to the hearts of many a management consultancy in the late 1980s and early 1990s. While this is another topic which is in danger of being viewed in retrospect as one characterized by hyperbole, it is important that it is covered in a book such as this, given that strategic information management should not be viewed as simply being about the *introduction* of information systems into organizations, but the *integration* of such systems with business processes. The mere automation of ineffective processes will lead to possibly more efficient, but no less ineffective processes. More on this argument can be found in the introduction to Part Two itself. The inclusion of business process redesign in Part Two is meant to reinforce the point made in Chapter 6 that this should be considered as an integral part of information systems strategy formation and implementation.

Having set the scene for our topic and having dealt with its strategic aspects, there remain a number of additional issues concerned with managing and organizing information systems services that need to be covered. These are dealt with in Part Three.

Part Three commences with a chapter by Brian Edwards, Michael Earl and David Feeny. In it they analyse the range of internal organizational arrangements for information systems services that might be considered. As a result of their analysis they form the opinion that, while by no means a panacea, the federal model (combining as it does aspects of a centralized approach with business units containing and controlling some information systems capability) is one that is worth pursuing.

Chapter 12 extends the argument concerning the most appropriate organizational arrangements for information systems services to incorporate the possibility of outsourcing some or all of such services – a topic about which there has been considerable interest of late. Written by Lawrence Loh and N. Venkatraman, this chapter seeks to develop and test a model of the determinants of outsourcing in the information systems context, following research into fifty-five major US corporations.

One aspect of the debate regarding the extent to which control of information systems should be centralized or decentralized relates to the factors that impact on the success of end-user computing. Chapter 13, which is written by Paul Cheney, Robet Mann and Donald Amoroso, deals with this issue and reflects on the range of research that has been undertaken in this aspect of strategic information mangement during the 1980s. A number of propositions are put forward as to how organizations can improve the likelihood of success and avoid some of the pitfalls associated with uncontrolled end-user computing.

For computing projects to be successful, whether they are bought in, result from some central initiative, or are end-user induced, a key consideration is the manner in which they are implemented. In Chapter 14, Lynne Markus reviews three theories of information systems resistance with a view to showing how the underlying assumptions of each differ, with consequent differences in the implied recommendations for the implementation process.

The human dimension of our subject matter is taken a stage further by Bob Tricker in Chapter 15. In it he argues that cultural differences need to be taken into account in information systems design. Given the growing phenomenon of globalized information systems this is clearly an extremely important consideration, but one which can all too easily be overlooked. Tricker reminds us that the classical paradigms in information systems are rooted in Western thought. Using his experience of living and working in Hong Kong and the surrounding region, he reviews the characteristics and culture of Chinese business methods as a means of developing insights into the cultural aspects of information.

Chapter 16, by Jack Rockart and James Short, reviews the different impacts that the introduction of information technology can have on organizations. They focus attention on information technology's impacts on organizational structure; on the emergence of team-based, problem-focused working groups; on the opportunities for inter-organizational systems; and on the increasing incidence of integrated systems and improved, cross-functional communications. A key message to emerge from their analysis is the issue of managing organizational interdependence as a result of these impacts – collaborative information systems in other words.

The book is brought to an end by a chapter contributed by Leslie Willcocks. A wide-ranging set of strategic information management issues has been dealt with in the preceding chapters. One key issue that remains is concerned with evaluating information technology investments. Many companies are in a position where they are impelled to invest in information technology in order to compete in their market-place, but find that the economics apparently do not justify the investment. Willcocks reviews a number of approaches to evaluation and current practice in this regard. Suggestions are made to improve the situation, including the use of some non-traditional techniques which may not otherwise have been considered.

As you will now be aware, the subject of strategic information management is diverse and complex. It is not simply concerned with technological issues – far from it in fact. The subject domain incorporates aspects of strategic management, globalization, the management of change and human/cultural issues which may not at first sight have been considered as being directly relevant in the world of information technology. Experience, often gained as a result of very expensive mistakes (for example the London Stock Exchange's ill-fated Taurus System), informs us that without due consideration to the kind of issues introduced in this book, these mistakes are likely to continue. Disregard these messages at your peril!

One final point that cannot be understated is this. Strategic information management is a *management* responsibility. It is no longer reasonable – if it ever was – for executives to abrogate this responsibility to technicians. The sooner that managements realize that information systems are their responsibility, the more likely it is that real business benefits will accrue from the massive investment in the technology that is continuing to grow year in year out. Technical competence is a requirement, of course, whether it is available in-house or bought in, but it certainly is not sufficient for information systems success.

We hope you find this book of interest and that it raises some important issues that you will wish to consider in your own organizational context. The much-trumpeted 'information society' will be just another pipe dream if you don't!

Bob Galliers and Bernadette Baker

References

Clark, Jr, T D (1992). Corporate systems management: an overview and research perspective. *Communications of the ACM*, **35**(2), 61–75.

Craumer, M A, Buday, R S, Waite, T J and Walseman, S M (1992). *Critical Issues of Information Systems Management for 1992*, CSC Index, Cambridge, Mass., February.

Galliers, R D (ed.) (1992). *Information Systems Research: Issues, Methods and Practical Guidelines*, Blackwell Scientific, Oxford.

Galliers, R D, Merali, Y and Spearing, L (1994). Coping with information technology? How British executives perceive the key information systems management issues in the mid-1990s, *Journal of Information Technology*, **9**(1), March.

Grindley, K (1992). Information systems issues facing senior executives. *Journal of Strategic Information Systems*, **1**(2), March, 57–62.

Pascale, R T and Athos, A G (1981). *The Art of Japanese Management*, Penguin, Harmondsworth.

Watson, R T (1989). Key issues in information systems management: an Australian perspective – 1988, *Australian Computer Journal*, **21**(2), August, 118–129.

Watson, R T and Brancheau, J C (1991). Key issues in information systems management: an international perspective. *Information and Management*, **20**, 213–223. Also in R D Galliers (ed.) (1992), op cit., 112–131.

Part One
Setting the Scene

Although information systems of some form or another have been around since the beginning of time, information technology (IT) is a newcomer to the scene. The facilities provided by such technology have had a major impact on individuals and organizations. There are few companies that can afford the luxury of ignoring IT and few individuals who would prefer to be without it . . . despite its occasional frustrations and the fears it sometimes invokes.

An organization may regard IT as a 'necessary evil', something that is needed in order to stay in business, while others may see it as a major source of strategic opportunity, seeking proactively to identify how IT-based information systems can help gain them a competitive edge. Regardless of the stance taken, once an organization embarks on an investment of this kind there is little opportunity for turning back.

As IT has become more powerful and relatively cheaper, its use has spread throughout organizations at a rapid rate. Different levels in the management hierarchy are now using IT where once its sole domain was at the operational level. The aim now is not only to improve efficiency but also to improve business effectiveness and to manage organizations more strategically. As the managerial tasks become more complex, so the nature of the required information systems (IS) changes – from structured, routinized support to ad hoc, unstructured, complex enquiries at the highest levels of management.

IT, however, not only has the potential to change the way organizations work but also the very nature of its business. Through the use of IT to support the introduction of electronic markets, buying and selling can be carried out in a fraction of the time, disrupting the conventional marketing and distribution channels (Malone *et al* 1989). Electronic data interchange (EDI) not only speeds up transactions but allows subscribers to be confident in the accuracy of information being received from suppliers/buyers and to reap the benefits of cost reductions through automated reordering processes. On a more strategic level, information may be passed from an organization to its suppliers or customers in order to gain or provide a better service (Cash, 1985). Providing a better service to its customers than its competitors may provide the differentiation required to stay ahead of the competition in the short term. Continual improvements to the service may enable the organization to gain a longer-term advantage and remain ahead.

The rapid change in IT causes an already uncertain business environment to be even more unpredictable. Organizations' ability to identify the relevant information needed to make important decisions is crucial, since the access to data used to generate information for decision making is no longer restricted by the manual systems of the organization. IT can record, synthesize, analyse and disseminate information quicker than at any other time in history. Data can be collected from different parts of the company and its external environment and brought together to provide relevant, timely, concise and precise information at all levels of the organization to help it become more efficient, effective and competitive.

Information can now be delivered to the right people at the right time thus enabling well informed decisions to be made. Previously, due to the limited information gathering capability of organizations, decision makers could seldom rely on up-to-date information but instead made important decisions based on past results and their own experiene. This no longer needs to be the case. With the right technology in place to collect the necessary data automatically, up-to-date information can be accessed whenever the need arises. This is the informating quality of IT that Zuboff (1988) writes so eloquently about.

With the use of IT, as with most things, comes the possibility of abuse. Data integrity and security is of prime importance to ensure validity and privacy of the information being held. Managing the information involves identifying *what* should be kept, *how* it should be organized, *where* it should be held and *who* should have access to it. The quality of this management will dictate the quality of the decisions being taken and ultimately the organization's survival.

With the growth in the usage of IT to support information provision within organizations, the political nature of information has come into sharper focus. Gatekeepers of information are powerful people; they can decide when and if to convey vital information, and to whom. They are likely to be either highly respected, or despised for the power that they have at their fingertips.

Such gatekeepers have traditionally been middle managers in organizations. Their role has been to facilitate the flow of information between higher and lower levels of management. With the introduction of IT such information can now be readily accessed by those who need it (if the right IT infrastructure is in place) at any time. It is not surprising then that there is resistance to the introduction of IT when it has the potential of changing the balance of power within organizations. Unless the loss in power, through the freeing up of information, is substituted by something of equal or more value to the individuals concerned then IT implementations may well be subject to considerable obstruction. This political aspect of our subject matter is pursued further in Chapter 14.

Developments in IT have caused revolutionary changes not only for individual organizations but for society in general. In order to understand the situation we now find ourselves in with respect to IT, it is as well to reflect on their developments. This is the subject matter of Chapter 1. Written by Somogyi and Galliers, it describes how the role of IT has changed in business and how organizations have reacted to this change. They attempt, retrospectively, to identify major transition points in organizations' usage of IT in order to provide a chronicle of events, placing today's developments in a historical context. The chapter charts the evolution of the technology itself, the types of application used by organizations, the role of the DP/IS function and the change in the methods of system development. Such histories are not merely academic exercises, they can serve as a foundation for future progress, allowing organizations to avoid past mistakes and to build on their successes.

Since this chapter was first published, in 1987, there have of course been further developments, some of which are discussed in more detail elsewhere in the book. Others are not and so are discussed below.

1   The *object-oriented concept* involves the groupings of data and the program(s) that use that data, into self-contained functional capsules called objects. These objects can be regarded as 'building blocks' which can be put together with other objects to create new applications or enhancements to existing ones. Unlike previous system development tools and techniques the object-oriented concept allows for *growth* and *change*. The reusing of objects for different applications will not only increase development productivity but also will reduce maintenance and improve the overall quality of the software being produced. In particular, the object-oriented concept has significant practical implementation on distributed processing. Rymel (1993) identifies four strategic benefits arising from such applications: development of distributed applications is greatly simplified; objects can be reused in multiple environments; distributed objects facilitate interoperability and information shaing; and the environment supports multimedia and complex interactive applications. It has to be said, however, that a fundamental change in mindset is required to support a move to object-oriented applications. Planning and commitment of top management are needed in the long term as returns from this approach are unlikely to be gained in the shorter term. Systems

development staff must be retrained to cope with the new concept and to fully understand the benefits it can convey.

2   *Client-server architecture* is a distributed approach to the organization of the IT infrastructure in which two or more machines 'collaborate' in fulfilling a user's request. Although Benjamin and Blunt's chapter (Chapter 2) does discuss this concept they do so in passing, therefore a more detailed description of it and the management implications with respect to it; is given here. The typical scenario is for workstations to be connected to local file servers and for these servers in turn to be connected to a central mainframe. The applications are divided between the client computer (i.e. the terminal and its end user) and the server (i.e. a dedicated machine running an application). However, at this time there is no standard or specific approach that identifies how the applications should be divided between the client and the server. This type of architecture enables resources to be more evenly spread across the network, improving response time for local requests by using the user's workstation to run part of the application. Besides the increase in user productivy gained through the improved response time, client-server architecture also provides ease of use with the performance, data integrity, security and reliability of a mainframe. This enables the information to be managed more effectively and provides greater flexibility (by allowing incremental growth) and control. One of the major problems, as with all new technologies or concepts, is the problem of implementation. There is a shortage of programmers who are skilled in network computing (Martin, 1992) and there is still a question as to the cost savings obtained despite some evidence that shows a benefit larger than initially expected (Cafasso, 1993). A distributed computing architecture often requires a complete reorganization of the IS function (LaPlante, 1992) because migration to a client-server architecture normally means downsizing or rightsizing. Therefore the transition must be carefully planned. The implementation of a client-server architecture will require not only retraining end-users, systems professionals and micro-oriented staff but also the overhauling of the data networks to provide the speed, integrity and reliability required by a distributed system.

3   *Data communications* form the backbone of modern computing networks. Local area networks (LANS) allow individuals to share information, printers and programs, improving the quality and accessibility of crucial information. Wide-area networks (WANS) allow communication of information between dispersed facilities (e.g data centres or regional offices). There are two main problems associated with data communication between LANS and WANS: security and the management of local area network traffic across wide area networks. Encryption capabilities, public-private key algorithms and digital signatures are used to improve security helping to ensure that the information has not been tampered with during transmission. Integrated systems digital network (ISDN) promises to provide unprecedented flexibility in the interconnection of networks. ISDN is a way of transmitting data over the public telephone network without having to convert it to sound. This allows vast amounts of data to be sent down a telephone line very quickly and with a high level of accuracy. However, to make enterprise networking a reality requires the interoperability between disparate computer systems and networks. Electronic data interchange (EDI) seeks to address the former while value-added networks (VANs) seek to address the latter. Communication between organizations is possible through EDI. This is the standard technique which enables computers in different organizations to send business or information transactions successfully from one to the other, reducing paperwork and costs, improving lead times and accuracy of transactions. VANs provide two main services: first, they provide connectivity between the different types of networks in different organizations and second, they can provide different types of external information services to the organization, information that previously was too expensive and/or difficult for organizations to collect themselves which help management to make more informative decisions. The access to such external information has opened up new opportunities and threats that

previously did not exist due to the cost barriers imposed by data collection. Management now not only have to think more proactively about the type of data that needs to be gathered from within the organization to make their decisions but also what external information is available and how it should be exploited.

4   *Image processing* technology allows documents to be stored in the form of pictures or images. These images can be indexed for efficient retrieval and transferred from one computer to another. It can change the way firms support marketing, design products, conduct training and distribute information. Since image processing helps to improve work methods it can also play a key role in re-engineering an organization (see Chapter 10), thereby improving customer service and increasing productivity. It is reported that in the UK, 95 per cent of all business information is still held on paper (Ash, 1991). Storing this information in digitized form (normally on optical disk) can not only save floor space but can reduce labour costs and the time needed to search for and retrieve documents, improve data security, allow for multiple indexing of documents and eliminate the problem of misfiled or misplaced documents. It is also easy to integrate these electronic documents with related information and, whereas paper documents must be processed sequentially, electronic documents can be processed in parallel. Ash (1991) reports improvements in transaction volume per employee by 25-50 per cent and reductions in transaction times of between 50 and 90 per cent. Other reported savings are in staff reduction of up to 30 per cent and a reduction in the storage space requirements of up to 50 per cent. Image processing, however, suffers as do all of the areas mentioned in this section, from a lack of industry standards. In addition, there are legal issues that need to be resolved with respect to document authentication.

5   *Multimedia applications* combine full-motion video images with sound, graphics and text, and are based on the integration of three existing technologies, namely the telephone, television and computer. Besides offering users a more human interface with their data, multimedia applications enable organizations to improve their productivity and customer service through the incorporation of different types of data (e.g. video) into their organizational systems. Conferencing applications (e.g. video conferencing) will probably be the first to benefit from this technology, bringing people who are physically miles apart electronically together in the same room. The most sophisticated example of a multimedia application is called *virtual reality*. This application takes the use of multimedia to its extreme. Computer-generated, interactive three-dimensional images (complete with sound and images) are used to enable users to become embedded in the reality that is being created on the screen in front of them. Although most applications are still at the research and development stage (due to such limitations as adequate computer power and developments in networking) some are beginning to find their way to the market place. The opportunities open to business through this application will be vast. Virtual reality will be able to offer benefits to business in the areas of training, design, assembly and manufacturing. Products or concepts will be able to be demonstrated in a way that would normally be impossible due to cost, safety or perception restrictions. Electronic databases will be able to be manipulated by hand or body movements, network managers will be able to repair technical network error without even having to leave their chair. Employees will be able to experience real-life situations within the training environment. These are just some of the applications of this technology. However, once again, one of the main problems with development in this area is the lack of standards.

These are just some of the more important developments in technology that will have a major impact on the business in years to come. Executives must be made aware of the opportunities and threats of such technology and plan accordingly.

The next two chapters in Part One, the first by Clark and the second by Benjamin and Blunt, look respectively at the other issues that executives are facing today and those that are likely to become important in the future.

Over the last few years a number of surveys have been conducted in different countries to identify the major issues being faced by management with respect to IS (e.g. Dickson *et al.* 1984; Hartog and Herbert, 1986; Brancheau and Wetherbe, 1987; Niederman *et al.*, 1991; Watson and Brancheau, 1991; Broadbent *et al.*, 1992; Galliers *et al.*, 1994). Clark reviews the results of some of the surveys conducted in North America and describes, following in-depth interviews with senior IS executive, how they are dealing with the issues.

Clark identifies six major issues which are discussed in detail in the chapter. In brief these are: the evolution of the IS function; management of end-user computing; IS planning; IS evaluation; outsourcing; and management of the technology development process. These findings support those of Niederman *et al.* (1991) who identified two important trends in the types of issues being identified: first, the rising importance of technology infrastructure issues and second, the strong comeback of internal effectiveness issues. Clark's chapter is particularly interesting in that it discusses both the practical and research implications of the issues raised.

In 1982, Benjamin predicted the state of IT in the year 1990 (Benjamin, 1982). In Chapter 3, Benjamin and Blunt not only revisit the forecasts made a decade ago to see how accurate they were, but also look forward to the year 2000. They predict the key challenges management will have to face with respect to IT.

This chapter provides an interesting insight into the future and the sort of advances we could expect if IT carries on developing at the rate it has been doing. It discusses the fundamental technology and business drivers these predictions are based on, some of which are discussed in more depth elsewhere in the book, and the implications with respect to the role of the IS function in the organization and that of the individual IS worker. The chapter also provides a brief description of the 'buzz words' currently being used in the IS and general business environments.

There has been much hyperbole surrounding the use of technology in organizations especially during the 1980s. In the next chapter, Earl seeks to put IT in its proper place. The main thrust of the chapter is that organizations need to refocus on the business and away from IT *per se*. He concludes by suggesting six ways in which this refocusing can be achieved, namely:

- *Vision:* focus on rethinking the business rather than accepting futures focused around IT.
- *Planning:* looking for business themes for IT rather than developing IT strategies for the business.
- *Justifying:* focus on the costs and benefits of business rather than IT's costs and benefits.
- *Controlling:* IT expenditure should be regarded as a cost of the business and should therefore be part of most decision-making models throughout the organization.,
- *Organizing:* outsourcing and facilities management can limit the potential use of IS in the organization. The IS function should focus on providing business IT rather than becoming a business in its own right in order to ensure a better fit between itself and the main business activity.
- *Learning:* gaining a real understanding of IT and its potential should be integrated into management understanding through the organizational development processes.

The final chapter in Part One takes us back to the changing role of IS in organizations and provides not only a useful end point to this introductory section of the book but a useful link with the subject matter of Part Two, *The Strategic Dimension*. The changing nature, and associated management issues, of IT use in organizations has been a topic of considerable interest in the literature and a number of models have been developed in an attempt to reflect this change. The best known model is probably that of Gibson and Nolan (1974) in whch, based on a study of several large organizations, four '*stages of growth*' were identified. This model was later extended by Nolan (1979) who added a further two stages.

This six '*stages of growth*' concept has been investigated by a number of researchers to test its validity. While weaknesses have been identified (King and Kraemer, 1984) it is still a useful model in terms of charting the issues that need to be addressed in order to move from one stage to the next. Since each transition indicates a crisis point in managing IS within the organization, the model is useful in identifying issues that may arise and which can therefore be circumvented before they actually occur

Galliers and Sutherland's chapter, which brings Part One to a close, provides a summary of Nolan's stages of growth concept, together with others that have been developed over subsequent years. They go on to develop a revised model which addresses strategic, organizational and human resource issues arising in organizations associated with IT usage. Similar to previous growth models, their framework provides management with a tool to *analyse* their organization's current status with respect to each of the elements. The model helps to raise questions as to where the organization should be, having identified the type of role they see IT playing. One departure from previous models is their argument against the inclusion of a final, mature stage of growth: the ultimate goal of presumably all organizations. The optimal stage of growth for any specific organization will depend on the view/vision it has for IT, given their particular circumstances.

While these descriptive models provide a general overview of the major issues that need to be considered in relation to each stage, Galliers and Sutherland are at pains to point out that they do not provide solutions. What they do provide is a framework for a range of questions to be asked, and discussed, by management teams. A shared vision of the key management issues associated with IT is more likely to emerge as a result of such discussions.

Part One is an attempt to set the scene for the remainder of the book. It provides a view of the developments that have taken place in business usage of IT and it provides a vision of the future. Key information systems management issues are identified and an agenda which places IT in perspective is provided. A framework for assessing the current state of play with respect to IT and its management in one's organization is introduced as a precursor to the formulation of an IS strategy – a topic covered in some detail in Part Two.

References

Ash, N (1991). Document image processing: who needs it?, *Accountancy*, **108** (1176), August, 80–82.

Benjamin, R I (1982). Information technology in the 1990s: a long range planning scenario, *MIS Quarterly*, June, 11–31.

Broadbent, M, Hansell, A, Dampney, C N G and Butler, C (1992). Information systems management: the key issues for 1992. *Australasian SHARE/GUIDE Ltd Conference*, Sydney 31 August – 2 September.

Brancheau, J C and Wetherbe, J C (1987). Key issues in information systems management. *MIS Quarterly*, March, 23–45.

Cafasso, R (1993). Client-server strategies pervasive. *Computerworld*, **27** (4), 2 January, 47.

Cash, J I (1985). Interorganizational systems: an information society opportunity or threat. *The Information Society*, **3** (3), 199–228.

Dickson, G W, Leitheiser, R L, Nechis, M and Wetherbe, J C (1984). Key issues for the 1980s. *MIS Quarterly*, **8** (3), September, 135–159.

Galliers, R D, Merali, Y and Spearing, L (1994). Coping with information technology? Key information systems management issues in the 1990s: viewpoints of British Managers. *Journal of Information Technology*, **9** (1), March.

Gibson, C F and Nolan, R L (1974). Managing the four stages of EDP growth. *Harvard Business Review*, Januay-February, 76–88.

Hartog, C and Herbert, M (1986). 1985 opinion survey of MIS managers: key issues. *MIS Quartely*, December, 351–361.

King, J L and Kraemer, K L (1984). Evolution of an organizational information systems: an assessment of Nolan's stage model. *Communications of the ACM*, **27** (5), May, 466–475.

LaPlante, A (1992) Enterprise computing: chipping away at the corporate mainframe. *Infoworld*, **14** (3), 20 January, 40–42.

Malone, T W, Yates, J and Benjamin, R I (1989). The logic of electronic markets. *Harvard Business Review*, May–June, 166–172.

Martin, M (1992). Client-server: reaping the rewards. *Network World*, **9** (46), 16 November, 63–67.

Niederman, F, Brancheau, J C and Wetherbe, J C (1991) Information systems management issues for the 1990s. *MIS Quarterly*, **15** (4), December, 474–500.

Nolan, R L (1979). Managing the crises in data processing. *Harvard Business Review*, March–April, 115–126.

Rymer, J (1993). Distributed computing meets object-oriented technology. *Network World*, **10** (9). 1 March, 28–30.

Watson, R T and Brancheau, J C (1991) Key issues in information systems management: an international perspective. *Information and Management*, **20** (3), March, 213–223. Reprinted in R Galliers (ed.) (1992). *Information Systems Research: Issues, Methods and Practical Guidelines*. Blackwell Scientific, Oxford.

Zuboff, S (1988). *In the Age of the Smart Machine: The Future of Work and Power*, Butterworth-Heinemann, Oxford.

1 Information technology in business: from data processing to strategic information systems

E. K. Somogyi and R. D. Galliers

Introduction

Computers have been used commercially for over three decades now, in business administration and for providing information. The original intentions, the focus of attention in (what was originally called) data processing and the nature of the data processing effort itself have changed considerably over this period. The very expression describing the activity has changed from the original 'data processing', through 'management information' to the more appropriate 'information processing'.

A great deal of effort has gone into the development of computer-based information systems since computers were first put to work automating clerical functions in commercial organizations. Although it is well known now that supporting businesses with formalized systems is not a task to be taken lightly, the realization of how best to achieve this aim was gradual. The change in views and approaches and the shift in the focus of attention have been caused partly by the rapid advancement in the relevant technology. But the changed attitudes that we experience today have also been caused by the good and bad experiences associated with using the technology of the day. In recent years two other factors have contributed to the general change in attitudes. As more coherent information was made available through the use of computers, the general level of awareness of information needs grew. At the same time the general economic trends, especially the rise in labour cost, combined with the favourable price trends of computer-related technology, appeared to have offered definite advantages in using computers and automated systems. Nevertheless this assumed potential of the technology has not always been realized.

This paper attempts to put into perspective the various developments (how the technology itself changed, how we have gone about developing information systems, how we have organized information systems support services, how the role of systems has changed, etc.), and to identify trends and key turning points in the brief history of computing. Most importantly, it aims to clarify what has really happened, so that one is in a better position to understand this seemingly complex world of information technology and the developments in its application, and to see how it relates to our working lives. One word of warning, though. In trying to interpret events, it is possible that we might give the misleading impression that things developed smoothly. They most often did not. The trends we now perceive were most probably imperceptible to those involved at the time. To them the various developments might have appeared mostly as unconnected events which merely added to the complexity of information systems.

The early days of data processing

Little if any commercial applications of computers existed in the early 1950s when computers first became available. The computer was hailed as a mammoth calculating machine, relevant to scientists and code-breakers. It was not until the second and third generation of computers appeared on the market that commercial computing and data processing emerged on a large scale. Early commercial computers were used mainly to automate the routine clerical work of large administrative departments. It was the economies of large-scale administrative processing that first attracted the attention of the system developers. The cost of early computers, and later the high cost of systems development, made any other type of application economically impossible or very difficult to justify.

These first systems were batch systems using fairly limited input and output media, such as punched cards, paper-tape and printers. Using computers in this way was in itself a major achievement. The transfer of processing from unit record equipment such as cards allowed continuous batch-production runs on these expensive machines. This was sufficient economic justification and made the proposition of having a computer in the first place very viable indeed. Typical of the systems developed in this era were payroll and general ledger systems, which were essentially integrated versions of well-defind clerical processes.

Selecting applications on such economical principles had side effects on the systems and the resulting application portfolio. Systems were developed with little regard to other, possibly related, systems and the systems portfolio of most companies became fragmented. There was usually a fair amount of duplication present in the various systems, mainly caused by the duplication of interrelated data. Conventional methods that evolved on the basis of practical experience with developing computing systems did not ease this situation. These early methods concentrated on making the computer work, rather than on rationalizing the processes they automated.

A parallel but separate development was the increasing use of operational research (OR) and management science (MS) techniques in industry and commerce. Although the theoretical work on techniques such as linear and non-linear programming, queueing theory, statistical inventory control, PERT-CPM, statistical decision theory, and so on, was well established prior to 1960, surveys indicated a burgeoning of OR and MS activity in industry in the United States and Europe during the 1960s. The surge in industrial and academic work in OR and MS was not unrelated to the presence and availability of ever more powerful and reliable computers.

In general terms, the OR and MS academics and practitioners of the 1960s were technically competent, enthusiastic and confident that their discipline would transform management from an art to a science. Another general remark that can fairly be made about this group, with the wisdom of hindsight, is that they were naive with respect to the behavioural and organizational aspects of their work. This fact unfortunately saw many enthusiastic and well-intentioned endeavours fail quite spectacularly, setting OR and MS into unfortunate disrepute which in many cases prohibited necessary reflection and reform of the discipline (Galliers and Marshall, 1985).

Data processing people, at the same time, started developing their own theoretical base for the work they were doing, showing signs that a new profession was in the making. The different activities that made up the process of system development gained recognition and, as a result, systems analysis emerged as a key activity, different from O&M and separate from programming. Up to this point, data processing people possessed essentially two kinds of specialist knowledge, that of computer hardware and programming. From this point onwards, a separate professional – the systems analyst – appeared, bringing together some of the OR, MS and O&M activities hitherto performed in isolation from system development.

However, the main focus of interest was making those operations which were closely associated with the computer as efficient as possible. Two important developments resulted. First, programming (i.e. communicating to the machine the instructions that it needed to perform) had to be made less cumbersome. A new generation of programming languages emerged, with outstanding examples such s COBOL and FORTRAN. Second, as jobs for the machine became plentiful, development of special operating software became necessary, which made it possible to utilize computing power better. Concepts such as multi-programming, time-sharing and time-slicing started to emerge and the idea of a complex large operating system, such as the IBM 360 OS, was born.

New facilities made the use of computers easier, attracting further applications which in turn required more and more processing power, and this vicious circle became visible for the first time. The pattern was documented, in a lighthearted manner, by Grosch's law (1953). In simple terms it states that the power of a computer installation is proportional to the square of its cost. While this was offered as a not-too-serious explanation for the rising cost of computerization, it was quickly accepted as a general rule, fairly representing the realities of the time.

The first sign of maturity

Computers quickly became pervasive. As a result of improvements in system software and hardware, commercial systems became efficient and reliable, which in turn made them more widespread. By the late 1960s most large corporations had acquired big mainframe computers. The era was characterized by the idea that 'large was beautiful'. Most of these companies had large centralized installations operating remotely from their users and the business.

Three separate areas of concern emerged. First, business started examining seriously the merits of introducing computerized systems. Systems developed in this period were effective, given the objectives of automating clerical labour. But the reduction in the number of moderately paid clerks was more than offset by the new, highly-paid class of data processing professionals and the high cost of the necessary hardware. In addition, a previously unexpected cost factor, that of maintenance, started eating away larger and larger portions of the data processing budget. The remote 'ivory tower' approach of the large data processing departments made it increasingly difficult for them to develop systems that appealed to the various users. User dissatisfaction increased to frustration point as a result of inflexible systems, overly formal arrangements, the very long time required for processing changes and new requests, and the apparent inability of the departments to satisfy user needs.

Second, some unexpected side-effects occurred when these computer systems took over from the previous manual operations: substantial organizational and job changes became necessary. It was becoming clear that data processing systems had the potential of changing organizations. Yet, the hit and miss methods of system development concentrated solely on making the computers work. This laborious process was performed on the basis of ill-defined specifications, often the result of a well-meaning technologist interpreting the unproven ideas of a remote user manager. No wonder that most systems were not the best! But even when the specification was reasonable, the resulting system was often technically too cumbersome, full of errors and difficult to work with.

Third, it became clear that the majority of systems, by now classed as 'transaction processing' systems, had major limitations. Partly, the centralized, remote, batch processing systems did not fit many real-life business situations. These systems processed and presented historical rather than actual information. Partly, data was fragmented across these systems, and appeared often in duplicated, yet incompatible format.

It was therefore necessary to re-think the fundamentals of providing computer support. New theoretical foundations were laid for system development. The early trial-and-error methods of developing systems were replaced by more formalized and analytical methodologies, which emphasized the need for engineering the technology to pre-defined requirements. 'Software engineering' emerged as a new discipline and the search for requirement specification methods began.

Technological development also helped a great deal in clarifying both the theoretical and practical way forward. From the mid-1960s a new class of computer – the mini – was being developed and by the early 1970s it emerged as a rival to the mainframe. The mini was equipped for 'real' work, having arrived at the office from the process control environment of the shopfloor. These small vesatile machines quickly gained acceptance, not least for their ability to provide an on-line service. By this time the commercial transaction processing systems became widespread, efficient and reliable. It was therefore a natural next step to make them more readily available to users, and often the mini was an effective way of achieving this aim. As well as flexibility, minis also represented much cheaper and more convenient computing power: machine costs were a magnitude under the mainframe's; the physical size was much less; the environmental requirements (air conditioning, dust control, etc.) were less stringent and operations required less professional staff. The mini opened up the possibility of using computing power in smaller companies. This, in turn, meant that the demand grew for more and better systems and, through these, for better methods and a more systematic approach to system development.

Practical solutions to practical problems

A parallel but separate area of development was that of project management. Those who followed the philosophy that 'large is beautiful' did not only think in terms of large machines. They aspired to large systems, which meant large software and very large software projects. Retrospectively it seems that those who commissioned such projects had little understanding of the work involved. These large projects suffered from two problems, namely, false assumptions about development and inadequate organization of the human resources. Development was based on the idea that the initial technical specification, developed in isolation from the users, was infallible. In addition, 'large is beautiful' had an effect on the structure of early data processing departments. The highly functional approach of the centralized data processing departments meant that the various disciplines were compartmentalized. Armies of programmers existed in isolation from systems analysts and operators with, very often physical, brick walls dividing them from each other and their users. Managing the various steps of development in virtual isolation from each other, as one would manage a factory or production line (without of course the appropriate tools!) proved to be unsatisfactory. The initial idea of managing large computer projects using mass production principles missed the very point that no two systems are the same and no two analysts or programmers do exactly the same work. Production line management methods in the systems field backfired and the large projects grew manyfold during development, eating up budgets and timescales at an alarming rate.

The idea that the control of system development could and should be based on principles different from those of mass production and of continuous process management dawned on the profession relatively late. By the late 1960s the problem of large computing projects reached epidemic proportions. Books, such as Brooks's *The Mythical Man Month* (1972), likening system development to the prehistoric fight of dinosaurs in the tar-pit, appeared on the book-shelves. Massive computer projects, costing several times the original budget and taking much longer than the original estimates indicated, hit the headlines in the popular press.

Salvation was seen in the introduction of management method that would allow reasoned control over system development activities in terms of controlling the intermediate and final products of the activity, rather than the activity itself. Methods of project management and principles of project control were transplanted to data processing from complex engineering environments and from the discipline developed by the US space programme.

Dealing with things that are large and complex produced some interesting and far-reaching side-effects. Solutions to the problems associated with the (then fashionable) large computer programs were discovered through finding the reasons for their apparent unmaintainability. Program maintenance was difficult because it was hard to understand what the code was supposed to do in the first place. This, in turn, was largely caused by three problems. First, most large programs had no apparent control structure; they were genuine monoliths. The code appeared to be carved from one piece. Second, the logic that was being executed by the program was often jumping in an unpredictable way across different parts of the monolithic code. This 'spaghetti logic' was the result of the liberal use of the 'GO TO' statement. Third, if documentation existed at all for the prgram, it was likely to be out of date, not accurately representing what the program was doing. So, it was difficult to know where to start with any modification, and any interference with the code created unforeseen side effects. All this presented a level of complexity that made program maintenance problematic.

As a result of realizing the causes of the maintenance problem, theoreticians started work on concepts and methods that would help to reduce program complexity. They argued that the human mind is very limited when dealing with highly complex things, be they computer systems or anything else. Humans can deal with complexity only when it is broken down into 'manageable' chunks or modules, which in turn can be inter-related through some structure. The uncontrolled use of the 'GO TO' statement was also attacked, and the concept of 'GO TO-less' programming emerged. Later, specific languages were developed on the basis of this concept; PASCAL is the best known example of such a language.

From the 1970s onwards modularity and structure in programming became important and the process by which program modules and structures could be designed to simplify complexity attracted increased interest. The rules which govern the program design process, the structures, the parts and their documentation became a major preoccupation of both practitioners and academics. The concept of structuring was born and structured methods emerged to take the place of traditional methods of development. Structuring and modularity have since remained a major intellectual drive in both the theoretical and practical work associated with computer systems.

It was also realized that the principles of structuring were applicable outside the field of programming. One effect of structuring was the realization that not only systems but projects and project teams can be structured to bring together – not divide – complex, distinct disciplines associated with the development of systems. From the early 1970s, IBM pioneered the idea of structured project teams with integrated administrative support using structured methods for programming (Baker, 1972), which proved to be one of the first successful ploys for developing large systems.

From processes to data

Most early development methods concentrated on perfecting the processes that were performed by the machine, putting less emphasis on data and giving little, if any, thought to the users of the system. However, as more and more routine company operations became supported by computer systems, the need for a more coherent and flexible approach arose. Management need for cross-relating and cross-referencing data, which arises from basic operational processes, in order to produce coherent information and exercise better control, meant that the cumbersome, stand-alone and largely centralized systems operating in remote batch mode were no longer acceptable. By the end of the 1960s the focus of attention shifted from collecting and processing the 'raw material' of management information, to the raw material itself: data. It was discovered that interrelated operations cannot be effectively controlled without maintaining a clear set of basic data, preferably in a way that would allow data to be independent of their applications. It was therefore important to de-couple data from the basic processes. The basic data could then be used for information and control purposes in new kinds of systems. The drive for data independence brought about major advances in thinking about systems and in the practical methods of describing, analysing and storing data. Independent data management systems became available by the late 1960s.

The need for accurate information also highlighted a new requirement. Accurate information needs to be precise, timely and available. During the 1970s most companies changed to on-line processing to provide better access to data. Many companies also distributed a large proportion of their central computer operations in order to collect, process and provide access to data at the most appropriate points and locations. As a result, the nature of both the systems and the systems effort changed considerably. By the end of the 1970s the relevance of data clearly emerged, being viewed as *the* fundamental resource of information, deserving treatment that is similar to any other major resource of a business.

There were some, by now seemingly natural side-effects of this new direction. Several approaches and methods were developed to deal with the specific and intrinsic characteristics of data. The first of these was the discovery that complex data can be understood better by discovering their apparent structure. It also became obvious that separate 'systems' were needed for organizing and storing data. As a result, databases and database management systems (DBMS) started to appear. The intellectual drive was associated with the problem of how best to represent data structures in a practically usable way. A hierarchical representation was the first practical solution. IBM's IMS was one of the first DBMSs adopting this approach. Suggestions for a network-type representation of data structures, using the idea of entity-attribute relationships, were also adopted, resulting in the CODASYL standard. At the same time, Codd started his theoretical work on representing complex data relationships and simplifying the resulting structure through a method called 'normalization'.

Codd's funamental theory (1970) was quickly adopted by academics. Later it also became the basis of practical methods for simplifying data structures. Normalization became the norm (no pun intended) in better data processing departments and whole methodologies grew up advocating data as the main analytical starting point for developing computerized information systems. The drawbacks of hierarchical and network-type databases (such as the inevitable duplication of data, complexity, rigidity, difficulty in modification, large overheads in operation, dependence on the application, etc.) were by then obvious. Codd's research finally opened up the possibility of separating the storage and retrieval of data from their use. This effort culminated in the development of a new kind of database: the relational database.

Design was also emerging as a new discipline. First, it was realized that programs, their modules and structure should be designed before being coded. Later, when data emerged as an important subject in its own right, it also became obvious that system and data design were activities separate from requirements analysis and program design. These new concepts had crystallized towards the end of the 1970s. Sophisticated, new types of software began to appear on the market, giving a helping hand with organizing the mass of complex data on which information systems were feeding. Databases, data dictionaries and database management systems became plentiful, all promising salvation to the overburdened systems professional. New specializations split the data processing discipline: the database designer, data analyst, data administrator joined the ranks of the systems analyst and systems designer. At the other end of the scale, the programming profession was split by language specialization as well as by the programmer's conceptual 'distance' from the machine. As operating software became increasingly complex, a new breed – the systems programmer – appeared, emphasizing the difference between dealing with the workings of the machine and writing code for 'applications'.

Towards management information systems

The advent of databases and more sophisticated and powerful mainframe computers gave rise to the idea of developing corporate databases (containing all the pertinent data a company possessed), in order to supply management with information about the business. These database-related developments also required data processing professionals who specialized in organizing and managing data. The logical and almost clinical analysis these specialists performed, highlighted not only the structures of data but also the many inconsistencies which often exist in organizations. Data structures reflect the interpretation and association of data in a company, which in turn reflect interrelationships in the organization. Some data processing professionals engaged in data analysis work began to develop their own view of how organizations and their management would be transformed on the basis of the analysis. They also developed some visionary notions about themselves. They thought that they would decide (or help to decide) what data an organization should have in order to function efficiently, and who would need access to which piece of data and in what form.

The idea of a corporate database that is accurate and up to date with all the pertinent data from the production systems, is attractive. All we need to do – so the argument goes – is aggregate the data, transform them in certain ways and offer them to management. In this way a powerful information resource is on tap for senior management. Well, what is wrong with this idea?

Several practical matters presented difficulties to the naive data processing visionary who believed in a totally integrated management information system (MIS) resting on a corporate database. One problem is the sheer technical difficulty of deciding what should be stored in the corporate database and then building it satisfactorily before an organizational change, brought about by internal politics or external market forces or both, makes the database design and the accompanying reports inappropriate. In large organizations it may take tens of person-years and several elapsed years to arrive at a partially integrated MIS. It is almost certain that the requirements of the management reports would change over that period. It is also very likely that changes would be necessary in some of the transaction processing systems and also in the database design. Furthermore, assuming an efficient and well integrated set of transaction processing systems, the only reports that these systems can generate without a significant quantum of effort are historical reports containing aggregated data, showing variances - 'exception reports' (e.g. purchase orders for items over a certain value outstanding for more than a predefined number of days) and the like. Reports that would assist management in non-routine decision making and control would, by their nature, require particular views of the data internal to the organization that could not be specified in advance. Management would also require market data, i.e. data external to the organization's transaction processing systems. Thus, if we are to approach the notion that seems to lie behind the term MIS and supply managers with information that is useful in business control, problem solving and decision making, we need to think carefully about the nature of the information systems we provide.

It is worth nothing that well organized and well managed businesses always had 'systems' (albeit wholly or partly manual) for business control. In this sense management information systems always existed, and the notion of having such systems in an automated form was quite natural, given the advances of computing technology that were taking place at the time. However, the unrealistic expectations attached to the computer, fuelled by the overly enthusiastic approaches displayed by the data processing profession, made several, less competently run, companies believe that shortcomings in management, planning, organization and control could be overcome by the installation of a computerized MIS. Much of the later disappointment could have been prevented had these companies realized that technology can only solve technical and not management problems. Nevertheless, the notion that information provision to management, with or without databases, was an important part of the computing activity, was reflected by the fact that deliberate attempts were made to develop MISs in greater and greater numbers. Indicative of this drive towards supporting management rather than clerical operations is the name change that occurred around this time: most data processing departments became Management Services departments. The notion was that they would provide, via corporate databases, not only automated clerical processing but also, by aggregating and transforming such data, the information that management needed to run the business.

That the data processing profession during the 1970s developed useful and powerful data analysis and data management techniques, and learned a great deal about data management, is without doubt. But the notion that, through their data management, data aggregation and reporting activities, they provided management with information to assist managerial decision making had not been thought through. As Keen and Scott Morton (1978) point out, the MIS activity was not really a focus on management information but on information management. We could go further: the MIS activity of the era was concerned with *data* management, with little real thought being given to meeting management information needs.

In the late 1970s Keen and Scott Morton were able to write without fear of severe criticism that

> . . . management information system is a prime example of a 'content-free' expression. It means different things to different people, and there is no generally accepted definition by those working in the field. As a practical matter MIS implies computers, and the phrase 'computer-based information systems' has been used by some researchers as being more precise.

Sprague and Carlson (1982) attempted to give meaning to the term MIS by noting that when it is used in practice, one can assume that what is being referred to is a computer system with the following characteristics;

- an information focus, aimed at middle managers;
- structured information flows;
- integration of data processing jobs by business function (production MIS, personnel MIS, etc.); and
- an inquiry and report generation facility (usually with a database).

They go on to note that

> . . . the MIS era contributed a new level of information to serve management needs, but was still very much oriented towards, and built upon, information flows and data files.

The idea of integrated MISs seems to have presented an unrealistic goal. The dynamic nature of organizations and the market environment in which they exist forces more realistic and modest goals on the data processing professional. Keeping the transaction processing systems maintained, sensibly integrated and in line with organizational realities, is a more worthwhile job than freezing the company's data in an overwhelming database.

The era also saw data processing professionals and the management science and business modelling fraternities move away from each other into their own specialities, to the detriment of a balanced progress in developing effective and useful systems.

The emergence of information technology

Back in the 1950s Jack Kilby and Robert Noyce noticed the semi-conducting characteristics of silicon. This discovery, and developments in integrated circuitry, led to large-scale miniaturization in electronics. By 1971 microprocessors using 'silicon chips' were available on the market (Williams and Welch, 1985). In the 1978 they hit the headlines – commentators predicting unprecedented changes to business and personal life as a result. A new, post-industrial revolution was promised to be in the making (Tofler, 1980).

The impact of the very small and very cheap, reliable computers – micros – which resulted from building computers with chips, quickly became visible. By the early 1980s computing power and facilities suddenly became available and possible in areas hitherto untouched by computers. The market was flooded with 'small business systems', 'personal computers', 'intelligent work stations' and the like, promising the naive and the uninitiated instant computer power and instant solution to problems.

As a result, three separate changes occurred. First, users, especially those who had suffered unworkable systems and waited for years to receive systems to their requirements, started bypassing data processing departments and buying their own computers. They might not have achieved the best results but increased familiarity with the small machines started to change attitudes of both users and management.

Second, the economics of systems changed. The low cost of the small machines highlighted the enormous cost of human effort required to develop and maintain large computer systems. Reduction, at any cost, of the professional system development and maintenance effort was now a prime target in the profession, as (for the first time) hardware costs could be shown to be well below those of professional personnel.

Third, it became obvious that small dispersed machines were unlikely to be useful without interconnecting them – bringing telecommunications into the limelight. And many office activities, hitherto supported by 'office machinery' were seen for the first time as part of the process started by large computers – that is, automating the office. Office automation emerged, not least as a result of the realization by office machine manufacturers, who now entered the computing arena, that the 'chip' could be used in their machines. As a consequence, hitherto separate technologies – that of telephony, telecommunication, office equipment and computing – started to converge. This development pointed to the reality that voice, images and data are simply different representations of information and that the technologies that deal with these different representations are all part of a new complex technology: information technology.

The resulting development became diverse and complex: systems developers had to give way to the pressure exercised by the now not so naive user for more involvement in the development of systems. *End user computing* emerged as a result, promoting the idea that systems are the property of users and not the technical department. In parallel, the realization occurred that useful systems can only be produced if those who will use them take an active part in their development. Integrating the user became a useful obsession, helping the development of new kinds of systems.

It also became clear that a substantial reduction in the specialist manual activity of system development is necessary if the new family of computers, and the newly-discovered information technology, are to be genuinely useful. Suddenly, there were several alternatives available. Ready-made application systems emerged in large numbers for small and large machines, and *packages* became a fashionable business to be in. *Tools for system development,* targetting directly the end user and supporting end-user computing, were developed in the form of special, high-level facilities for interrogating databases and formatting reports. Ultra high-level languages emerged carrying the name 'fourth generation languages' (4GLs) to support both professional and amateur efforts at system development.

For the first time in the history of computing, serious effort was made to support with automation the manifold and often cumbersome activities of system development. Automated programming support environments, systems for building systems, analysis and programming workbenches appeared on the market, many backing the specialist methodologies which, by now, became well-formulated, each with its own cult following.

New approaches to system development

In addition, new discoveries were made about the nature of systems and system development. From the late 1960s it was realized that the development of a system and its operations can be viewed as a cycle of defined stages. The 'life-cycle' view of systems emerged and this formed the basis of many methods and methodologies for system development. It became clear only later that, while the view of a lifecycle was the correct one, a *linear* view of the life-cycle was counter-productive. The linear view was developed at the time when demand for large-scale systems first erupted and most practitioners were engaged mainly in development. The first saturation point brought about the shock realization that these systems needed far more attention during their operational life than was originally envisaged. As the maintenance load on data processing departments increased from a modest

20 to 60, 70 and 80 per cent during the 1970s, many academics and practitioners started looking for the reasons behind this (for many, undesirable and unexplained) phenomenon.

It was discovered that perhaps three different causes can explain the large increase in maintenance. First, the linear view of the life-cycle can be misleading. Systems developed in a linear fashion were built on the premise that successive deductions would be made during the development process, each such deductive step supplying a more detailed specification to the next one. As no recursive action was allowed, the misconceptions, errors and omissions left in by an earlier step would result in an ever-increasing number of errors and faults being built into the final system. This, and the chronic lack of quality control over the development process, delivered final systems which were far from perfect. As a result, faults were being discovered which needed to be dealt with during the operational part of the life-cycle, thereby increasing unnecessarily the maintenance load. It was discovered that early faults left in a system increase the number of successive faults in an exponential way, resulting in hundredfold increases in effort when dealing with these faults in the final system.

Second, there are problems associated with specifications. The linear life-cycle view also assumed that a system could be safely built for a long life, once a specification had been correctly developed, as adjustments were unlikely to be required provided the specification was followed attentively. This view had negated the possibility that systems might have a changing effect on their environment, which, in turn, would raise the requirement for re-tuning and readjusting them. The followers of this approach had also overlooked the fact that real business, which these systems were supposed to serve, never remains constant. It changes, thereby changing the original requirements. This, in turn, would require re-adjusting or even scrapping the system. Furthermore, the idea that users could specify precisely their requirements seems to have been largely a fallacy, negating the basis on which quite a few systems had been built.

Third, maintenance tends to increase as the number of systems grows. It is misleading to assume that percentage increase in the maintenance load is in itself a sign of failure, mis-management or bad practice. Progressing from the state of having no computer system to the point of saturation means that, even in a slowly changing environment and with precision development methods, there would be an ever-decreasing percentage of work on new development and a slow but steady increase in the activities dealing with systems already built.

Nevertheless, the documented backlog of system requests grew alarmingly, estimated by the beginning of the 1980s at two to five years worth of work in major data processing departments. This backlog evolved to be a mixture of requests for genuine maintenance, i.e. fixing errors, adjustments and enhancements to existing systems, and requirements for new systems. It was also realized that behind this 'visible' backlog, there was an ever-increasing 'invisible', undocumented backlog of requirements estimated at several times the visible one. The invisible backlog consisted largely of genuine requests that disillusioned users were no longer interested in entering into the queue.

As a response to these problems, several new developments occurred. Quality assurance, quality control and quality management of system development emerged, advocating regular and special tests and checks to be made on the system through its development. Walk-throughs and inspections were inserted into analysis, design and programming activities to catch 'bugs' as early (and as cheaply) as possible.

The notion that systems should be made to appeal to their users in every stage of development and in their final form encouraged the development of 'user friendly' systems, in the hope that early usability would reduce the requests for subsequent maintenance. Serious attempts were made to encourage an iterative form of development with high user involvement in the early stages, so that specifications would become as precise as possible. The idea of building a prototype for a requirement before the final system is built and asking users to experiment with the prototype before finalizing specifications helped the system development process considerably.

By now, the wide-ranging organizational effects of computer systems became clearly visible. Methods for including organizational considerations in system design started to emerge. A group of far-sighted researchers, Land and Mumford in the UK, Agarin in the USA, Bjorn-Andersen in Denmark, Ciborra in Italy and others, put forward far-reaching ideas about letting systems evolve within the organizational environment, thereby challenging the hitherto 'engineering-type' view of system development. For the first time since the history of computing began, it was pointed out that computerized information systems were, so to speak, one side of a two-sided coin, the other side being the human organization where these systems perform. Unless the two are developed in unison, in conjunction with each other, the end result is likely to be disruptive and difficult to handle.

Despite these new discoveries, official circles throughout the world had successively failed to support developments in anything but technology itself and the highly technical, engineering-type approaches (Land, 1983). It seems as though the major official projects were mounted to support successive problem areas one phase behind the time! For example, before micros became widespread, it was assumed that the only possible bottleneck in using computers would be the relatively low number of available professional programmers. Serious estimates were made that if the demand for new systems should increase at the rate shown towards the end of the 1970s, this could only be met by an ever-increasing army of professional programmers. As a result, studies were commissioned to find methods for increasing the programming population several-fold over a short period of time.* Wrong assumptions tend to lead to wrong conclusions, resulting in misguided action and investment, and this seems to be hitting computing at regular intervals. Far too much attention is paid in the major development programmes of the 1980s to technology and far too little attention is paid to the *application* of the technology.

New types of systems

The 1980s have brought about yet another series of changes. It has become clear that sophisticated hardware and software together can be targeted in different ways towards different types of application areas. New generic types of systems emerged on the side of data processing systems and MISs. Partly, it was realized that the high intelligence content of certain systems can be usefully deployed. Ideas originally put forward by the artificial intelligence (AI) community, which first emerged in the late 1950s as a separate discipline, now became realizable. Systems housing complex rules have emerged as 'rule-based' systems. The expressions 'expert systems' and 'intelligent knowledge-based systems' (IKBS) became fashionable to denote systems which imitate the rules and procedures followed by some particular expertise. Partly, it was assumed that computers would have a major role in supporting decision-making processes at the highest levels of companies and the concept of decision support systems (DSS) evolved. When remembering the arguments about management information systems, many academics and professionals have posed the question whether 'decision support system' was a new buzz word with no content or whether it reflected a new breed of systems. Subsequent research showed that the computerized system is only a small part of the arrangement that needs to be put in place for supporting top-level decision makers.

Manufacturers got busy in the meantime providing advanced facilities that were made available by combining office systems, computers and networks, and by employing the facilities provided by keypads, television and telecommunications. Electronic mail systems appeared, teleconferencing and videotex facilities shifted long-distance contact from the telephone, and – besides the processing of data – voice, text and image processing moved to the forefront. The emphasis shifted from the provision of data to the provision of information and to speeding up information flows.

---

*This approach is reminiscent of the famous calculation in the 1920s predicting the maximum number of motor cars ever to be needed on earth. The number was put at around 4 million on the basis that not more than that number of people would be found to act as chauffeurs for those who could afford to purchase the vehicles. It had never occurred to the researchers in this case that the end user, the motor car owner, might be seated behind the wheel, thereby reducing the need for career chauffeurs. Or that technological progress and social and economic change might reduce the need for specialist knowledge and the price and might also change the economic justification, factors which all affect the demand for motor cars.

Important new roles for information systems

The major task for many information systems (IS) departments in the early 1980s is making information available. The problems of interconnecting and exchanging information in many different forms and at many different places turned the general interest towards telecommunications. This interest is likely to intensify as more and more people gain access to, or are provided with, computer power and technologically pre-processed information.

As a result of recent technological improvements and changes in attitudes, the role of both data processing professionals and users changed rapidly. More systems were being developed by the users themselves or in close co-operation with the users. Data processing professionals started assuming the role of advisers, supporters and helpers. Systems were being more closely controlled by their users than was the practice previously. A new concept – the information centre – emerged, which aimed at supporting end-user computing and providing information and advice for users, at the same time also looking after the major databases and production systems in the background.

The most important result of using computer technology, however, was the growing realization that technology itself cannot solve problems and that the introduction of technology results in change. The impact of technological change depends on why and how technology is used. As management now had a definite choice in the use of technology, the technological choices could be evaluated within the context of business and organizational choices, using a planned approach. For this reason more and more companies started adopting a planned approach to their information systems. 'System strategy' and 'strategic system planning' became familiar expressions and major methods have been developed to help such activities.

It has been realized also that applying information technology outside its traditional domain of backroom effectiveness and efficiency, i.e. moving systems out of the back room and into the 'sharp end' of the business, would create, in many cases, distinct competitive advantage to the enterprise. This should be so, because information technology can affect the competitive forces that shape an industry by

- building barriers against new entrants;
- changing the basis of competition;
- changing the balance of power in supplier relationships;
- tying in customers;
- switching costs; and
- creating new products and services.

By the mid-1980s this new strategic role of information systems emerged. From the USA came news of systems that helped companies to achieve unprecedented results in their markets. These systems were instrumental in changing the nature of the business, the competition and the company's competitive position. The role of information systems in business emerged as a strategic one and IS professionals were elevated in status accordingly. At the same time the large stock of old systems became an ever-increasing burden on companies wanting to move forward with the technology.

More and more researchers and practitioners were pointing towards the need for linking systems with the business, connecting business strategy with information system strategy. The demand grew for methods, approaches and methodologies that would provide an orderly process to strategic business and system planning. Ideas about analysing user and business needs and the competitive impact of systems and technologies are plentiful. Whether they can deliver in line with the expectations will be judged in the future.

Summary

The role of computerized information systems and their importance in companies have undergone substantial transition since the 1950s. Over the same period both the technology and the way it was viewed, managed and employed changed considerably. The position and status of those responsible for applying the technology in various organizations have become more prominent, relevant and powerful, having moved from data processing, through management services, to information processing. At the same time, hitherto separate technologies converged into information technology.

As technology moved from its original fragmented and inflexible form to being integrated and interconnected, the management of its use in terms of both operations and system development changed in emphasis and nature. Computer operations moved from a highly regulated, centralized and remote mode to becoming more *ad hoc* and available as and when required. The systems effort itself progressed from concentrating on the programming process, through discovering the life-cycle of systems and the relevance of data, to more planned and participative approaches. The focus of attention changed from the technicalities to social and business issues.

Systems originally replaced clerical activities on the basis of stand-alone applications. The data processing department's original role was to manage the delivery and operation of these predominantly back-room systems. When data became better integrated, and more management-orientated information was provided, the management services departments started concentrating on better management of their own house and on making links with other departments and functions of the business which needed systems. This trend, combined with the increased variety and availability of sophisticated and easier to use technology, has led to the users taking a more active role in developing their own systems.

Lately, since it is realized that information is an important resource which can be used in a novel way to enhance the competitive position of business, information technology and information systems are becoming strategically important for business. Information systems are moving out of the back-room, low-level support position, to emerge as the nerve centres of organizations and competitive weapons at the front end of businesses. The focus of attention moved from being tactical to becoming strategic, and changed the nature of systems and the system portfolio.

It is evident that activity in the information systems field will continue in many directions at once, driven by fashion and market forces, by organizational need and technical opportunity. However, it appears that the application of information technology is at the threshold of a new era, opening up new opportunities by using the technology strategically for the benefit of organizations and businesses. It is still to be seen how the technology and the developers will deliver against these new expectations.

References

Baker, F. T. (1972) Chief programmer team management of production programming. *IBM System Journal*, Spring.

Brooks, F. R., Jr. (1972) *The Mythical Man-Month*. Addison-Wesley.

Codd, E. F. (1970) A relational model of data for large shared data banks. *Communications of the ACM*, **13**, 6.

Galliers, R. D. and Marshall, P. H. (1985) *Towards True End-User Computing: From EDP to MIS to DSS to ESE*. Western Australian Institute of Technology, Bentley, W. A.

Grosch, H. R. J. (1953) High-speed arithmetic: the digital computer as a research tool. *J. Opt. Soc. Am.*, April.

Keen, P. G. W. and Scott Morton, M. S. (1978) *Decision Support Systems: An Organisational Perspective*. Addison-Wesley.

Land, F. F (1983) Information Technology: The Alvey Report and Government Strategy. An Inaugural Lecture. The London School of Economics.

Sprague, R. H. and Carlson, E. D. (1982) *Building Effective Decision Support Systems*. Prentice Hall.

Tofler, A. (1980) *The Third Wave*. Bantam Books.

Williams, G. and Welch, M. (1985) A microcomputing timetable. *BYTE*, **10**, 9, September.

Reproduced from Somogyi, E.K. and Galliers, R. D. (1987). Applied information technology: from data processing to strategic information systems. *Journal of Information Technology*, **2** (1), March, 30-41. Reprinted with permission.

2 Corporate systems management

T. D. Clark Jr

A number of recent papers and articles have dealt with the views of information systems (IS) managers about the important issues facing them [5,9]. These studies typically involve survey techniques that do not allow in-depth exploration of the issues identified. A difficulty encountered in survey research is understanding why the executives view the issues as important and exactly how to advance knowledge about management of the issues. The research reported in this chapter was intended to provide not only a view of some of the more important issues, but to place them into a research perspective and explore why the issues are important. To accomplish this, detailed structured interviews with a select group of senior IS executives were conducted.

The material in this chapter deals with the views of this group about the key issues facing them, how the executives deal with the issues and how they manage and develop IS resources relative to the issues. The research was guided by two specific objectives. The first was to provide a composite, senior management view of several of the major IS management issues being considered by IS researchers or identified in the previous referenced surveys. These included dispersion of IS resources and management responsibility, end-user computing management, IS planning, the IS management infrastructure, outside services management and the management and control of technology. The second objective was to develop frameworks for understanding the issues in the corporate context and to use the frameworks to suggest specific research questions important both to IS executives and academics.

This chapter is organized into three sections, the first of which deals with the specific research methodology. The second section 'Systems Management Issues,' contains a synthesis of the insights gained from the structured interviews. The last section, 'Conclusions and Research Directions,' contains a proposed research agenda derived from the interview data.

Structured interview methodology

A structured interview methodology based on Kerlinger's [11] principles was chosen to provide the opportunity for ample discussion of material that might be peculiar to a specific subject, organization or industry. Interviews allow for extended development of ideas introduced in the process without constraining the exploration of material that initially was not included in a research plan. Given the objectives in this research, this methodology was most appropriate. While the interview technique has great flexibility, its major drawback is the difficulty involved in control of the discussions and topics introduced. To counter this problem, the key to effective interview research is a well-developed interview guide.

Using extensive research journal references as well as other sources, a detailed interview guide was developed, validated, and subsequently employed to manage the interview process. The principles suggested by Kerlinger [11] were employed to steer construction of the guide which was organized into three major sections dealing with *corporate systems management, outside services management and management of the technology development process.* It is from the discussion of these areas that an understanding of the major issues evolved.

After a methodology had been selected, the individuals to interview were selected. The process began with development of a list of 300 companies primarily in the southeastern United States. From the initial list, 40 companies were selected. This selection was judgmentally made to provide a balance between size based on revenue (or assets), profitability, the number of employees, the geographical setting (urban, suburban, rural) and industry type. Some of the companies declined to participate and interviews could not be arranged with managers from others resulting in a final sample of 30 companies. The senior IS executive from each of these companies was interviewed. As expected, the title given this individual varied widely. He or she was called either the Chief Information Officer, the Chief Financial Officer, the Director of Information Systems, the Vice President for Information Systems or the Director of Data Processing. There was no pattern in the titles. Given the selection criteria, 30 people provided an adequate number to ensure a balance and yield valid data.

Before contact was made with any company, data about the company was compiled from references such as *Dun & Bradstreet Reports, Standard & Poor's Reports, Value Line Reports* and from popular business publications such as *The Wall Street Journal, Forbes, Business Week* and *Fortune.* The interview guide was adapted to each company based on the material gathered in this phase.

The issues discussed in the next section of this article were developed from the data gathered using the guide in the interview process. After each interview, the notes taken during the conference were reviewed and a detailed overview of the discussions written. These detailed summaries along with other materials gathered (strategic plans, budgets, organizational charts) were analyzed with a focus on cataloging common themes and issues. The remainder of this chapter contains a report of this analysis focused on the important issues and management concerns.

Systems management issues

There were six issues that dominated the discussions with the IS executives. The first was the evolution of the IS organizational structure stemming from the dispersion of IS management and resources, the second was the management of end-user computing, the third was IS planning and the link between IS and business functions, the fourth was the measurement of the effectiveness of the IS infrastructure, the fifth was the management of outside services and the last was management of the technology development process. Each of these will be discussed in detail in the following subsections of this article.

Organizational structures for IS management

The functional placement of MIS operations varied considerably across organizations, and there was little evidence that the concepts associated with the title Chief Information Officer existed in any of the organizations, even when the title was in fact used. Typically, the MIS function remained in the financial reporting line even when a vice president of MIS existed or the head of IS reported to the Chief Operating Officer. The placement of the function was not an important issue to the people interviewed, but the functions and the responsibilities assigned to the centralized IS function were of concern. The responsibilities differed considerably, however, depending on organizational placement.

The most significant structural issue has to do more with the size and responsibilities of the IS function than with its placement. There was a consensus that the size of the central IS function had decreased significantly in the past several years and would continue to do so at an even faster pace. The managers felt this stemmed principally from a *shift in the primary function of the central organization from systems design and development to systems integration and from the role of developer to that of advisor.* They agreed that the changes provided an environment where certain types of people are no longer required in the same numbers they had been in the past. In the evolving organization, a significant amount of emphasis was placed on training the IS professional as a business manager rather than as a technical expert and on the need to recruit people proficient in business functions. This was seen as necessary to be effective in the integrator and advisor roles. Most people felt that the role of the CIO, if the concept survived, would evolve to that of a bridge person between the technological community and the business functional managers.

A composite picture of the IS management structures seen in the organizations is shown in Table 1. Some form of this tier structure was repeatedly described and the concepts shown in the table used to characterize the elements included in the table. Most of the organizations retained some form of a centralized IS function, but most of the managers encouraged, where possible, a dispersed or a decentralized approach to the management of information systems. In some cases, decentralization was used to describe what actually was dispersion which involves placing IS resources in business functional areas but retaining control of them in the central IS function. Decentralization is the assignment of resources, responsibility and authority to the business functions. *Dispersion was much more common than decentralization, although decentralization was observed.*

There was little evidence of a strong trend to match the structure of the IS

Table 1 Organizational structure

The number and name	*Concept*

1   End-User Computing
        User Autonomy
        (Type 1)
	Equipment (primarily microcomputers) is purchased without articulation of corporate standards. The user is fully responsible for design and support of systems. The user totally controls the budget.

User Partnershp (Type II)	Equipment and software are purchased by the user using a corporate standard. Applications are devoloped by the user. Systems training and support are given by the IS function. Budget responsibility is shared.
Central Control (Type III)	Equipment and Software are purchased by the IS function. Applications are developed by both the user and IS staff. The IS staff provides support and training. The budget is controlled by the IS function.
II Corporate Systems Decentralized	The IS function supports the organizational infrastructure (computers, peripheral equipment and communications) located throughout the organization. The operating functions are responsible for applications, systems design and implementation. Budget responsibility is shared and the user has full control of the requirements specification process.
Centralized	The IS function operates and manages all computing resources which are usually located centrally. The IS function controls the budget.
Dispersed	The central IS function supports and operates all computing resources which are distributed throughout the organization. The IS function is responsible for applications, systems design and implementation. The IS function controls the budget.
III Executive Information	Specialized systems developed for management of the enterprise. The responsibility and budget for these systems is shared by the IS function and executives involved. The systems are primarily data driven and graphically oriented.

organization to that of other organizational elements [15]. Even when the company had or professed a decentralization strategy, the IS function remained *a centralized staff function*. The corporate function was most concerned with traditional transaction processing systems that typically deal with accounting, routine administrative and personnel functions. A subsequent discussion of end-user computing will address this issue more fully. An analysis of corporate economic data, organizational size and industry characteristics showed no significant indicators that might be used to predict the type of organizational structure.

The placement of the authority and responsibility for development and implementation of information systems did, however, vary somewhat depending on the type of system, the type of equipment used for a system and the characteristics of the organization. But as noted, the responsibility for system development or integration still largely resided in the central IS function. Many executives discussed efforts to make the user more responsible for development and at times, for management of the implementation of systems. In fact, in one organization, the functional managers were free to contract with the internal IS function or an outside service for a system that would be implemented fully within the function. There was agreement that central IS control of systems that are of 'core importance' to the organization or those that cut across functional lines would remain strong. To make any definitive statements about dispersion/decentralization trends would be difficult without a much more extensive data set.

There was strong evidence from the statements of the managers, however, that more and more frequently the user of a system was given both the authority and responsibility for management of development, usually through chairing a 'steering committee' for a project. Such committees were composed of a variety of people depending on the type of system. Regardless of their compostion, they generally had both budget and operational control of the project. Rockart [21], as well as a number of others, and some of those interviewed (40%), believed that such trends contribute to a decline in the size of the IS organization and evolution of its role to that of 'advisor' rather than 'implementor' of systems. A second contributor to the shrinkage of the IS function was identified by several managers as the increasing use of IS productivity tools.

The evolution described by the managers also suggested that the central IS function will be increasingly responsible for managing the infrastructure for decentralized or dispersed computing that includes telecommunications, office systems, software and hardware. This was not true in the majority of the organizations in the study, but was seen by a majority of managers as the direction of movement. In discussing the determinants of evolution toward dispersion/decentralization of resources with centralized infrastructure management, several respondents identified the major detractors to be loss of economies of scale and diffusion of expertise. Most felt that these may be increasingly less important concerns, depending on how rapidly technology advances and systems literacy develops. The effectiveness of the IS function as a manager of infrastructure also was seen to depend, to a large degree, on how the organization integrated IS and business planning.

For the sample in this study, the user was fully responsible for the entire system development and management life cycle for highly specialized functions and applications. The IS function simply provided some technical systems advice and the computer cycles necessary to operate the system. Examples were found in the production functions of several companies. Responsibility for automated manufacturing and control systems resided fully with the production manager who had, in at least two cases, employed his own IS manager within the function. Some felt that this trend probably is reinforced by the reluctance or inability of IS managers to employ the types of people necessary to define and develop the variety of specialized systems that are possible in a diverse business environment. One manager, for example, described a project that required extensive simulation modeling in which he could not even fill an advisor's role or afford to employ an individual to do so.

In summary, there was a consensus that the tremendous growth in end-user computing has contributed to a changing role for the IS function. The development of end-user computing (EUC) reinforces the noted trends of reduced IS size, change in function and decentralization of authority and responsibility for systems development and management – this will be discussed next.

End-user orientation vs. centralized management

The second area that virtually all of the managers identified as important was the method used to manage and control end-user computing in the organization. From the outset, it was clear that the term 'end-user computing' meant very different things to different people. Some employed it in the same sense as that in the IS literature where the focus is on stand-alone microcomputing [10, 22]. Others used the term in discussion of decentralization and dispersion. For the managers in the sample, the term was not used to denote user microcomputing but more broadly to describe the involvement of users in the responsibility for design, development and implementation of systems.

There had been a tremendous growth (50-90% per year) in both end-user orientation and micro-computing in all of the firms surveyed. For example in one organization, 60% of the total IS capital budget was controlled by line managers in various operations and staff functions. The majority of the budget was devoted to development of end-user applications and support. According to Rockart and Flannery [22], such extraordinary growth is due in large part to improvements which make EUC more feasible and less costly, a vastly increased awareness of EUC potential, the need for a variety of information quickly, and dissatisfaction with traditional methods. The majority of the executives agreed with that view.

In only two cases were the early growth of EUC and the proliferation of microcomputers managed by the corporate IS staff. In both of those organizations, the managers felt confident that decentralized, end-user-oriented computing was being adequately managed, but in all other cases, there was some question about both effective control and the investment involved. Most of the IS managers simply felt it was impossible to manage the proliferation. This contributed to their articulation of the tiered concept of IS organization for the company. End-user computing was always defined as 'tier one,' but the concepts associated with tier one varied according to the patterns previously introduced in Table 1.

The predominant model for microcomputing was Type 1. Within this environment there were some Information Centers, but the trend toward disbanding the centers and reassigning the people to either users' organizations or the IS function was apparent [8]. The preponderance of the Type 1 model is probably a primary reason that most of the managers identified EUC as a very important issue and one that demanded their attention. It just was not clear to them how EUC would evolve in many of the organizations. With a large investment of IS resources in this area, the managers were understandably concerned. Very few of the companies had a strategy for managing Type 1 end-user computing. As a result, the managers were dissatisfied with operations in this area. Especially important was the ability to assess the impact that the advance in end-user technology might have on both traditional information management methods and the organization of centralized MIS functions.

End-user computing obviously will become increasingly important as the desktop computer becomes more and more powerful and end users become more proficient at developing their own systems. Most agreed that the movement in end-user computing may never replace the large, transaction-processing system, but many decision applications and management reporting tasks that have been major systems tasks will no longer be done with large computers. At least one study of EUC evolvement links development patterns to organizational characteristics and accompanying theory [20]. Extensive research, however, would be required to show the links between organizational characteristics and EUC patterns [20–22]. There were no such patterns evident in the companies of this study.

Even though there has been an explosion of general software (database managers, spreadsheets, graphics and presentation generators) for microcomputers, the majority of the managers identified this as an underdeveloped area in the market. Given the continued proliferation of such software and the continued decline in the cost of hardware, more systems will be developed in some type of a decentralized setting. There was a consensus that as the power of small computers grows, their use in new settings will become even more evident and important.

IS planning and structure

For a number of years, the prevalent model of systems structure has been hierarchical and appears often in the form shown in Figure 1. As portrayed, there are three levels of systems that roughly correspond to the management levels of the organization. At the strategic level, systems are predominantly either decision support systems (DSS) or executive information systems (EIS). The EIS is data-driven with graphical representation of the data created on-demand a key feature. The DSS generally deals with a specific problem domain and contains a modelling component as well as a data management capability. At the operational control or middle level of an organization, the systems are for managerial control (budgeting, manufacturing) or for specific decision support in a problem domain (financial management, logistics management). Many operational control systems are embedded in the production technology of the firm and are variance-oriented. The transactional level contains the more traditional IS applications such as personnel systems, accounting systems (general ledger, chart of accounts, billing, ordering) and integrated logistics systems (inventory management, transportation). This model is, of course, very broad, but served as a convenient vehicle for discussion of planning and infrastructure issues, as well as for other topics presented later in this chapter.

The majority of systems discussed either were large transaction-processing systems or systems dealing with operational control or production. Such systems were the focus of IS management in virtually all of the organizations. There were very few true decision support or executive information systems. The majority of the managers felt that the production of transaction-type systems was mature and well understood. This produced confidence that

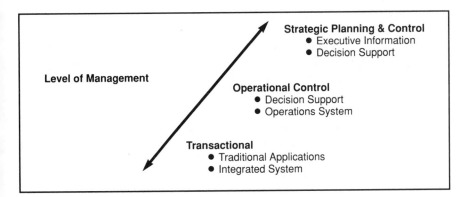

Figure 1. Traditional system view

when such systems were required, they could be effectively delivered. *Most agreed that the next important frontier in systems was executive support.* Although the concept of an EIS was not well understood, all but one executive believed it was a very important area. In that one organization, a decision had been made to avoid development of EIS because of the investment and concern that senior managers simply would not use the product. Even here, the executive believed this was not a closed issue.

Although the organizations in the study were quite diverse, there was a surprising consistency in the description of an organization's systems strategy. Most of the executives described some variation of a four-level, integrated hardware and systems strategy. In reality, the strategy was very narrowly implemented, dealing more with the types of machines than with the types and placement of systems and applications. The four 'levels' or components mentioned most often were mainframe, mini-(mid-range), and microcomputers and communications systems. Most felt that the key to having an effective systems strategy was integration of these components and the focus of software on 'business problems.' No one spoke of a systems strategy in terms of the diagram shown in Figure 1 or in a broad sense of its relationship to organizational strategy [3].

A clear majority of the companies are seeking better ways to tie IS planning to the normal business planning of the organization. This is an increasingly important topic as the modern organizational form continues to evolve. Although there were several different methods used to accomplish this, most involved the formal integration of users into the planning and management process of systems. A prevalent method was the use of a steering committee for the IS function comprised of the senior executives of the major functional areas of the organization. The effort was to have the area vice presidents plan both for business initiatives and systems simultaneously. In reviewing the data gathered for each organization, it was apparent that when the steering committee method was labeled '*effective,*' there was a *formal (documented) cyclic planning process.*

The link with business planning was strongest in the transaction-processing area. This could be expected because many of the initiatives here had documented efficiency goals that strongly depended upon IS support. There was an effort, in these organizations, to leverage IS for some type of competitive advantage or to link new systems to reduced administrative costs. About half the organizations linked IS initiatives to reduction of personnel although there was rarely a 'personnel payoff model' used to justify the introduction of new systems.

In about half of the organizations, IS managers arranged the systems development area into 'enterprise zones' that were linked to the key functions of the business. IS functional experts were either hired or developed in business areas such as marketing and production. These people were not necessarily traditional systems analysts who developed through the

IS function as programmers or technocrats, but rather were business managers who possessed knowledge of (or had) IS skills. These were the individuals primarily responsible for IS planning. In three cases, the senior IS executive did not rise through the IS channel but came to the area as either the vice president or as a director who shortly became the vice president. This is perhaps the strongest evidence to support the conclusion that firms are serious about integrating the systems function into the business planning cycle.

Technology planning has been dealt with in both the popular press and in academic journals [4]. This material was used as a basis for discussion of the topic. The emphasis repeatedly was placed on open-systems architecture and industry standard platforms. Integration of existing technology was a major issue as was migration of older data management models to new database management technology. These issues will be discussed later in this chapter.

IS infrastructure effectiveness measurement

The work of Bjern-Anderson and Davis [2] and Kleijnen [14] are representative of the extensive literature addressing an appropriate methodology to employ in assessing the effectiveness of an organization's information infrastructure and providing a real measure of success or failure. This problem is quite different from simply providing a cost-benefit analysis for separate IS projects. The latter problem is difficult enough, but when the contribution made by the enterprise-system infrastructure to the profitability or productivity of the organization must be determined, the problem becomes virtually impossible to solve. As impossible as it may seem, the majority (78%) of the executives were faced with answering the Chief Executive Officer's question, 'What does IS contribute to the bottom line?' Even though all felt IS effectiveness evaluation was becoming increasingly important and necessary and the majority had been asked the question, only one executive in the study had initiated a project to devise a method for solving the problem.

Since the current IS literature provides very little specific guidance on the topic, considerable additional research work in this area is required. The literature does, however, identify some of the major areas that must be assessed and suggests some representative measures. The work of Campbell [6] is representative of this literature. The major areas are presented in Table 2. The approach suggested is to provide performance measures in each of the major functional areas of a business firm and in each area to link the measures to the information necessary for effective managerial decision making and planning. Identifying these links is, of course, what makes the problem a difficult one.

There are, of course, a number of other measures that might be employed, but the ones in the table were discussed to one degree or another with each manager. Most managers simply did not deal with any of them except the

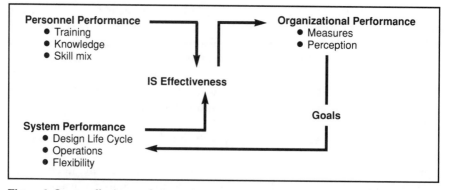

Figure 2. System effectiveness framework

technical performance variables and the performance indicators for the computer and communications systems. Technical performance assessment was generally done through statistical process control and monitoring packages that are a part of a computer's software environment. Most believed this to be quite important but of limited value when addressing the question of the contribution of the enterprise IS to overall, organizational performance.

Based on the data in Table 2, the systems effectiveness framework shown in Figure 2 was developed. It was discussed in detail with the managers who said they had been asked the question about the IS contribution to the enterprise. Most agreed that such a framework was a useful way to approach the problem, but that the measurement and linkage issues would make it difficult to test. This is an obvious area for more extensive study.

A number of the executives (40%) felt that the assessment of systems at the enterprise level was not useful because of the difficulties involved. Their assumption was that if each systems project was evaluated on a cost-benefit basis the sum of the projects was by definition, beneficial and effective. Although this may be an appealing argument, it ignores subsystem interfaces and the issues of synergy and suboptimization identified in the literature [14]. Such things can either detract from or add to the effectiveness of the overall organization.

For a number of the managers, the preferred method to assess effectiveness, especially for administrative systems, was to track personnel levels. These executives felt that if the total number of people in the firm (or an area of it) was declining over time, the information system was making a contribution to efficiency. In no case, however, was there a systematic method employed to show direct linkages between the information system and personnel levels.

Finally, almost half (48%) of the managers used some method to compare their operations to those of other companies in their industry. This was done formally in some cases and informally in others. The formal methods involved comparing their figures for such elements as percentage of sales invested in IS and total IS investment to industry averages. The informal methods involved talking to other executives in their industry about their experiences and directions. Most were unwilling to discuss what specifically was done. Based on the difficulty exhibited by many of the executives in answering investment and percentage allocation questions, the method of comparing investments in technology to industry averages may or may not be a valid indication of relative performance. The reluctance to discuss the topic is likely because of the antitrust implications of discussions among competitors.

Table 2 Organizational performance measures

Organizational area	Performance measure

Finance and Accounting	Rate of Return
	   Return on Equity
	   Return on Investment
	Profitability
	   Net Income
	   Profit Margin
	Debt Structure

Sales and Marketing	Sales Market Share Demand Analysis Effectiveness

Production and Materials Management	Capacity Utilization
	Output (Productivity)
	Inventory
	   Levels
	   Costs

Engineering and Product Development	Development Costs
Personnel and Labor	Human Resource Skills Mix Employee Turnover Staffing Levels
Information system	Reliability of Service Technical Performance Perception Management Support of the Business Plan Critical Success Factors
Business Planning	Cycle Effectiveness Forecasting Reliability

It was obvious that the ideas about effective management of corporate systems are evolving as the systems environment changes. The move to end-user developed systems requires a new view of electronic linkages within the firm (horizontal structuring) and how systems at all levels are integrated and coordinated. The use of production technology in the IS function also is causing significant shifts in the way systems are developed and delivered. The explosion in communications systems has created opportunities for linking suppliers, producers, and customers (vertical structuring). This is creating new opportunities in systems applications and will, over time, increase standardization among systems (at least systems interfaces). Effective methods to design and evaluate systems in this environment will be necessary. All of these issues raise interesting research questions that will be discussed later.

Outside service activities and management

The management of external relations deals with the relationship between the internal IS function of an organization and its vendors and consultants. It also includes any products the internal IS function develops for markets external to the organization. Although the executives believed this is an increasingly important topic, it has not been adequately addressed in either the academic or practitioner literature. It is also an area in which a variety of approaches and philosophies of management were found to exist. This makes it difficult to draw any definitive conclusions from the material gathered in this study, although it is possible to offer several propositions about the important issues.

There are several prominent issues that were discussed and which will be covered in this section. These include the use and integration of externally developed software, the management of external services such as contract programmers and consultants, and integration of external services objectives into the operational plans of the organization. The discussion will be oriented to the traditional model of the structure of systems in the organization introduced in Figure 1 previously.

External software packages

Packaged software has been the topic of recent studies [16], and therefore was of particular interest in this study. There was extensive use of externally developed software in all the companies participating in the study. Extraorganizational software services were used most often for applications at the transactional level and to a limited degree for operational control systems. There also was extensive use of second-party software for database management, computing systems management and operations analysis. The use of analysis packages such as Lotus 1-2-3 and the Interactive Financial Planning Package (IFPS) is very common with microcomputing, end-user developed applications. Most of the executives prefer to purchase software rather that to develop it internally – they all believed it was more efficient, especially for very complex operations.

The major reasons for using outside rather than internally developed software were given as *reduced cost* and *rapid implementation*. Discussions with these IS executives confirm the findings of Lynch [17] that the original cost and schedule goals of outside software projects as well as expectations are rarely met, leaving some dissatisfaction with much, if not most, of the products. There was recognition that costs and implementation schedules were dependent on the amount of modification that a package required to have it conform to organizational operations. The estimation of exact modification requirements was thought to be very difficult if not impossible, although critical to effective performance.

A general rule used by these managers in deciding when to employ an external rather than internal package was not found. Most did agree, however, that the objective was to modify the software as little as possible and use of a strategy changing internal operations to fit the software to avoid modification. The majority used a rule of thumb that required the software to perform at least 80% of its intended function without modification. The trick, of course, was to predict how much modification will be required.

There was no agreement about how to perform an accurate *a priori* evaluation and there is virtually no empirical study that would provide direction. In this study, it seemed to be based on each case and was related to at least three elements, which previously have been discused by Ivari [11]. These are complexity, radicalness and originality. Complexity is particularly difficult to assess for it is dependent on size, system variability (stochasticity, uncertainty) and how outcomes are measured. How radical an application is depends on the extent of internal change required to implement it. Originality is dependent on whether or not the system is replacing an older application or is entirely new. Although the managers agreed that these were not directly measurable for a given situation, they seemed to be reasonable items to consider.

Applications development process

Responses indicated that applications were increasingly developed either through modification of second-party software, use of contract programmers or use of consultants. Contract programmers were used by all of the firms participating in the study, and all the firms purchased some type of secondary vendor-developed software. About 40% of the firms either had used, were using, or planned to use consultants, which were broadly defined to include people from a software vendor, from consulting firms or individuals hired for short-term specific tasks. About 30% of the managers said they would never use consulting services, citing high costs as the primary reason. For the managers who felt this way, a common characteristic or set of characteristics, such as industry or firm size, could not be determined.

Also since it could not be determined from the interviews how the individuals actually made cost comparisons, this is an obvious area for extended study. The rest of the executives were indifferent or had not had an occasion to use consultants.

There were two major cost considerations repeatedly given as important elements in the management of applications development. The first was the cost of actual production and the second was the cost associated with coordinating internal and external activities. There was agreement that the first cost is the easier of the two to identify and control, while the second is almost impossible to accurately forecast. The key to production cost control was felt to be a very detailed systems requirements specification and careful project planning to efficiently satisfy the requirements. Given this, one would expect to find a well-developed process to specify requirements and plan projects prior to requesting proposals from outside vendors or consultants or to hiring contract programmers. This, however, was not the case. In several instances, outside vendors or consultants actually developed system specifications as part of the project. Costs in such cases would be difficult to accurately forecast and their unpredictability may have been the seed of dissatisfaction with the final product. The management of such interventions will be discussed in a later section of this chapter.

The three areas in which outside services most often were employed were in database development (or conversion); operational decision support system design and development; and transactional level systems (personnel, accounting and production) specification, design, development and implementation. Clearly, the last area was the one in which outside resources were most often employed. *All of the managers who used outside services said they would not employ them for 'strategic systems.'* Examples given were for systems to provide executive support, support strategic planning or support 'core' business functions.

There were, however, examples where outside services apparently were used in these areas, and it was difficult for these executives to distinguish 'core' from 'noncore' systems. Apparently, these executives exhibit considerable caution when they feel a system is vital to the health of the firm or when it is a highly visible application.

Outside services management

Several important issues surfaced in the discussions of the management of interventions and contracts. The first was planning for the use of outside services, the second was contract management and production control and the fourth was the process used to develop requirements. Although these are strongly interrelated, they will be discussed separately.

A number of methods were used to manage outside services. Usually, these were linked strongly to company policy. The first was an IS-managed intervention, the second was user management, the third was contractor management, the fourth was committee management and the fifth was some mixture of the others. Generally, the mixed model occurred when the project had several different parts, each part being managed with one of the approaches. These 'parts' were identified as specification development, request for proposal (RFP) development, contract administration and the development work itself. The management model, its description and predominant use are shown in Table 3.

Table 3 Outside services management models

Management model	Description	Predominant Use
User Managed	The functional user managed the entire project	Project
IS Managed	IS personnel managed all phases	Specifications Project RFP Development Contract Administration
Consultant Managed	A senior consultant managed the work flow	Project
Committee Managed	User, IS and consulting people participated. The chair was an IS person or a user.	Specifications Project
Mixed Management	Either an IS, consulting person, or the user managed some part of the project	Contract Administration RFP Development Specifications Project

To some degree, the type of management depended on the type of project, the nature of the industry and the product. IS people always managed the purchase and modification of software, unless the purchase was embedded in a larger project involving consultants. When consultants were employed by functional users, the project generally was managed by the consultant, primarily because of the lack of expertise within the organization and secondarily because the project tended to be more uniquely directed at a specific product. Each one of these generally produced satisfaction.

This was not the case, however, when management of a project was mixed between consultants and IS staff. Some dissatisfaction by both consultants and IS staff was expressed with this approach, even though it seemed quite common. The managers recognized that organizational cultural differences as well as management approaches produced friction. Considerable energy generally was expended in the coordination of work in such circumstances. Most managers agreed that it seemed reasonable to seek, where possible, *single-source management of a project rather than an integrated approach* even when two or more organizations mix people. This approach clearly produced the highest levels of satisfaction among the managers.

Most of the managers felt the real key to successful management was the thoroughness with which specifications for the project and the products were written, and when one was produced, the breadth and clarity of the RFP for a given project. The method that produced the greatest satisfaction among the executives interviewed was one in which a contrast administrator was used and was separated from the project manager. The administrator acted as a procurement manager and either an IS person or consultant (in one case a user) acted as the project manager. The procurement manager, who was assigned to the IS function, had very little to do with the project after the contract was signed.

There is difficulty in reaching definitive conclusions for most of the topics addressed in this section. This stems from the diversity of approaches in the use of outside services and the fact that each person interviewed had a somewhat different view of how and when to employ an outside service and how to manage the process once use of a service was selected. Several research topics have been developed from the data and some suggestions were made. The one strong conclusion reached is that this is an increasingly important topic, and the use of outside services of all types will become more prevalent.

Technology management

Two types of technology were of interest in the study. The first was, of course, the equipment (computers, peripherals, communications and support) used to create the 'computing environment' or 'IS infrastructure' for the organization. The second was the software used to manage operations and administration, and to develop the information system or model of the organization. The two were regarded quite differently by the managers, with several people indicating they were actually separate issues. When viewed as separate issues, most managers believed they were interdependent but not directly linked. Several managers mentioned the 'software lag' as a problem that forced separation of hardware and software issues.

There were several important topics addressed in the discussions of technology developments. The first was the type of model used in the organization to import technology. The predominant models are 'technology push,' where the managers respond to the movement of technology in the marketplace, and 'demand pull,' where the manager either develops technology to meet a defined need or uses existing technology to fill some predefined requirement. The second was the method or system used to manage the importation and control of technology. The third topic was the sources of both the technology and information about the technology. The fourth was how technology was integrated into the organization, and the last was the nature of future systems design. Each of these will be discussed.

Technological Management Structure. The central IS managers tend to see themselves as technology advocates in the organization. In this role, the manager is responsible for identifying (either demand pull or technology push) new technology and 'forcing' it into the organization. This means that even in end-user computing environments, the central IS function would retain control of technology in the firm. Even when managers saw themselves in this role, very few actually had created systems for effectively controlling the process. When an effective system was in place, very few felt that the system was efficient.

A number of people simply relied on vendors to keep them aware of new technology. The managers recognized that a problem with the approach was that the organization was reacting to, rather than anticipating, new developments. Very little technology forecasting was evident in the organizations and forecasting was rarely discussed by the managers.

The management of technology was found to be governed by three different philosophies, each of which resulted in a very different technological environment for an organization. The first was a 'leading edge' philosophy which usually was linked to the 'technology need-pull' model. The manager here attempted to develop a strong link between the business strategy and technology required to implement the strategy. One example used to discuss the method was to provide the dimensional specifications for hardware (or software) to serve a specific need, prepare an RFP to satisfy the need and manage the vendor contracting process. The development of hand-held check-in devices in the rental car industry was mentioned. Competitive advantage of some type was the objective in pursuing this strategy.

The leading-edge approach was seen in very few of the businesses in this study, and then in only the most competitive situations. For example, a large defense contractor produced a 'paperless factory' to ensure production efficiencies that enabled the company to successfully proceed with a critical defense contract. This project called for creation of hardware and software that otherwise would not have been available.

Most of the companies (65%) in the study had a 'lagging-edge' philosophy which was prevalent with most administrative and transaction-processing systems. It was found most often coupled with the 'technology push' model and was prevalent in less competitive environments. The company with this approach would meet business goals, usually seen as problems of efficiency enhancement, with proven technology that was widely available, documented and serviced. The approach was seen to be strongly dependent on a thorough knowledge of the vendors and products in a given technological area. The executive generally depended only on his or her knowledge of existing sysems and the technology was directed at current rather than anticipated business needs. Technological standards to ensure compatibility with existing systems were a concern when pursuing this strategy.

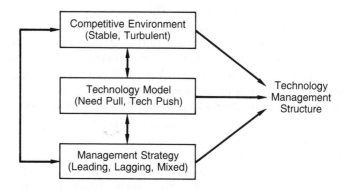

Figure 3. Technology management structure

The third model noted was a mixed approach that might be termed 'on the wave.' In this approach, there was not a predominant technology model but a mixture of the two. The manager used unproven technology that was new but did not provide the specifications for it. He or she would attempt to exploit newly developed products and shift technology with its growth. This approach was vendor-oriented and was found where strategic systems or decision support systems had been or were being developed. The firms using this approach also had developed functions to manage RFP processes and were closely linked to one or two vendors. In at least two cases, the senior IS executive had signed nondisclosure agreements with one vendor and had access to extensive technological knowledge prior to its release to the general public.

It was apparent from the data that the technological structure of the firm was determined by the interaction between the technology model (Need Pull, Demand Push), the management strategy (Leading, Lagging or Mixed) and the competitive environment (Stable, Turbulent). These factors are illustrated in Figure 3. The factors in the figure require further study and will be the focus of a later discussion of research directions.

Technology Integration. Technology integration is the process used by an organization to assess and assimilate new technology. This is a more complex issue than it might initially appear to be. The definition of what constitutes 'new technology' is what makes it difficult to judge in other than specific cases in specific firms. The conversations about integration also included discussions of the primary sources of technology and information about it.

The material developed by Huff and Monro [10] was used as a basis for discussion of the topic. They studied technology assessment and adoption and identified six phases and six roles important in the process. The phases are awareness, interest, evaluation, trial, implementation and diffusion; the roles are users, influencers, deciders, gatekeepers, planners and sponsors.

Each of these was addressed in some fashion and were found to exist to one degree or another within the framework presented in Figure 3. The 'stage theory' of Nolan [18] also was used as a source. Although the stage theory has wide acceptance, several extensive studies of it have shown that it is not a valid explanation of technology evolution [1, 15]. Some of the concepts contained in the theory, however, were useful when addressing technology integration as were those of McFarlan and McKenney [19].

Only one of the organizations had a well-defined, systematic integration process that blended business issues and technological opportunity in a planning process that would fit fully into the framework. The most consistent integration methodology was an opportunistic one where fortuitous business issues and technology matches occurred. This is consistent with the Huff and Monro findings and consistent with the prevalent 'lagging-edge' philosophy expressed by most of the individuals. It is also consistent with decision theory that describes policy development as 'ad hoc' meetings of issues and solutions [7].

The informal methods used to assess technology were personality driven. The most frequent response to the question about technology awareness was that the senior executive was responsible for this and read trade publications, spoke to vendors and attended conferences. These were not systematically done, however, and in most cases, were quite intermittent. Whether or not the method used was effective was impossible to determine because of the difficulty in measuring the true state of technology in a given firm. Three organizations had either a person or committee responsible for technology assessment. In each case, the people on the committee were all IS staff. As a result, even in these cases, the methods used to match technology to business issues were not clear.

The managers generally offered three reasons for the pursuit of technology. The first was to secure some competitive advantage, the second was to improve efficiency (operations) and the third was to enhance effectiveness (development). The latter two are well documented and as noted, were cited repeatedly and most often as the reasons for seeking new technology.

Because one emerging area of technology was discussed and emphasized by a majority of the managers (80%), it will be addressed separately here. The executives believed that application of expert systems in various traditional IS areas had real merit and planned to actively pursue the technology. Examples included control of vehicle dispatching, product pricing, cash control, sales analysis and marketing control, network management, personnel scheduling, operations control, data management and business analysis. They felt that movement in artificial intelligence and expert systems was a natural evolution of decision support and would become more prevalent for structured decision problems. A number (5%) of the organizations had implemented some type of expert system, mainly dealing with various maintenance functions.

The executives agreed that development in this area had been constrained by the technology available to implement systems and the difficulty in knowledge engineering. Most agreed that development of a general-purpose system generator would encourage growth and proliferation. All recognized that the investment to develop such a tool would be significant but that the rewards also would be significant. The ES generator would have to be system- and language-independent – both of which create a further barrier to development.

Conclusions and research directions

Analysis and discussion of the material in this article were based on three separate efforts. The first was a detailed analysis of the data gathered in the interview research process. The interviews extended over a two-and-one-half month period and were summarized in the material contained in this chapter. The second involved a review of additional literature in the topic areas and organization of the material for presentation. The third involved discussion of the material with MIS academics and practicing managers. A list of potential research topics was developed from the latter process. These topics along with appropriate research questions are presented in Table 4. The basis for selecting these questions will be discussed in the short summary of each area that follows. Together the questions form a research agenda that executives would support and that have important implications for development of the IS management field.

Organizational structures for IS management. Several important issues came from the discussions in this area. These issues form the basis for the research questions regarding the various methods used to organize IS activities. The ambiguity surrounding the issues of dispersion and decentralization were important as was a tiered concept of structure. The methods for distribution of IS resources and the measurement of results given the resource allocations also were important. These topics are addressed in the three research questions shown in Table 4.

End-user orientation versus centralized management. The discussion of end-user computing showed a different view of the concept than that used in the IS academic literature. The executives had a multidimensional view of end-user computing that involved the users autonomy, the level of user participation in application development and the degree of centralized control of resources. The research question developed at this stage deals with the nature of structure given the type of organization and industry.

IS planning and infrastructure. In this area, the IS linkages to business units were of greatest concern to the executives. There was consensus that more needs to be known about how to effectively create and manage the linkages. The inclusion of IS in the normal business planning process was also of concern. These concerns produced two research questions.

Table 4 Research agenda

Topic area	*Questions*
Organizational Structures for IS Management	1 Are there different organizational patterns and structure for the IS function in differing for IS Management organizational and industry environments? Is there a best model for a given situation? 2 How prevalent is the tiered model and can it be linked to organizational characteristics? 3 What causes the differing patterns of the distribution of IS resources between IS and other organizational functions? Is this linked to the nature of success?
End-User Orientation vs. Centralized Management	1 What is the link between the extent of end-user computing in an organization and the Centralized Management nature of the external and internal environment of the system? This is discussed in the literature but has not been defined. If there is a link, what are its effects?
IS Planning and Structure	1 What are the Internal IS organizational characteristics that produce the strongest and most effective links with business units? 2 How are IS and business planning linked to produce an effective IS infrastructure?
IS Infrastructure Effectiveness Measurement	1 How should the enterprise IS structure be evaluated? 2 Does an integrated systems strategy produce greater intrastructure effectiveness? 3 Is an 'assessment framework' useful in evaluating IS effectiveness?
Outside Services Activities and Management	1 What is the link between the cost of activities and consulting services and value added by consultants? The interaction with the type of service provided would be important. What is the overall effect on effectiveness and efficiency produced by the use of external vs Internal resources? 2 What are effective (and efficient) management processes for controlling a consulting intervention? Would certain methods of managing interventions and external resource development projects be more effective in one vs. another type of organizational environment? 3 The requirements specification process prior to RFP of outside services impacts the nature and overall effectiveness of a project. What are the types of processing leading to success or failure? (A sample of companies would be difficult to form.) 4 What are the effectiveness and efficiency trade-offs between the use of outside services and internal staff? Issues are cost vs. time and the average for training internal staff. 5 What are effective corporate strategies for vendor management? Single, two or multiple vendor strategies and their outcomes would be the focus of the study. What is produced by the strategies could be investigated with a survey instrument.
Technology Management	1 What effect does the current organizational 'technological environment' have on the importation and dispersion of IS technology? What are effective models for managing technology infusion? 2 What link is there between the technology strategy and organizational success? What effect does the strategy have on overall organizational success? A collateral problem is identification of the source of the strategy. For example, does it stem from internal organizational forces or from the forces in the environment? 3 Is the need pull-technology push approach determined primarily by the competitive nature of the environment and nature of the industry or does it stem from other factors? Is the need for efficiency the key factor? 4 Is the technology operating domain of an organization determined by the simultaneous interaction of the management strategy (leading, lagging, mixed), technology model (need pull, demand push) and competitive environment (stable, turbulent) What are the operating domain characteristics?

IS infrastructure effectiveness measurement. The managers were comfortable with current methods for cost-benefit analysis of individual IS projects. They expressed concern, however, about the ability to assess the overall performance of the IS infrastructure and in their ability to link resource investment to organizational effectiveness. The research questions in this area reflect these concerns.

Outside services and management. This area was extensively discussed by the managers and it was obvious that the issues emerging in the area were of concern. When to employ external services was not clear and when employed, management of the intervention process produced wide dissatisfaction. Since the employment of outside service and the use of outsourcing has not received extensive attention in the academic IS literature, a number of potentially fruitful research questions emerged.

Technology management. The management of technology development in the organization was, of course, of concern to the executives. Most related the topic to their philosophy of technological positioning, the nature of the competitive environment in their industry or the source of demand for technology. The issues that grew out of these discussions yielded the research questions for the area shown in Table 4.

The research reported in this chapter was conducted to add depth to the survey results reported in the literature. The purpose was to broaden understanding of many of the important issues facing both IS managers and researchers in the field. The in-depth interviews yielded data that allowed broader discussion of the issues than has previously appeared and led to the research agenda presented in Table 4.

References

1   Benbasat, I., Dexter, A. S., Drury, D. H., and Goldstein, R. C. A critique of the stage hypothesis: Theory and empirical evidence. *Commun. ACM 27*, 5 (May 1984), 476–485.
2   Bjern-Anderson, N. and Davis, G. B. Eds. *Information Systems Assessment: Issues and Challenges.* Elsevier Science, Inc., N. Y., 1988.
3   Boland, R. J. and Hirscheim, R. A. Information systems strategy formulation. In *Critical Issues in Information Systems Research*, R. J. Boland and R. A. Hirscheim, Eds. John Wiley & Sons, N. Y. 1987, 157–178.
4   Boynton, A. C. and Zmud, R. W. Information technology planning in the 1990's: Directions for practice and research. *MIS Q. 11*, 1 (Mar. 1987), 59–71.
5   Brancheau, J. C. and Wetherbe, J. C. Key issues in information systems management. *MIS Q. 11*, 1 (Mar. 1987), 23–45.
6   Campbell, J. P. On the Nature of Organizational Effectiveness. *New Perspectives on Organizational Effectiveness.* P. S. Goodman and J. M. Pennings, Eds. San Francisco, Calif.: Josey-Bass Publishing, 1977, 13–35.
7   Cohen, M. D., March, J. G. and Olsen, J. P. A garbage can model of organizational choice *Admin. Sci. Q.* 17, 1 (Jan. 1972), 1–25.
8   Guimaraes, T. and Ramanujam, V. Personal computing trends and problems: An empirical study. *MIS Q. 10*, 2 (June 1986), 179–186.
9   Hartog, C. and Herbert, M. 1985 Opinion survey of MIS managers: Key issues. *MIS Q. 10*, 4 (Dec. 1986), 351–361.

10   Huff, S.L. and Munro, M. C. Information technology assessment and adoption: A field study, *MIS Q. 9*, 4 (Dec. 1985), 327–339.

11   Ivari, J. Implementability of in-house developed vs. application package based information systems. In *Proceedings of ICIS* (1986), 67–80.

12   Kerlinger, F. N. *Foundations of Behavioral Research*, 3rd ed. N. Y., N. Y. Holt, Rinehart and Winston, Inc., 1986.

13   King, J. L. and Kraemer, K. L. Evolution and organizational information systems: An assessment of Nolan's stage model. *Commun. ACM 27*, 5 (May 1984), 466–475.

14   Kleijnen, J. P. C., *Computers and profits: Quantifying Financial Benefits of Information*. Addison-Wesley, Reading, Mass., 1980.

15   Leifer, R. Matching computer-based information systems with organizational structures. *MIS Q 12*, 1 (Mar. 1988), 63–73.

16   Lucus, H. C., Jr., Walton, E. J. and Ginzberg, M. J. Implementing packaged software. *MIS Q. 12*, 4 (Dec. 1988), 537–549.

17   Lynch, R. K. Implementing packaged application software: Hidden costs and new challenges. *Syst. Obj. Solutions 4*. 4 (Nov. 1984), 227–234.

18   Nolan, R. L. Managing the computer resource: A stage hypothesis. *Commun. AGM 16*, 7 (July 1973), 399–105.

19   Raho, L. E., Belohlav, J. A., and Fiedler, K. D. Assimilating new technology into the organization: An assessment of McFarlan and McKenney's model. *MIS Q. 11*, 1 (Mar. 1987), 47–57.

20   Rivard, S. and Huff, S. L. Factors of success for end-user computing. *Commun. ACM 31*. 5 (May 1988), 552–561.

21   Rockart, J. F. The line takes the leadership: IS management in a wired society. *Sloan Management, Rev. 29*, 3 (Summer 1988). 57–64.

22   Rockart J. F. and Flannery, L. S. The management of end user computing. *Commun. ACM 26*, 10 (Sept. 1983), 276–284.

23   Zmud, R. W. Design alternatives for organizing information systems activities. *MIS Q. 8*, 2 (June 1984), 79–84.

3 Critical information technology issues: the next ten years

R. I. Benjamin and J. Blunt

It's a Monday morning in the year 2000. Executive Joanne Smith gets in her car and voice activates her remote telecommunications access workstation. She requests all voice and mail messages, open and pending, as well as her schedule for the day. Her workstation consolidates the items from home and office databases, and her 'message ordering knowbot,' a program she has instructed, delivers the accumulated messages in the order she prefers. By the time Joanne gets to the office she has sent the necessary messages, revised her day's schedule, and completed a to-do list for the week, all of which have been filed in her 'virtual database' by her 'personal organizer knowbot.'

The 'virtual database' has made Joanne's use of information technology (IT) much easier. No longer does she have to be concerned about the physical location of data. She is working on a large proposal for the Acme Corporation today, and although segments of the Acme file physically exist on her home database, her office database, and her company's marketing database, she can access the data from her portable workstation, wherever she is. To help her manage this information resource, Joanne uses an information visualizer that enables her to create and manage dynamic relationships among data collections. This information visualizer has extended the windows metaphor (graphical user interface) of the early 1990s to three-dimensional graphic constructs.

Papers that predict the form of IT in the year 2000 and how it will affect people, organizations, and markets are in plentiful supply. *Scientific American* has devoted a whole issue to this subject, describing how the computing and communications technology of the year 2000 will profoundly change our institutions and the way we work.[1] What is missing is a vision of what the IT function in a large organization must become in order to enable this progress. With some trepidation, we will attempt to fill this gap.

In the early 1980s, one of us published a paper that forecasted the IT environment in 1990.[2] In this chapter, we revisit those predictions and apply the same methodology to a view of the IT environment in the year 2000. We describe the fundamental technology and business assumptions that drive our predictions. Scenarios illustrate how the IT function will evolve in terms of applications, application architectures, application development, management of IT-based change, and economics. Finally, we highlight some key challenges in the next decade for the IT executive and other senior managers.

The 1980 vision of today

Table 1 shows to what degree the predictions made in 1980 were realized. The technology predictions tended to be too conservative, and the predictions that required organizational change tended to be too optimistic. They were as follows:

1 *The rapid spread of workstations.* Everyone who sits at a desk in a corporation will have a workstation by 1990. Workstations will be as common in the office as telephones. The cost of a supported workstation will be about 20 percent of a clerical's salary and less than 10 percent of a professional's salary.

2 *The user interface.* The distinction between office systems and end-user systems will disappear. The terminal will be ubiquitous and multifunctional, able to support end-user, data processing, and office systems tasks.

3 *The distribution of processing.* Databases and processing power within the organization, which are relatively centralized today, will become much more distributed. This distribution will follow some basic rules. Data will be *stored* at a higher organizational level only if it needs to be *integrated* at that level. Application at lower organizational levels will not rely on a staffed data center.

4 *IT spending.* IT spending will increase as a percent of revenue over the decade – by about 50 percent.

5 *Organization of the IT function.* IT management will be concerned with managing the demand for its services rather than rationing its supply. The end user will dominate the use of computing resources. The primary value of the centralized IT function will be to provide interconnectability.

6 *Key application drivers.* The 1980s will be a decade of integrating applications across functions. Organizational frameworks will be developed to encourage application integration across business functions.

7 *Application development.* All aspects of software will continue to improve steadily. However, the demand for software is so great as to appear infinite, and the improvement will be perceived as having little effect on the backlog.

Table 1   The predictions for the last decade

		Achieved	Partly achieved	Not achieved
1	Workstations will be as common as telephones.	✓		
2	The distinction between office systems and end-user systems will disappear.	✓		
3	Databases and processing power will become more distributed.		✓	
4	IT spending as a percent of sales will increase by at least half, relative to sales.	✓		
5	The primary value of the centralized IT function will be to provide interconnectability.		✓	
6	The 1980s will be a decade of integrating applications across functions.			✓
7	All aspects of software will continue to improve steadily.		✓	

As the figure shows, not all of these predictions were realized. The developments of the 1980s give us clues to how well we'll progress in the next decade.

IT in the year 2000 – best case scenario

Joanne's computing environment represents a best-case scenario for the year 2000. The essential elements can be described as follows:

● She has a hierarchy of powerful computing capabilities at her disposal; portable computer, home computer, office computer, and various organizational and information service computers.

● All the stationary computers are physically interconnected to very high bandwidth public networks. This means they are linked through a medium – fiber optic cable – that allows large amounts of information to be communicated very quickly.

● Advances in remote telecommunications access technologies allow her to access these resources without a physical connection.

● She uses sophisticated interfaces that incorporate advanced ergonomic design concepts. That is, the computers are extremely user friendly; they have been designed to fit the way people actually work, even to fit the way individuals work.
● Knowbots greatly simplify Joanne's use of information technology. Knowbots are 'programs designed by their users to travel through a network, inspecting and understanding similar kinds of information, regardless of the language or form in which they are expressed.'[3] Among other functions, they provide the data she wants to look at in the order she wants to look at it.[4]

In short, the IT environment gives Joanne access to any information, anytime, anywhere, in any presentation mode she desires.

This scenario is technically feasible. All the elements exist either in commercial products or as prototypes. It is highly likely that a sizeable number of Joannes will exist in ten years, that is, that some key knowledge workers will have access to IT resources of the quality described. However, Joanne's environment is not representative of the typical worker environment we expect for the year 2000. Many organizations will not have progressed so far. How far an organization progresses, and the benefits it obtains from

Table 2 The predictions for the next decade

Technology
● The cost performance of everything related to IT (e.g., memories, microprocessors, etc) will improve by two orders of magnitude.
● The billion bit backbone network will be completed; it will be the international highway of business communication.
Architecture and standards
● Client/server will be the predominant technology architecture, and it will evolve into an important application architecture.
Services
● Electronic mail will become ubiquitous, integrating graphics, voice, and text, and it will provide extensive collaborative support capabilities.
Economics
● Major investments will be made to complete and maintain the infrastructure.
● Because technology is increasingly cheaper for all, the advantage will go to those who (a) apply it well and (b) effectively purchase value-added services for implementing it.
Applications
● Applications will be designed and built using high-level business models. Emphasis will be on design of robust applications that adapt to both short-term operational difficulties and evolutionary change.
● The implementation process within and between large businesses is generating larger and more complex applications. Because the design issues are so complex, it is reasonable to expect one or two application disasters.
Change management
● The executives in charge of IT organizations will have to learn change management skills and make sure that these skills are built into the IT organization.

---

doing so, will depend more upon its ability to identify appropriate strategic goals and to manage change than upon any technical factor. Table 2 summarizes our predictions for the year 2000.

The driving assumptions

The year 2000 scenario is based on several assumptions about technology. They are as follows:

Cost performance will improve by two orders of magnitude.

Since the 1960s, the core information technologies have shown cost-performance improvements of between 30 percent and 50 percent per year. If this trend continues through the 1990s, the cost-performance ratios of everything – memories, microprocessors, and so forth – will improve by two orders of magnitude, that is, by at least 100 times or 1,000 percent. Thus the workstation that can now process 25 million to 100 million instructions per second (MIPS) will be able to process from 500 MIPS to 2,000 MIPS. Instead of providing 10 million bytes of primary storage in your workstation, it will provide hundreds of millions of bytes of primary storage. And it will have billions of bytes of secondary storage attached, such as disk or optical memory.[5] But this workstation will cost the same $10,000 in real dollars that today's high-performance workstation costs.

These improvements are often indexed to labor costs. If we assume a modest increase in labor costs of 4 percent, the total IT cost-performance improvement relative to labor costs will be 2.5 orders of magnitude per decade.[6] Because the cost performance of IT continues to improve relative to labor and other forms of capital, companies will continue to invest heavily in it. The lesson of the 1970s and 1980s was that IT was a superior investment when it could replace or augment other forms of capital. In addition, as the power of the technology increased, so did the range of its application to new business situations. These trends can only become stronger in the next decade.

All computers will be interconnected via high bandwidth networks

During the mid- to late-1990s, national and international telecommunications backbone networks that operate at a billion bits per second will be implemented. The initial funding for the first of these networks was assured by passage of the Gore bill in December 1991. The prototype is the National Research and Education Network (NREN) in the United States, which today operates at 45 million bits per second.[7] In 1991 NREN for the first time allowed commercial enterprises to access the network.

Within offices, major computing elements will be interconnected with very high-speed local area networks (LAN). Homes will be connected to all of these networks with fiber optic cable, enabling people to work at home and to access a full range of entertainment and educational services. At home and in the office, portable computers will access databases using high-speed remote telecommunications technologies. While traveling, individuals will be connected to backbone networks and the desired databases by remote telecommunications technologies.

To summarize, fixed devices will be connected by fiber, and moving or movable devices will be connected by remote access technologies. Fiber will provide capabilities of up to a billion bits per second, and remote access technologies will provide between 10 million and 100 million bits per second.

Client-server will be the standard architectual model

By the year 2000, hardware configurations will almost universally follow the client-server model. In this model, the 'client' or user operates a workstation that has a certain configuration of hardware and software, and a number of 'servers' – mainframes, minicomputers, communications devices, very powerful workstations, novel printing devices, and servers that provide access to other networks – provide the client with supporting services. This model is already increasing in popularity, and it will dominate because of several key advantages:

- it simplifies the separation of the user interface from the service provided to the user;
- it eases functional separation of technology and of applications, thus simplifying growth and maintenance;
- within its current range of application capability, installations are reporting savings of 25 percent to 50 percent over mainframe and minicomputer architectures; and
- there is an ever-increasing quantity of software for client-server architectures. Consequently, applications will be distributed across several platforms. That is, programs will be able to share data easily; they will be interconnected and interoperable. Such issues will dominate technology purchase decisions.

Standards for interconnection and interoperability will be developed

The current confusion in standards for interconnection and interoperability of hardware and software will be significantly improved by the year 2000. Vendors are inevitably coming to the conclusion that their markets will be severely constrained unless they make it substantially easier for users to interconnect and interoperate. (The 1982 paper thought that this realization would have occurred long ago.)

Although not ideal, the level of interconnection will be far superior to where it is today. The vast amount of computer power available will make the required conversions and translations as seamless as possible. Consequently, the user 'wizardry' required today to build networks will be much less necessary.

What the final result will be is unclear. Today 'open systems' is almost

---

A general manager's glossary

Excerpts from P.G.W. Keen, *Every Manager's Guide to Information Technology: A Glossary of Key Terms and Concepts for Today's Business Leader* (Boston: Harvard Business School Press, 1991). 1991 by Peter G.W. Keen. Reprinted by permission of the publisher.

Bandwidth. Bandwidth is a measure of the carrying capacity of a telecommunications link. It determines the speed at which information can be transmitted and how much information can share the link, and consequently, the practical range of the applications it can support. Fiber optic links currently transmit at rates of from 100 million bits per second (bps) to 2.4 billion bps. At 720 million bps, the entire works of Shakespeare could be transmitted in a quarter of a second!

Computer-Aided Software Engineering (CASE). CASE is the use of computer technology to help improve application systems development. It consists of a set of workstation-based software tools designed to support application developers: data dictionaries to store and validate definitions of items used in programs; diagnostic tools to check for inconsistencies and redundancy; and diagrammatic representations of system designs that can be created quickly and kept up to date and reused in other applications.

Decision Support System (DSS). A decision support system is an information system or analytic model designed to help managers and professionals be more effective in their decision making. The logic of decision support is that the combination of managerial judgement, intuition, and experience and computer analysis, data access, display, and calculation will result in more effective and creative decision making than either a manager or a computer could achieve.

End-User Computing. End-user computing refers to uses of IT that are entirely under the control of business units and do not require traditional IT application systems development and operations expertise.

Millions of Instructions Per Second (MIPS). Millions of instructions per second, or MIPS, is a rough measure of the power of a computer, rather like horsepower is an approximate measure of the performance of an automobile engine.

Open Systems. Users and vendors have a mutual need for vendor-and product-independent standards. 'Open systems' are implicitly vendor-independent and, by extension, interconnectable and 'interoperable.'

Operating System. An operating system is an extensive and complex set of programs that manages the operation of a computer and the applications that run on it. A computer is defined more by its operating system than any other single feature. Major mainframe operating systems include MVS, DOS/VSE, OS/400, and VM for IBM computers and VMS for Digital Equipment Corporation computers.

User Interface. User interface refers to the dialogue between a human being and a computer system. The traditional user interface is the keyboard, from which commands are typed into a computer. Emerging types of user interface include tablets that may be written on with a special pen, light pens that can write directly on the computer screen, and voice commands to the computer.

---

synonymous with the operating system Unix and the government standard version, Posix.[8] By 2000, open systems solutions will more likely involve the adoption of key standards that enable a mix of environments to cooperate effectively. Perhaps systems will coalesce around Unix, but we think this is unlikely because it is not in the interests of vendors to have one architecture dominant. Traditionally, organizations have sought stability in their technology investment by standardizing to a single family of operating systems. In the next decade, stability will be as or more dependent on standardizing to a single user interface and set of personal support tools.

It is likely that as the necessary standards are developed and accepted, the open solutions will be developed more quickly than proprietary architectures have been. Open solutions change the nature and quality of investment for organizations. Open systems deprive vendors of monopoly profits and create more competition in areas where standards take hold. In order to stay profitable, vendors will have to develop niche products that fit the open systems architecture, and they will have to concentrate on price-performance improvements. The benefit for vendors will be that so many users will be working within the open systems architecture that a much larger potential market will be accessible.

What to expect

IT executives can expect the following in 2000:

- The size of computer will not dictate the use of different application programs for the same task (i.e., there will be a high level of 'scalability'). Each major vendor will sell a single computer architecture that spans from the desktop to the largest mainframe. An application programmer will only have to learn and use a single set of tools and standards.
- There will be similar scalability for small- to moderately large-size applications across vendor architectures in the Unix open systems environment.
- The highest performance systems, such as online reservation systems, will continue to operate within the large vendor architecture. Partly this reflects expectations about technology, in particular software robustness and the practicality of distributing massive databases. It also reflects conservatism in systems design and the high risk of making substantial shifts in architectures for core applications.
- The choice of user interface will be independent of the choice of hardware. Next and Sun, for instance, are creating versions of their interfaces to run on IBM PCs.
- Some services will become standardized and available across architectures, such as file transfer, document mail services, and so forth.
- A more sophisticated and extensive market in outsourcing and leasing of resources will develop. Companies will be able not only to buy resources outright from corporations but also to pay on a usage basis for basic processing and telecommunications capacity and for software. A significant advantage of adopting and implementing an open or industry

standard architecture will be the flexibility this provides for planning capacity and responding to changing demand, that is, the ability to outsource in demand-driven chunks.

What not to expect

- IT executives cannot expect to distribute certain mission critical applications: the very high-volume, real-time, inventory management systems, such as airline reservation systems. The largest databases will still require proprietary (i.e., nonrelational) solutions to meet performance needs.

Together, these assumptions describe a vast increase in computer power and telecommunications resources, which are made easier to use by wide adoption of client-server architectures and much improved standards for interconnection, display, and data sharing. James Emery, writing in *MIS Quarterly*, suggests that 'these technical advances are rapidly moving us to the position of having a magic genie capable of satisfying almost any logically feasible information need.'[9] The issue is to get the genie focused on critical business concerns.

Fundamental business drivers

Just as there are fundamental technology drivers, there are fundamental business drivers, and we need to understand how they will influence the IT function. Most articles on IT and business strategy provide a list of key business drivers. Although there are many, we have consolidated them into a few basic ones:

- The restructuring of the industrial enterprise. This most important of drivers is referred to in many ways – business reengineering, the lean-production paradigm, the total quality company, and so on. What is consistent is that the traditional, mass-production stovepipe organization is adopting a leaner form of production, and the traditional managerial buffers of inventory, time, and staff are being ruthlessly eliminated.[10]
- The globalization of business. By the year 2000, we will live in a global market society. This is already true of the financial and automotive markets.
- The changing global labor market.
- The increasing volatility of business environments.

Organizations will have to continually test and refine applications and business processes in response to these changes. Companies will need to become tightly interconnected not only internally but also with suppliers and customers. The short supply of labor and skills will force organizations to design better business processes and systems, both within and between organizations, and to make use of extensive expert systems, knowbots, collaborative support, and other capabilities. Malone and Rockart describe how the textile industry, already advanced in integration, could become an electronic marketplace in which databases and consultants are available on-line, and specialty terms form instantly to solve the problem of the moment.[11]

More organizations will embrace the idea of the 'informated' organization; that is, they will use their internal information to learn how to do their processes better.[12] The informated organization shifts the locus of control from the manager to the worker, who is empowered by accessible information to exercise this control. Thus, organizations will rely to a much greater extent on the accessibility of information at all levels of the hierarchy. This will conflict with more traditional management processes and structures. The design and use of information systems will not be free of organizational politics as each company decides where and how it will compromise on the issues of managerial control and information accessibility.

In summary, these business changes suggest a sustained growth in new applications (for example, to replace the transaction systems of the stovepipe business, to empower workers in information-rich activities, and to help the less skilled) and a continuing high interest by senior managers in where and how the IS budget is spent.

Applications in 2000

It is difficult to predict the specific new applications that will be most important for the IT function. However, we can identify certain classes of applications and how they will change in the coming decade.

Application types

To understand the evolution of applications in the next decade, it is useful to consider applications as falling into three categories:

1 *Business operations systems.* These are the traditional core of the IT function; they have also been described as transaction and control systems. These systems can manage business processes that run in real-time, such as process control, and those that operate on weekly or monthly schedules, such as accounting and settlement systems.
2 *Information repository systems.* These evolved somewhat later in the history of the IT function, as applications were built that isolated data from processing. Unlike transaction systems, the value and function of these systems is largely determined by the content and organization of the database rather than by the structure of the predesigned interactions.

3 *Personal support systems.* These have evolved from the end-user support, timesharing systems of the late 1970s to more advanced support systems today. Their evolution has followed a path from personal task systems (e.g., word processing, spreadsheets, and simple databases) to database access and specialized support systems such as design support and executive managerial support. These higher-level support systems have often incorporated personal task systems and electronic mail capabilities. There is a growing belief that these will become collaborative workgroup support systems.

Application architectures

IT groups charged with developing the information infrastructure have to develop policies and supporting tactical plans to migrate these three categories of applications from the existing base to the level of functionality and integration that we believe will be required in the year 2000.

Business operations systems

IT executives need to understand that business operations systems will get larger and more complex in the coming years in order to respond to pressures to integrate internally and externally, to eliminate wasteful intermediaries, and to speed up business processes. Because of the enormous past investments in these systems, there will be an emphasis in design on building on current capabilities and creating more flexibility.

Organizations may find it advantageous for business operations systems to decompose into two subsets – back office operation and decision support. Consider the order entry process. In the new architecture, the back office component will automatically set up the order in the file, schedule it into production, and assign a delivery date for the customer. The decision support component will give a person the tools to negotiate with the customer regarding the order, terms and conditions, and delivery date. The back office process will change much less frequently than the decision support process, thus providing functional isolation and easier maintenance.

This organization cannot be seen as fixed. What is structured and transactional and what is unstructured and conversational change as we uncover the inherent structure in the process. This has implications for application design and for bringing knowledge-based systems into the application mainstream.

Further, the decision support component can 'surround' the current data structures and transactions and can be built with little or no modification to them. A few companies have successfully implemented surround applications today. The technology to surround existing applications has been developed by small companies operating at the periphery of the major vendors. Some of these technologies are now being acquired by major vendors. They have considerable potential to manage the legacy problem (that is, figuring out how to deal with the legacy of old technology systems that do not fit current business requirements but that seem too expensive to redo) but they cannot be relied upon to make it go away.

We observe three trends in business operations systems:

- IT executives will invest large sums of money in multimedia business operations systems. USAA's image transaction system is an early example.[13] These systems will be able to handle all forms of information used in business processes, from illustrations to voice acknowledgement. Programs that model the human working process, such as voice annotation, will become very important.
- Systems will be designed to adapt more effectively to unforeeen changes in the business, the operating environment, and the organization. Traditionally, backup procedures have dealt only with failures, and we have thought of backup as a completely different mode of operation. This is no longer adequate. Given the level of change predicted for the future, backup will evolve into a proactive process that will ensure that systems be available at all times.
- The nature of the legacy systems will have changed, but managing the retirement and replacement of mission critical systems will continue to be near the top of the IT management agenda.

Despite all of these changes, many operational systems developed in the next ten years will be organizational time bombs. Our dependence on information systems is continuing to grow faster than our ability to manage them, and in many organizations responding to immediate needs will divert resources and attention from identifying and implementing quality solutions consistently.

Information repository systems

These will grow rapidly as the concept of the learning organization becomes operationalized. They will (1) be multimedia, (2) provide expert agent assistance (knowbots), (3) come in many levels of aggregation, including very fine line-item detail, and (4) be distributed to where the need for data access is highest. People will be able to define their own virtual repository in terms of other repositories and look to knowbots to find the data that interests them. As Zuboff suggested, much effort will be expended in deciding who has access rights to what data, a critical design and implementation issue.

Personal and collaborative support systems

We currently see several contradictory trends that must mutually coexist:

- Support systems will become more segmented by specialty. That is, software will include more of the intellectual content of tasks, in some cases as components are added to basic packages and in others as specialized applications are developed. For example, a will-writing program is more than just another word processor, but it can be created using one. Similar niche products will appear that are targeted at specific occupations and tasks.

- Basic support capabilities will become standardized as standard user interfaces and modules become accepted. For example, electronic mail that integrates graphics, voice, and text will become ubiquitous.

- The distinction between some types of support systems will blur over time. For example, managerial support systems are currently encompassing elements of executive support and decision support systems.

- Desktop tools, which have lost their 'virginal' simplicity and, in the race for product differentiation, have become an almost unmanageable menagerie, will have to be rethought to provide users with the truly flexible capabilities needed to do their work. Mark Weiser describes research at Xerox PARC that is trying to develop what he calls 'ubiquitous computing . . . where you are unaware of it.'[14]

- Collaborative work tools will become more important. The first generation of PCs led to development of significant new applications such as spreadsheets. Now that the norm is networked terminals, we should expect new applications that support teamwork to evolve. Already electronic mail, bulletin boards, and conferencing software provide a basic infrastructure for communication. Increasingly we will see software that allows people to work together collaboratively and interactively. Tools that allow two users to display and amend the same document simultaneously will be commonly available. More sophisticated applications may use technology related to 'artificial reality' to enable groups to create, share, and manage very large amounts of information.

Integrating systems with the business

Currently we are in the third stage of a four-stage evolution of conceptual thinking in the IT function. Each stage is defined by what the IT function has to deliver in order to support the organization effectively. They are as follows:

1 *Automation.* Initially, application design was directed at automating existing manual systems. Progress could easily be measured by monitoring the systems portfolio. Masses of information were made available, but access was, and largely still is, exceedingly difficult. Much of the data was locked up in files accessed only by particular programs. Information could not be shared across applications or platforms. The dominant method of giving out information to its users was as line printer reports that found their most productive use as children's drawing paper.

2 *Access to information.* Before automation could be completed, it became clear that we were better at collecting information than disseminating it.

Since about 1970, the dominant concern of IT groups has been to reverse this trend. On-line systems replaced batch systems. PCs and workstations are no longer stand-alone devices. Data modeling and database management systems are enabling the integration of information at appropriate levels in order to support the organization's information needs. The problem of providing secure information access is a dominant driver of IT investment today and will continue to be a major consideration.

3 *Filtering information.* Today, instead of being starved of information, managers and workers are in danger of dying from a surfeit of communication. The average information content of 'information' is rapidly falling. When the number of electronic mail messages per day exceeds two hundred, they cease to attract attention. To stay productive, organizations are going to have to invest in the development of knowbots and other forms of active information filtering. If information access is a key driver for current investment, providing the right information filtering capabilities emerges as a major challenge.

4 *Modeling information.* When information is accessible and filtered, then the question must be asked, 'What do I do with it?' Expert systems, modeling systems, and executive and managerial support systems all have a role to play in modeling information to make it more useful. The application of information models will require a proactive effort far beyond that required to order and filter data, but it will be necessary to ensure a good fit with business processes.

Information modeling cannot be managed without bringing together all three application segments – business operations, information repositories, and personal support systems. In addition, information modeling will require development of new models that integrate business process and systems design. Examples of these are Jay Forrester's systems dynamics and Stafford Beer's work on cybernetic models. These have been around for several decades, but they have not been brought into the IT mainstream. IT has developed mostly static models focused on describing system function and content, even though information systems are only one element in the total system of the organization. The implementation of large-scale applications and new technologies is not only technically complex, it can change the social and political structure of organizations. Yet often companies commit large sums to fund applications without understanding the full implications of their decision. We do not expect managers to continue to tolerate this level of risk, and what is accepted today as best practice will in the next few years come to be viewed as naive and unprofessional.

Managers need models that include a description of both structure and policy, thus enabling them to explore the implications of change. These models should be integrated with the organization's operational systems. It will be a challenge for many IT organizations to service this need as it requires mastery of disciplines outside the compass of most IT professionals.

Client-server application model

This model, shown in Figure 1, integrates the three classes of applications described above. The support systems are in the workstations, and the business operations systems and information repositories are in the servers. The various clients and servers can communicate with each other through standard EDI-like transactions or object references.

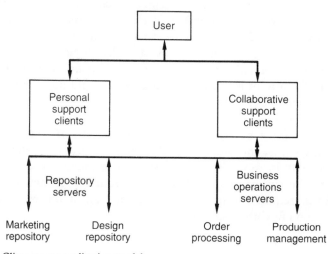

Figure 1. Client-server application model

This model represents a dramatic break from design concepts that were developed when the mainframe was the dominant information processing technology. IT has long advocated systems and information integration. Consequently it has searched for ever larger, more complex applications that will integrate everything into a single solution. The alternative – designing many smaller applications that can communicate and cooperate – has been considered too difficult, unstable, and probably inferior to a single solution. Client-server architecture is going to force a reevaluation of that trade-off. To give an example: a company and supplier may integrate their complementary processes by communicating via EDI and electronic mail. Today, if the same two functions were within a single company, there would be a tendency to develop a single application with one integrated database. In the future we will reverse this process. Instead of trying to build as much logic as possible into large applications, we are going to break up applications into smaller distributable modules. Defined interfaces will be seen as opportunities, not as barriers. Distributed systems, when well designed, will be reliable and will allow system components to operate asynchronously. Methods of application design that are common in factory and process automation will become common for providing support to traditional business and management processes. Increasingly we will conceptualize information systems as communicating cells, each dependent upon the whole but capable of providing independent support for local tasks and operations.

The more advanced companies will achieve integration of the three types of applications through a client-server application model. However, at best this implementation will be only partially achieved by large organizations in the next ten years.

Distribution of processing

Computer processing will increasingly be distributed to where the work is done, subject to seveal constraints:

- Systems will need to operate at relatively high-performance levels even when segments are down, including the center of the system. For example, when an airline computer reservation system is down at a major airport, the rest of the system must be protected.
- Recovery will need to be nearly automatic after a breakdown. This is the concept of the self-healing process.
- Recovery will need to restore high-value information first. Take a system monitoring a multinational portfolio of bank loans. Following a breakdown, the system will recapture information in order of importance, using criteria such as loan size, the risk of breaching the credit limit, and the borrower's credit worthiness. Transactions will be posted in a sequence that updates the data most critical for decision making first. This implies that the recovery system 'understands' the business's needs.
- The operational aspects of managing a data center, such as backup procedures, mounting of tapes, and so on, must be automated. Distributed computing on the scale we are discussing is viable only if operational costs are reduced through automation.

To summarize, the distribution of processing will be driven by the economics of computation and telecommunications and by the need to fit processing into organizational work patterns – none of which favor centralized processing. Integrity in large multilocation applications will still demand that master data and updating process be stored at one or at most a few locations.

Application development

Our systems today are like London's phone system. When British Telecom (BT) considered replacing the existing analog exchanges in London with modern digital switches, it found the task almost impossible. During the bombing in World War II, engineers had gone out each day to repair the damage done the previous night. Working against time, they did whatever was needed to get service back. After the war, BT had no plans of the real network, only a map of how it was originally designed. Our current systems have the same relationship to their documentation. Usually, on the day systems are computerized, the documentation is already in error. From then on, through upgrades, maintenance, and emergency patches, we increasingly lose track of how the system operates. The result: critical systems that are expensive to maintain and impossible to replace.

Many companies are working intensively on modular design, reusable code, and client-server architectures, and these contributions are helping us to move away from this trap. Yet these depend upon a revolution in systems development practices.

Application models will contribute to this revolution. Unlike applications, which have the services and data structures embedded in them, application models can be used to generate the services and data infrastructure specific to an organization's needs. Each 'application' will have to conform to the same standards used by the applications with which it shares data. It will not be acceptable to make applications conform by modifying the source code.

PC applications running under common user interfaces such as Windows are already using this concept. They have a special installation routine that identifies other packages and builds appropriate links with them. With the development of multimedia application and program-to-program protocols such as Dynamic Data Exchange (DDE) and Object Linking and Embedding (OLE) in Windows, and Publish and Subscribe in the Macintosh, these tools are going to become even more complex.

Generally these install routines work bottom up; each application tries to understand its environment and build what it needs. For enterprise-wide, distributed applications, top-down models will be needed that understand how the applications are to work together. The key building blocks for these models are the information repositories and object request brokers that the major vendors are just beginning to deliver.[15] This is a technology in its infancy, but these models will become key organizationl resources for managing a diverse distributed resource.

Another important influence on systems development is computer-aided software engineering (CASE). CASE tools automate many of the necessary tasks that used to involve tinkering with the programs code, such as linking data to process requirements. In the future, designers will develop systems using high-level modeling tools, from which code will be generated in one clean step. Systems will have self-documenting tools that automatically keep track of all changes. More important, *all* maintenance will be done by changing the design model, not the code. Even a failure of a critical production system will have to be rectified with fully auditable tools, without any loss of service. To reach these goals, we will need to adopt such technologies as tight modularization and dynamic linking so that changes can be made incrementally and almost immediately to the system as it operates. The ultimate test of success will be the retirement of all systems programmers' tools that give direct access to physical memory or disk sectors and that act outside the normal security system.

CASE tools have been developed and marketed largely as productivity tools and mostly for systems professionals. Organizations often have not reaped the promised benefits because they have not understood the need to develop new processes for developing systems. Computer-aided engineering (CAE) has had a similar history. The real pay-off from CAE became available only when organizations began to see its possibility for changing the relationship between design and manufacturing engineering. Implementing CASE, like implementing CAE, is a severe organizational change problem, and it can be successful only when senior executives are willing to pay the price that complex culture change entails. In a recent meeting of senior IT executives, nearly all conceded that there was little understanding among themselves, their management, their users, and their senior staff that CASE was an essential to their organizations' success as was CAE.

Given where we are, the best we can expect is that the 1990s will be the decade of CASE the way the 1980s was the decade of CAE. If this is so, we can expect only moderate success in implementing CASE within very large organizations. However, there are examples of small to medium companies using the available tools to develop fairly complete portfolios of systems.[16] These companies are the forerunners. They succeed because (1) they make a serious organizational commitment; (2) they either start with a clean slate, or they clearly identify ways to work around legacy systems; and (3) they understand that this is an iterative learning process that will challenge basic assumptions.

Despite the trends toward modular design, reusable code, and client-server architectures, larger systems will continue to be built, and they will be built faster and more accurately. As this happens, it will become abundantly clear that accelerating the rate of technical implementation will only be possible if priority is given to managing the consequent changes in work and organization.

Managing technology-based change

Research from the Massachusetts Institute of Technology Management in the 1990s Program suggests that the major reason that the benefits of IT implementation have been so slow in coming is that organizational change is not adequately managed.[17] This thesis seems unarguable to most observers, but there is considerable skepticism that anything can be done about the problem. The reality is that progress *must* be made on this front if the IT executive is to succeed in this decade.

Successful implementation of systems has never been easy. Laudon comments, 'Building an information system, . . . an on-line, distributed, integrated customer service system, . . . is generally not an exercise in "rationality." It is a statement of war or at the very least a threat to all interests that are currently involved in any way with customer service.[18] However, the problem will become more severe in this decade: the technology is allowing us to build ever larger and more complex systems, and supporting interdependent business processes will require those larger and more complex systems. Thus IT will continue to be involved in a change process that, at the same time, it makes more complex. IT complicates the change process in a number of ways; it moves the locus of knowledge and hence power in the organization, it changes the time dimension of processes and decisions, and it enables new organizational constructs to be implemented.

Consequently, organizational issues, resistance, and other change management problems become more pronounced. IT executives need to be aware that there is a body of literature and practice in organizational change that has been and can be applied to their problems and that they need to be the champion for technology-enabled change.[19]

Even with a commitment to change management, companies are likely to find that people's inability to change, not technology, is the limiting factor in transforming organizations.

Economic considerations

The IT executive will need to be aware of some important long-term economic considerations in devising strategies.

1   Technology will be increasingly cheaper and equally available for all companies. More software will be available through retail and mail-order supplies. Even Unix software will be available ready to install on most platforms using vendor-supplied install routines. The same economies in software development and merchandising currently enjoyed for the IBM PC and Apple Macintosh platforms will spread to the other major platforms. Thus, advantage will accrue to those companies that develop improved business processes and decision processes more effectively (cheaper, faster, and of higher quality) than their competitors. In the year 2000, the cost differential in the acquisition of computer technology will be smaller than today. There will be fewer economies of scale available to larger companies. Also, in the race to increase the power of systems, the cost difference between competing platforms will tend to decrease. All workstations are getting cheaper at roughly the same pace. The absolute cost differential for any size machine will decrease. In addition, chips – the raw material – are likely to become more standardized and shared across product lines. In a commodity business there will be less advantage

to selecting one vendor or another. There will continue to be significant differences in how well companies implement technology and therefore in the benefits they achieve. How well a technology is used is a function of organizational learning. In this sense the choice of vendor will continue to remain crucial – not the hardware vendor, but the systems integrator consultant.

2   Companies will have to make major investments to complete their IT infrastructures and to keep them current. For example, the workstation population can be expected to turn over at least twice in the coming ten-year period owing to technology cost-performance improvements and the availability of new software. Consider a company that is roughly at maximum penetration of 1 workstation per employee with a total of 10,000 workstations. It would then have a minimum capital cost of 20,000 times at least $5,000 per workstation, or $100 million over the decade, irrespective of other infrastructure items. Facing up to the implications of infrastructure completion and reinvestment will not be easy.

IT function in the year 2000

There are an ample number of future predictions for the IT function.[20] The IT function in the year 2000 will most probably continue its evolution as a hybrid – manager of infrastructure and staff advisor to senior executives and user organizations. As Dixon and John note, 'IT manages the technology, and line executives manage the application of the technology through partnerships with IT.'[21] Learning how to work effectively with all the stakeholders, including vendors, to accomplish the necessary changes will be a major task of the decade.

IT will retain a strategic role because it is the gatekeeper for introducing and integrating new technology and processes. The IT function's critical knowledge, which is knowing how to navigate a course to technical integration, will evolve to become a mix of technical, business, organizational, and consulting skills.

Key challenges for the decade

The initial vision of the future in this chapter was deliberately high tech. Most organizations will not be operating at that level, and the major challenge for IT executives will be helping their organizations exploit the technology opportunites.

Although the list could be quite long, we highlight a few key challenges for the IT executive in these interesting years to come:

●   Managing the evolving infrastructure – overseeing the movement to scalable client-server architectures, introducing exciting new enabling technologies, preserving current investments, generating capital to complete the infrastructure and revitalize it as it becomes obsolete, and learning how to operate a worldwide utility that ranks in complexity with moderate-sized telephone companies of today.

- Managing infrastructure financing – deciding when to take advantage of outsourcing, resource leasing, and other techniques that give the organization access to scalable power on demand without compromising the organization's development of competitive advantage technology.
- Moving toward the new application architectures necessary to transform organizational business and decision processes – continuing to distribute function to where work is done, segmenting application logic along client and server lines, and so forth. Some solutions will come from vendors as they upgrade their systems planning and integration methodologies. The most important of these technologies will require the organization to develop its own models that describe its business process and to link them to its technology systems. This information architecture will be the road map for the systems development process and the anchor for justifying IT investment. Without an understandable information architecture, IT will be unable to bridge the gulf between the new technologies and the business's strategic directions.
- Addressing the implications of managed organizational change both for CASE and for reengineered business process. CASE is moving rapidly from a future goal to a current critical success factor. The technology will continue to change rapidly. This is going to put the IT organization under considerable stress. Current skills will become obsolete, and the cost structure of IT will be transformed. The senior IT executive has to manage a complete transformation of the function while ensuring quality support for customers. This will not happen through benign neglect. Active strategies for managing the institutionalization of CASE, prototyping the developing technology, and moving up the learning curve until the technology is absorbed by the IT and user organizations will require energy and new skills. Reengineered business processes are technologies that must be transferred into the organization, with similar implications for changes in skills and learning. Largely missing in organizations today is a person to take responsibility for managing technology-driven organizational change, for learning what can be done and how to apply it, and for acting as a change champion. It may be that the success or viability of the IT organization will depend on how well it fills this vacuum.
- Managing the new buy-versus-make paradigm. Each company has a history and a culture that make it more or less successful at using packages and at building applications from scratch. The quantity of technology now available and the increasing level of integration mean that most major applications will be hybrids. Successful companies will

be those that manage integration most effectively and apply in-house resources to the tasks with the highest payoff.

Overarching all these issues is the fact that no company is an island. As a web of networks develops and people begin to focus on linkages across and outside organizations, key standards will be developed that will come to define 'open systems.' Successful IT managers will understand the standard development process and position their organization to benefit from other's investments.

Surprises

This chapter started with the hypothesis that it was possible to make reasonable predictions of the future of IT based upon a few long-term trends. But prospective futurologists are advised to consider the track record of their profession. In many ways the future is bound to surprise us. Yet we can guess where some of the surprises will come from. They are those areas where there is no useful track record or analog from the past.

Mobile MIPS

With powerful portable workstations becoming commonplace, how will they be transformed? Will we see special purpose systems targeted to the needs of particular professions or modular designs with plug-in hardware for particular tasks? The ergonomics and economics of personal tools are still maturing.

We do not even pretend to guess the full consequences of the next generation of cellular laptops. Currently, the extra power is being devoted to better interfaces, pen and voice. Yet the cost-performance trend of the technology is such that there will be resources to do significant work. What will that be? Does this enable a new class of independent or franchised professionals who take industry-specific solutions to clients? How will schools integrate the use of portable knowledge bases in classes?

Data – available, accessible and interconnected

The amount of data – text, numbers, pictures, voice, and video – in databases and accessible is going to explode. The universal data highways will bring a vast array of information to anyone who wishes to tap it. Yet access to information has always been a source of power and influence, and access to megadatabases will change relationships among individuals, organizations, and the state. As a society we are only beginning to understand the practices and ethics of data collection and management. The outcry over Lotus's Marketplacetm system and current concerns about credit reporting systems are examples of the issues to be addressed and the stakes involved. At another level there are likely to be new classes of services and products. In a glut of data there will be a market for editors to sift, choose, compare, validate, and present information, whether those editors are knowbots or people.

Integration

In combination, the mobility of computing and the availability of vast amounts of data will produce combinations and applications that are truly unpredictable today.

New systems development

What effect will the new systems development tools have on the design of business processes? If we can build systems using flexible, adaptable, and innovative technology, what does that say for the way we change business processes? Are we going to see the end of the big application? Will it be replaced by iterative, evolutionary development of improved processes? Indeed, will the technology of systems development at last put business managers back in control of creating and managing the systems they use?

References

1 *Scientific American.* September 1991. The issue is devoted to a series of articles on how computers and telecommunications are changing the way we live and work.
2 R. I. Benjamin, 'Information Technology in the 1990s: A Long-Range Planning Scenario.' *MIS Quarterly.* June 1982. pp. 11–31.
3 M. L. Dertouzos. 'Communications. Computers and Networks.' *Scientific American.* September 1991, pp. 30–37.
4 T. W. Malone, J. Yates, and R. Benjamin. 'The Logic of Electronic Markets.' *Harvard Business Review.* May–June 1989, pp. 166–172.
5 'A Talk with INTEL.' *Byte.* April 1990, pp. 131–140.
6 J. Yates and R. I. Benjamin. '*The Past and Present as a Window on the Future.*' in *The Corporation of the 1990s*, M. S. Scott Morton, ed. (New York: Oxford University Press, 1991) pp. 61–92.
7 V. G. Gerf, 'Networks,' *Scientific American*, September 1991, pp. 42–51.
8 Unix, developed by Bell Labs in the early 1970s, is an 'operating system, a religion, a political movement, and a mass of committees,' according to Peter Keen. 'It has been a favorite operating system of technical experts . . . owing to its "portability" across different operating environments and hardware, its support of "multitasking" (running a number of different programs at th same time), and its building-block philosophy of systems development (building libraries of small "blocks" from which complex systems can be built).' See: P. G. W. Keen, *Every Manager's Guide to Information Technology* (Boston: Harvard Business School Press. 1991), pp. 156–157.
9 J. C. Emery, 'Editor's Comments,' *MIS Quarterly*, December 1991, pp. xxi–xxiii.
10 M. J. Piore and C. F. Sabel, *The Second Industrial Divide. Possibilities for Prosperity* (New York Basic Books, 1984); and J. P. Womack, D. T Jones and D. Roos, *The Machine That Changed the World* (New York: Rawson Associates, 1990).
11 T. W. Malone and J. F. Rockart, 'Computers, Networks, and the Corporation,' *Scientific American.* September 1991, pp. 92–99.

12 S. Zuboff, *In the Age of the Smart Machine: The Future of Work and Power* (New York: Basic Books, 1988).

13 'Billing Systems Improve Accuracy, Billing Cycle,' *Modern Office Technology,* February 1990; and C. A. Plesums and R. W. Bartels, 'Large-Scale Image Systems: USA A Case Study,' *IBM Systems Journal 23* (1990): 343–355.

14 M. Weiser, 'The Computer for the Twenty-First Century,' *Scientific American,* September 1991, pp. 66–75.

15 Object request brokers are technologies that allow the user to access programs developed by other companies or groups much as the telephone directory allows a user to speak with someone. These tools give more people access to pre-existing solutions. See: H. M. Osher, 'Object Request Brokers,' *Byte,* January 1991, p. 172.

16 K. Swanson, D. McComb, J, Smith, and D. McCubbrey, 'The Application Software Factory: Applying Total Quality Techniques to Systems Development,' *MIS Quarterly,* December 1991, pp. 567–579.

17 M.S. Scott Morton, ed., *The Corporation of the 1990s* (New York: Oxford University Press, 1991), pp. 13–23.

18 K. Laudon. *A General Model for Understanding the Relationship between Information Technology and Organizations* (New York: New York University, Center for Research on Information Systems. January 1989).

19 See E. H. Schein. *Innovative Cultures and Organizations* (Cambridge, Massachusetts: MIT Sloan School of Management, Working Paper No. 88–064, November 1988); and E. H. Schein, *Planning and Managing Change* (Cambridge, Massachusetts; MIT Sloan School of Management. Working Paper No. 88–056, October 1988).

20 J. F. Rockart and R. Benjamin, *The Information Technology Function of the 1990s: A Unique Hybrid* (Cambridge, Massachusetts; MIT Sloan School of Management, Center for Information Systems Research, Working Paper No. 225, June 1991); and E. M. Von Simson, 'The "Centrally Decentralized" IS Organization,' *Harvard Business Review,* July–August 1990, p. 158–162.

21 P. J. Dixon and D. A. John, 'Technology Issues Facing Corporate Management in the 1990s,' *MIS Quarterly,* September 1989, pp. 247–255.

4 Putting information technology in its place: a polemic for the nineties

M. J. Earl

Introduction

These two pieces of business rhetoric neatly capture the hype and the despair of the 1980s. Claims were made that IT yields competitive advantage (McFarlan, 1984; Porter and Millar, 1985; Ives and Feeny, 1990) and some well known examples still seem credible – at least if they are critically assessed such as the Clemons and Row study of McKesson (1988) or the Copeland and McKenney (1988) analysis of airline reservation systems. As the 1990s unfold, new metaphors are now replacing the old. The IT industry, management consultants and academics suggest that IT can transform the ways in which business is done so that business processes can be redesigned or re-engineered (Hammer,1990; Davenport and Short, 1990). At the same time, we are advised that globalization depends on IT infrastructures, that groupware is the key to levering managerial and professional knowledge, and that telecommunications networks are creating virtual organizations, businesses, regions and markets. Again, each of these claims has some merit and research programmes such as Scott Morton's (1991) *Management In The Nineties* have documented and conceptualized the changing nature of the business in an observable information society.

On the ground however, in many businesses in 1992, IT is undergoing heavy scrutiny and sometimes radical surgery. IT budgets are being capped or pruned. Headcounts in the IT function are under attack, often for the first time. IT and an examination of the IS departments are being rationalized or sold off. IT operations and development are being outsourced. IT directors are being replaced. These are not just reactions to recessionary pressures or changing economics of technology. Chief executives are tiring of IT rhetoric and hype; many of them feel it has been oversold and underdelivered.

Consider three short cases:

1 One of the first actions of a new CEO was to call for an inquiry into the rising costs of IT department's productivity. This was in a bank struggling to recover its leadership in a sector where IT was not only underpinning most business operations but was the platform for the future product development. The outcome of the enquiry was the hiring of a new IT director, the replacement of the second tier of IT management and a cost cutting programme.

2 A new CEO of a manufacturing company considered that the IT function had lost the support of the user community. Once again, a new IT director was appointed. One division's IT department was taken over by a leading vendor in the facilities management sector and another division's IT department was encouraged to make a management buy-out.

3 A financial services company went into deficit for the first time. The CEO recognized that cost restructuring was essential and the IT function became the first target. The headcount was reduced by 90% and the IT budget reduced by 55%. A moratorium was put on IT development and the core information systems activities were outsourced. 'I had to change the culture of the IT department', remarked the CEO, 'they thought the world owed them a living.'

In other words, there are real top management concerns about information technology – and they may be valid. It is not so much hostility or resistance to IT that is being displayed. It is scepticism and frustration. In the first case, top management were not seeing enough benefit from IT. In the third case IT disinvestment was seen to offer a short-term expedient to a business survival problem. Interestingly the CEO in question is now considering how to rebuild IT activities because the CEO sees the recovery strategy as being

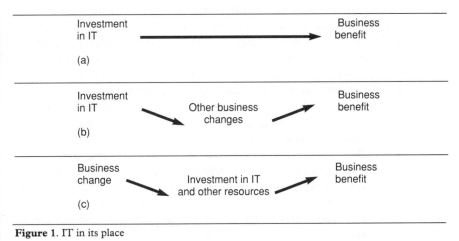

Figure 1. IT in its place

dependent on IT. And in the second case, there is recognition that much of the last year's IT strategy had been appropriate but not appreciated.

So the question can be asked: what is going on? It seems that whilst management in the past have claimed that their approach to IT has been business-led, their policies, action and language suggest a different picture. The hype of strategic IT, the very words 'information technology' and the compound growth of IT expenditure in the 1980s all contributed to putting information technology on a pedestal; to 'putting the cart before the horse'. The time has come to put it in its place – in its proper place. Figure 1 portrays the problem, the partial solution and the way forward.

Figure 1a represents many of the arguments employed in the early 1980s. It was seen as a new and strategic weapon which could be deployed for competitive advantage as much in the market place as within the firm. Build a reservation system, develop online links to customers or suppliers, or construct a flexible manufacturing system, and competitive advantage would follow. Soon the shrewder and more experienced observers suggested that investment in IT alone usually yields very little return. If substantial business benefit was to be earned, other changes were also required, as Figure 1b suggests. A reservation system might be more successful if it were accompanied by customer service programmes or alliances with other businesses to distribute travel related services. On-line links to suppliers and customers would require changes in inventory, manufacturing and distribution policies and procedures, in order to be really effective. Flexible manufacturing systems would provide little benefit unless supported by new working practices and different management controls. It is difficult to argue against such advice. There are calls for holistic approaches to information systems investment.

Figure 1c, however, portrays a third perspective. It turns much of the rhetoric about IT on its head. The suggestion is that firms should identify business change needs or opportunities first. They should then agree what capabilities and actions, including IT, are needed to achieve the change and be managed as a whole if full business benefits are to be delivered. Figure 1c is a simple model of both the dynamics of strategic exploitation of IT as well as its systematic structure. Earl (forthcoming) has shown that where IT has been involved in radical business change or transformation of business operations, technology has rarely been the only, or ultimately the most important, factor at work. The genesis of the change project was an analysis of a crippling business problem and the search for any solution which made sense. Gradually a vision of business change took shape and many other changes were implemented alongside technology and systems, all driven by top management. Those involved talk more of managing change than of anything else. They may not talk of the project as an IT project at all, but of the cost reduction programme or the quality initiative or the customer service mission. Conversely when one hears IT projects described by IT directors as vehicles for organizational change, as forcing cultural change, or as taking the business into the 21st century, they are often descriptions of projects in trouble where technology has been the driver. I even heard one IT strategy being described as the journey to the promised land. They have not arrived there yet!

In the successful change projects, IT may have been the key enabler, but the business benefits derived from understanding the business, committing it to change, and aggressively pursuing the ends not the means. In those projects which brought disappointments and frustrations, the endeavour was managed as an IT project, the IT director stood most to lose, and despite investments in education and propaganda, accompanying investment in other resources lagged that in IT. In short an 'IT project' is often a failed project.

So whilst Figure 1 could be seen as graphic sophistry or a kaleidoscope of project management progressively grounded in organizational realities, it seeks to say more. The dilemmas posed in the opening three captions arise because IT has been seen as somehow 'above' business, beyond question, as different and special, as separate from the rest of organizational activity. Thus corporate doubts about IT exist today because IT has not been put in its proper place. The philosophy of Figure 1a prevails whilst perhaps the questioning CEOs are looking for the manifestation of Figure 1c.

The thinking which tends to dominate various issues of information management when IT is put above the business is summarised as the perspectives labelled 'from IT' in Figure 2. The perspectives labelled 'business change' (the Figure 1c model) suggest the change of orientation implied by placing IT *within* the business. As we shall see the former set is often expressed as constraints by IT directors and concerns by their CEOs. The latter set does not question the potential of IT as a force for change, or dismiss the IT function. Rather, by putting the business first, these perspectives treat IT as an enabling technology and call on the business to put the business back into IT. Each perspective is examined in turn.

Management issue	From IT	To	Business change
Vision	Technology futures	→	Rethinking business
Planning	IT strategies	→	Business themes
Justifying	Financial appraisal	→	Business case
Implementing	Project management	→	Managing Benefits
Controlling	IT expenditure	→	Cost of business
Organizing	IT business	→	Business IT
Learning	IT literacy	→	Organizational development

Figure 2. Putting business back into IT

Vision: 'from technology futures to rethinking business'

It has been fashionable to demand that businesses should have a vision of the future and their managements pursue vision statements crafted by their

CEOs. This has been a plea in the IT world as much as in business strategy in general. It may be valid. However, visions of the future which centre on technology tend to be unhelpful.

For example, an electronics company set up a team to specify a 'factory of the future'. The final recommendations included robotics, computer-integrated manufacturing concepts and lights-out capabilities. When presented, the executive committee was unable to critically evaluate the proposals. They obviously represented a new manufacturing strategy but was it right or wasn't it? Nobody was sure on what principles and assumptions the scenario was based. The report was filed for possible later reference and a new team was assembled to investigate the 'business of the future'.

Earl (forthcoming) has indicated that most radical applications of IT which achieved strategic change for the business did not arise from any visioning of technology at all. They often were conceived from a conviction by a CEO or top manager that a significant business problem had to be solved or, less frequently, that a new business opportunity was available. Usually a team of senior managers, including an IT executive, was established to investigate a vaguely defined problem or idea and make recommendations. IT was rarely mentioned at the outset. A multi-disciplinary task force was given a business remit. In time, the problem or idea was redefined and solutions including IT applications not only took shape but emerged into a larger strategic thrust. It enabled the change but did not beget it.

In an insurance company the issue was how to drive down head office costs. This led to recommendations for automation, relocating many information processing tasks to branches and intermediaries. It then became clear that, by putting sales and policy-related processing nearer to the customer, an embryonic value added network had been established and this could be extended to open up new distribution channels and novel ways of selling.

In a chemical company, exhortation and education, focussing on particularly visionary exemplars, consistently failed to stimulate business unit managers to embrace IT and seek competitive advantage. However, when these same managers were seconded to task forces to examine current business issues such as quality or customer responsiveness, they frequently requested IT projects as part of their recommended strategies.

So the moral of this perspective is to forget technology futures. Concentrate on rethinking business by analysing current business problems and environmental change – and by considering IT as one ingredient of the solution, not the solution.

Planning: 'from IT strategies to business themes'

A common corporate concern is to seek alignment of IT investments with business needs and goals (Brancheau and Wetherbe, 1989). Top management have constantly doubted that IT has been applied in the most beneficial areas. Equally IT directors – recognizing that IT projects are often multi-year developments, demand resources which need forward planning, and are not easily stopped and restarted – look for some certainty of direction. Added to these pressures is the fact that firms felt the need to discover competitive advantage opportunities from IT and the corporate interest in the strategic planning of IT is understandable.

Many methodologies for IS planning are available and most work in the right situation and at the right time. However they are usually battling against the odds. They are often applied where there are no useful business plans to relate to, or where business strategies are too abstract. Frequently they are led by the technologists who are the only people with sufficient incentive to pursue the battles. Commonly they fail because they produce IT oriented models, recommendations and priorities which lose the support of the business.

From research in European companies (Earl, 1990) there appear to be three effective approaches to IT strategy-making. The first is that no IT strategic planning is done at all! Instead normal business planning processes are expected to include an analysis of IT opportunities and consideration of the IS implications of business plans. This happens, for example, in an oil major. The expectation is that a few themes fall out of the annual business planning cycle which deserve, or depend, on IT investment. In this case, there have been major programmes of management education done in-house on IT and strategic analysis. Earlier the company experimented with less than successful formal IS planning techniques – which in hindsight was perhaps part of their education.

In the second workable approach, no IT strategic planning was done because long range planning of any sort was counter-cultural. The more entrepreneurial or reactive company might almost stumble on a significant IT need by accident. However, accidents were designed for, in that all management meetings, agendas and deliberations of note deliberately included discussion of the relationship of IT to the other matters being examined.

The third approach is the use of task forces where every few years, business rethinking exercises are done, e.g. in an automobile company each year a task force is put to work on the topic that is occupying the CEO's mind. IT is always represented on the task force.

With all these approaches, general managers as well as IT managers, usually end up articulating only one or two business initiatives which are driving the IT effort. These can be thoughts of themes not plans, driving the IT effort for several years running. Management can explain why these are in progress and what needs to be done. Thus the moral of this perspective is find business themes for IT rather than formulate IT strategies for the business.

Justifying: 'from financial appraisal to business case'

IT managers frequently complain that good IS projects are turned down by faulty investment appraisal. There is too much emphasis on cost so that projects look expensive and only cost savings are accepted as returns. This can impede development of IT applications which are aimed at generating revenue or building market position. Alternatively the IT community concedes that some benefits are difficult to quantify with any accuracy or certainty. Classically, this is the problem with justifying infrastructure projects. General managers then add their concerns. They feel that it is difficult to set priorities between competing claims for IT resources. More recently they ask how we can decide whether an IT project is more deserving than any other project calling for financial and other resources?

All these are understandable doubts. However, they are not unique to information technology. Many a proponent of capital investment projects will cast doubts on DCF techniques, payback criteria and profitability indices. Many R & D directors or personnel managers will question methods for allocating funds to functions. In most IT situations, the problem is connected to the earlier issues of vision and planning. The perspective is at fault.

If an IT investment is an integral part of a vision of the future business, justification is simplified. If an IT project is essential to achievement of the business plan, the case is clearer. Why is this so? First, the business understands why the investment is being proposed. Secondly it may already be committed to it. Thirdly, the benefits may be stated, even if not in numbers, more confidently in terms of business rationale. Fourthly, both the expenditure and the returns can be built into the business strategic and operating plans more easily. Finally, arguments often fall away about competing priorities. If there is truly a business case as opposed to a financial case alone, different stakeholders can usually see, or at least accept, priority decisions. Furthermore, most of them are likely to be involved in the initiative anyway and thus will be gaining or committing resources.

Let us consider some cases. A travel company was unsure whether to introduce IT systems into distribution channels. The costs were clear but there was no agreement on the size and probability of the benefits. However, when the Board asked themselves what would be the outcome if their main rival implemented a similar project, an answer was clear. A new form of channel warfare would begin; they had to be the first mover.

When a textile company evaluated a proposal for introducing production planning and control systems, the calculated NPV and payback fell well below corporate hurdle rates. The Board then discussed what would happen if they rejected the project. There was unanimous agreement that increasingly manufacturing would be incapable of responding to more fashion-intensive customer needs and shorter lead times. The business would suffer. As the CEO said, 'either our financial calculations are wrong or the appraisal methods are. The business case is clear, if we don't do it we die'.

Finally, from research of IT innovations (Lockett, 1987; Ives and Vitale, 1992) it is clear that new ways of doing business would not have happened if tight financial yardsticks had been applied. Often the benefits, and the costs, were initially unclear but someone, usually outside the IT department, had an idea for business change. Construction of a prototype system demonstrated what the real benefits – often unforeseen – and costs were. After a trial period a clear business rationale emerged and the system's supporters had the confidence to estimate enough benefits to justify full investment in the innovative application. Meanwhile the prototype had demonstrated what were the significant business and organizational changes involved and had informed the project's sponsors how to manage them.

So the moral of this perspective is clear. Focus on business changes, not IT costs and benefits in justifying IT applications. If you are in doubt, experiment to discover or prove the business benefits. A business case then becomes more persuasive than applying conventional financial appraisal - or at least allows a better estimate of the numbers.

Implementing: 'from project management to managing the benefits'

Some IS developments today qualify as major projects. They are large in work content, substantial in potential impact and carry several risks. IT executives therefore frequently call for both better project managers and improved project management techniques. They may be right to do so, but there are other issues to address.

Managements still claim that IT projects tend not to achieve their intended objectives. They also complain of cost over-runs and time delays; however, they generally put up with these if the application is eventually seen to have been worthwhile. Achieve the ends, or put another way, deliver the benefits and problems over the means are soon forgotten. But project managers and project planning and control techniques all too often focus on the means, on costs and on time targets, particularly on the IT activities. They also assume the users will do whatever is necessary on all the other fronts of change and that the benefits will flow and initial objectives will be met.

Earl (1991) shows the problem is still more serious. Many projects are conceptual; they do not advance beyond the feasibility stage. Resources are not made available, new priorities take over, and disagreements between users and IS professionals begin to surface. Project initiation can be more difficult than project approval.

However, research into IS projects has discovered some patterns of success (Runge, 1985; Lockett, 1987; Edwards, 1991; Earl, forthcoming). Three factors stand out. High change IT applications have project champions – user managers who are tasked to make sure systems are implemented and the benefits realized. These champions often appoint themselves; they arise informally, usually because they or their area of the business has been clear about the benefits (and risks) from the outset. Indeed they may have argued and battled for the system in the first place. However, they commonly need higher level support as well – a project sponsor. A sponsor is a senior executive to go to when substantial resource difficulties, organizational constraints or system disputes arise. The sponsor identifies with the benefits so that he or she will commit the organization to the application. The sponsor was probably asked to initially justify the investment.

But how do sponsors and champions evaluate and understand the benefits? Often one of them was a member of the team or task force who proposed the application. They therefore own the system - and have a team behind them. This suggests that championship and sponsorship (i.e. collective leadership) are more important than sole champions or sponsors. In other cases the champion led a trial (a prototype) which established costs and benefits and then initiated a tighter phase of project management.

Pervading these dynamics, is a determined effort to articulate project benefits, own them as goals and aggressively manage their realization. It is a recognition that only users can deliver benefits; the IT function builds the tools. So the moral is this: project management as conventionally understood, though necessary, is too narrow. The focus has to be on managing the benefits, which seems to imply having benefits managers attending to, and having authority for, non-IT resources as much as IT itself.

Controlling: 'from IT expenditure to cost of business'

IT directors, and the industry at large, have been obsessed in recent years by the size of their IT budgets. To be sure, the growth has been remarkable in some companies and presenting the figures does demonstrate that information resources need to be managed efficiently and effectively. However it is the size and escalation of the numbers which leads to some of the CEO attitudes represented in the opening captions. Naive budget capping, crude value for money questions, short term pressures to outsource and draconian functional restructuring are inevitable responses if the cost of IT is emphasized at the expense of its value. This is not to say any of these actions are invalid; rather it is a concern to avoid emotional actions in desperate situations. What is required in the 1990s is both a strategic appreciation of the value of IT and a detailed understanding of the resultant cost base.

First the value question. One figure is revealing; today, in many organizations, there is as much spent on IT outside the IT department's boundaries as within. If a market knows the best philosophy is assumed, then these end-users have worked out the cost-benefit equation. Indeed if their personal computers, treasury work stations or CAD terminals were taken away from them there would probably be loud cries 'foul'. These users perceive IT as part of their daily work-life; in some companies new recruits receive a terminal or personal computer with their desk. Much end-user or functional niche computing is already embedded in business functioning and integrated with its local environment. IT in this arena has become a cost of daily business.

Another perspective on value is the cost of not investing in IT. A survey of the adoption of electronic data interchange (EDI) in four sectors in Europe (Peterson, 1990; Krucik, 1990) found that several businesses had to join EDI networks to keep their customers or suppliers. For them, IT became a cost of staying in business. However, so did accompanying improvements in operational procedures, or customer service, or human resource skills. Business change brought cost implications for IT and non-IT factors.

In a chemical company (Earl, 1989) a new competitive strategy was discovered through its investment in manufacturing technology. One project led to another as automation goals were replaced by service goals which, in turn, were superseded by competitive differentiation based on building knowledge of the process and product. Previously starved of capital, the firm's strategic renewal is leading to a pattern familiar in many industries; over half of its capital expenditure is now on IT. This is the cost of business (and survival) in information intensive businesses.

So recognizing that IT is increasingly not a discretionary expenditure is important. Conversely, however, understanding the cost consequences of IT investments becomes more necessary than ever. A retail bank introduced possibly the most modern front office technology to be found anywhere. The rationale for this investment was improved customer service. However, the level of infrastructure required could not be funded on an 8% market share. The market share had to double to make the investment viable - an unlikely proposition. This bank did not understand that IT investments were becoming a barrier to entry in some markets unless infrastructures were shared or economies of scale were achieved some other way.

Where IT is embedded in, or supporting, products and processes it becomes necessary to trace the IT costs to assess the economics of new product or service introductions or operational changes. For example, an airline did a distribution cost analysis of IT expenditure to help managers evaluate alternative ways of doing business. Likewise activity-based costing could be introduced where IT applications underpin the production or delivery of services. Indeed one argument for chargeout of information systems is that consciousness of IT costs is raised as a result, not so much at the macro-level, but at the micro-level of individual business decisions.

So the moral is this: obsession with total IT expenditure figures and ratios is meaningless and unhelpful. For most businesses many IT expenditures are mandatory; IT is a cost of business. However this means these costs should be visible, traceable, analysed and part of most decision-making models at both the operational and strategic levels of business.

Organizing: 'from IT to business IT'

A canon which originated in the 1970s was manage IT as a 'business within a business'. As large, central DP departments evolved, it was clear that they could be seen as economic units with revenues, expenses, customers, suppliers, capital and people. The business within a business metaphor was one way of introducing more professional expectations of DP management. Cost centre accountability was soon introduced, perhaps to be replaced with a profit centre mission. For some corporations (and some IT directors) in the spirit of the 1980s, it then seemed attractive to spin-off the IT department, as it was called, as a business venture. It might trade only within the corporation or it could sell services outside. This, it was claimed, would make IT professionals stand on their own feet and demonstrate to customers that they were commercially mature.

For some the recipe worked – at least for a time. However, research done in European companies (Feeny *et al.*, 1987) suggests that the prescription does not easily fit the demands of the 1990s. The most important requirement for the IT function, if IT is to be effectively exploited, is that it is well integrated with the rest of the business. Figure 1c implies this. The required fit is about structure and also management style (Hodgkinson, 1991). Above all, IT management must know the host orgnization's business, their peers be aware of what IT can offer, and the management processes for IT activities be congruent with the culture of the organization as a whole.

One implication is that the IT function must get close to the business. For example in decentralized organizations a totally centralized IT function is too remote from the sharp end of business. At the minimum, management teams should have an IT executive in their midst sharing problems, shaping solutions, joining study teams and task forces and committed to the business. Some development resource probably needs to be devolved too, to respond to business threats and opportunities in a timely and relevant manner. Indeed in centralized organizations, a case can be made for distributing some IT resource into other functional lines for the same reasons. It is not so obvious, however, that IT operations need to be devolved. The factory side of IT can be run anywhere, locally, regionally, centrally or even outsourced – and should be decided according to criteria of efficiency and reliability. Often local handling of IT operations can divert attention from the more important business unit responsibilities of strategic planning of IT applications and managing IS development and implementation.

These research studies (Feeny *et al.*, 1987; Earl *et al*, 1992) also show that

IT groups set up as profit-making ventures, as businesses in their own right, are often suboptimal in terms of satisfying the host organization's needs. Their eye is perceived to be on profit goals alone. They are accused of favouring external clients or leaking competitive advantages. They become less involved with daily understanding of their host business. They may succeed as businesses but gradually their strategic contribution to the parent falls away - not least as the operational, service and profit contribution role expected of them conflicts with their strategy-guiding, leadership and developmental role.

The generic problem is that the functional characteristics of IT: specialist knowledge, professional leadership, career development, technology stewardship, are valid but the pay off of IT is in the business, whether in business units or other functions. The functional characteristics are concerned with efficiency and standards. Only the business can deliver the effectiveness and benefits. If a choice has to be made, the pendulum has to swing towards the latter proposition. Otherwise the syndrome of 'an IT department too good for the business' or 'IT disconnected from the business' is the inevitable result.

So the moral is this: the potential of running IT as a business can be limited. More important, decisions about IT use need to be in the business. Benefits are limited unless it is the business' IT – not least to ensure that IT is represented in the processes of strategy - making (formal or informal) and to ensure good fit between IT and other resource changes.

Learning 'from IT literacy to organizational development'

In the early 1980s, it was fashionable to talk of 'IT literacy', to arrange 'IT awareness' courses and to call for managers to improve their 'IT fluency'. Indeed these metaphors are not dead; the IT awareness industry is alive and well one decade later. Hands-on training may have decayed, but education courses and conference proselytizing still prevail. These may have helped some managers and raised the profile of IT. Such events can provide useful kickstarts to new thinking on IT and its exploitation and reinforce lessons of the past. However they are not sufficient, can often confirm managers' prejudices about IT and can easily focus on the wrong objective.

There is evidence emerging of an alternative paradigm founded on three premises. First, managers learn about IT through business lenses not technospeak. Second, understanding the potential of IT demands knowledge of business operations as much as of technology and systems. Finally, many of us learn by doing not listening or watching.

A decade of experience in information management education suggests that management teams learn more than individual managers if the objective is understanding and internalizing the business potential of IT. However, they learn more by analysing their business first, then thinking about the place of IT and agreeing what needs to be done to put ideas into action.

Workshops with management teams can generate a shared understanding of the contribution of IT to the business, a common language for thinking and talking about this, and a collective commitment to do something. This is one way of putting IT in its place (the business) and putting management back into IT.

What such events often reveal, however, is that whilst management may have a strategic sense of their business, they have lost touch with the operational realities. Ask a top manager how an order is taken and processed, or a purchase invoice actually handled or operations actually organized and they are frequently unsure. Yet it is at this level that IT opportunities and consequences are best understood. This is especially true if radical redesign of business processes is the objective. The richest educational experience I had encountered for some time was in a workshop not with a management team but with a hierarchical slice of a company from top to bottom. When secretaries, supervisors, and middle managers began to share business problems with senior executives and functional specialists a different perspective emerged. Real problems, previously unheeded opportunities and burning ideas were articulated and a hitherto hidden but obvious strategic thrust for IT was agreed. Many ideas for IT application and much potential understanding of what is involved comes from within organizations not from the top.

Finally, my own research (Earl, forthcoming) suggests that many radical and significant applications of IT evolve in an incremental manner where managers and organizations learn by doing. One application idea leads to another. So education and development in IT may come from experimentation rather than conceptualization. There are at least three consequences of this phenomenon. First some of the IS budget should be allowed for prototyping and experimentation by users and joint IS-user teams when interesting ideas arise. This might be called education as much as IT. Second, educational events which are closer to action learning than classroom teaching make sense. An example might be setting up an IT development project as an organizational development programme where development, implementation, evaluation and tuition all intermingle. Third, the debate about hybrid managers (Earl and Skyrme, 1991) is relevant. Where the aim is to create line managers and users to have some IT capability to help them in the developmental and innovative side of their jobs, the hybrid concept makes sense, i.e. giving managers a period in the IS function not necessarily to become IT managers or professionals but to become more confident users.

So the moral here is this: IT literacy campaigns have random influences. Integrating IT and its management into organizational development processes is more likely to succeed.

Conclusion

In many ways, this chapter is a polemic. It argues for a shift of emphasis or perspective in applying and managing IT. But the polemic is based on a collection of empirical studies done in business organizations in recent years. The messages may seem like common sense. Unfortunately common sense is all too uncommon or a matter of hindsight. In the case of information technology it is eroded by the enthusiasm (or hype) of the IT industry, the specialist knowledge based power of the IT function and the technological temerity of general management at large. Information technology is also 'different'. It is always changing, makes progress through enthusiasts and radical thinkers, is complex and demanding in many ways and can breed a rationality which does not fit easily on the conventional behaviour of individuals and organizations.

The need to integrate IT with the business is not a new message either. We relearn the truism evey decade. The Management in the Nineties programme (Scott - Morton, 1991) is a well researched reminder (in the idiom of an information society) that technology, strategy, organization structure, individuals and their roles, corporate culture and management processes need to be developed as a whole. My polemic can be seen as a set of managerial mandates congruent with this philosophy.

The central thrust of the polemic then is not to treat IT in isolation, or, even worse, above the business. Grounded in the dynamics of organizational behaviour and the experiences of those companies who seem to have more success than failure with IT, it seeks to put IT in its place. This is not so much to knock IT off its pedestal; there is evidence that information technology can enable orders of magnitude change in business. It is more to straighten out managerial thinking. The graphics of Figure 1 emphasize that business change not technological change is a more promising perspective. The framework of Figure 2 suggests that the focus must be on the business first and so each of the seven consequential shifts of mindset represents a management corrective to what might be called the 'information tendency', that is IT thinking at odds with the realities of management.

Without these correctives, the costs will be high. They include some of the potentially short-term naive reactions represented in the opening captions. More important, they include both missed opportunities to achieve the order of magnitude business benefits which can be enabled by IT and the dangers of becoming uncompetitive against those who have managed to put IT in its place - not by cutting it down to size but by putting the management back into information technology.

References

Beath, C. (1992) The Information Technology Champion, in *Information Management: The Organisational Dimension*, Earl, M. J. (ed) (Oxford University Press, Oxford).

Brancheau, J. C. and Wetherbe, J. C. (1987) Key issues in information systems management. *MIS Quarterley*, **11**, 1, 23–45.

Clemons, E. K. and Row, M. (1988) McKenson Drug Company A case study of Economost – a strategic information system. *Journal of Management Information Systems*, **5**, 1, 36–50.

Copeland, D. G. and McKenney, J. L. (1988) Airline reservation systems: lessons from history. *MIS Quarterly*, **12**, 3, 353–370.

Davenport, T. H. and Short, J. E. (1990) The new industrial engineering. Information technology and business process redesign. *Sloan Management Review*, Summer, 11–27.

Edwards, B. (1992) The role of the sponsor in IS projects, in *Information Management: The Organisational Dimension* Earl, M. J. (ed) (Oxford University Press, Oxford).

Earl, M. J. (1990) Approaches to strategic information systems planning: experience in twenty-one United Kingdom companies, in *Proceedings of the International Conference on Information Systems*, Copenhagen, 1990.

Earl, M. J. (forthcoming) IT and competitiveness: the origins of innovative applications.

Earl, M. J. and Skyme, D. (1992) Hybrid managers: what do we know about them? *Journal of Information Systems*, **2**, 3.

Earl, M. J., Feeny, D. F. and Edwards, B. (1992) Structuring the IS function in complex organisations, in *Information Management: The Organisational Dimension*. Earl, M. J. (ed) (Oxford University Press, Oxford).

Edwards, B. (1992) The role of the sponsor in IS projects, in *Information Management: The Organisational Dimension* Earl, M. J. (ed) (Oxford University Press, Oxford).

Feeny, D. F., Earl, M. J. and Edwards, B. (1987) *Complex Organisations and the Information Systems Function. A Research Study.* Oxford Institute of Information Management Research and Discussion Paper RDP 87/7. Templeton College Oxford.

Hammer, M. (1990) Reengineering work: don't automate, obliterate. *Harvard Business Review* July - August, 104–112.

Hodgkinson, S. L. (1991) The role of the corporate IT function in the large multi-business company. Unpublished PhD thesis, University of Oxford.

Ives, B. and Feeny, D (1990) In search of sustainability. *Journal of Management Information Systems*, 7, 27–46.

Ives, B. and Vitale, M. (1992) Competitive information systems: some organisational design considerations, in *Information Management: The Organisational Dimension*, Earl M. J. (ed) (Oxford University Press, Oxford).

Lockett, M. (1987) *The Factors Behind Successful IT Innovation.* Research and Discussion Paper RDP 87/9. Oxford Institute of Information Management. Templeton College Oxford 1987.

McFarlan, F. W. (1984) Information technology changes the way you compete. *Harvard Business Review*, **62**, 98–103.

Porter, M. E. and Millar, V. E. (1985) How information gives you competitive advantage. *Harvard Business Review*, **63**, 19–160.

Runge, D. A. (1985) *Using Telecommunications for Competitive Advantage*, unpublished doctoral thesis, University of Oxford, 1985.

Scott-Morton, M. S. (1991) *The Corporation of the 1990s: Information Technology an Organisational Transformation* (Oxford University Press, Oxford).

Peterson, G. and Krucik, D. (1990) Electronic unpublished MPhil Dissertations, University of Oxford, Oxford.

Reproduced from Earl. M. J. (1992). Putting information technology in its place: a polemic for the nineties. *Journal of Information Technology*, 7, 100–108. Reprinted with permission.

5 Information systems management and strategy formulation: applying and extending the 'stages of growth' concept

R. D. Galliers and A. R. Sutherland

Introduction

For some time, reason has held that the organizational growth with respect to the use of Information Technology (IT) and the approach organizations take to the management and planning of information systems could be conceived of in terms of various, quite clearly defined, stages of maturity. Whilst there has been some criticism of the models that have been postulated, many view the various 'stages of growth' models as being useful in designating the maturity (in IT terms) of organizations. Four such 'stages of growth' models are described briefly below, i.e. those postulated by: (a) Nolan (1979); (b) Earl (1993; 1986, as amended by Galliers, 1987a, 1989*); (c) Bhabuta (1988), and (d) Hirschheim, *et al.* (1988).

The Nolan model is perhaps the most widely known and utilized of the four – by both practitioner and researcher alike. Despite its critics, by 1984, it had been used as a basis for over 200 consultancy studies within the USA by Nolan, Norton and Company, and had been incorporated into IBM's information systems planning consultancies (Nolan, 1984); Hamilton & Ives (1982) report that the original article describing the model (Gibson & Nolan, 1974) was one of the 15 most cited by information systems researchers.

*Galliers, R.D. (1989) The developing information systems organization: an evaluation of the 'stages of growth' hypothesis, paper presented at the London Business School, January 1989.

The Nolan model

Nolan's original four-stage model (Gibson & Nolan, 1974) was later developed into a six-stage model (Nolan, 1979), and it is this latter model which is most commonly applied. Like the models that followed it, it is based on the premise that the organizations pass through a number of identifiable growth phases in utilizing and managing IT. These 'stages of growth' are then used to identify the organization's level of maturity in this context, with a view to identifying key issues associated with further IT development.

Nolan posited that the growth phase could be identified primarily by analysing the amount spent on data processing (DP) as a proportion of sales revenue, postulating that DP expenditure would follow an S-curve over time. More importantly, however, it was claimed that this curve appeared to represent the learning path with respect to the general use of IT within the organization. As indicated above, the original four-stage model (Figure 1) was expanded into a six-stage model in 1979 with the addition of two new stages between 'control' and 'maturity', namely 'integration' and 'data administration'.

The six-stage model is illustrated in Figure 2. As can be seen, Nolan indicates that, in addition to DP expenditure, there are four major growth processes that can be analysed to identify the organization's stage of maturity with respect to IT use.

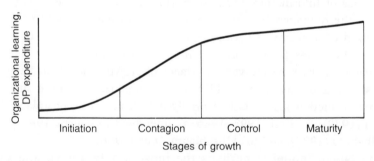

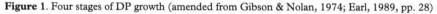

Figure 1. Four stages of DP growth (amended from Gibson & Nolan, 1974; Earl, 1989, pp. 28)

1   The scope of the *application portfolio* throughout the organization (moving from mainly financial and accounting systems to wider-ranging operational systems, to management information systems).
2   The focus of the *DP organization* (moving from a centralized, 'closed shop' in the early stages to data resource management in maturity).
3   The focus of the *DP planning and control* activity (moving from a primarily internal focus in the first three stages to an external focus in the latter stages), and

4   The level of *user awareness* [moving from a primarily reactive stance (reactive, that is, to centralized DP initiatives) in the first two stages, to being a driving force for change in the middle stages, through to a partnership in maturity].

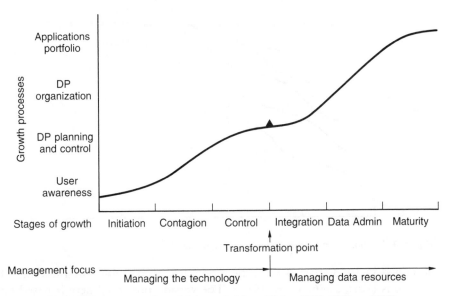

Figure 2. Nolan's six-stage growth model (amended from Nolan, 1979; Galliers, 1989)

Nolan argues that the information systems management focus is very much concerned with technology *per se* during the earlier stages of growth, with a transformation point occurring at the completion of stage three, after which the focus is on managing the organization's data resources, utilizing database technology and methods.

As indicated earlier, the model has been criticized because it has not proved possible to substantiate its claims to represent reality, either as a means to describe the phases through which organizations pass when utilizing IT, or as a predictor of change (Benbasat, *et al.*, 1984; King & Kraemer, 1984). In addition, its focus on database technology clearly dates the model. Earl (1989), for example, argues that organizations will pass through a number of different learning curves with respect to *different* ITs, as illustrated in Figure 3. In addition, it is now clear that different parts of a single organization may well be at different stages of growth with respect to a particular IT.

The Earl model

Unlike Nolan's model, Earl's concentrates attention on the stages through which organizations pass in *planning* their information systems. First

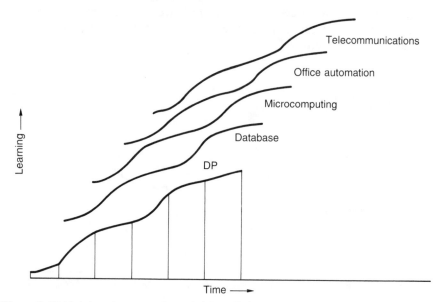

Figure 3. Multiple learning curves (amended from Earl, 1989, p. 31)

described in 1983 (Earl, 1983), the model has been revised on a number of occasions (Earl, 1986, 1988, 1989). The version presented here is based on the two earlier versions, as amended by Galliers (1987a, 1989), bearing in mind Earl's own subsequent changes. As can be seen from Table 1, Earl illustrates the changing agenda for information systems planning by concentrating attention on what is seen as the primary *task* of the process: its major *objective*, the *driving forces* of the planning process (in terms of those involved), the *methodological emphasis*, and the *context* within which the planning takes place. Following research on current information systems planning practice, Galliers adds to this a supplementary early stage of planning (which is essentially *ad hoc* in nature) and an additional factor, concerning the *focus* of the planning effort. In the latter context, he argues that the focus has tended to change over the years from a predominantly *isolated*, Information Systems function orientation, through an *organizational* focus, to a competitive, *environmental* focus.

Earl's argument is essentially that organizations begin their planning efforts by the first attempting to assess the current 'state of play' with respect to information systems coverage and IT utilization. Increasingly, the focus shifts to management concern for a stronger linkage with business objectives. Finally, the orientation shifts to a strategic focus, with a balance being maintained in relation to the make-up of planning teams (between information systems staff, management and users), environmental and organizational information (with the likelihood of inter-organizational systems being developed, cf. Cash & Konsynski, 1985), and the range of approaches adopted (with multiple methods being accepted).

Table 1   Earl's planning in stages model (amended from Earl, 1986, 1988, 1989) and Galliers (1987a, 1989)

Factor	*I*	*II*	*III*	*IV*	*V*	*VI*
			Stages			
Task	Meeting demands	IS/IT audit	Business support	Detailed planning	Strategic advantage	Business-IT strategy linkage
Objective	Provide service	Limit demand	Agree priorities	Balance IS portfolio	Pursue opportunities	Integrate strategies
Driving force	IS reaction	IS led	Senior management led	User/IS partnership	IS/exective led; user involvement	Strategic coalitions
Methological emphasis	*Ad hoc*	Bottom-up survey	Top-down analysis	Two-way prototyping	Environmental scanning	Multiple methods
Context	User/IS inexperience	Inadequate IS resources	Inadequate business/IS plans	Complexity apparent	IS for competitive advantage	Maturity, collaboration
Focus	IS department		Organization-wide		Environment	

The Bhabuta model

Based on earlier work by Gluck *et al.* (1980), which proposes a four-stage process of evolution towards strategic planning, and a somewhat similar model of IT assimilation and diffusion postulated by McFarlan *et al.* (1982, 1983), Bhabuta (1988) developed a model which attempts to map the progress towards formal strategic planning of information systems. This is illustrated in Table 2.

Underpinning Bhabuta's argument is the contention that strategies based on productivity improvement (and the information systems needed to support them) 'will become the dominant paradigm in the turbulent and fiercely competitive markets of the next decade' (Bhabuta, 1988, p. 1.72). His model is more widely focused than either the Nolan or Earl models, in that it attempts to bring together elements of, for example, strategy formulation, information systems, and the mechanisms by which the information systems function is managed. The value sytems associated with each phase of the model are also identified (cf. Ackoff, 1981).

Table 2   Bhabuta's model linking the evaluation of strategic planning with information systems and the organization of the information systems function (amended from Bhabuta, p. 1.76; Sutherland & Galliers, p. 10)

	Phase 1	*Phase 2*	*Phase 3*	*Phase 4*
Evolutionary phases of strategic planning	Basic financial planning	Forecast-based planning	Externally oriented planning	Strategic management
Value System	Meet the budget	Predict the future	Think strategically	Create the future
Competitive strategy mechanisms	Operational level productivity and diffuse innovation	Focused (niche) innovation and operational/tactical level productivity	Focused innovation and strategic productivity (quality focus)	Systemic innovation and productivity
Lead by	Top management	Top and senior management	Entrepreneurial managers (top/ senior/middle)	Corporate-wide employees
Application of IT/IS	Resource management Efficient operations Transaction processing Exception monitoring Planning and analysis	Effectiveness of divisional operations IT infrastructure Support key division makers	IT-based products and services Communications network Direct competitive tool	Inter-organizational IS (link buyers, suppliers, manufacturers, consumers). Facilitate organizational learning
Formalized IS and decision making	Processing of internal data	*Ad hoc* processing of external data	Systematic external data analysis	Link tactical/operational activities to external data analysis
Management of IT, location in hierarchy and scope	Technology manage-ment Individual projects Middle management responsibility	Formal planning of IS Data sharing and administration Focus on IT infusion Senior management responsibility	Couple IT and business planning IT planning at SBU/ corporate level Senior/Top manage-ment responsibility	Systemic support of organizational processes IT planning at SBU/ portfolio level Top management responsibility

In interpreting the Bhabuta model, it should be noted that the categories used are not distinct nor absolute. With the maturing of IT utilization, and managerial sophistication with respect to IT, it can be expected that some of the attributes associated with, for example, Phase 3 and 4 organizations will emerge within Phase 1 and 2 organizations. This point takes account of some of the criticism of the Nolan model (Benbasat *et al.*, 1984), which is itself based on earlier work by Greiner (1972), regarding the discontinuities that organizations experience in growth.

The Hirschheim *et al.* model

The Hirschheim *et al.* (1988) model also builds on the earlier work of Nolan (1979) and arises from research, undertaken during the first half of 1986, into the evolution and management of the IT function in a number of British organizations. As a result of this research. Hirschheim and his colleagues contend that in companies where top management had begun to realize that information systems are vital to their business, organizations move through three evolutionary phases in their management of the IS/IT function. The three phases are labelled 'delivery', 'reorientation' and 'reorganization' (see also Earl, 1989, p. 197).

The 'delivery' phase is characterized by top management concern about the ability of the IS/IT function to 'deliver the goods'. Senior executives have begun to take the subject very seriously, but there is often dissatisfaction with the quality of the available information systems and the efficiency of the IS/IT function, together with mounting concern regarding IT expenditure and the consistency of hardware and infrastructure policies. It would appear that often this phase is initiated by replacing the DP manager with an external recruit with a good track record and substantial computing experience.

The emphasis in this phase is on the 'delivery' of information systems and, accordingly, the newly appointed IS executive spends most of the time on matters internal to the IS department. The primary role is to restore credibility to the function and/or to create confidence in user/top management that the function really is supporting current needs and is run efficiently. During this phase, IS education is sparse, but where it is provided, it is targetted on DP personnel with a view to improving skills, techniques and project management.

In the 'reorientation' phase, top management (or the Director ultimately responsible for IS) changes the focus of attention from the delivery of basic IS services to the exploitation of IT for competitive advantage. An attempt is made to align IS/IT investment with business strategy. In short, it is in this 'reorientation' phase that 'the business is put into computing'. With this change of direction/emphasis, it is common to appoint an IS executive over the DP Manager. The new post is filled, typically, by an insider: a senior executive who has run a business unit or been active in a corporate role, such as marketing or strategy formulation. They are likely to have only limited experience of DP, but are respected by top management for an ability to bring about change. The focus during this second phase is on the market place; on the external environment of the enterprise; on using IT for competitive advantage, and in extending the value chain through inter-organizational systems (cf., Cash & Konsynski, 1985).

In the 'reorganization' phase, the senior IS executive (by now the IT Director) is concerned with managing the interfaces or relationships between the IS function and the rest of the organization. Some areas will be strategically dependent on IS, others will be looking to IS more in a support role. Some will have significant IT capability, particularly with the advance of end-user computing, and some business executives will be driving IT and IS development. Increasingly IS will be managed along 'federal' lines (Edwards *et al.*, 1989) with IS capability in the centre *and* in business units/functions. These changed and changing relationships require careful management and often 'reorganization', and once again attention is focused on internal (organizational), as opposed to external (market place), concerns.

The concerns and considerations associated with each of the phases of the Hirschheim *et al.* model are summarized in Table 3.

Table 3   The Hirschheim *et al.* model of changing considerations towards information systems management (amended from Hirschheim *et al.*, p. 4.33; Sutherland & Galliers, p. 11)

Phase/factor	Delivery	Reorientation	Reorganization
IS executive	External IS recruit	Inside business	Same person
Management focus	Within IS/DP	Into the business	The interfaces
Education needs	Credibility	Strategy	Relationship
CEO posture	Concerned	Visionary/champion	Involved
Leadership	The board	The function	Coalition

Towards a revised 'stages of growth' model

The major inadequacies of the early Nolan models relate to their lack of organizational and management focus, and the overly simplistic and subjective assumptions on which they were based. More importantly, they provided little help for the beleaguered DP manager attempting to create a successful IS function within the organization. This, as has been demonstrated, has been remedied in part by the subsequent work of Earl, Bhabuta and Hirschheim *et al.* In all but the latter case, however, the models described how an organization could place itself within a particular stage of IT planning maturity, rather than describing what is needed to be done in order to progress through to the more mature stages of growth.

The models that have been discussed thus far describe elements (technical, managerial and organizational) in the growth of 'computing' within an organization. Were these to be arranged and combined with a structure describing the important elements of an organization generally, then a model depicting the kinds of activities and organizational structures needed for an enterprise to move through IT growth stages (a more comprehensive and useful model) would result.

Such a model, dealing as it would with the growing maturity in the management and use of IT in an organization, would indicate how an organization might develop its use of the technology and its organization of the IS function. However, a means has to be found of bringing together a range of key elements associated with the operation and management of an organization generally in order that the revised model could be developed.

After some considerable literature searching, the so-called Seven 'Ss' used by McKinsey & Company in their management consultancy (Pascale & Athos, 1981) were used to assist in the development of the model. The Seven 'Ss' used in the analysis of organizational processes and management are summarized in Table 4.

Table 4 The seven 'Ss' (Pascale & Athos, p. 81)

Strategy	Plan or course of action leading to the allocation of a firm's scarce resources, over time, to reach identified goals
Structure	Characterization of the organization chart (i.e. functional, decentralized, etc.)
Systems	Procedural reports and routine processes such as meeting formats
Staff	'Demographic' description of important personnel categories within the firm (i.e. engineers, entrepreneurs, MBAs, etc.). 'Staff' is *not* meant in line-staff terms
Style	Characterization of how key managers behave in achieving the organization's goals; also the cultural style of the organization
Skills	Distinctive capabilities of key personnel or the firm as a whole
Superordinate goals	The significant meanings or guiding concepts that an organization imbues in its members. Superordinate goals can be also describd as the shared values or culture of the organization

Research method

As a first step, the elements of each of the Seven 'Ss' were considered in the context of each stage in the growth of IT utilization and management, according to the models described. In other words, a description of each of the 's' elements was attempted in terms of the IT function and the provision of IT services generally, rather than the organization overall. Following a description of each of the 'S' elements in each stage of the model, an indication of what might be done to move into the next stage of the model can be provided. These indicators are based on what constitutes the Seven 'Ss' in the next stage.

Having produced a tentative model, it was then applied to four Perth-based organizations, and amendments made. The approach was to interview four or five senior executives from different areas in each of the organizations studied. These executives were, typically:

(a) the Chief Executive Officer, or the Deputy,
(b) the Head of a Strategic Business Unit (SBU),
(c) the IT Director, or Head of the IS function,
(d) the Head of Corporate Planning, or equivalent.

In some instances, for example, where the particular circumstances warranted broader coverage, more than one SBU head was interviewed. The interviews focused on the experiences of each organization in planning, managing and utilizing IT, and on their preparedness to utilize IT strategically. As a result of these interviews, the tentative model was continually refined and each organization eventually assessed in the context of the revised model. As a result of this assessment, conclusions were drawn as to what steps each organization might take (in relation to each of the Seven 'Ss') in order to move on to later growth stages.

Since then, the model has been 'tested' by numerous participants at conferences and short courses, and by clients both in the United Kingdom and Australia. As a result it has been further refined.

Revised stages of growth model

The growth in IT maturity in an organization can be represented as six stages, each with its particular set of conditions associated with the Seven 'Ss'. These stages are described in Table 5.

Table 5   Stages of IT growth in Organizations (Sutherland & Galliers, 1989, p. 14)

Stage	Description
One	'Ad Hocracy'
Two	Starting the foundations
Three	Centralized dictatorship
Four	Democratic dialectic and cooperation
Five	Entrepreneurial opportunity
Six	Integrated harmonious relationships

The following sections describe each of the stages in the model in detail, using each of the Seven 'Ss' as a basis for the description. Each of the elements constitute an important aspect of how the IT function within the organization might operate at different stages of growth. The stages described are not intended to include any overt (nor covert) negative overtones associated with the early stages of the model. Some of the descriptions may appear to paint an uninviting and somewhat derogatory picture of IT utilization and management within organizations during earlier stages, especially in relation to the DP personnel involved. This is primarily due to the fact that the earlier stages tend to represent a historical perspective of how organizations first began to 'come to grips' with IT. Conversely, the latter stages are essentially a distillation of what are currently considered to be the best features of IS management as organizations begin to utilize IT more strategically.

In the past, few in the DP/IT profession paid much attention to the subtle organizational and psychological aspects of implementing and managing IT within organizations. The same could be said of management. Computing was seen as essentially a technical, support function for the most part. The situation is not quite so parlous at the present time, but some DP professionals still exhibit this type of behaviour, despite the increasing concern for IS professionals to exhibit 'hybrid' (i.e., a combination of managerial, organizational and business skils in addition to technical expertise) qualities (BCS, 1990).

Even with very aware DP staff, organizations will still display symptoms of the early stages. Indeed many aspects of the early stages, if implemented correctly, are actually quite important foundations. Correct implementation of IT during the early stages of development may well mean the difference between success or failure during the later stages of an organization's IT development. Indeed, organizations that attempt to move to later stages of the model too soon, without laying the appropriate groundwork of the earlier stages, are more likely to be doomed to IT failure.

Stage 1 'Ad hocracy'

Stage 1 of the model describes the uncontrolled, *ad hoc* approach to the use of IT usually exhibited by organizations initially. All organizations begin in Stage 1. This is not to say that all organizations remain in Stage 1 for any length of time. Some move very quickly to later stages. This may occur through pressure being exerted by a computer vendor, for example, actively attempting to push the client organization into a later stage of maturity.

Strategy

The major (only) strategy in this stage is to acquire hardware and software. Acquisition of IT staff and development of IT skills throughout the organization are for the most part disregarded by management in this initial start-up phase. There is a desire for simple applications to be installed, typically those relating to controlling financial aspects of the business (i.e. accounting systems). The 'strategy' normally employed at this stage is concerned with the acquisition of standard packages and, in many instances, external suppliers may be contracted to develop specific applications, rather than in-house applications being attempted (which would have been the norm prior to the 1980s).

Structure

There is no real organizational structure associated with IT in this stage. IT is simply purchased and installed wherever someone (usually with sufficient purchasing power) requires it to be used. As expenditure on IT represents a relatively large capital outlay for the typically small organizations currently at this stage of development, the CEO/owner is usually actively involved in purchasing. Little thought is given to the organizational impact of the IT, nor to the infrastructure necessary to manage its acquisition and use.

Systems

Any systems development that takes place during this stage tends to be *ad hoc*. Systems are most often unconnected (i.e. developed and operated in isolation). Development and operation of systems is uncoordinated, whether this is across the organization as a whole or within the area requiring the application. Systems tend to be operational in nature, concentrating on the financial aspects of the organization, rather than its core business. The *ad hoc* approach to development and use of information systems results in many being located within, and supporting, just one functional business area. Most of these systems will overlap and are inconsistent in operation and output. Manual systems are typically retained to 'backup' the computerized systems. Systems tend to cover only a limited aspect of the range of work required of the individuals within the area concerned.

Staff

IT staff typically consist of a small number of programmers. A number of programming staff may be employed, but often external contractors are used. Purchase of packaged software means that very few internal IT staff are deemed to be required.

Style

The predominant style associated with the utilization of IT in this stage is that of being unaware and, more significantly, unconcerned with being unaware. IT operates in a virtual vacuum, with almost total disregard as to how it will affect the organization, its processes and human resources. From the IT personnel perspective, the only issues that appear to be of any relevance are technical ones: nothing else is of significance so far as they are concerned. Much of this style can be attributed to the use of external contractors as IT staff. These external contractors will typically show little interest in the organization they are contracted to (they will not be there that long, and their future advancement does not depend on the organization or its management).

Skills

The skills associated with IT use tend to be of a technical nature and rather low level at that. The accent is well and truly on *technology*, as opposed to organizational, business or informational issues. Skills are individually based: while certain staff have or develop particular skills, these are jealously guarded from others. The only IT skills gained by user personnel relate very specifically to particular applications, whether this is a package or a bespoke development. Computers and computer applications tend to be so arcane that non-IT personnel find it extremely difficult to gain the requisite skills to be able to use the few systems that do exist. IT training provided by organizations in Stage 1 is virtually non-existent.

Superordinate goals

Given that very few people working in Stage 1 organizations have a clear conception of what is happening in the IT area (including the IT people themselves), it is difficult to ascribe a set of superordinate goals to this stage of the model. At best, one might describe these as being concerned with obfuscation. IT personnel typically keep whatever they may know and do hidden from those they are supposed to serve, either by design or through ignorance or misguided elitism (mostly the latter). A more unkind evaluation (although possibly a more accurate one!) would suggest that the practitioners in this stage are not capable of formulating well constructed superordinate goals.

Stage 2 Starting the foundations

Stage 2 of the model marks the beginning of the ascendancy of an IT 'priesthood' in the organizaion.

Strategy

In this stage, the IT staff (for there is now a permanent cadre of such staff) attempt to find out about user needs and then meet them. This is the era of the IT Audit (cf. Earl, 1989), i.e. simply checking what has and is done, with the future seen simply as being a linear extension of the past. As indicated above, some systems have been installed in Stage 1 (typically packages), and these relate mostly to basic financial processes. Organisations in Stage 2 now concentrate on developing applications associated with other areas of the business. Although the emphasis is still on financial systems, they are now not so narrowly constrained. They are, however, still very much operational systems. No effective planning is performed, even though the IT staff may claim that they do at least plan their own work. What planning is undertaken is usually part of an annual budgetary process. The 'bottom-up' nature of ascertaining computing needs and the lack of adequate planning lead to the perception of a large backlog of systems still to be built, and demands for major increases in DP spending.

Structure

This is the first stage when a separate IT section within the organization is recognized. This section is given various names, but it is typically located under the Finance or Accounting function, as it reflects the main emphasis of IT applications within the organization. The IT section is still quite small, and provides limited services to the broad range of functions in the organization. The growth of internal IT staff usually heralds an era of reducing reliance on outside assistance. The internal IT staff now attempt to gain control of IT matters within the organization and do not usually welcome 'outside' interference.

Systems

Many more applications are developed (or purchased) and installed in the organization during this stage. Whereas Stage 1 may usually be quite short lived, Stage 2 may continue for quite some time. Early on, managers and staff in the organization begin to see computerized applications being installed after what may have been quite a lengthy period of waiting. This early delivery of applications provides an initial boost to the credibility of the IT function, thus lulling them and the rest of the organization, into a false sense of security. The self-image of an important and powerful 'priesthood' is reinforced. Even though applications are being installed at a greater rate than previously, there are still substantial gaps in computerization in Stage 2 organizations. At the same time, many of the applications tend to overlap in purpose, function and data storage. Development and operation of applications is invariably centralized, spawning the development of the 'computer centre', and its attendants. Applications remain operational in nature, once again with the concentration being in the financial area, but with some other core business-orientated applications being attempted (although rarely completely implemented to the satisfaction of the end-user). The *ad hoc* and unprepared nature of going about building the first systems (in Stage 1 and early in Stage 2) also leads to a large maintenance load being placed on the IT section. This large maintenance load invariably leads to a growth in the number of IT staff. Usually this occurs in an uncontrolled manner, and leads, as this stage progresses, to a slowing of the pace in which new systems are developed.

Staff

This stage heralds the appearance of a DP Manager, who usually reports to the Financial Controller or equivalent. Apart from the programmers inherited from Stage 1, the DP Manager will be joined by Systems Analysts and Designers: people charged with the responsibility of ensuring that they have adequately understood the requirements of the 'user' and of designing appropriate systems.

Style

The predominant style of the IT staff in this stage is one of 'don't bother me (I'm too busy getting this system up and running at the moment)'. The pressure is really on these staff, and they show it. Their orientation is still technical. They assume that whatever they are doing is what they should be doing to assist the organization. Their job is to go about building the system as quickly as possible, and as technically competently as possible. Involvement with other staff in the organization, especially when these others attempt to be involved in building systems, is not welcomed, since users 'keep changing their minds about what they want'. In other words, the IT staff do not appreciate the changing nature of information needs at this stage (cf. Land, 1982; Oliver & Langford, 1984; Galliers, 1987b).

Skills

Rather than purely technical skills associated with the programming and installation of computing equipment, the IT staff now concentrate on skills associated with building and installing complete systems for the organization. Thus, expertize in systems development methodologies, structured techniques and the like become important at this stage.

Superordinate goals

There is now a cohesive set of superordinate goals shared within the IT function, concerned with the primacy and (in their terms) the inherent appropriateness of technological developments. The predominant situation elsewhere in the organization would be one of confusion, however. Many people are doing many things, but nobody quite knows exactly what is going on, and the whole picture of IT use in the organization is only dimly perceived.

Stage 3   Centralized dictatorship

Strategy

Stage 3 attempts to right the imbalances caused by the *ad hoc* nature of developments in Stage 1 and the 'blind' rush into systems of Stage 2. The need for comprehensive planning is recognized and embraced whole-heartedly by some (usually powerful) members of the management team (including some IT staff). IT is under central control up to this stage, but it is actually *out* of the control of those who are supposedly 'controlling' it. The answer is perceived to be in planning, and typically top-down planning. There is an awareness that many of the systems developed thus far do not actually meet real business needs. There is general recognition that IT should support the organization (rather than the converse) and as such, all IT development must be somehow linked to the corporate/business plans in a fundamentally linear manner. Thus, the over-riding strategy is to ensure that a top-down, well-documented IT plan is put into place, from which future IT developments will emanate, and against which further development initiatives will be gauged.

Structure

A comprehensive DP department is incorporated into the organization at this stage. It is centralized, with all 'official' IT power invested in the department and its head (still the DP Manager). The latter may still report to the Financial Controller (Vice President Finance), but their standing in the management team will have grown slightly, although they are still treated as a technical person, and are not usually asked to participate in making 'business' decisions. Senior management have tended to renege on their responsibility to manage and control IT. This may be due to a number of factors, not the least being their almost total lack of understanding of IT, and in many instances, their unwillingness to begin to attempt to understand it. This attitude has then excluded DP staff from the organization's 'business' decision-making process, even though they may have wanted to participate, or may have been capable of making a positive contribution. The attitudes of Stage 2 are further developed in Stage 3, leaving a legacy which causes the DP Manager some discomfort. 'End users' have had some experience with IT for some time now and feel restless under the autocratic centralist regimes of the DP department. Typically, the DP Manager (and others in the department) will tend to ignore 'end users': in some instances letting them run free to do whatever they think fit (cf. Stage 1), but more likely attempting to exercise light control over any end-user developed system, with consequent ill feeling. The DP Manager and the DP department become out of touch with the 'ordinary' user in the organization, and problems in implementation and acceptance of systems developed centrally continue to manifest themselves.

Systems

Most systems are centrally developed, installed, operated and controlled by the DP department. By this stage, DP staff have implemented systems to cover most major operational activities in some form or another (they may not meet all the needs of the users, but they nonetheless operate in major business areas). At the same time, there are a number of systems which have been put together by end users in an uncontrolled, uncoordinated manner. These systems exhibit all the problems associated with Stage 1 developments, with the further difficulty that they have not been developed using technical expertise, and do not include all the elements that ensure a well maintained on-going success for the system in the future. For example, system security is a major problem here. When these systems fail (which they do regularly), the end users typically lay the blame at the feet of the DP Department and demand that they (the DP Department) fix and maintain the system.

Staff

Not only does the DP Department retain (and increase) the previous complement of staff (programmers, analysts, designers), but it grows further, with the addition of Information System Planners, and Database and Data Administration staff. Towards the end of this stage, the DP Manager may have a change in title to that of Information Systems/ Technology Manager or the like. Similarly, the DP Department may be renamed the Information Systems (or Technology) Department.

Style

The predominant style at this stage is one of abrogation (or at least, delegation) of responsibility, from the DP department to other people in the organization, usually the end user. The view taken is that the latter can do whatever they like as regards IT acquisition and IS development – so long as they pay for it. The DP personnel see it as the user's problem if one of *their* systems malfunctions or fails. Similarly, the DP Manager will look to senior management for direction, requiring management commitment and guidance for new developments. Also, senior management of the organization have abrogated their ultimate responsibility for IT within the organization to the DP manager and personnel, despite the fact that they are becoming concerned about control and performance problems with IT.

Skills

Apart from the skills gained through the previous two stages, the major skill demonstrated in Stage 3 is that of project management. Those projects that are centrally instigated are normally well controlled, following strict project management guidelines. The major emphasis is to ensure that the systems that are to be built, are built on time and within budget.

Superordinate goals

At this stage, the principle over-riding values are those of senior management *concern* with the IT function. Senior management have seen substantial money invested in IT over the period of the first two stages and are now justifiably concerned about whether they will see an adequate return on its investment. As a result, they begin to attempt to ensure that this is achieved. The DP Department becomes defensive about adverse comments regarding how well it is performing, and often expresses how difficult it is to perform well, given the complexities and competing demands.

Stage 4 Democratic dialectic and co-operation

Strategy

The conflicting forces concerned with gaining centralized control and with the move towards end-user computing of the previous stage, has left IT in a state of disarray, with little coordination between the DP department and those using the technology. Thus, the emphasis of Stage 4 is towards integration and co-ordination. DP thus moves out of its defensive 'ivory tower' posture, into the real world turmoil of the business organization.

Structure

The emphasis in Stage 4 moves towards bringing all users back into the fold. In practice this means that the previously centralized DP department becomes a little more decentralized, with the addition of Information Centres, integration of Records Management, Office Automation (Word Processing) and Library Services to a group now known as the Information Systems or Information Services Department. The Information Systems (or Services) Manager (previously the DP Manager) often moves up a rung in the organizational structure (at the Vice President level or just below), and this often involves a change in title. The new title may be Information

Resources Manager or, more commonly in America, the Chief Information Officer (Sobkowick, 1985). In many instances, a new manager is appointed as Information Systems Manager. The incumbent DP manager is overlooked, and is sometimes replaced (cf. Hirschheim *et al.*, 1988). The new IS Manager typically has more widespread business management experience, and may well not hail from the IT area. This new manager may come from another part of the organization, or may be recruited from external sources.

Systems

The organization now adopts a 'federal' approach to information systems management and development (cf. Edwards *et al.*, 1989). Line departments may (and usually do) gain control over the deployment of IT within their department. This results in miniature DP Departments spread throughout the organization. These exhibit characteristics of Stage 2 maturity. In Stage 4, Systems Analysts are now called Business Analysts. They know more about the business of the line department, but they perform much of the same role as the Systems Analyst of old. The Information Services Department now co-ordinates the use of IT throughout the organization and suggests methods which the separate DP departments should follow. Office Systems are now installed in an integrated and coordinated manner throughout the organization. Previously, they were implemented on a stand-alone basis, with no regard to integration considerations. Some Decision Support Systems (DSS) are attempted, but more often than not in an *ad hoc* manner. The organization is just coming to grips with working together with IT (rather than disparate groups pulling against each other), but a co-ordinated approach to DSS development through the organization is not as yet a reality.

Staff

As mentioned above, the traditional DP staff of analysts, designers and programmers are joined by Business Analysts. These staff are actually employed by the line departments they serve, but must closely interact with the rest of the DP department personnel. A higher level manager for the Information Services area is installed in the organization, usually at the Vice President level (or just below), as indicated above.

Style

The mood of the previous stage (defensiveness) has now changed to one of co-operation and collaboration. The Head of IT is deliberately chosen as being a person who can ensure that IT works in conjunction with, and to the benefit of, the rest of the organization. One of the major tasks allocated to this manager is to instil this sense of co-operation throughout the IT organization. This task is characterized by skills associated with a democracy. A dialectic is initiated and established throughout the organization for all IT-related issues. The dialectic ensures that proper understanding and co-operation are developed and maintained between IT staff and the rest of the organization. The dialectic can result in some constructive confrontation. Many IT personnel employed during the previous stages may be ill-equipped to handle this type of situation, and thus may be replaced or retrained.

Skills

The skills required of IT personnel in moving from Stage 3 to Stage 4 change dramatically. Although technical capabilities are still required, they are de-emphasized in relation to business skills, and to the over-riding need for them to fit in with the rest of the organization (Galliers, 1990). Organizational integration is a major theme, with improved understanding between IT and other organization staff being the result. The IT function gradually gains an understanding of how the business works, and users finally gain a proper insight into IT-related issues. The IT function also gains some business-oriented management for its area, as opposed to the techno-professional (isolated, defensive) attitude taken in the previous stages.

Supordinate goals

Co-operation is the prevailing attitude throughout Stage 4. All areas in the organization now attempt to gain an understandig of other areas and to work together for the common good and towards a common goal or set of related goals. This is possible only because of the intensive top-down planning work performed in Stage 3 (and carried through into Stage 4). Without the extensive and rigorous planning having been performed earlier, the gains made through the initiation of a dialectic could well be ephemeral.

Stage 5 Entrepreneurial opportunity

At last, the IT function is at the stage of coming out from under the burden of simply providing supporting services to other parts of the organization and can begin to provide a strategic benefit in its own right. The major operational systems are now in place, running relatively smoothly, and providing the opportunity to build strategic systems based on the foundations provided by these operational systems.

Strategy

The predominant strategy at this stage is to actively seek opportunities for the strategic use of IT, to provide a competitive advantage for the organization. This strategy involves substantial environmental scanning. The forces driving IT are predominantly outward looking, with internal operations successfully delegated to other managers.

Structure

Rather than comprising a relatively fixed structure, be it centralized or decentralized, coalitions are now formed between IT and business units in the organization. The 'federal' organization has come of age. Many coalitions are formed, each of them separate, but fitting within the overall plans of the organization, and driven by strategic, corporate (and subsidiary IT) plans. These strategic coalitions flow relatively freely into and out of existence, allowing the organization to respond to changing environmental pressures more readily. The necessary infrastructure (combining elements of both centralization and decentralization) has been put into place in the previous stages to ensure that these fluid coalitions do in fact operate as required, and produce results, both in the short term and the long term (i.e. from a maintenance and an enhancement point of view).

Systems

Systems are now more market-orientated than before. IT is used in an attempt to add value to organizational products and services. This factor, combined with the coalition aspect of the organizational structure in this phase, means most new systems are basically decentralized but with proper central co-ordination and control. Systems intended to provide a strategic advantage to the organization or to a business unit are developed in this stage. Most of these systems rely heavily on gathering and processing external data in addition to internal data. But in most instances, there is still a distinct lack of real integration between external and internal data. Decision Support Systems (DSS) for senior staff are developed and implemented at this stage. These DSS are possible only because necessary operationl systems are in place and integrated appropriately. Most staff have had enough experience associated with IT to be able to specify effectively and use DSS and other Executive Information Systems (EIS).

Staff

The new role at this stage is that of a combined Business and Information Systems Planner. These people are responsible for recognizing and planning for strategic information systems, for the organization as a whole and for individual business units. They have had some years experience, both in the business (or very similar businesses), and in the IT area (cf, the 'hybrid' concept). They may have come from either area, but are definitely cross-disciplinary.

Style

The predominant style is that of the Product Champion, the rugged individual who conceives of a good idea and pushes it through the necessary approval procedures in order to get it off the ground and working. In this case the idea is for information systems that will lead to a strategic advantage for the organization. Such systems are typically very hard to justify on a standard cost-benefit analysis basis. They require the whole-hearted support of powerful members of the organization to ensure that they are implemented (and even then, they run the risk of being stalled in mid-development).

Skills

This is the stage where IT moves out of the era of being a second string service and support unit, into being an integral part of the successful operation of the orgnization. The skills required to manage this transition are those of a senior executive. Entrepreneurial and marketing skills within selected IT personnel are also the basic requirements for ensuring success in this stage. Very knowledgeable IT users become quite commonplace. Successful organizations use these people to their full potential, as there is no longer any defensiveness about users acquiring in-depth knowledge about IT use.

Superordinate goals

Opportunity is pre-eminent during this stage. An entrepreneurial (as well as intrapreneurial) attitude is positively encouraged. Everyone is willing to identify and act on opportunities for strategic advantage.

Stage 6   Integrated harmonious relationships

Stage 6 is now reached, the dawning of a new age of sophistication and use of IT. At this stage, one notices harmonious working relationships between IT personnel and other staff in the organization. IT is deeply embedded throughout every aspect of the organization.

Strategy

During this stage, management is concerned with maintaining the comparative strategic advantage that has been hard won in the previous stage(s). This involves a constant reassessment of all uses of IT, both within the organization and in its marketplace(s). Cooperative strategies (strategic alliances) are also in place. Interactive planning, involving monitoring both likely futures as well as present circumstances (cf. Ackoff, 1981), is the focus of strategy formulation.

Structure

The strategic coalitions between IT and business units were somewhat separate and relatively uncontrolled in the previous stage. In this stage, however, they are now centrally co-ordinated (although not necessarily 'controlled' in any strict sense). An overall corporate view is integrated with the individual business unit views (both the operational and the IT viewpoint).

Systems

Building on the outward-looking strategic of the previous stage, IT now embarks on implementing *inter*-organizational systems (with suppliers, customers, government, etc.). New products and services may now be developed which are IT-based (rather than the technology being first a supporting element).

Staff

During this stage, the IT Head becomes a member of the Board of Directors. This is not a token measure for providing the occasional piece of advice when asked, but rather, as a full member of the Board, the IT Head will play an active part in setting strategic directions. Strategic decisions will then have the required IT element when appropriate from the very beginning, rather than as an afterthought.

Style

The style is now one of interdependence, with IT being but one part of the business team, working together towards making and keeping the organization successful.

Skills

All the skills required of a member of a Board, together with being a senior manager who understands IT and its potentialities, as well as the business, are necessary at this stage. And in keeping with the team approach, IT personnel are very much in tune with the needs and aspirations of the strategic business units with which they work.

Superordinate goals

Interactive planning, harmonious relationships and interdependent team work are the predominant values associated with this stage. The internal focus is on collaborative IT initiatives between groups, brought together to develop strategic information systems products. The external focus is on strategic alliances utilizing shared information systems, and the value chain is extended to include suppliers and customers.

This revised 'stages of growth' model is summarized in Table 6.

Application of the revised model

Application of the revised model in the context of the four Perth-based organizations is described in more detail elsewhere (Galliers & Sutherland, 1991). In this context, however, and in subsequent applications, the model has proved useful not only in clarifying the location of each organization in

IT maturity terms, but also in providing insights into aspects of IS management and planning which appear to require particular attention. Specific insights into the model's application include the following.

1 Any organization is likely to display characteristics associated with a number of stages for each of the Seven 'S' elements. It is unlikely that any particular organization will find itself entirely within one stage. In addition, it is most likely that different parts of a single organization will be at different stages of growth at any one time. Use of the model in this context provides management with insights into areas/elements requiring particular attention.

2 Elements in early stages of the model must be adequately addressed before related elements in later stages are likely to be successfully undertaken. For instance, Decision Support Systems (DSS) or Executive Information Systems (EIS) are extremely unlikely to be effective without the right kind of basic operational systems/databases in place. Furthermore, an organization simply trying to overcome the large backlog and heavy maintenance load of systems (associated with Stage 2) is unlikely to be able to develop substantial strategic information systems, without further development in, for example, skill levels and planning approaches.

3 Organizations do not need to work slavishly through all the elements of each stage, making the same mistakes as many organizations have done in the past. For example, 'young' organizations can make effective use of top-down information systems planning to circumvent some of the pitfalls associated with this aspect of the first two stages. Typically, however 'skipping' portions of the model can only be successfully accomplished when the senior management of the organization has already experienced the conditions that affect performance in the earlier stages, and thus understand the benefits/advantages of following 'correct' procedures.

4 The positive aspects of earlier stages of the model are not discarded when moving through to the later stages. More 'mature' organizations will incorporate those elements from all proceeding stages to the degree that they are consistent with the later stages. Thus, organizations at Stage 5 will still perform Information Systems Planning, they will still have a DP function (of sorts) and will be likely to require Information Centres. The more mature organization will be flexible enough to determine the most appropriate nature of IT use and organization, rather than blindly following the structures and procedures adopted by other organizations.

5 To be effective, organizations should consolidate in most elements up to a particular stage, and then select certain key elements (in accordance with their own planning critiera/priorities), which they should then

Table 6 A revised 'stages of growth' model (Sutherland & Galliers, 1989, p. 23, reproduced in Galliers, 1991, pp. 61–62)

Element	Stage 1	2	3	4	5	6
Strategy	Acquisition of hardware, software, etc	IT audit Find out and meet user needs (reactive)	Top-down IS planning	Integration, co-ordination & control	Environmental scanning & opportunity seeking	Maintain comparative strategic advantage Monitor futures Interactive planning
Structure	None	Label of IS Often subordinate to accounting or finance	Data processing department Centralized DP shop End-users running free at Stage 1	Information centres Library records. OA etc. in same unit information services	SBU coalition(s) (many but separate)	Centrally co-ordinated coalitions (corporate & SBU views concurrently)
Systems	Ad hoc unconnected Operational Multiple manual & IS Uncoordinated Concentration in financial systems Little maintenance	Many applications Many gaps Overlapping systems Centralized Operational Mainly financial systems Many areas un-satisfied Large backlog Heavy maintenance load	Still mostly centralized Uncontrolled end-user computing Most major business activities covered Database systems	Decentralized approach with some controls, but mostly lack of co-ordination Some DSS-ad hoc Integrated office technology systems	Decentralized systems but central control & co-ordination Added value systems (more marketing oriented) More DSS-internal, less ad hoc Some strategic systems (using external data) Lack of external & internal data integration integration of communications technologies with computing	Inter-organizational systems (supplier, customer, government links) New IS-based products External-internal data integration
Staff	Programmers/contractors	Systems analysts DP Manager	IS planners IS Manager Data Base Administrator Data Administrator Data analysts	Business analysts Information Resources Manager (Chief Information Officer)	Corporate/business/ IS planners (one role)	IS Director/ member of board of directors
Style	Unaware	Don't bother me (I'm too busy)	Abrogation/ delegation	Democratic dialectic	Individualistic (product champion)	Business team
Skills	Technical (very low level), individual expertise	Systems development methodology	IS believes it knows what the business needs Project management	Organizational integration IS knows how the business works Users know how IS works (for their area) Business management (for IS staff)	IS Manager-member of senior executive team Knowledgeable users in some IS areas Entrepreneurial marketing skills	All senior management understand IS and its potentialities
Superordinate	Obfuscation	Confusion	Senior management	Co-operation	Opportunistic	Interactive planning

address in moving to the next stage. Indeed, all elements should be addressed in order to pass more smoothly on to the following stage.

6 It is not necessarily the case that organizations will develop *automatically* towards the more mature stages. Indeed, it has been found that organizations move 'backwards' at times, as a result of a change in personnel or managerial attitudes, see Galliers (1991) for example. Furthermore, it has proved useful at times to chart the development of the organization over a period of time by identifying when (i.e. in what year) each particular stage was reached.

The model has been found to be particularly useful in that it takes a holistic view of information systems management issues, dealing as it does with the development of information systems applications and information systems planning/strategy formulation, the changing nature of required skills, management style/involvement, and organizational structures. While the model cannot pretend to give all the *answers*, it does provide a framework which enables appropriate *questions* to be raised when setting out an appropriate strategy for information systems, giving pointers as to what is feasible as well as desirable in this regard.

Further testing and refinement of the model is taking place, but after 2 years of application, the authors are confident that the model is sufficiently refined to provide both IT and general management with a usable and useful framework to assist in the task of marshalling their IT resources in line with business imperatives.

While one might argue with the precise detail of the contents of each element at each stage of the model, this does appear not to affect the utility. Its key contribution is in focusing management attention onto a broad range of issues associated with the planning and management of information systems, in surfacing assumptions and attitudes held by key executives about the role IT does and might play in achieving/supporting business objectives and thereby enabling a shared understanding/vision to be achieved, and (most importantly) providing an easily understood means of putting IS/IT management on the senior and middle management agenda.

References

Ackoff, R. L. (1981) *Creating the Corporate Future.* Wiley, New York.

British Computer Society (1990) *From Potential to Reality: 'Hybrids' – A Critical Force in the Application of Information Technlogy in the 1990s.* A Report by the British Computer Society Task Group on Hybrids, 2 Janury.

Benbasat, I., Dexter, A. Drury, D. & Goldstein, R. (1984) A critique of the stage hypothesis: theory and empirical evidence. *Communications of the ACM*, 27(5), 476-485.

Bhabuta, L. (1988) Sustaining productivity and competitiveness by marshalling IT. In: *Proceedings: Information Technology Management for Productivity and Strategic Advantage*, IFIP TC-8 Open Conference, Singapore, March.

Cash, J. I. (Jr.) & Konsynski, B. R. (1985) IS Redraws competitive boundaries, *Harvard Business Review*, **63** (2), 134–142, March- April.

Earl, M. J. (1983) Emerging trends in managing new information technologies, Oxford Centre for Management Studies Research Paper 83/ 4. In: *The Management Implications of New Information Technology*, Peircy N. (ed.), 1986, Croom Helm, London.

Earl, M. J. (1986) Information systems strategy formulation. In: Boland R. J. & Hirschheim, R. A. (eds.), (1987). *Critical Issues in Information Systems Research*. Wiley, Chichester.

Earl, M. J. (ed.) (1988) *Information Management: The Strategic Dimension*, The Clarendon Press, Oxford.

Earl, M. J. (1989) *Management Strategies for Information Technology*. Prentice Hall, Hemel Hempstead.

Edwards, B., Earl, M. & Feeny, D. (1989) Any way out of the labyrinth of managing IS? RDP89/3, Oxford Institute of Information Management Research and Discussion Paper, Templeton College, Oxford University.

Galliers, R. D. (1987a) Information systems planning in the United Kingdom and Australia: a comparison of current practice. In: *Oxford Surveys in Information Technology*, Zorkorczy P. I. (ed.), 4, 223-255. Oxford University Press, Oxford.

Galliers, R. D. (ed.) (1987b) *Information Analysis: Selected Readings*. Addison-Wesley, Wokingham.

Galliers, R. D. (1990) Problems and answers of the IT skills shortage. *The Computer Bulletin*, 2(4), 25 May.

Galliers, R. D. (1991) Strategic information systems planning: myths, reality and guidelines for successful implementation. *European Journal of Information Systems*, 1, 55–64.

Galliers, R. D. & Sutherland, A. R. (1991) Organizational learning and IT: steps towards managing and planning strategic information systems. *Warwick Business School Working Paper*, University of Warwick, January.

Gibson, C. & Nolan, R. L. (1974) Managing the four stages of EDP growth, *Harvard Business Review*, 52(1), January– February.

Gluck, F. W., Kaufman, S. P. & Walleck, A. S. (1980) Strategic management for competitive advantage. *Harvard Business Review*, 58(4), July–August.

Greiner, L. E. (1972) Evolution and revolution as organisations grow. *Harvard Business Review*, 50(4), July–August.

Hamilton, S. & Ives, B. (1982) Knowledge utilisation among MIS researchers. *MIS Quarterly*, 6(12), December.

Hirschheim, R., Earl, M., Feeny, D. & Lockett, M. (1988) An exploration into the management of the information systems function: key issues and an evolutionary model. *Proceedings: Information Technology Management for Productivity and Strategic Advantage*, IFIP TC-8 Open Conference, Singapore, March.

King, J. & Kraemer, K. (1984) Evolution and organizational information systems: an assessment of Nolan's stage model, *Communications of the ACM*, 27(5), May.

Land, F. F. (1982) Adapting to changing user requirements. *Information and Management*, 5, Reproduced in Galliers, R. D. (ed.) (1987) *Information Analysis: selected readings*, Addison-Wesley, Wokingham, pp. 203-229.

McFartan, F. W. & McKenney, J. L. (1982) The Information archipeligo: gaps and bridges. *Harvard Business Review*. 60(5), September– October.

McFarlan, F. W., McKenney, J. L. & Pyburn, P. (1983) The information archipeligo: plotting a course. *Harvard Business Review*, 61(1), January–February.

Nolan, R. (1979) Managing the crises in data processing. *Harvard Business Review*, 57(2), March–April.

Nolan, R. (1984) Managing the advanced stages of computer technology: key research issues. In: *The Information Systems Research Challenge*, McFarlan, F. W. (ed.) pp. 195–214. Harvard Business School Press, Boston.

Oliver, I. & Langford, H. (1984) Myths of demons and users. *Proceedings: Australian Computer Conference*, Australian Computer Society Inc., Sydney, November. Reproduced in Galliers, R. D. (ed) (1987) *Information Analysis: selected readings*. Addison-Wesley, Wokingham, pp. 113–123.

Pascale, R. T. & Athos, A. G. (1981) *The Art of Japanese Management*. Penguin, Harmondsworth.

Sobkowich, R. (1985) When the company picks a CIO, will you be IT? *Computerworld*, June 24.

Somogyi, E. K. & Galliers, R. D. (1987a) Applied information technology: from data processing to strategic information systems. *Journal of Information Technology*, 2(1), March, 30–41.

Somogyi, E. K. & Galliers, R. D. (1987b) *Towards Strategic Information Systems*. Abacus Press, Cambridge MA.

Sullivan, C. H. (1985) Systems planning in the information age. *Sloan Management Review*, Winter.

Sutherland, A. R. & Galliers, R. D. (1989) An evolutionary model to assist in the planning of strategic information systems and the management of the information systems function. *School of Information Systems Working Paper*. Curtin University of Technology, Perth. Western Australia, February.

Ward, J., Griffiths, P. & Whitmore, P (1990) *Strategic Planning for Information Systems*. Wiley, Chichester

Reproduced from Galliers, R. D. and Sutherland, A. R. (1991). Information systems management and strategy formulation: the 'stages of growth' model revisited. *Journal of Information Systems*, 1, 89–114.

Part Two
The Strategic Dimension

During the 1980s the role of IT in business entered a new era: the support and driving of organizations' business strategy. While, as we have seen in Part One of the book, Earl (1992) among others, argues that we should not elevate IT to a status it does not deserve, we certainly should not ignore the opportunities IT can provide. These opportunities, and the frameworks and techniques used to identify them, were well-documented throughout academic and professional journals during the mid-1980s (e.g. Parsons, 1983; Benjamin *et al*, 1984; Ives and Learmonth, 1984; McFarlan, 1984; Notowidigdo, 1984; Cash and Konsynski, 1985; Porter & Millar, 1985; Rackoff *et al.*, 1985; Large, 1986). A topology of strategic frameworks can be found in Earl (1990a, pp. 33–53).

It is clear from past research that not all organizations view IT in the same way. An organization's view of IT and the opportunities it may provide will be determined by many factors, both internal and external. Such factors include the limitations placed on innovative thought within the organizaion and the current thinking in general of the industry with respect to the application of IT. The very nature of the information requirement in a particular industry sector (Earl, 1989) will also have a major impact on IT usage.

Porter and Millar's (1985) information intensity matrix provides a way to judge the potential for exploiting IT for strategic advantage within a particular industry. This is done by assessing the information intensity of the value chain against the information content of the product, as shown in Figure 1. Although a rather simplistic view of the situation, it is a useful model in that it allows important questions to be raised as to how an organization should be viewing the usage of IT within their particular context.

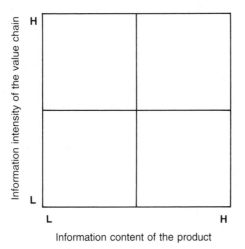

Figure 1. The information intensity matrix

Earl (1989, pp. 34-37) identifies four ways in which an organization may view its IT: drive, dependent, delivery and delayed. These categories fit nicely into the Porter and Millar matrix and help to describe the nature and importance of IT to different organizations within different industries. For organizations who find the information intensity of their value chain and their product low, IT will be used primarily to support business operations (*delivery*), while those organizations who find the information intensity of their value chain and their product high will seek to exploit new technologies in order to develop their business and manage it in more effective ways (*drive*). Those organizations whose information intensity of their value chain is high but the information content of the product is low may not have perceived any threat or opportunity with respect to information as a product as such, although they may be using IT to improve on customer service (*delayed*). Finally, those organizations whose information intensity of their value chain is low but the information content of the product is high will find their business strategy becoming increasingly reliant upon IT (*dependent*).

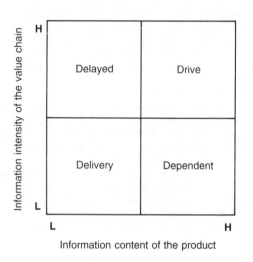

Figure 2. Earl's classification of IT strategies mapped on to the information intensity matrix

All such frameworks and models provide a useful basis for discussion amongst senior management. Once a shared view has been reached by management on the current position of their organization *vis à vis* the position deemed to be appropriate for their industry, the extent of the IT strategy task can begin to be brought into sharper focus.

After establishing the role of IT within the industry, it is then the remit of senior management to decide on the role of IT within their particular organization. McFarlan (1984) suggests that an organization may view its own approach to IT in four ways: strategic, turnaround, support or factory (see Figure 3). The predominant position the organization currently occupies on this matrix can be determined once again from discussion amongst the management team. Clearly, certain systems will be located in one quadrant while others will be located elsewhere. As a result of this assessment and against the backdrop of the industry's perspective, the position the organizaton should occupy in the future can be discussed and agreed.

These and the other frameworks mentioned are mainly descriptive and should not be used prescriptively. They provide a structure to the type of discussion that needs to be undertaken when developing an IS strategy, allowing executives to ask pertinent questions about the role of IT in their organization in the context of industry best practice.

While the industry sector and role of information therein will determine the extent and impact

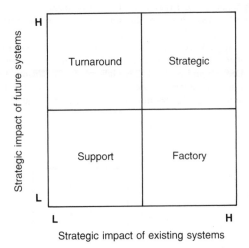

Figure 3. IT strategic grid

of IT, exploitation of IT for strategic/competitive advantage has been one of the major issues on IS managers' minds over recent years. In addition, improved quality and a reduction in production costs have been among the objectives set for the application of IT in many companies. These two perspectives, one essentially optimistic and proactive, the other essentially defensive, utilizing IT as more of a support mechanism, represents the Jekyll and Hyde nature in which IT is often viewed by senior executives (Galliers, 1992).

More recently, however, we have seen the application of IT helping organizations to gain the loyalty of customers by adding value to their products before, during and after a sale has taken place. With the change in application focus from one of improved efficiency and effectiveness to improved competitiveness and strategy making, the rules of the game have changed. Using IT to support, deliver or drive the business strategy (through the application of new products and services) has increased the risk of *not* considering IT in this strategic light.

Many of the much-heralded strategic applications of IT in the literature (*e.g.* American Airline's SABRE system and Thomson Holidays' TOPS booking system) have arisen from a single source of inspiration which has subsequently been exploited to its full potential by a project champion. However, Senn (1992) reminds us that many such strategic information systems arise from incremental enhancements to *existing* systems, rather than major, new developments. Having said this, these strategic information systems have changed current thinking with respect to the application of IT and have forced management to think more strategically about IT. Ward *et al.* (1990, p. 22), from a sample of 150 strategic examples in the literature, classified strategic information systems into four types. These were systems that:

1 link the organization to its customers and/or suppliers (inter-organizational systems);
2 improve effectiveness by adding value to the business processes (intra-organizational systems);
3 develop, produce, market and deliver new/enhanced products and/or services;
4 support the development and implementation of the business strategy.

It has become imperative for most organizations to proactively seek opportunities instead of leaving them to chance. As a result, it is necessary for organizations to take a more formal, proactive view of planning for their systems than they may have done in the past. It is not surprising then that over the last decade or so, information management surveys (Ball and Harris, 1982; Dickson *et al.*, 1984; Hatog and Herbert, 1986; Brancheau and Wetherbe, 187; Niederman *et al.*, 1990; Watson and Brancheau, 1991; Broadbent *et al.*, 1994) have ranked Information Systems Planning (ISP) as one of the most (if not *the* most) critical issue facing IS managers/executives.

From the above analysis, we have seen how important ISP is, but it is clear from research into this particular IS management topic that organizations have found it to be one which presents a range of problems (e.g. Lederer and Sethi, 1988; Galliers, 1987; Wilson, 1990; Earl, 1993). Galliers (1987) provides a good summary of other previous surveys conducted in this area, while Galliers *et al.* (1994) provide a useful framework (illustrated in Figure 4) to assist in the classification of issues.

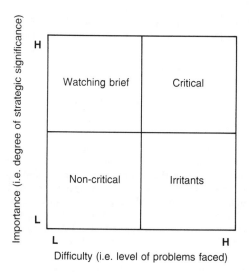

Figure 4. Classifying IS management issues

Information systems planning (ISP)[1] has been carried out in one form or other since information systems were first used in the 1960s to support the activities of the business, the planning process itself maturing hand in hand with the technology. During the early years of business computing the role of ISP was limited in scope. The focus was on managing the technology; and the process tended to be divorced from on-going business decisions. There was little choice as to the sort of hardware that could be bought and no 'off-the-shelf' software applications were available. Hardware was so costly that only the largest of organizations could afford to invest in it.

At this time, ISP was essentially concerned with the identification of possible applications that would improve the efficiency of company operations, such as order entry/processing and invoicing. However, there was little direction as to how to conduct ISP, and little interest on the part of senior executives in the topic since it was viewed as being the domain of the computer specialist. Planning was carried out on an ad-hoc, irregular basis and, as a result of this and the limited view of its objectives and scope, understanding about ISP progressed only slowly through the 1960s and into the 1970s.

[1]Similar terms are information systems strategic planning (ISP), strategic information systems planning (SISP) and information systems strategy (ISS). These terms are generally used loosely in the planning literatue to mean the same or something very similar (normally referring to planning for information systems at different levels in the organization).

During the latter part of the 1970s and early in the 1980s, much improved technology (based on the microchip), meant that even the smallest of companies could purchase a wide range of IT if they so wished. With improved technology and falling prices came a much wider range of choice and sophisticated architectures. As a result of this, investment in IT increased, systems began to be developed to support planning and control activities at various levels of management, and, as a consequence, companies had to rethink their ISP approach.

Due to this increase in progressing power and capability, enabling potential access to a vast amount of data, organizations sought information systems that would provide timely, accurate information for better decision making. As a result, the ISP process was now considered not only to be concerned with improving efficiency but also the identification of applications that could improve company effectiveness and competitiveness (Sinclair, 1986). New activities needed to be supported and, indeed, new products and services (utilizing IT) began to be identified.

Different methodologies started to emerge to aid management in formulating an ISP that would support this range of business activities and concerns. The format of ISPs also changed with the rapid progress in technology and a growing realization as to the key role that information could play. However, as we moved into the 1980s, the realization dawned that key aspects associated with the successful implementation of ISPs had, until then, been missing. There was a tendency for IS plans to become mere 'shelfware', collecting dust on executives' shelves, seldom referred to and often leading to little action.

One such implementation issue was the management of human resources. Along with the identification and prioritization of proposed information systems, the necessary skills and training required to implement and run these needed to be specified. This became increasingly crucial as new technology came on stream at an increasing rate. Consequently, ISP needed to incorporate aspects of human resource planning.

Another major issue was associated with the impact of ISPs on organizational structures, culture, job descriptions and power status at all levels, whether 'by accident' or design. Management learned that if such changes are not managed adequately then failure is likely to ensue because of user resistance. A change management plan had, therefore, to be incorporated in the ISP also. Not only that, the very nature and purpose of the IS function, and the way it is organized also had to be carefully considered in the light of the strategic IS decisions made.

As technology continues to evolve and the business environment shows no sign of stabilizing, it is not surprising that successful IS is difficult to achieve. Despite the avalanche of tools, techniques and frameworks devised since the very first surveys indicated that information systems plans were falling short of expectation, many of the original problems and issues still exist today. Planning, however, is not only growing in importance due to the strategic orientation of IT. Reviews conducted by Price Waterhouse (Grindley, 1992, 1993) reveal that other reasons are forcing organizations to plan for their IS, for example:

- Cost containment of IT has been of increasing concern to senior executives, especially over the last few years, due to the recession and to senior management concern that IT has sometimes failed to deliver the expected business benefits (Galliers, 1992).
- The integration of IT into the organization especially with the adoption of open systems versus proprietary architecture, is also becoming increasingly important in the eyes of senior executives.

Other factors making it necessary for organizations to plan their IS/IT activities are highlighted from a variety of other studies in ISP spanning the last decade. Some of these are listed below. Factors influencing the necessity to plan include:

- the growing awareness of management as to the strategic and competitive opportunities that IS can provide which has already been mentioned (Porter, 1985; Lederer and Mendelow, 1986; Boynton and Zmud, 1987; Atkinson, 1990; Earl, 1990; Earl, 1990b; Premkumar and King, 1991).

- the unstable and increasing competitiveness of the business environment (Ackoff, 1981; Grindley, 1991).
- the rate of technological change (Atkinson, 1990; Grindley, 1991).
- resource deployment considerations (Galliers, 1987; Earl, 1990b) which result in the need to prioritize IS developments (Kay *et al.*, 1980: Gupta and Guimaraes 1991).
- the search for a coordinated approach to organization-wide IS (e.g., to enable the development of a common IS architecture) (Kay *et al.*, 1980; Galliers, 1987; Atkinson, 1990).
- the need for more effective IS (Galliers, 1987; Atkinson, 1990; Earl, 1990b).
- the need to facilitate communication between IS personnel and others (Gupta and Guimaraes, 1991).
- the need to develop a capital budget for the IT function (Gupta and Guimaraes, 1991).
- the potential impact of IT on business process redesign (Hammer, 1990; Davenport and Short, 1990; Scott Morton, 1991).
- the need to assist organizational change (Yadav, 1983; Lederer and Mendelow, 1986; Gupta and Guimaraes, 1991).
- the increasing role of telecommunications and distributed processing in the day-to-day operations of many organizations (Boynton and Zmud, 1987).

The chapters that form Part Two of the book aim to address the types of IS planning problems that exist today and the major needs or issues that such planning will need to address in the future.

Chapter 6, by Galliers, looks at the critical success factors associated with (S)ISP. Galliers provides an overview of (S)ISP and discusses the different types of ISP methodologies used by organizations. The definition of competitive versus strategic IS, as given by Huff and Beattie (1985), cited in the chapter, provides a useful conceptual distinction to aid planners in identifying both types of system. The chapter also gives a brief account of the changing focus of (S)ISP over the years.

Based on research conducted in the UK and Australia (Galliers, 1987) four major critical success factors for ISP are identified and are used in developing a holistic framework for ISP to aid planners in their understanding of the planning activity in all its complexity.

In addition, Chapter 6 provides examples of strategic information system applications and of methods and frameworks developed to help in the identification of these. It concludes with a discussion of the type of methodology that should be pursued given an organization's particular context. Empirical evidence for this contingent view of planning is given by Raghunathan and Raghunathan (1990) who identified differences in planning aspects depending on an organization's position in the strategic grid (McFarlan, 1984).

Chapter 7 summarizes survey research conducted in the US (Lederer and Sethi, 1988). It discusses specific problems experienced by organizations in carrying out (strategic) information systems planning and suggests some solutions to overcome these. The problems identified from previous research were classified into three planning dimensions: resource, process or output related, and IS planners were asked to rank these problems on a scale of 'not a problem' through to 'an extreme problem'. The results indicated that although IS planners were generally 'fairly satisfied' with their planning process, problems were being experienced in implementation. Furthermore, information systems that were not identified in the plan were being developed and implemented. Based on these and other findings of the survey, Lederer and Sethi suggest actions to be taken in order to avoid the range of problems identified.

Many strategic applications of IT have developed into strategic necessities. In the next chapter in this part of the book, Clemons and Row attempt to answer the question '*when can an information technology-based strategy confer sustainable competitive advantage?*' They discuss the types of inter- and intra-organizational interactions IT can facilitate and how these interactions can improve resource efficiency which in turn can provide sustainable advantage for the innovating organization.

Chapter 8 provides advice regarding the strategies an organization can adopt in capitalizing on its structural differences with a view to obtaining and subsequently sustaining competitive advantage from IT. As we have seen, IT can be used to support or drive the processes of the organization. It is this application of IT that Clemons and Row suggests provide sustainable competitive advantage through supporting structural change, a topic we pick up again in Chapter 10.

Chapter 9, by Karimi and Konsynski, discusses the issues of competing in a global marketplace and the effect this has on the control and structure of an organization and the implications with respect to the information systems strategy. The chapter provides a good overview of the triggers to globalization and the major issues that need to be considered when developing *global information systems*. The authors suggest guidelines as what the key components of a global information systems management strategy should be.

Business process redesign/engineering has become a recent management buzzword although there is some debate in academic circles, particularly in the systems and operations management areas, as to the originality of the concept. It involves the reorganizing of a firm along its key business processes rather than its functional hierarchy. This is the subject matter of the final chapter in this part of the book, which is taken from a seminal article by Davenport and Short.

Traditional functional hierarchies tend to be highly bureaucratic in nature and this leads to problems of communication. Communication is a particular problem across functional boundaries. It is often the case that the only real integration between functions happens at the executive levels of management. In such circumstances, there is a tendency to encourage optimization within individual functions rather than across the whole organization. Consequently, managers are more concerned with achieving their own functional objectives rather than focusing on corporate goals. This lack of cooperation/coordination leads to inefficiencies within the organization.

As a result, while the product or service still gets delivered, the efficiency of delivery may be far from optimum. Organizing around business processes, however, adds value to the activities through the improvement of communication between different parts of the organization. Multifunctional teams are set up to carry out each of the different business processes from beginning to end with the objective of optimizing their own process. While this adds value to the organization via improved vertical integration, it is also important to remember the potential added value that can be gained through horizontal integration as well. Horizontal integration requires identifying ways of adding value across the major processes. This can be done if major processes contain similar sub-processes. Instead of managing the similar sub-processes individually within the main processes themselves, ways should be sought to optimize the execution of these sub-processes across the major processes, thereby reducing the amount of resources required. Opportunities for horizontal integration should be investigated alongside that of vertical integration and may be facilitated by encouraging membership of more than one multidisciplinary team.

Applying process redesign to an organization will make it more effective too by identifying redundant activities. All this has been made possible by developments in communications technology which improves internal linkages within the organization providing access to the right information at the appropriate time. The chapter by Davenport and Short discusses the role of IT with respect to business process design and suggests a five-step methodology to help redesign an organization. They also address the important issue of changes in the managerial role and organizational structure and the skills required to support such changes. It is included in this part of the book to reinforce the point that any such review of current processes should be undertaken very much as part of the SISP process, which in turn should be integrated with business strategy. An isolated review, focusing on IT alone, should come with a Government Health Warning!

References

Ackoff, R. L. (1981). *Creating the Corporate Future*, Wiley & Sons, Chichester.

Atkinson, R. A. (1990). The motivations for strategic planning, *Journal of Information Systems Management*, Fall, 53–56.

Ball, L. and Harris, R. (1982). SMIS members: a membership analysis. *MIS Quarterly*, March, 19–39.

Benjamin, R. I., Rockart, J. F., Scott Morton, M. S. and Wyman, J. (1984). Information technology: a strategic opportunity, *Sloan Management Review*, Spring, 27–34.

Boynton, A. C. and Zmud, R. W. (1987). Information technology planning in the 1990s: directions for practice and research, *MIS Quarterly*, March, 59–71.

Broadbent, M. Hansell, A. Dampney, C. N. G. and Butler, C. (1992). Information systems management: the key issues for 1992, *Australasian SHARE-GUIDE Ltd Conference*, Sydney 31 August – 2 September 1992.

Brancheau, J. C. and Wetherbe, J. C. (1987). Key issues in information systems management. *MIS Quarterly*, March, 23–45.

Cash, J. I. and Konsynski, B. R. (1985). IS redraws competitive boundaries, *Harvard Business Review*, March–April, 134–142.

Davenport, T. H. and Short, J. E. (1990). IT and BPR, *Sloan Management Review*, Summer, 11–27.

Dickson, G. W., Leitheiser, R. L., Nechis, M. and Wetherbe, J. C. (1984). Key issues for the 1980s, *MIS Quarterly*, **8** (3), September, 135–159.

Earl, M. J. (1989). *Management Strategies for Information Technology*, Business Information Technology Series, Prentice Hall, New York.

Earl, M. J. (ed.) (1990). *Information Management: The Strategic Dimension*, Oxford University Press, Oxford.

Earl, M. J. (1990b). Strategic information systems planning in UK companies: results of a field study, Working Paper #RDP 90/1, Oxford Institute of Information Management, Templeton College, Oxford University.

Earl, M. J. (1992) Putting IT in its place: a polemic for the nineties, *Journal of Information Technology*, Summer, 100–108.

Earl, M. J. (1913). Experiences in strategic information systems planning, *MIS Quarterly*, March, 1–24.

Galliers, R. D. (1987). Information systems planning in the UK and Australia – a comparison of current practice, *Oxford Surveys in Information Technology*, **4**, Oxford University Press, Oxford, 223–255.

Galliers, R. D. (1992) Information technology – managements boon or bane? *Journal of Strategic Information Systems*, **1** (2), March, 50–56.

Galliers, R. D., Merali, Y. and Spearing, L. (1994). Coping with information technology? Key information systems management issues in the 1990s: viewpoints of British managers, *Journal of Information Technology*, **9** (1), March.

Grindley, K. (1991). *Price Waterhouse Information Technology Review 1991-92*, Price Waterhouse, London.

Grindley, K. (1992), *Price Waterhouse Information Technology Review 1992/93*, Price Waterhouse, London.

Grindley, K. (1993), *Price Waterhouse Information Technology Review 1993/94*, Price Waterhouse, London.

Gupta, Y. P. and Guimaraes, T. (1991) Issues in management information systems planning, Working Paper (in press), University of Louisville.

Hammer, M. (1990). Reengineering work: don't automate, obliterate. *Harvard Business Review*, July-August, 104–112.

Hartog, C. and Herbert, M. (1986) 1985 opinion survey of MIS managers: key issues, *MIS Quarterly*, December, 351–361.

Huff, S. L. and Beattie, E. S. (1985). Strategic versus competitive information systems, *Business Quarterly*, Winter 97–102.

Ives, B. and Learmonth, G. P. (1984). The information system as a competitive weapon. *Communications of the ACM*, **27** (12), December, 1193–1201.

Kay, R. H., Szyperski, N., Horing, K. and Bartz, G. (1980). Strategic planning of information systems at the corporate level, *Information and Management*, **3**, 175–186.

Large, J. (1986). Information's market force. *Management Today*, August.

Lederer, A. L. and Mendelow, A. L. (1986). Issues in information systems planning, *Information and Management*, **10**, 245–254.

Lederer, A. L. and Sethi, V. (1988). The Implementation of strategic information systems planning methodologies, *MIS Quarterly*, September, 445–461.

McFarlan, F. W. (1984) Information technology changes the way you compete. *Harvard Business Review*, May–June, 98–103.

Niederman, F., Brancheau, J. C. and Wetherbe, J. C. (1990) Information systems management issues for the 1990s, *MIS Quarterly*, **15** (4), December, 474–500.

Notowidigdo, M. H. (1984) Information systems: weapons to gain the competitive edge, *Financial Executive*, **52** (3), 20–25.

Parsons, G. L. (1983) Information technology – a new competitive weapon, *Sloan Management Review*, Fall, 3–14.

Porter, M. E. (1985). *Competitive Advantage: Creating and Sustaining Superior Performance*, Free Press, New York.

Porter, M. E. and Millar, W. E. (1985). How information gives you competitive advantage, *Harvard Business Review*, July–August, 149–160.

Premkumar, G. and King, W. R. (1991). Assessing strategic information systems planning, *Long Range Planning*, **24** (5), October, 41–58.

Rachoff, N., Wiseman, C. and Ulrich, W. A. (1985). Information systems for competitive advantage: Implementation of a planning process, *MIS Quarterly*, **9** (4), 285–294.

Raghunathan, B. and Raghunathan, T. S. (1990). Planning implications of the IS strategic grid: an empirical investigation, *Decision Sciences*, **21** (2), Spring, 287–300.

Scott Morton, M. S. (ed.) (1991). *The Corporation of the 1990s: Information Technology and Organizational Transformation*, Oxford University Press, Oxford.

Senn, J. A. (1992) The myths of strategic information systems: what defines true competitive advantage? *Journal of Information Systems Management*, Summer, 7–12.

Sinclair, S. W. (1986). The three domains of information systems planning, *Journal of Information Systems Management*, Spring.

Waema, T. M. and Walsham, G. (190) Information systems strategy formulation, *Information and Management*, **18** (1), January, 29–39.

Ward, J., Griffiths, P. and Whitmore, P. (1990). *Strategic Planning for Information Systems*, Wiley Series in Information Systems, Chichester.

Watson, R. T. and Brancheau, J. C. (1991) Key issues in information systems management: an international perspective, *Information and Management*, **20** (3) March, 21-223. Reprinted in R Galliers (ed.) (1992). *Information Systems Research: Issues, Methods and Practical Guidelines*, Blackwell Scientific, Oxford, 112–131.

Wilson, T. D. (1990). The implementation of IS strategies in UK companies: aims and barriers to success. *International Journal of Information Management*, **9**, 245–258.

Yadav, S. B. (1983 Determining an organisation's information requirements: a state of the art survey, *Data Base*, **14** (3).

6 Strategic information systems planning: myths, reality and guidelines for successful implementation

R. D. Galliers

Introduction

Much has been claimed concerning the competitive advantage companies can obtain through the judicious application of information technology (IT). Examples such as American Hospital Supply and American Airlines in the USA and Thomson Holidays in the United Kingdom are often cited with a view to making organizations rethink their information systems strategy to include competitive considerations (see, for example, Large, 1986).

However, there have been some notable exceptions to these success stories. For example, while the Bank of America was confident of information systems strategy success in 1984 (Lansman, 1984), by 1988 $80m had been spent on its MasterNet accounting system, whose failure resulted in 29 of the Bank's most lucrative trust fund customers being handed over to a competitor (BBC, 1988).

The introduction of competitive forces analysis into our thinking on strategic information systems planning (SISP) arises in part from the work of Michael Porter and his colleagues from the Harvard Business School (e.g. Porter, 1980; McFarlan, 1984; Porter, 1985; Porter & Millar, 1985; Cash & Konsynski, 1985). In particular, attention in SISP is now much more focused on using IT to harness (or negate) the following competitive forces identified by Porter:

- potential entrants/new rivals
- substitute products/services
- suppliers
- buyers/customers
- traditional industry competitors.

If one reads the wealth of literature that now exists on the subject, one might be forgiven for believing that much of current strategy formulation practice reflects this kind of thinking. The reality is that many companies do not formulate strategy according to this rational/analytical model, nor do they adequately plan their information systems, let alone incorporate competitive considerations into their planning efforts. What is more, they experience difficulty in implementing their plans, once these have been formulated. This is certainly true in the United Kingdom, and probably in many other countries as well (Galliers, 1987a).

The basis for this contention rests on survey evidence collected in the latter half of the 1980s (Galliers, 1987a,b; Wilson, 1989). Both studies indicate that in excess of 75% of British companies undertake SISP. Similar figures apply to other countries as well – for example, USA (Martino, 1983) and Australia (Galliers, 1987a). However, as will be shown below, much current SISP practice falls well short of what is the conventional wisdom for SISP success.

This chapter puts forward an explanation for this, and a broader concept for what properly constitutes SISP is proposed, as is a framework that has been used to assist companies in choosing an appropriate IS strategy.

First, though, it is important that we understand what is meant by the term associated with SISP and IS strategy formulation. Two such terms are strategic and competitive information systems. Huff and Beattie (1985) provide the following useful distinction between the two:

- Strategic information systems 'directly support the creation and implementation of an organization' strategic plan'. The emphasis here is on information systems that enhance executive management processes and decisions. For example, according to this definition, information systems that test the assumptions underpinning strategic plans or business objectives would be classified as strategic.
- Competitive information systems 'directly support the execution of strategy by improving the value/cost relationship of the firm in its competitive environment'. Here, the emphasis is on improving competitiveness through the use of IT in reducing costs or adding value to products/services.

It is also useful to consider how our thinking has developed over the years regarding the focus of SISP.

In the early writings on SISP, attention was concentrated primarily on improving computer efficiency and matters of computer management generally (e.g. Kriebel, 1986). SISP was seen as being a matter for the IS function, somewhat isolated from the continuing business of the organization. As time passed and experience of IS management was gained, there was growing concern on the part of management to have business-driven SISPs, capable of dealing with the business problems or issues they faced. Such approaches as IBM's Business Systems Planning (c.f. Zachman, 1982) and Rockart's Critical Success Factors (Rockart, 1979) became increasingly accepted. The approaches were somewhat reactive in nature, given their emphasis on top-down planning (Ng, 1984), feeding from business plans/strategies. In addition, they were somewhat mechanistic in approach, following clearly defined procedures and frequently requiring fairly detailed analysis of, for example, processes and data.

While meeting with a measure of success, these approaches were criticised in some quarters for not having a sufficiently strong link with business objectives and for concentrating too much on issues of the day, rather than on future goal or concerns (Davis, 1979). Partly as a result of this, business-driven approaches began to focus more on the latter, and developments of, for example, the Critical Success Factors approach, began to include a consideration of future scenarios with effort being made to identify the critical assumptions upon which business plans or strategies were being built (Henderson *et al.*, 1984). While still being dependent on business plans (and, therefore, in this sense, still reactive in nature), such approaches attempted to identify future opportunities for the application of IT, rather than simply focusing on current issues or concerns.

As organizations sought to identify IT opportunities through their SISP efforts, so-called 'middle-out' approaches became more common (Henderson & Sifonis, 1986), the seminal work being that of Porter and colleagues (e.g. Porter, 1979: Porter & Millar, 1985). In this context, SISP became more proactive, with attention being concentrated on an organization's business environment as much as on internal processes, and on technological advances that might be harnessed to good effect.

Current thinking recognises that elements of each of these foci are likely to be more or less required in different circumstances, and in the mid to late 1980s came calls for the adoption of 'eclectic' (Sullivan, 1985) or 'multiple' (Earl, 1987, 1988 and 1989) methods. In fact, the very nature of SISP is now seen to be more complex than formerly. No longer should organizations be looking simply for a prioritised portfolio of information systems applications as the sole outcome of the process. Human, organizational and infrastructural issues (e.g. skills requirements and the manner in which information systems services can best be organized) are now seen as critical components of the task (see Figure 3 and Galliers, 1987a, p. 230). These developments in SISP are summarised in Figure 1, which is based on a framework first proposed by Hirschheim (1982) and later amended by Galliers (1987a,c) and Ward (1988).

A note of caution, however – much of our thinking in the SISP world appears to be based on an overly optimistic, formal and rational model of strategy formulation. As intimated above, in many companies strategy is arrived at by a more informal and creative process. Indeed, it might be said that some companies have no formal strategy at all. The process of SISP must, therefore, take into account the prevalent style of strategy formulation in any given context (cf. Pyburn. 1983) and, moreover, should not adopt an entirely rational model itself.

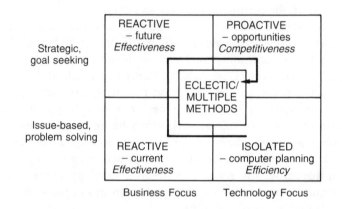

Figure 1. A development path for strategic information systems planning (amended from Galliers, 1987a)

Having summarised some of the developments that have taken place in SISP thinking, let us now turn to how SISP practice compares with the 'conventional wisdom' for SISP success.

Successful strategic information systems planning: theory versus practice

In a 1986 survey of UK SISP practice (Galliers, 1987b), respondents indicated that, from an information systems management perspective, their efforts were either partially or highly successful in 71% of the cases where SISP was being undertaken. Relative figures from a senior and middle management perspective were 68% and 58% respectively. In Wilson's more recent survey of companies in *The Times 500*, 73% of respondents indicated that they believed their SISP efforts to be either reasonably or highly successful. The conclusions from the two surveys are therefore remarkably similar, despite the intervening three years.

Where practice does appear to have changed, however, is related to the competitive advantage component of SISP. In 1986, competitor analysis was present in only 5% of cases, while 6% claimed that competitive edge was a focus for their planning efforts (Galliers, 1986a). Conversely, Wilson reported 88% of his respondents as claiming that competitive advantage was a feature of their IT strategies.

This comparison is somewhat misleading however, in that Wilson reported 44% (i.e. half of those respondents claiming the competitive advantage was part of their strategy), as seeing the reduction of costs through the application of IT as a component of this strategy. Likewise, Galliers reported that 17% of his respondents saw improved efficiency or cost reduction as being one of their objectives in undertaking SISP. Where the figures are radically different, however, relates to the use of IT to improve products or services. In 1986, Galliers reported this as an SISP objective in just 4% of cases, while in 1989, Wilson reported 73% as claiming this (i.e. 83.3% of the 88% claiming competitive advantage as a feature of SISP).

As a result of this comparison, it would be reasonable to suggest that competitive advantage has been a growing consideration over recent years in UK companies' SISP. Indeed, the 1990/91 Price Waterhouse *IT Review* indicates that concerns about IT for competitive edge began to come to the forefront precisely in 1987 (Grindley, 1990).

Table 1 Barriers to successful IS strategy (amended from Wilson, 1989)

Rank		Barrier
ISP		
Formulation	*Implementation*	
1	3	Measuring benefits
2	2	Nature of business
3	1	Difficulty in recruiting
4	6	Political conflicts
5	5	Existing IT investment
6	4	User education resources
7	11	Doubts about benefits
8	9	Telecommunications issues
9	7	Middle management attitudes
10	8	Senior managemnt attitudes
11	10	Technology lagging behind needs

A further useful comparison can be made in respect of the barriers that were identified as reducing the likelihood of successful SISP formulation and implementation. Wilson's findings are summarised in Table 1, while the viewpoints of IS planners as to SISP success factors, as reported by Galliers, are summarised in Table 2.

By referring to both Tables 1 and 2, it is possible to group factors together to form a perspective on key considerations in SISP:

- the attitude, commitment and involvement of management (to include debating the process or outcomes of SISP to overcome the 'politics' of planning, and management education)
- the current status of the company with respect to IT, in terms of the technology itself, the manner in which the IS function is organized, and the SISP skills available.
- the ability to measure, review or assess the benefits of SISP (in terms of outcomes and the process itself)
- linking or taking into account the business strategy.

Table 2 Strategic information systems planning success factors (amended from Galliers, 1987b, p. 249)

Rank (importance)	Success factor (IS planner viewpoint)
1	Senior management commitment
2	Senior management involvement
3	Senior and middle management involvement
4	Increased management understanding of IS/IT
5	Assessment/evaluation of ISP
6	ISP supported by IS management function
7	Business plans a basis for ISP
8	ISP outcomes/process debated by management
9	Middle management involvement
10	ISP outcome: prioritised applications portfolio

Management involvement

While the Galliers survey suggests that the extent of involvement on the part of management in the SISP process is often not a problem (see Figure 2), there is a weight of evidence to suggest that the attitude of UK managers to IT can reasonably be described as one of disinterest, except in terms of concern about costs (Grindley, 1990). In addition, it is often the case that the SISP approach adopted involves the planner or consultant interviewing individual managers, thereby reducing the opportunity for debate. Further, despite a very large majority in favour of SISP teams being led by a senior manager, in practice, it is most often the case that an IS professional will have to take the lead (Galliers, 1987c). In other words, while it seems likely that management will involve themselves in SISP, the quality of that involvement, and the extent of their commitment to resultant change, may be called into question.

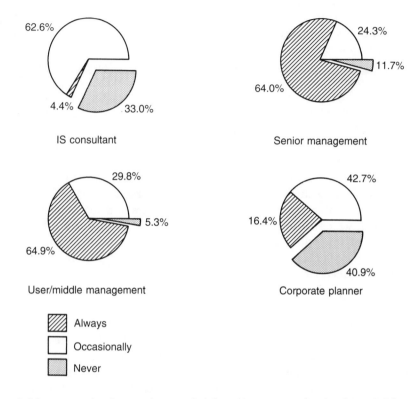

IS consultant

Senior management

User/middle management

Corporate planner

Always

Occasionally

Never

Figure 2. Management involvement in strategic information systems planning (amended from Galliers, 1987a, p 246)

Current status

It is paradoxical that the IS profession is often criticised for developing information systems which too closely reflect the *status quo*. In other words, we automate ineffective processes too often (Galliers, 1987d). When it comes to planning information systems, however, we increasingly appear to be more concerned with where we want to get to, rather than the route which we need to take to get there. For example, Wilson (1989) talks of SISP as '[bringing] together the business aims of the company . . . It is a plan for the development of systems towards some future vision'. Porter (1985), however, reminds us that business strategy is 'the route to competitive advantage'.

Strategy formulation is concerned, then, with 'getting from A to B'. It is not sufficient that we know just A or B. We must know A and B. And, just as importantly, B must be appropriate and achievable, given our A. In other words the chosen strategy must be feasible as well as desirable (cf.

Checkland, 1981). Furthermore, given alternative visions of the future, alternative Bs may be identified (and alternative routes planned).

So-called 'stages of growth' models have been used to good effect in determining a company's current status as regards aspects of IT utilisation and management (e.g. Nolan, 1979; Earl, 1989), despite the reservations of academic researchers (e.g. Benbasat *et al.*, 1984). One of the problems of earlier models relates to the fact that they referred only to aspects of the IS situation. For example, the Nolan model focuses for the most part on database technology, the amount spent on data processng and the extent of user awareness with regard to IT.

In the light of these criticisms, particularly in relation to the narrowness of focus, a revised model has been developed which takes account of a number of broader issues associated with IS strategy formulation or implementation (Sutherland & Galliers, 1989; Galliers & Sutherland, 1991). These include the skills available (both on the part of managers and IS professionals), the manner in which IS services are organized, and the focus of the SISP effort. Because of this wider focus, the model has been used to good effect in identifying both feasible and desirable IS strategies. The revised model is briefly described later.

Assessment

Reviewing both the process and outcomes of SISP is considered to be one of the most important success factors. However, while 84% of respondents to the Galliers survey indicated that formal reviews did take place, an assessment of the benefits of SISP were reported as occurring in only 16% of cases. What is more, formal assessments of benefits occurred in just 9% of cases. Given that measuring benefits is considered to be the single greatest barrier to the successful development of IS strategies (Wilson, 1989), this is of major concern.

It is important to understand that benefits should be measured in the context of what is expected of the SISP process. The Galliers study showed that what was important in terms of required SISP outcomes to one stakeholder group may not be so important to another (Galliers, 1987e). For example, while, in general, IS managers were looking for clear, achievable plans, middle managers simply wanted improved information systems as a result of the SISP process, and senior managers sought an improved capability for justifying IT investment. One could argue the point further. Individual managers from within the same stakeholder group may well have different outcomes in mind.

When one considers the range of SISP approaches that can be used, many of which have a distinct type of outcome (e.g. applications portfolio, database architecture, extent or type of IT investment required), an ability to assess likely benefits, associated with an ability to choose an approach likely to produce the desired outcome, appears to be significant. However, the

Galliers survey showed that formal evaluation of alternative approaches took place in only 7% of the companies surveyed (Galliers, 1986b).

Business linkage

It is almost a truism to suggest that SISP should be closely linked to business planning and that it should therefore take very careful note of the nature of the business which is to be supported by IT. Nevertheless, as many as 58% of those surveyed by Galliers were prepared to admit that their SISPs were at best only tenuously linked with their business plans. Part of the reason for this is that business planner involvement is still relatively rare, with 83% of respondents admitting that this takes place on an occasional basis at best, as shown in Figure 2 (Galliers, 1987a).

Summary

This section has looked at how current SISP practice differs from the conventional wisdom of what is thought to constitute successful SISP. It would appear that we often find it difficult to put theory into practice when it comes to:

- obtaining appropriate commitment to, and involvement in ISP from management. This is possibly due to the over-concentration on technical and technological, rather than business management and organizational issues associated with much of current SISP practice (see Figure 3). It may also be due in part to the fact that insufficient emphasis is given to management debate about the key issues associated with alternative futures or IS strategies.
- ascertaining an appropriate IS strategy, given current capabilities associated with IS, as well as future goals. While it may well be possible in the longer term to introduce IS applications which utilise the most up-to-date and complex technology and which promise to provide the organization concerned with a competitive edge, it may also be the case that the organization is not ready (e.g. in terms of skills, human resources and management practices) for such an eventuality. In these cases, such strategies may well represent a considerable risk (c.f. Ives & Learmonth, 1984) and may well prove to be unimplementable. Frameworks for assisting in choosing an appropriate approach or strategy should be of considerable assistance here, and examples of these are introduced below.
- reviewing or assessing the benefits of SISP and choosing an appropriate SISP approach in the light of the desired outcomes of the SISP process. It is often said that SISP should be a continuous, learning process, and very much part of continuing management activity. It is often still the case, however, that SISP is associated with an annual budgetary, or a

once-off special exercise which tends to be seen as being unrelated to key business processes. Even in situations where SISP is undertaken continuously, the learning process is rendered less effective by a lack of assessment against desired outcomes or targets. In addition, the process itself suffers because inadequate attention has been paid to the choice of an approach that is likely to be capable of delivering the required outcomes, as illustrated above. The combination of executive workshops and other opportunities to debate important issues may play a key role here.

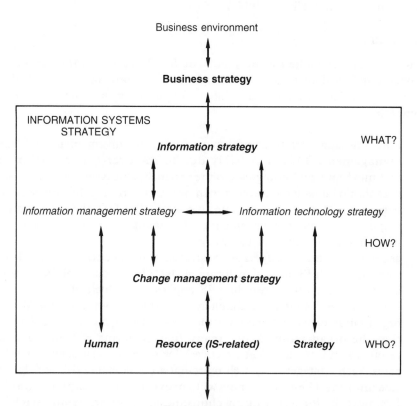

Figure 3. The components of information systems strategy: a socio-technical perspective (after Earl, 1989)

● linking SISP with business planning. While it is invariably argued that SISP should be closely associated with the business planning process (if only one part of it), it is still too often the case that the link is tenuous at best, with the two processes being undertaken in isolation from each other and with little business planner involvement in SISP and vice versa. Again, part of the reason for this relates to too great attention being paid to technological, rather than business, management and organizational issues during the SISP process. In addition, the style of the two proesses may well differ, with an overly rational, mechanistic approach to SISP and a more creative, informal approach to business strategy formulation. This leads to a lack of committed management involvement, because the language used is that of the technologist or methodologist, which in turn reduces the linkage with business strategy, thus compounding the problem.

A broader conception of strategic information systems planning

In the section above, it was argued that part of the reason our SISP efforts fall short of what is considered to be good practice is due to an over-emphasis on what might be termed IT strategy rather than IS strategy. Earl (1989) makes a useful distinction between the two concepts when he writes of IT strategy being more concerned with *how* to provide required information, while IS strategy should be concerned with understanding *what* is required

If one takes a socio-technical perspective of information systems (i.e. a more holistic stance), it can be argued that information systems are as much concerned with human activity and organization as they are with technology – if not more so (cf. Checkland, 1981; Land & Hirschheim, 1983). If this argument is accepted, it follows that IS strategy should contain not only IT strategy, but also such organizational issues as change management and a human resource strategy associated with IS – in other words, a strategy that takes into account the manner in which one might move from A to B, and the necessary organization, people and skills associated with this movement. A model which illustrates this thinking is provided in Figure 3.

It is important to note that the IS strategy is very much embedded in business strategy: it both feeds off, and feeds into, the business strategy process, which in turn is depicted as having a two-way interrelationship with the company's business environment. The model is, therefore, in line with Earl's multiple approach to IS strategy, incorporating 'top-down', 'bottom-up' and 'inside-out' planning (Earl, 1989).

Note, too, that information strategy is incorporated in the model as providing the answer to what information is required to support both business strategy formulation and business processes (cf. Galliers, 1984).

Table 3 A revised 'stages of growth' model (Sutherland & Galliers, 1989, p. 23; Galliers & Sutherland, 1991)

Elements	Stage I	II	III	IV	V	VI
Strategy	Acquisition of hardware, software etc	IT audit Find out and meet user needs (reactive)	Top-down IS planning	Integration, co-ordination and control	Environmental scanning and opportunity seeking	Maintain comparative strategic advantage Monitor futures Interactive planning
Structure	None	Label of IS Often subordinate to accounting or finance	Data processing department Centralized DP shop End users running free at stage 1	Information centres Library records OA etc in same unit Information services	SBU coalition(s) (many but separate)	Centrally co-ordinated coalitions (corporate & SBU views concurrently)
Systems	Ad hoc, unconnected Operational Multiple manual and IS Uncoordinated Concentration on financial systems Little maintenance	Many applications Many gaps Overlapping systems Centralized Operational Mainly financial systems Many areas unsatisfied Large backlog Heavy maintenance load	Still mostly centralized Uncontrolled end user computing Most major business activities covered	Decentralized approach with some controls, but mostly lack of coordination Some DSS (ad hoc) Integrated office technology systems	Decentralised systems but central control and coordination Added value systems (more marketing oriented) More DSS (internal, less ad hoc) Some strategic systems (using external data) Lack of external and internal data integration Integration of communications technologies with computing	Inter-organizational systems (supplier, customer, government links) New IS based products External/internal data integration

Table 3 (continued)

Elements	\	\	\	Stage	\	\
	I	II	III	IV	V	VI
Staff	Programmers contractors	Systems analysts DP manager	IS planners IS manager	Business analysts Information resource manager (chief information officer)	Corporate business IS planners (one role)	IS director-member of board of directors
Style	Unaware	Don't bother me (I'm too busy)	Abrogation Delegation	Democratic Dialectic	Individualistic (product champion)	Business team
Skills	Technical (very low level) (individual expertise)	Systems development methodology	IS believes it knows what the business needs Project management	Organizational integration IS knows how the business works Users know how IS works (for their area) Business management (for IS staff)	IS manager-member of senior executive team Knowledgeable users in some is areas Entrepreneurial marketing skills	All senior management understand IS and its potentialities
Superordinate goals	Obfuscation	Confusion	Senior management concern DP defence	Cooperation	Opportunistic Entrepreneurial Intrapreneurial	Interactive planning

Emphasis should be placed on the strategies located in the centre of Figure 3 (i.e. those in bold) when seeking management commitment, leadership and involvement, rather than on technological concerns (IT strategy) or infrastructure issues (IM strategy). All too often, it is the case in practice that the focus of debate is on the latter rather than the former, with consequent disinterest on the part of management.

As indicated above, a revised 'stages of growth' model has been developed to take into account the socio-technical view of SISP depicted in Figure 3 (Sutherland & Galliers, 1989; Galliers & Sutherland, 1991). This is summarised in Table 3 (cf chapter 5).

In addition to what are taken as the usual components of SISP (i.e. those associated with the technology and the kind of systems that have been, and are being, developed), the model attempts to take account of the company's superordinate goals (i.e. its culture or shared values – those values that underpin its business strategy and its strategy style), and the staff, skills and organizational structure necessary to implement the chosen strategy (cf. Pascale & Athos, 1981. p 81).

Most models of this kind depict the final stage as representing 'maturity' – a stage of near perfection in which the hard-won lessons of the earlier stages are put to good effect. The 'maturity' label has not been used to describe Stage VI in this model. While this stage does represent a phase which incorporates the accumulated wisdom of the earlier stages, it does not represent an ultimate goal to which all organizations should aspire. For example, a Stage VII might be postulated, concerned with the provision of a flexible IT infrastructure and with integrating IT into both formal and informal organizational forms (Frank Land, personal communication).

The model has been used to good effect by a number of organizations during the past two years or so. In particular, it has proved helpful in raising a number of questions about, for example:

● those aspects of the current IS strategy which appear to require particular attention (i.e. those factors which appear to be lagging behind others)
● those parts of the business which appear to be lagging behind others with respect to IS and IT issues
● the appropriateness, or otherwise, of revised or new IS strategies (i.e. in terms of feasibility as well as desirability).

With regard to the latter, it has been noted that too little attention has been paid in practice to the choice of an appropriate ISP strategy or approach. However, there are some frameworks available that can help in this regard.

For example, McLaughlin *et al.* (1983) propose that an appropriate ISP strategy can be chosen by reflecting

(i)   on how IS/IT can have an impact on products and markets, and on the competitiveness of the company in the market, and

(ii) on the 'ability to deliver' of the company's IS resources (see also, Ives & Learmonth, 1984; Galliers, 1987c; Ward, 1988).

The framework reproduced in Table 3 can assist in gauging the latter, while the work of Porter (1979, 1980, 1985), for example, is helpful with the former. The McLaughlin framework is depicted in Figure 4.

Briefly, their argument is that organizations with good opportunities and strong resources should attempt to attack their competitors by exploiting

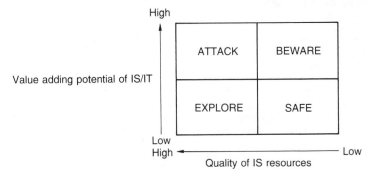

Figure 4. Choosing an appropriate ISP strategy (McLaughlin *et al.*, 1983)

IS/IT. Similarly, in situations where there is both low potential and resources, they argue that the company concerned is safe from attack. Conversely, however, where the company has good quality resources but potential appears to be limited, they should explore all opportunities to consolidate their IT assests and to be in a positon to attack should the impact of IS/IT increase in their industry. Should opportunities be high but competence low, companies should beware because they are vulnerable to attack at any time via the exploitation of IS/ IT on the part of their competitors.

Another means of assessing the appropriateness of SISP approaches in any particular context is to review the motivations of various stakeholders in the process. As highlighted above, it is likely that different stakeholders will have different reasons for wanting an SISP study to take place, that is, they may well be looking for different outcomes from the process.

As a result of Galliers' research into SISP practice during 1986, a number of different motivations were identified. These can be compared with

(i) the prevalent motivations that exist amongst different stakeholder groups in any given situation and

(ii) the kinds of outcomes different SISP approaches are likely to produce.

For example, certain SISP approaches, such as BSP and information engineering, concentrate attention on producing an applications portfolio or

ISP Orientation[1]	IT ↔ Organization ↔ Environment		
Motivation			
Efficiency, cost reduction	x x	x x	x
Effectiveness	x	x x x	x x
Improved products/ services	x	x x	x x x
Applications portfolio	x	x x x	x x
IT acquisitions	x x x	x	x
IT architecture	x x x	x	x
Competitive advantage	x	x x	x x x
Improved mgmt./ IS relations	x	x x	x x
Resourcing decisions	x x	x x	x
Human resource considerations	x	x x	x
Database architecture	x x x	x x	x

Note: [1] SISP orientation related to the type of SISP approach being considered, i.e. whether the focus is on the technology itself (isolated), or on matters internal to the organization (reactive), or on the business environment (proactive) (Figure 1).

x minor   x x reasonable   x x x major

Figure 5. A contingency framework for choosing an appropriate SISP approach based on stakeholder motivations (amended from Galliers, 1987f, p. 344)

on a database architecture (e.g. Zachman, 1982; Martin, 1982). While these may well be entirely appropriate if they are the desired outcomes of the SISP process, they are likely to be less helpful in, or example, identifying necessary organizational changes, IS-related skill requirements, or opportunities to gain a competitive advantage through the utilisation of IT. A matrix of the kind illustrated in Figure 5 may be of use in choosing an appropriate SISP approach based on the differing motivations that may exist at any one point in time, or are likely to at some stage in future.

The set of motivations included in Figure 5 is not meant to be comprehensive but indicative only. The framework is meant to be used as a basis for questioning what the motivations (in regard to SISP) of individual stakeholders are so that candidate approaches can be identified and debated.

Conclusions

This chapter has shown how current SISP practice compares with those factors generally agreed to be critical for SISP success. It has been demonstrated that practice is deficient, particularly in respect of:

● gaining appropriate commitment to, and involvement in, SISP on the part of senior and middle management

- implementing IS strategies, due to an inappropriate choice of strategy – from a feasibility as well as desirability standpoint
- reviewing and assessing the benefits of SISP in the context of the differing expectations of different stakeholders
- the linkage with business strategy.

Reasons for this deficiency have been postulated, and a broader perspective of what properly constitutes SISP has been proposed. The resultant model aims to assist management in undertaking and implementing SISP by circumventing some of the common problems encountered in applying SISP theory in practice. Most importantly, however, the paper has introduced contingent frameworks that assist in making an appropriate choice of SISP approach or strategy.

Strategy formulation should not be seen as an entirely rational or formal process, however. It should also aim to capture creative, intuitive thinking. The contingent models introduced here should be used to question beliefs and bring key assumptions about the current and future business to the surface. In so doing, it is hoped that they may assist creative strategy formulation and ease strategy implementation.

References

BBC (1988) Bank counts cost of IT disaster. *Business Computing and Communications* **March**.

Benbasat I. Dexter A. Drury D. and Goldstein R. (1984). A critique of the stage hypothesis: theory an empirical evidence. *Communications of the ACM* 27(5), 476–485.

Cash Jr J. I. and Konsynski B. R. (1985) IS redraws competitive boundaries. *Harvard Business Review* 63(2), 134–142.

Checkland P. B. (1981) *Systems Thinking. Systems Practice.* Wiley, Chichester.

Davis G. B. (1979) Comments on the critical success factors method for obtaining management information requirements in the article by John F. Rockart. *MIS Quarterly*, 3(3).

Earl M. J. (1987) Information system strategy formulation. In *Critical Issues in Information Systems Research* (Boland R. J. and Hirschheim R. A. Eds). pp. 157–168. Wiley Chichester.

Earl M. J. (Ed.) (1988) *Information Management The Strategic Dimension.* The Clarendon Press, Oxford.

Earl M. J. (1989) *Management Strategies for Information Technology.* Prentice-Hall, Hemel Hempstead.

Galliers R. D. (1984) An approach to information needs against analysis. In *Human-Computer Interaction – INTERACT '84* (Shackel B. Ed.). *Proceedings of the IFIP WG 6.3 Conference,* London, 4–7 September 1984. pp. 619–628. Elsevier, Amsterdam. Reproduced in Galliers (1987d), *op cit.* pp. 291–304.

Galliers R. D. (1986a) Information systems and technology planning within a competitive strategy framework. In *Information Management.* Pergamon Infotech. State of the Art Reports, 14, pp. 36–51. Pergamon Infotech. Maidenhead.

Galliers R. D. (1986b) Information technology strategies today: the UK experience. Presented at the *Oxford/PA Conferences: Formulating IT Strategies,* Oxford. 30 September–2 October. Reproduced in M. J. Earl (Ed.) (1988). *op cit.* pp. 179–201.

Galliers R.D. (1987a) Information systems planning in the United Kingdom and Australia – a comparison of current practice. In *Oxford Surveys in Information Technology* Volume 4. pp. 223–225.

Galliers R.D. (1987b) Information technology for comparative advantage: serendipity or strategic vision? Keynote address of the *AUSCAM National Conference*. Perth, Western Australia, 23 October.

Galliers R. D. (1987c) Information technology planning within the corporate planning process. In *Integrated Project Control* Pergamon Infotech State of the Art Reports 15, pp. 27–38. Pergamon Infotech, Maidenhead.

Galliers R. D. (Ed.) (1987d) *Information Analysis: Selected Readings*. Addison-Wesley, Workingham.

Galliers R. D. (1987e) Discord at the top. *Business Computing and communications*. **February**, 22–25.

Galliers R. D. (1987) Information Systems Planning in Britain and Australia in the mid-1980s: Key Success Factors. Unpublished PhD Thesis, London School of Economics, June.

Galliers R. D. and Sutherland A. R (199) Information systems management and strategy formulation: the 'stages of growth' model revisited. *Journal of Information Systems* (in press).

Grindley C. B. B. (Ed.)(1990) *Information Technology Review 1990/ 91*. Price Waterhouse, London.

Henderson J. C. Rockart J. F. and Sifonis J. G. (1984). A planning methodology for integrating management support systems. *MIT CISR Working Paper* No. 116, September. Reproduced in *The Rise of Management Computing* (Rochart J. F. and Bullen C. V. Eds.) pp. 257–282. Dow Jones-Irwin. Holmwood, Illinois (1986).

Henderson J. C. and Sifonis J. G (1986). Middle out strategic planning: the value of IS planning to business planning. In *Proceedings of the 1986 NYU Symposium on Strategic Uses of Information Technologies* New York. May 21–23.

Hirschheim R. A. (1982) Information Management Planning in Organisation – Part One: A Framework for Analysis. Unpublished LSE working paper.

Huff S. L. and Beattie (1985) Strategic versus competitive information systems. *Business Quarterly* **Winter.**

Ives B and Learmonth G. P. (1984) The information system as a competitive weapon. *Communications of the ACM* **27(12)**, 1193–1201.

Kribel C. G. (1968) The strategic dimension of computer systems planning. *Long Range. Planning* **September.**

Land F. F. and Hirschheim R. A. (1983) Participative systems design rationale, tools and techniques. *Journal of Applied Systems Analysis* 10. 91–107.

Lansman G (1984) Banking on innovation. *Datamation* 15 **August.**

Large J. (1986) Information's marketer force. *Management Today* **August.**

Martin J. (1982) *Strategic Data-Planning Methodologies*. Prentice-Hall. Englewood Cliffs, New Jersey.

Martino C. A. (1983) *Information Systems Planning to Meet Objectives: A survey of Practices 1983*. Cresao. McCormick and Paget, New York.

McFarlan F. W. (1984) Information technology changes the way you compete. *Harvard Business Review* **62(3)**, 98–102.

McLaughlin M. Howe R. and Cash jr J. I. (1983) Changing competitive ground rules – the impact of computers and communications in the 1980s. Unpublished Working Paper. Graduate School of Business Administration, Harvard University.

Ng M. W. (1984) Strategic systems planning should start from the top. *Australasian Computerworld* **June** 22, 12–13.

Nolan R (1979) Managing the crises in data processing. *Harvard Business Review* **57(2)**, 115–126.

Pascale R. T. and Athos A. G. (1981) *The Art of Japanese Management*. Pengium, Harmondsworth.

Porter M. E. (1979) How competitive forces shape strategy. *Harvard Business Review* **57(2)**.

Porter M. E. (1980) *Competitive Strategy*. The Free Press, New York.

Porter M. E. (1985) *Competitive Advantage*. The Free Press, New York.

Porter M. E. and Millar V. E. (1985) How information gives you competitive advantage.

Harvard Business Review **63(4)**.

Pyburn P. J. (1983) Linking the MIS plan with corporate strategy: an exploratory study. *MIS Quarterly* **7(2)**, 1–14.

Rockart J. F. (1979) Chief executives define their own data needs. *Harvard Business Review* **57(2)**. Reproduced in Galliers (1987d), *op cit*, pp. 267–289.

Sullivan, jr C. H. (1985) Systems planning in the information age. *Sloan Management Review* **27(4)**, 3–12.

Sutherland A. R. and Galliers R. D (1989) An evolutionary model to assist in the planning of strategic information systems and the management of the information systems function. School of Informatic Systems Working Paper, Curtin University of Technology, Perth, Western Austrialia, Feburary.

Ward J. M. (1988) Information systems and technology application portfolio management – an assessment of matrix-based analyses. *Journal of Information Technology* **3**, 205–215.

Wilson T. D. (1989) The implementation of information systems strategies in UK companies: aims and barriers to success. *International Journal of Information Management* **9(4)**, 245–258.

Zachman J. A. (1982) Business systems planning and business information control study: a comparison. *IBM Systems Journal* **21**.

7 Meeting the challenges of information systems planning

A. L. Lederer and V. Sethi

Strategic information systems planning (SISP) is a critical issue facing today's businesses. Because SISP can identify the most appropriate targets for computerization, it can make a huge contribution to business and to other organizations. Effective SISP can help organizations use information systems to implement business strategies and reach business goals. It can also enable organizations to use information systems to create new business strategies. Recent research has shown that the quality of the planning process significantly influences the contribution which information systems can make to an organization's performance.[1] Moreover, the failure to carry out SISP carefully can result in lost opportunities and wasted resources.[2]

To perform effective SISP, organizations conventionally apply one of several methodologies. However, carrying out such a process is a key problem facing management.[3]

SISP also presents many complex technical questions. These deal with computer hardware, software, databases, and telecommunications technologies. In many organizations, as a result of this complexity, there is a tendency to let the computer experts handle SISP.

However, SISP is too important to delegate to technicians. Business planners are increasingly recognizing the potential impact of information technology, learning more about it, and participating in SISP studies despite their lack of technical experience.

This chapter defines and explains SISP. It illustrates four popular SISP methodologies. Then, based on a survey of 80 organizations, we discuss the problems of carrying out SISP. We also suggest some potential actions which business planners can take to deal with the problems.

What is SISP?

Information systems planning has evolved over the last 15 years. In the late 1970s, its primary objectives were to improve communication between computer users and MIS departments, increase top management support for computing, better forecast and allocate information system resource requirements, determine opportunities for improving the MIS department and identify new and higher payback computer applications.[4]

More recently, two new objectives have emerged. They are the identification of strategic information systems applications – those that can give the organization a competitive edge – and the development of an organization-wide information architecture.[6]

While the importance of identifying strategic information systems applications is obvious, the importance of the organization-wide information architecture of information systems that share common data and communicate easily with each other is highly desirable. Just as new business ventures must mesh with the organization's existing endeavours, new systems applications must fit with the existing information architecture.

Unfortunately, an organization's commitment to construct an organization-wide information architecture vastly complicates SISP. Thus organizations have often failed to build such an architecture. Instead, their piecemeal approach has resulted in disjointed systems that temporarily solved minor problems in isolated areas of the organization. This later has caused redundant efforts and exorbitant costs.

Thus, this article embraces two distinct yet usually simultaneously performed approaches to SISP. On one hand, SISP entails the search for high-impact applications with the ability to create an advantage over competitors.[7] Thus, SISP helps organizations use information systems in innovative ways to build barriers against new entrants, change the basis of competition, generate new products, build in switching costs, or change the balance of power in supplier relationships.[8] As such, SISP promotes innovation and creativity. It might employ idea generating techniques such as brainstorming,[9] value chain analysis,[10] or the customer resource life cycle.

On the other hand SISP is the process of identifying a portfolio of computer-based applications to assist an organization in executing its current business plans and thus realizing its existing business goals. SISP may mean the selection of rather prosaic applications, almost as if from a pre-defined list, that would best fit the current and projected needs of the organization. These applications would guide the creation of the organization-wide information architecture of large databases and systems of computer programs. The distinction between the two approaches results in the former being referred to as attempting to *impact* organizational strategies and the latter as attempting to *align* MIS objectives with organizational goals.

Carrying out SISP

To carry out SISP, an organization usually selects an existing methodology and then embarks on a major, intensive study. The organization forms teams of business planners and computer users with MIS specialists as members or as advisors. It is likely to use the SISP vendor's educational support to train the teams and consulting support to guide and audit the study. It carries out a multi-step procedure over several weeks or months. The duration depends on the scope of the study. In addition to identifying the portfolio of applications, it prioritizes them. It defines databases, data elements, and a network of computers and communications equipment to support the applications. It also prepares a schedule for developing and installing them.

Organizations usually apply one of several methodologies to carry out this process. Four popular ones are Business Systems Planning[11] PROplanner,[12], Information Engineering,[13] and Method/1.[14] These will be described briefly as contemporary, illustrative methodologies although four undergo continuous change and improvement. They were selected because, together, they accounted for over half the responses to the survey described later.

Business Systems Planning (BSP), developed by IBM, involves *top-down* planning with *bottom-up* implementation. From the top-down, the study team first recognizes its firm's business mission, objectives and functions, and how these determine the business processes. It analyses the processes for their data needs. From the bottom-up, it then identifies the data currently required to perform the processes. The final BSP plan describes an overall information systems architecture comprised of databases and applications as well as the installation schedule of individual systems. Table 1 details the steps in a BSP study.

BSP places heavy emphasis on top management commitment and involvement. Top executive sponsorship is seen as critical. MIS analysts might serve primarily in an advisory capacity.

PROplanner, by Holland Systems Cor. in Ann Arbor, Michigan, helps planners analyse major functional areas within the organization. They then define a Business Function Model. They derive a Data Architecture from the Business Function Model by combining the organization's information requirements into generic data entities and broad databases. They then identify an Information Systems Architecture of specific new applications and an implementation schedule.

PROplanner offers automated storage, manipulation, and presentation of the data collected during SISP. PROplanner software produces reports in various formats and levels of detail. *Affinity* reports show the frequencies of accesses to data. *Clustering* reports guide database design. Menus direct the planner through on-line data collection during the process. A data dictionary (a computerized list of all data on the database) permits planners to share PROplanner data with an existing data dictionary or other automated design tools.

Information Engineering (IE), by KnowledgeWare in Atlanta, provides techniques for building Enterprise Models, Data Models, and Process Models. These make up a comprehensive knowledge base that developers later use to create and maintain information systems.

In conjunction with IE, every general manager may participate in a critical success factors (CSF) inquiry, the popular technique for identifying issues that business executives view as the most vital for their organization's success. The resulting factors will then guide the strategic information planning endeavour by helping identify future management control systems.

IE provides several software packages for facilitating the strategic information planning effort. However, IE differs from some other methodologies by providing automated tools to link its output to subsequent systems development efforts. For example, integrated with IE is an application generator to produce computer programs written in the COBOL programming language without handcoding.

Table 1 Description of BSP study steps

Enterprise Analysis The team documents the strategic business planning process and how the organization carries it out. It presents this information in a matrix for the executive sponsor to validate.

Enterprise Modelling The team identifies the organization's business processes, using a technique known as value chain analysis, and then presents them in a matrix showing each's relationship to each business strategy (from the Enterprise Analysis). The team identifies the organization's entities (such as product, customer, vendor, order, part) and presents them in a matrix showing how each is tied to each process.

Executive Interviews The team asks key executives about potential information opportunities needed to support their enterprise strategy (from the Enterprise Analysis), the processes (from the Enterprise Modelling) they are responsible for, and the entities (from the Enterprise Modelling) they manage. Each executive identifies a value and priority ranking for each information opportunity.

Information Opportunity Analysis. The team groups the opportunities by processes and entitles to separate 'quick fix' opportunities. It then analyses the remaining information opportunities, develops support recommendations, and prioritizes them.

I/S Strategies and Recommendations The team assesses the organization's information management in terms of its information systems/enterprise alignment, ongoing information planning, tactical information planning, data management, and application development. It then defines new strategies and recommends them to executive management.

Data Architecture Design The team prepares a high level design of proposed databases by diagramming how the organization uses its entities in support of its processes (entities and processes were defined during Enterprise Modelling) and identifying critical pieces of information describing the entities.

Process Architecture Design The team prepares a plan for developing high priority applications and for integrating all proposed applications. It does this by tying business processes to their proposed applications.

Existing Systems Review The team reviews existing applications to evaluate their technical and functional quality by interviewing users and information systems specialists.

Implementation Planning The team considers the quality of existing systems (from the Existing Systems Review) and the proposed applications (from the Process Architecture Design) and develops a plan identifying those to discard, keep, enhance, or re-develop.

Information Management Recommendations The team develops and presents a series of recommendations to help it carry out the plans that it prepared in Implementation Planning.

Method/1, the methodology of Andersen Consulting (a division of Arthur Andersen & Co.), consists of 10 phases of work segments that an organization completes to create its strategic plan. The first five formulate information strategy. The final five further formulate the information strategy but also develop action plans. A break between the first and final five provides a top management checkpoint and an opportunity to adjust and revise. By design, however, a typical organization using Method/1 need not complete all the work segments at the same level of detail. Instead, planners evaluate each work segment in terms of the organization's objectives.

Method/1 focuses heavily on the assessment of the current business organization, its objectives, and its competitive environment. It also stresses the tactics required for changing the organization when it implements the plan.

Method/1 follows a layered approach. The top layer is the methodology itself. A middle layer of techniques supports the methodology and a bottom layer of tools supports the techniques. Examples of the many techniques are focus groups, Delphi studies, matrix analysis, dataflow diagramming and functional decomposition. FOUNDATION, Andersen Consulting's computer-aided software engineering tool set, includes computer programs that support Method/1.

Besides BSP, PRO planner, IE and Method/1, firms might choose Information Quality Analysis,[15] Business Information Analysis and Integration Technique,[16] Business Information Characterization Study,[17] CSF, Ends/Means Analysis,[18] Nolan Norton Methodology,[19] Portfolio Management,[20] Strategy Set Transformation,[21] Value Chain Analysis, or the Customer Resource Life Cycle. Also, firms often select features of these methodologies and then, possibly with outside assistance, tailor their own in-house approach.[22]

Problems with the methodologies

Planners have long recognized that SISP is an intricate and complex activity fraught with problems.[23] Several authors have described these problems based on field surveys, cases, and conceptual studies. An exhaustive review of their most significant articles served as the basis of a comprehensive list of the problems for our research.

To organize the problems, we classified them as tied to resources, process, or output. Resource-related problems address issues of time, money, personnel, and top management support for the initiation of the study. Process-related problems involve the limitations of the analysis. Output-related problems deal with the comprehensive and appropriateness of the final plan. We derived these categories from a similar scheme used to define the components of IS planning. (Research Appendix 1 lists the problems studied in the surveys, cases and conceptual studies. The problems have been paraphrased, simplified, and classified.)

A survey of strategic information systems planners

To understand better the problems of SISP, we developed a questionnaire with two main parts. In the first part, respondents identified the methodology they had used during an SISP study. They also rated the extent to which they had encountered each of the aforementioned problems as 'not a problem', 'an insignificant problem', 'a minor problem', 'a major problem', or 'an extreme problem'. Similar studies have used this scale.

The second part asked about the implementation of plans. Planners indicated the extent to which different outputs of the plan had been effected. This conforms to the recommendation that a criterion for evaluating a planning system is the extent to which the final plan actually guides the strategic direction of an organization. In this part, the subjects also answered questions about their satisfaction with various aspects of the SISP experience.

We mailed the questionnaire to 251 organizations in two groups. The first included systems planners who were members of the Strategic Data Planning Institute, a Rockville, Maryland group under the auspices of Barnett Data Systems. The second was another group of systems planners.[24]

While 163 firms returned completed surveys, 80 (or 32 per cent) had carried out an SISP study and they provided usable data. Considering the length and complexity of the questionnaire, this is a high response rate.

Evidence of SISP problems: carrying out plans

In general, the respondents were fairly satisfied with their SISP experience. Their average rating for overall satisfaction with the SISP methodology was 3.55 where a neutral score would have been 3.00 (on the scale of zero to six in which zero was 'extremely dissatisfied' and six was 'extremely satisfied'). Satisfaction scores for the different dimensions of SISP were also only slightly favourable. Satisfaction was 3.68 with the SISP process, 3.38 with the SISP output, and 3.02 with the SISP resource requirements.

However, satisfaction with the carrying out of final SISP plans was lower (2.53). In fact, only 32 per cent of respondents were satisfied with the extent of carrying them out while 53 per cent were dissatisfied. Table 2 summarizes the respondents' satisfaction with these aspects of the SISP.

Further evidence focusing on the plan implementation problem stems from the contrast between the elapsed planning horizon and the degree of completion of SISP recommended projects. The average planning horizon of the SISP studies was 3.73 years while an average of 2.1 years had passed since the studies' completion. Thus, 56 per cent of the planning horizons had elapsed. However, out of an average of 23.4 projects recommended in the SISP studies, only 5.7 (24 per cent) had been started. Hence, it appears that firms were failing to start projects as rapidly as necessary in order to complete them during the planning horizon. There may have been insufficient project start-ups in order to realize the plan.

Table 2   Overall satisfaction with SISP

	Average	Satisfied	Neutral	Dissatisfied
The methodology	3.55	54%	23%	23%
The resources	3.02	38%	24%	38%
The process	3.68	48%	17%	25%
The output	3.38	55%	17%	28%
Carrying out the plan	2.53	32%	15%	53%

In addition to *not* starting projects in the plan, organizations instead had begun projects that were *not* part of their SISP plan. These latter projects were about 38 per cent of all projects started during the 2.1 years after the study.

Actions for planners

Below are the 18 most severe problems – which at least 25 per cent of the respondents described as an 'extreme' or 'major' problem. Because each can be seen as closely tied to Leadership, Implementation, or Resource issues, they are categorized into those three groups. They are then ordered within the groups by their severity. (Research Appendix 2 ranks all of the reported problems. The 'Extreme or Major Problem' column in the table shows the percentage of subjects rating the problem as such. The 'Minor Problem' displays the similar percentage. Subjects could also rate each as 'Insignificant' or 'Not a Problem'.)

We offer an interpretation of each problem and suggestions to both top management and other business planners considering an SISP study. Many of the suggestions are based on the successful SISP experiences of Raychem Corp., a world-wide materials sciences company based in Menlo Park, California with over 10,000 employees in 41 countries. Raychem conducted SISP studies in 1978 and 1990.[25] The company thus had the chance to carry out and implement an SISP study, and to learn from the experience.

The interpretations and suggestions provide a checklist for debate and discussion, and eventually, for improved SISP.

Leadership issues

It is Difficult to Secure Top Management Commitment for Implementing the Plan (No. 1 – the Most Serious – of the 18)
Over half the respondents called this an extreme or major problem. It means that once their study was completed and in writing, they struggled to

convince top management to authorize the development of the recommended applications. This is consistent with the percentages in the previous section.

Such a finding suggests that top management might not understand the plan or might lack confidence in the MIS department's ability to carry it out. It thus suggests that top management carefully consider its commitment to implementing a plan even before authorizing the time and money needed to prepare the plan.

Likewise, planners proposing an SISP study should assess in advance the likelihood that their top management will refuse to fund the newly recommended projects. They may also want to determine tactics to improve the likelihood of funding. In Raychem's 1978 study, the CEO served as sponsor and hence the likelihood of implementing its findings was substantially improved.

The success of the Methodology is Greatly Dependent on the Team Leader (No. 3)
If the team leader cannot convince top management to support the study or cannot obtain a top management mandate to convince functional area management and MIS management to participate, the study is probably doomed. The team leader motivates team members and pulls the project along. The team leader must be a respected veteran in the organization's business and a dynamic leader comfortable with current technology.

Organizations should reduce their dependency on their team leader. One way to do so is by using a well-structured and well-defined methodology to simplify the team leader's job. Likewise, by obtaining as much visible, top management support as possible, the organization will depend less on the team leader's personal ties to top management. In Raychem's case, dependency on the team leader was reduced because the team consisted of members with broad, corporate rather than parochial, departmental views. Such members can enable the team leader to serve as a project manager rather than force the individual to be a project champion.

It is Difficult to Find a Team Leader who Meets the Criteria Specified by the Methodology (No. 4)
As with the previous item, management will have to look hard to find a business-wise and technology-savvy leader. Such people are scarce. Management must choose that person carefully.

It is Difficult to Convince Top Management to Approve the Methodology (No. 8)
It is not only difficult to convince top management to implement the final plan (as in the first item above) but also difficult to convince top management to even fund the initial SISP study. SISP is slow and costly. Meanwhile, many top managers want working systems immediately, not plans for an uncertain future. Thus, advocates of SISP should prepare convincing arguments to authorize the funding of the study.

In Raychem's case, four executives – including two vice presidents – from different areas of the firm met several times with the CEO in 1978. Because he felt that information technology was expensive but was not sufficiently providing him with the information required to run the company, the executives were able to convince him to approve the SISP study and be its sponsor.

Implementation Issues

Implementing the Projects and the Data Architecture Identified in the Plan Requires Substantial Further Analysis (No. 2)
Nearly half the respondents found this an extreme or major problem. SISP often fell short of providing the analysis needed to start the design and programming of the individual computer applications. The methodology did not provide the specifications necessary to begin the design of the recommended projects. This meant duplicating the investigation initially needed to make the recommendations.

This result suggests that prospective strategic information systems planners should seek a methodology that provides features to guide them into implementation. Some vendors offer such methodologies. Otherwise, planners should be prepared for the frustrations of delays and duplicated effort before seeing their plans reach fruition.

In Raychem's case, the planners drew up a matrix showing business processes and classes of data. The matrix reduced the need for further analysis somewhat by helping the firm decide the applications to standardize on a corporate basis and those to implement in regional offices. As another means of reducing the need for more analysis, Raychem set up model databases for all corporate applications to access.

The Methodology Fails to Take into Account Issues Related to Plan Implementation (No. 7)
The exercise may produce an excellent plan. It may produce a list of significant, high-impact applications.

However, as in earlier items, the planning study may fail to include the actions that will bring the plan to fruition. For example, the study might ignore the development of a strategy to ensure the final decisions to proceed with specific applications. It might fail to address the resistance of those managers who oppose the plan.

Again, planners need to pay careful attention to ensure that the plan is actually followed and not prematurely discarded.

The Documentation does not Adequately Describe the Steps that Should be Followed for Imlementing the Methodology (No. 12)
The documentation describing some proprietary SISP methodologies is inadequate. It gives insufficient guidance to planners. Some of it may be erroneous, ambiguous, or contradictory.

Planners who purchase a proprietary methodology should read its documentation carefully before signing the contract. Planners who develop their own methodology should be prepared to devote significant energy to its documentation.

In Raychem's case, it chose BSP in 1978 simply because there were no other methodologies at the time. For its 1990 study, Raychem planners interviewed a number of consulting companies with proprietory methodologies before choosing the Index Group from Boston. Raychem then used extensive training to compensate for any potential deficiencies in the documentation.

The Strategic Information Systems Plan Fails to Provide Priorities for Developing Specific Databases (No. 13).
Both top management and functional area management must agree with the plan's priorities. For example, they must concur on whether the organization builds a marketing database, a financial database, or a production database. They must agree on what to do first and what to delay.

Without top management agreement on the priorities of the targeted databases, the plan will never be executed. Without functional area management concurrence, battles to change the priorities will rage. Such changes can result in temporarily halting ongoing projects while starting others. One risk is pre-eminent: Everything is started but nothing is finished.

Planners should be certain that the plan stipulates priorities and that top management and functional area management sincerely accept them.

Raychem approached this problem by culling 10 agreed upon, broad initiatives from 35 proposals in the 1990 study. Instead of choosing to establish database priorities during the study, it later established priorities for the numerous projects spawned by the initiatives.

The Strategic Information Systems Plan Fails to Determine an Overall Data Architecture for the Organization (No. 14)
Although the major objective of many SISP methodologies is to determine an overall data architecture, many respondents were disappointed with their success in doing so. They were disappointed with the identification of the architecture's specific databases and with the linkages between them. To many respondents, despite the huge effort, the portfolio of applications may appear piecemeal and disjointed.

Although these may appear to be technical issues, planners should still understand major data architecture issues and should check to be sure that their SISP will provide such an overall, integrated architecture, and not just a list of applications.

The Strategic Information Systems Plan Fails to Sufficiently Address the Need for Data Administration in the Organization (No. 18)
Because long-range plans usually call for the expansion of databases, the need for more data administration personnel – people whose sole role is

ensuring that databases are up and working – is often necessary. In many organizations, the data administration function has grown dramatically in recent years. It may continue to expand and the implications of this necessary growth can be easy to ignore. Planners should thus be sure that their long-range plan includes the role of data administration in the organization's future. In Raychem's case, a data administration function was established as a result of its 1978 study.

Resource Issues

The Methodology Lacks Sufficient Computer Support (No 5)
SISP can produce reams of reports, charts, matrices and diagrams. Planners cannot manage that volume of data efficiently and effectively without automated support.

When planners buy an existing methodology, they should carefully scrutinize the vendor's computer support. They should examine the screens and reports. On the other hand, if they customize their own methodology, they must be certain not to underestimate the need for such support. In some organizations, the expense of developing computer support in-house might compel the organization to then buy an existing methodology rather than tailor its own.

The Planning Exercise Takes Very Long (No. 6)
The study takes weeks or even months. This may be well beyond the span of attention of many organizations. Too many business managers expect results almost immediately and lose interest if the study drags on. Moreover, many organizations undergo major changes even during the planning period.

Most importantly, an overrun during the planning exercise may reduce top management's confidence in the organization's ability to carry out the final plan. Hence planners should strive to keep the duration of the planning study as short as possible.

Raychem's 1978 study required 3 months but its 1990 study required 9. In 1990, planners chose to risk the consequences of a longer study because it enabled them to involve more senior level executives albeit on a part-time basis. Planners could have completed a briefer study with lower level executives on a full-time basis. However, the planners felt the study under such circumstances would have been less credible. They clearly felt that the potential problem of insufficient top management commitment described above was more serious than the problem of a lengthy study!

The Strategic Information Plan Fails to Include an Overall Personnel and Training Plan for the MIS Department (No. 8)
Many MIS departments lack the necessary skills to carry out the innovative and complex projects recommended by an SISP study. A strategic information systems plan thus needs to consider new personnel to add to the MIS Department. The SISP study will probably recommend additions to

existing positions, permanent information systems planners, and a variety of such new positions as expert systems specialists, local area and wide area network specialists, desktop-publishers, and many others. An SISP study also often recommends training current MIS staff in today's personal computer, network, and database technologies.

Planners will need to be certain that their study accurately assesses current MIS department skills and staffing. They will also need to allocate the time and resources to ensure the presence of critical new personnel and the training of existing personnel. Raychem included a statement supporting such training in its 1990 study.

It is Difficult to Find Team Members who Meet the Criteria Specified by the Methodology (No. 10)
Qualified team members, in addition to team leaders (as in an earlier item above), are scarce. Team members from functional area departments must feel comfortable with information technology while computer specialists need to understand the business. Both need excellent communication skills and must have the time to participate. Hence, management should check the credentials of their team members carefully and be certain that their schedules allow them to participate fully in the planning process.

To find qualified team members, Raychm's planners in its 1990 study first drew up lists of business unit functions and geographical locations. They used it to identify a mix of team members from a variety of units in various locations. World-wide, senior managers helped identify team members who would be seen as leaders with objective views and diverse backgrounds. Such team members made the final study more credible.

The Strategic Information Systems Plan Fails to Include an Overall Financial Plan for the MIS Department (No 11)
Responsible top management frequently demands financial justification for new projects. Because computer projects appear different from other capital project, planners might treat them differently. Because top management will scrutinize and probably challenge costs and benefits in the long-range plan, planners must be sure that any costs and benefits are defensible.

In 1990, Raychem did not provide specific cost and benefit figures because of its concern that technological change would render them inaccurate later on. However, the firm did use various financial tests to reduce its initially suggested initiatives from 35 to 10. Moreover, planners did cost justify individual projects as they were spawned from the initiatives.

The Planning Exercise is Very Expensive (No. 15)
The planning exercise demands an exorbitant number of hours from top management, functional area management, and the MIS department. These are often the organization's busiest, most productive, and highest paid managers, precisely the people who lack the time to devote to the study.

Hence, management must be convinced that the planning study is both essential and well worth the time demanded of its top people.

The Strategic Information Systems Plan Fails to Sufficiently Address the Role of a Permanent MIS Planning Group (No 16)
Like general business planning, strategic systems planning is not a one-time endeavour. It is an ongoing process where planners periodically review the plan and the issues behind it. Many information systems planners feel that a permanent planning group devoted solely to the information systems is essential, but that their planning endeavours failed to establish one.

As with many other planning efforts, planners should view the SISP exercise as an initial effort in an ongoing process. They should also consider the need for a permanent planning function devoted to SISP. In Raychem's 1978 study, the company formed a planning committee of executives from around the company. In their 1990 study, the management refined their procedures to ensure that planning committee members would serve as sponsors of each of the 10 initiatives and that they also report progress on them to the CEO.

Many Support Personnel are Required for Data Gathering and Analysis During the Study (No 17)
To understand the current business processes and information systems support, many staff members must collect and collate data about the organization. Planners are concerned about their time and expense.

Planners should be sceptical if the vendor of a methodology suggests that staff support will be negligible. Moreover, planners may want to budget for some surplus staff support. Raychem controlled the cost of data gathering and analysis by having team members gather and analyse the data in the business units with which they were familiar.

Implications

There are two broad approaches to SISP. The *impact* approach entails the identification of a small number of information systems applications that can give the organization a competitive edge. It involves innovation and creativity in using information systems to create new business strategies by building barriers against new entrants, changing the basis of competition, generating new products, building in switching costs, or changing the balance of power in supplier relationships.

The *align* approach entails the development of an organization-wide information architecture of applications to guide the creation of large databases and computer systems to support current business strategies. It typically involves identifying a larger number of carefully integrated conventional applications that support these strategies.

Some organizations may attempt to follow both approaches equally while others may follow one more so than the other. Thus the two approaches suggest that perhaps the different groups of problems may carry different weights during the SISP process. The matrix in Figure 1 shows the approaches, categories with summarized problem statements, and weights in each cell.

For example, when seeking new and unconventional applications under the impact, leadership may play a more critical role. Without experienced, articulate and technology savvy leadership in the SISP study, it may be difficult to convince top management to gamble on radical innovation. This does not suggest that leadership is unimportant when attempting to plan applications for alignment but rather that it may be more critical under the impact approach.

Because the align approach typically affects larger numbers of lower-level employees, the potential for resource problems is perhaps greater. The possible widespread effects increase the complexity of the align approach. Thus resource issues are probably of more critical concern in this approach.

Finally, regardless of whether the approach is 'impact' or 'alignment', implementation is still often perceived as the key to successful SISP. Thus whether an organization is attempting to identify a few high-impact applications or many integrated and conventional ones, implementation issues remain equally important.

Conclusion

Effective SISP is a major challenge facing business executives today. It is an essential activity for unlocking the significant potential that information technology offers to organizations. This chapter has examined the challenges of SISP.

In summary, strategic information systems planners are not particularly satisfied with SISP. After all, it requires extensive resources. Top management commitment is often difficult to obtain. When the SISP study is complete, further analysis may be required before the plan can be executed. The execution of the plan might not be very extensive. Thus, while SISP offers a great deal – the potential to use information technology to realize current business strategies and to create new ones – too often it is not satisfactorily done.

In fact, despite its complex information technology ingredient, SISP is very similar to many other business planning endeavours. For this reason alone, the involvement of top management and business planners has become increasingly indispensable.

| | Approaches | |
Issues	*'Impact'*	*'Align'*

LEADERSHIP
Difficult to Secure Top
  Management Commitment
  for Implementation
Success Dependent on Team
  Leader
Difficult to Find Team
  Leader Meeting Criteria
Difficult to Obtain Top
  Management Approval
	Critical	Important

IMPLEMENTATION
Requires Further Analysis
Ignores Plan Implementation
  Issues
Documentation is Inadequate
  for Implementation
No Priorities for Developing
  Databases
No Overall Data Architecture
  is Determined
No Data Administration
  Need Addressed
	Very
	important
		Very
		important

RESOURCES
Methodology Lacks Sufficient
  Computer Support
Planning Exercise Takes
  Long Time
No Training Plan for
  IS Department
Difficult to Find Team
  Members Meeting Criteria
No Financial Plan for IS
  Department
Very Expensive
No Permanent IS Planning
  Group
Many Support Personnel
  Required
	Important	Critical

Figure 1. Where information systems planning fails

References

1 G. Premkumar and W. R. King. Assessing strategic information systems planning. *Long Range Planning.* October (1991).
2 W. R. King. How effective is your information systems planning? *Long Range Planning.* **21** (5). 103–112 (1988).
3   A. L. Lederer and A. L. Mendelow. Issues in information systems planning. *Information and Management.* pp. 245–254. May (1986): A. L. Lederer and V. Sethi. The implementation of strategic information systems planning methodologes. *MIS Quarterly.* **12** (3) 445–61. September (1988): and S. W. Sinclair. The three domains of information

systems planning. *Journal of Information Systems Management. 3* (2) 8–16. Spring (1986).

4   E. R. McLean and J. V. Soden. *Strategic Planning for MIS*. John Wiley and Sons. Inc. (1977).

5   PRISM. Information systems planning in the contemporary environment final report. December (1986). Index Systems. Inc. Cambridge, MA and M. R. Vitale, B. Ives and C. M. Beath. Linking information technology and corporate strategy an organizational view. *Proceedings of the Seventh International Conference on Information Systems.* pp. 265–276. San Diego. CA. 15–17 December (1986).

6   R. Moskowitz. Strategic systems planning shifts to data-oriented approach. *Computerworld.* pp 109–119. 12 May (1986).

7   E. K. Clemons. Information systems for sustainable competitive advantage. *Information and Management.* 1 (3). 131–136. October (1986). B. Ives and G. Learmonth. The information system as a competitive weapon. *Communications of the ACM.* 27 (12). 1193–1201. December (1985). F. W. McFarlan. Information technology changes the way you compete. *Harvard Business Review* 62 (3). 98–103. May–June (1984). G. L. Parsons. Information technology a new competitive weapon. *Sloan Management Review.* 25 (1). 3–14. Fall (1983): and C. Wiseman. *Strategy and Computers Information Systems as Competitive Weapons.* Dow Jones-Irwin, Homewood. IL (1985).

8   M. E. Porter. *Competitive Advantage Creating and Sustaining Superior Performance.* New York Free Press (1985).

9   N. Rackoff. C. Wiseman and W. A. Ulrich. Information systems for competitive advantage and implementation of planning process. *MIS Quarterly.* 9 (4). 285–294. December (1985).

10 M. E. Porter. *Competitive Advantage Creating and Sustaining Superior Performance.* New York Free Press (1985).

11 IBM Corporation. *Business Systems Planning – Information Systems Planning Guide* Publication No GE20 0527–4 (1975).

12 Holland Systems Coporation. *4FRONT strategy Method Guide.* Ann Arbor. MI (1989).

13 J. Martin. *STRATEGIC Information Planning Methodologies.* Prentice-Hall Inc. Englewood Cliffs. NJ (1989).

14 Andersen Consulting. *Foundation Method/1 Information Planning.* Version 8.0. Chicago. IL (1987).

15 J. R. Vacca. IBM's information quality analysis. *Computerworld.* 10 December (1984).

16 W. M. Carlson. Business information analysis and integration technique (BIAIT) a new horizon. *Data Base.* pp. 3–9. Spring (1979).

17 D. V. Kerner. Business information characterization study. *Data Base.* 10–17. Spring (1979).

18 J. C. Wetherbe and G. B. Davis. Strategic Planning through Ends/ Means Anlysis. MISRC Working Paper. 1982. University of Minnesota.

19 R. Moskowitz. Strategic systems planning shifts to data-oriented approach. *Computerworld.* pp. 109–119. 12 May (1986).

20 F. W. McFarlan. Portfolio approach to information systems. *Harvard Business Review* 59 (5). 142–150. September October (1981).

21 W. R. King. Strategic planning for management information systems. *MIS Quarterly* pp. 27–37. March (1978).

22 C. H. Sullivan Jr. An evolutionary new logic redefines strategic systems planning. *Information Strategy. The Executive's Journal.* 3 (2). 13–19. Winter (1986).

23 F. W. McFarlan. Problems in planning the information system. *Harvard Business Review.* 49 (2). 75-89. March–April (1971).

24 J. R. Vacca. BSP How is it working. *Computerworld.* March (1983).

25 Interviews with Paul Osborn, an executive at Raychem, who provided details about the firm's SISP experiences.

Related Reading

M. Hosoda, CIM at Nippon Seiko Co. *Long Range Planning* 23 (5). 10–21 (1990).
G. K. Janssens and L. Cuyvers. EDI – A strategic weapon in international trade. *Long Range Planning.* 24 (2). 46–53 (1991).

Appendix 1:

SISP Survey Items: Resources, Processes and Output

Resources
1 The size of the planning team is very large.
2 It is difficult to find a team leader who meets the criteria specified by the methodology.
3 It is difficult to find team members who meet the criteria specified by the methodology.
4 The success of the methodology is greatly dependent on the team leader
5 Many support personnel are required for data gathering and analysis during the study.
6 The planning exercise takes very long.
7 The planning exercise is very expensive.
8 The documentation does not adequately describe the steps that should be followed for implementing the methodology.
9 The methodology lacks sufficient computer support.
10 Adequate external consultant support is not available for implementing the methodology.
11 The methodology is not based on any theoretical framework.
12 The planning horizon considered by the methodology is inappropriate.
13 It is difficult to convince top management to approve the methodology.
14 The methodology makes inappropriate assumptions about organization structure.
15 The methodology makes inappropriate assumptions about organization size.

Process
The Methodology
1 fails to take into account organizatioal goals and strategies:
2 fails to assess the current information systems applications portfolio:
3 fails to analyse the current strengths and weaknesses of the IS department:
4 fails to take into account legal and environmental issues:
5 fails to assess the external technological environment.
6 fails to assess the organization's competitive environment:
7 fails to take into account issues related to plan implementation:
8 fails to take into account changes in the organization during SISP:
9 does not sufficiently involve users:
10 Managers find it difficult to answer questions specified by the methodology:
11 requires too much top management involvement:
12 requires too much user involvement:
13 the planning procedure is rigid:
14 does not sufficiently involve top management.

SISP Output:
1 fails to provide a statement of organizational objectives for the IS department:
2 fails to designate specific new steering committees:
3 fails to identify specific new products:
4 fails to determine a uniform basis for priorities projects:
5 fails to determine an overall data architecture for the organization:
6 fails to provide priorities for developing specific databases:
7 fails to sufficiently address the need for Data Administration in the organization:

8 fails to include an overall organizational hardware plan.
9 fails to include an overall organizational data communications plan:
10 fails to outline changes in the reporting relationships in the IS department:
11 fails to include an overall personnel and training plan for the IS department:
12 fails to include an overall financial plan for the IS department:
13 fails to sufficiently address the role of a permanent IS planning group:
14 plans are not flexible enough to take into account unanticipated changes in the organization and its environment:
15 is not in accordance with the expectations of top management:
16 Implementing the projects and the data architecture identified in the SISP output requires substantial further analysis:
17 It is difficult to secure top management commitment for implementing the plan:
18 The experiences from implementing the methodology are not sufficiently transferable across divisions:
19 The final output document is not very useful:
20 The SISP otput does not capture all the information that was developed during the study.

Research Appendix 2

Extent of SISP Problems

Abbreviated problem statement

Item No		Extreme or major problem	Minor problem
O17	Difficult to secure top management commitment	52%	16%
O16	Requires further analysis	46%	31%
R4	Success dependent on team leader	41%	30%
R2	Difficult to find team leader meeting criteria	37%	17%
R9	Methodology lacks sufficient computer support	36%	27%
R6	Planning exercise takes long time	33%	30%
P7	Ignores plan implementation issues	33%	18%
R13	Difficult to obtain top management approval	32%	36%
O11	No training plan for IS department	30%	29%
R3	Difficult to find team members meeting criteria	30%	24%
O12	No financial plan for IS department	29%	28%
R8	Documentation is inadequate	28%	33%
O6	No priorities for developing databases	27%	26%
O5	No overall data architecture is determined	27%	22%
R7	Very expensive	26%	29%
O13	No permanent IS planning group	26%	24%
R5	Many support personnel required	26%	23%
O7	No data administration need addressed	26%	16%
O18	Experiences not sufficiently transferable	24%	19%
O9	No organizational data communications plan	22%	38%
O10	No changes in IS reporting relationships	22%	31%
O4	No prioritization scheme provided	22%	19%
O15	Output belies top management expectations	22%	15%
P3	No analysis of IS department strengths/weaknesses	21%	32%
O8	No hardware plan	20%	36%
P11	Heavy top management involvement	20%	21%
O14	Resulting plans are inflexible	20%	18%
P5	No analysis of technological environment	19%	20%
P12	Too much user involvement	18%	28%

O19	Final output document not very useful	18%	20%
P10	Questions difficult for managers to answer	17%	39%
O20	Information during study not captured	17%	25%
P4	Methodology ignores legal/environmental issues	14%	16%
R14	Bad assumptions about organization structure	14%	14%
P8	Ignores organization changes during SISP	13%	25%
O1	No objectives for IS department are provided	13%	21%
P9	Insufficient user involvement	13%	5%
R1	Very large planning team required	12%	21%
P6	Methodology ignores competitive environment	12%	19%
O3	No new projects identified in final plans	12%	13%
O2	Output fails to designate new steering committees	11%	18%
P13	Rigidity of planning procedure	9%	17%
P2	No assessment of current applications portfolio	9%	16%
P14	Lack of top management involvement	9%	13%
P1	Ignores organizational goals and strategies	8%	10%
R12	Inappropriate planning horizon	6%	7%
R10	Inadequate consultant support	5%	11%
R15	Inappropriate size assumptions	4%	8%
R11	No theoretical framework	3%	5%

8 Sustaining information technology advantage: the role of structural differences

E. K. Clemons and M. C. Row

Introduction

There is widespread and continuing interest in information systems and their effects on business strategy, particularly those that can confer sustainable competitive advantage for innovative firms (Ives and Learmouth 1984; Johnston, *et al.*, 1988; Porter and Millar, 1985). But there is a growing realization that achieving competitive advantage through information technology (IT) may be more difficult than initial reports suggested (Vitale, 1986).

Clemons and Kimbrough (1986) have argued that many applications of IT are, in fact, *strategic necessities*. Such systems radically change cost structures, relative bargaining power, or the basis of competition to an extent where most competitors are compelled to imitate them. However, because competitors often imitate them or otherwise respond before customers change their behavior, these systems seldom confer competitive advantage. Many applications we have examined in financial services, retail banking, and distribution systems have proved to be strategic necessities (Banker and Kauffman, 1988; Clemons, 1989; Clemons and Row, 1988), despite our initial expectations to the contrary.

Vitale (1986) supports the notion that attaining competitive advantage through IT may be difficult, suggesting that in many cases the initial innovator may, in fact, even place his firm in a *disadvantaged* position. Where there are no first mover effects or barriers to imitation to give advantage to the innovator, and if the innovation becomes a necessity and the innovating firm lacks special skill in producing this necessity, it may actually find itself in a weakened competitive position. While these observations are interesting and reasonable, they do not help in identifying when and how an application will lead to advantage, disadvantage, or merely a different parity. Vitale treats unfortunate outcomes as unforeseeable risks of the strategy formulation process. An alternative view is that the outcomes stem from analyzable traits of participants in the industry and the application. This second approach offers far more valuable guidance to decision makers, but it demands explanatory frameworks. The objective of this article is to make progress toward such a framework, elaborating on ideas first presented by Clemons and Row (1987).

Drawing on recent work in the study of strategy and the economics of innovation (e.g., Teece, 1987), we argue that differences among competitors in access to *complementary strategic resources* needed to exploit an IT innovation are important in explaining and predicting the division of benefits from the innovation and, ultimately, the creation of competitive advantage. While we define and develop these concepts later, we can think of resources broadly as any long-lived productive capability, including tangible assets, such as a manufacturing plant or fleet of trucks, as well as intangible assets, such as patent rights or a brand image. Resources are needed to exploit any innovation. For example, a new product requires manufacturing capacity, marketing support systems, and access to distribution channels. Such resources are complementary to the innovation when the value or uniqueness of the resources are altered by the innovation. Moreover, these resources are strategic when they are both critical for the successful implementation of the innovation and are highly specialized or unique. Often, the benefits of an innovation will flow primarily to whomever controls these key resources. The innovator, or first mover, may not necessarily be the long-term beneficiary.

To develop a resource-based theory of innovation and competition for IT, it is necessary to establish a theoretical link between applications of IT and specific complementary resources. To do this we focus on IT applications to manage the interactions among economic activities. Many applications of IT influence interactions, either directly or indirectly. This has been recognized implicitly in much of the literature on strategic IT (e.g., Cash and Konsynski, 1985; Malone, *et al.*, 1987). American Airline's SABRE, McKesson Drug Company's Economist, and American Hospital Supply's ASAP all manage the flow of information between those firms and their customer bases. Merrill Lynch's CMA Financial Product linked functions for banking (check processing and debit card processing) and investment (brokerage account processing and money market fund processing).

Transactions cost economics provides a theoretical base for investigating the economic effects of IT on the structures and processes linking different business activities. Transactions cost theory posits that the organization of economic activity is strongly influenced by the costs of managing interactions between economic activities, including the cost of searching, negotiating and agreement, and monitoring execution of the transaction (Williamson, 1975).

By reducing transactions costs, IT allows higher levels of coordination, increasing the value of the coordinated resources through economies of scale and scope. This result can be used to investigate opportunities for IT in the presence of resource differences among firms. In this chapter, we investigate several general forms of such differences, in particular:

1 Differences in degree of vertical integration
2 Differences in diversification
3 Differences in resource quality and organization (i.e., soft resources like human capital, as well as more tangible resources, like scale, capital, or technology infrastructure available)

These differences among firms are *structural* in that they are based on resource differences and are thus difficult and potentially expensive to change. This is opposed to situations where firms have similar resource bases but differ in terms of strategy pursued or how these resources are utilized, both of which can be changed when the need is perceived. With this work we are not attempting a complete explanatory model of the strategic effects of IT applications. We are instead making the more modest point that strategic resources are an important factor that should be included in any such model but have been largely neglected in the literature to date.

Theoretical foundations

We believe that strategic resource differences among firms are important in explaining and predicting the competitive outcomes of strategic applications of IT. The next section examines the link between innovation and competitive advantage, showing that differences among firms are important in explaining the division of the benefits from an innovation. This is followed by a discussion that shows how these differences can be understood in terms of differences in resources controlled by a firm. We then show that by focusing on resources and the related markets for those resources, we can better understand the competitive outcomes of an innovation. The theory presented here derives from recent work in strategy and innovation (e.g., Barney, 1986; Rumelt, 1987; Teece, 1986; 1987). The theory is general and applicable to all innovations. Subsequent sections apply this theory in the specific context of IT.

Innovative and competitive advantage

Competitive advantage is normally defined as the ability to earn returns on investment persistently above the average for the industry (e.g. Porter, 1985). The ability of any innovation to contribute toward competitive advantage, therefore, depends on the innovator receiving a larger share of the economic benefits from the innovation than competitors or incurring a lower cost (investment) in implementing the innovation than competitors. In this section, we discuss the relationships between innovation and competitive advantage. Differences among firms emerge as important in explaining or predicting the competitive outcome of an innovation.

Innovations, in general, create economic value by decreasing the costs of existing goods or services, improving their quality, or creating new goods or services for which there is sufficient demand. However, this economic value is not necessarily captured by the innovator. Competitors and potential entrants are motivated to imitate the innovation. With imitation, the process of competition will force down the price of the new good or service. Thus, customers receive much of the economic benefit of the innovation in the form of lower prices rather than the innovator receiving those benefits through higher profits. In many cases imitators also face lower costs and significantly lower risks as a result of learning from the innovator's experience.

Another threat to the profits from an innovation is that other parties may seek to use political power or market power to appropriate a portion of the economic value created by the innovation. Unions, customers, suppliers, and governments are common examples of organizations that have a motivation and, frequently, the power to seize a piece of the pie. For example, Michael Bloomberg developed a debt instrument trading support system that included sophisticated analytics and risk management capability (Winkler and Miller, 1988). The viability of the system depended to a large extent on the ability to include accurate and timely price quotations, even for bonds not traded on any exchange. Merrill Lynch, one of the country's largest bond trading houses, agreed to provide the pricing information. In return, Merrill Lynch was allowed to purchase a 30 percent minority interest in Bloomberg's company when Bloomberg was unwilling to take other investors. Moreover, Merrill Lynch received access to functions not available to other customers, and most importantly, the right to limit the sale of the system to 13 of Merill Lynch's main competitors. The key point is that Merrill Lynch, as a supplier of a crucial resource, was in a position to negotiate away a portion of the potential profits from Bloomberg's system.

Given the threats of imitation and appropriation, gaining advantage from an innovation appears much more difficult than frequently presented in both the academic and popular press. In particular, these theats to the profits from an innovation have, until recently, been largely ignored in the literature on strategic applications of IT.

There are several factors that may enable an innovator to defend the economic value of his or her innovation, thus earning sustainable above average returns, i.e. competitive advantange.[1]

---

[1] There is no generally accepted typology of the sources of competitive advantage through innovation. This list is adapted from Porter (1985, pp. 171–172), but can be mapped onto Rumelt's (1987) 'isolating mechanisms' as well as Teece's (1987) 'appropriability regime' and 'access to complementary resources.' Changes in industry structure (Porter's fourth source of competitive advantage from innovation) are beyond the scope of this article.

- There are barriers to duplication. Competitors cannot imitate the innovation due to patents, trade secrets, or lack of technical expertise.
- There are significant first-mover effects. The innovator can preempt the market and defend this position through customers' switching costs, or there are substantial dynamic economies (such as learning and continuing innovation) that allow the innovator to stay ahead of the competition.
- The innovation changes underlying industry characteristics (e.g., available technologies, consumer preferences, or business processes) that influence costs or differentiation[2] to favor the innovator. This includes leveraging a comparative advantage or minimizing the negative effects of a comparative disadvantage.

The focus of this chapter is on the role of differences among firms in influencing competitive advantage from IT innovation. We believe this underlies all three factors to a greater or lesser extent. While early economic work treated firms in an industry as homogenous, such an assumption is contradicted by even casual observation of most industries. Businesses, even in the same primary industries, are clearly not alike. They differ in terms of degree of vertical integration, breadth of product line, diversity of customer base, channels of distribution, technology, and, of course, strategy selected.

In general, such differences will normally be most important for the third factor identified above: changes in industry cost or uniqueness drivers. Clearly, an asymmetrical impact of innovation presupposes that there are differences in the key factors driving a firm's strategy. For example, American Hospital Supply's strategy of a common sales point for all of its diverse product lines was very different from its key competitor's strategy. Johnson & Johnson operated each of its divisions as very autonomous units, including separate sales and marketing functions. It can be argued that AHS's innovation of its ASAP system, which provided electronic order entry and, later, inventory control support, dramatically affected the feasibility of J&J's decentralized approach to sales of hospital supplies: J&J could not simply copy the innovation without first altering the structure of its sales operations. It is also likely that significant differences among firms reinforce the first two factors. We would expect that, in many cases, the more alike competitors are, the less imitation lag is involved for any innovation.

In the remainder of this chapter, we consider only innovations that are socially efficient.[3] We will also exclude innovations for which barriers to

---

[2] Porter (1985) refers to these industry characteristics as cost drivers (chapter 3) and uniqueness drivers (chapter 4).

[3] Socially efficient means that the innovation creates economic benefits in excess of the costs of development. This does not mean the innovation is necessarily profitable for the innovator or anyone else. It is entirely possible that, with rapid imitation, prices are driven down to marginal cost and all benefits are realized solely by customers.

imitation and first mover effects will provide sufficient defense to sustain competitive advantage. These assumptions allow us to focus on the role differences play in the division of economic benefits from an innovation. Moreover, previous research indicates that these assumptions are satisfied for a significant number of IT innovations (Clemons, 1991).

Our focus on differences among firms is not intended to suggest that other means of protecting an innovation are unimportant. Examples of using information technology to achieve sustainable advantage through either barriers to imitation or first mover advantages do exist, but they are far less common than a trusting first scan of MIS literature would imply. After some thought, this is probably not surprising: patent protection for information systems is almost non-existent; information technology is widely available; it is difficult to keep an idea secret (particularly for systems used by customers or suppliers); it is difficult to keep improving an idea faster than competitors not tied to an older technology; it is difficult to get a product adopted fast enough to preempt a market.

This discussion asserts that differences among firms are important in understanding the outcome of innovations. How can we conceptualize these differences among firms? How can we relate specific differences to specific innovations? The concept of *strategic resources* is important in answering these questions.

Differences among firms and strategic resources

The most important differences among firms can be viewed as differences in endowment of *strategic resources*. In this section we begin by defining what is meant by strategic resources. We then show how this approach allows us to understand better the relationships between differences among firms and competitive advantage from innovation. This conceptual approach also provides a framework for making predictive statements about the competitive outcomes of innovations, including predictions of competitive advantage as well as statements about changing industry structure or relationships among firms.

Resources can be defined as any long-lived productive capability. Resources may be physical, such as plant and equipment, or intangible, such as customer relationships, know-how, or brand-name recognition. Conceptually, at least, any characteristic of a firm can be viewed as a resource. In fact, a firm can be viewed as a collection of resources under common control (Penrose, 1959). This is in contrast to the traditional economic view of firms as production functions. Such a perspective is extremely useful. Pfeffer and Salancik (1978) have used this resource-based perspective to investigate questions of organizational structure and processes. And, as we shall see, resources can be useful in understanding the effects of innovation.

Resources must be either produced internally from other resources or acquired from the firm's environment. Acquisition of resources from other parties is possible by the existence of *resource markets*. Some resources, such as computers, are freely available in competitive resource markets in effectively unlimited supply. Other resources may be acquired on markets, but natural limitations on supply and control of the relevant resource market by a few sellers tend to make such acquisition expensive. Still other resources cannot be readily acquired or sold because they are highly specialized and non-separable from the firm that produces and controls them (Rubin, 1973; Rumelt, 1982; Williamson, 1975). The strategic importance of a resource will clearly depend on the extent to which it is competitively available on some market. Specifically, we can say a resource is *strategic* when it is a significant portion of the investment base of the firm and is not freely available on a competitive resource market.

Focusing on resources allows us to explain differences in profitability and strategy among firms in terms of resource differences. Above-average profits are the result of having acquired (or produced) the resources necessary to implement a particular strategy at less than the true current economic value of those resources. This is an important point that requires a brief digression into traditional economics.

All resources, either procured directly from the resource markets or produced internally from other resources, are acquired at a cost. If the resource markets were perfect, in the economic sense, the price paid for a resource would be the true economic value of the productive capability represented by that resource. (In economic terms, this price would be the discounted value of all future cash flows produced by the resource.) This means that the firm would earn only a normal rate of return on its investment. If at some point there were imperfections in the strategic resource markets, it would be possible that the acquisition price of the resource in the strategic resource market would not equal what later events revealed to be its true value. For example, consider a rancher who cheaply acquired a large parcel of range land, only to learn that oil was discovered on the land, radically increasing the economic value. For the rancher, this windfall would be realized as an extremely high return on investment. However, should someone wish to acquire that land after the oil was found, he would have to pay a much higher price, reflecting the new economic value. The new owner would not necessarily earn a higher return on his investment. Thus, the process of economic change and innovation alters the value of firms' existing resource portfolios and changes the strategic options they face (Barney, 1986).

Attention must therefore be focused on *discontinuities* (sharp, unforeseeable changes) in the strategic resource markets. In many cases, IT will be important as an enabler in adjusting to non-IT related discontinuities. For example, the strategic use of IT in the airline industry and in the financial services industry has closely paralleled deregulation in those industries (Clemons, 1991; Copeland and McKenney, 1988). IT was critical in managing the complex and volatile web of fares and routes that emerged in the deregulated environment. Similarly, Merrill Lynch's CMA Financial Product exploited the deregulation of banking activities in the late 1970s. In other cases, IT innovation may be the primary source of discontinuity in resource values. The introduction of scanner systems into the retail grocery trade has had far-reaching consequences throughout the industry. The information generated by these systems has altered the way grocers manage their business and dealings with manufacturers and is creating new mechanisms for product promotion. It is often difficult to separate environmental and IT sources of discontinuity. The competitive changes triggered by the airline computerized reservation systems (CRS) were clearly more than merely adjusting to deregulation. One could easily argue that the CRSs were significant discontinuities in themselves. In the next section we look more closely at the role of innovation in creating discontinuities in resource values, but it should be kept in mind that the analysis is applicable to other sources of discontinuities as well.

Strategic resources and innovation[4]

A technological innovation can change the value of strategic resources, increasing the value of some resources and decreasing the value of others. These shifts in resource values can have a large impact in the division of benefits from an innovation. An invention or any new way of doing things has little value without the resources to implement the idea. An innovative system for optimizing a warehouse requires a warehouse to optimize. A new product requires manufacturing capacity, distribution, and marketing. Frequently, the resources needed to implement an innovation will have a higher value when used in conjunction with the innovation than when used without the innovation. To extend the above example, a warehouse with the new system will be more productive than a warehouse without the system. These resources are termed *complementary* resources (Teece, 1986). Sometimes the complementary resources will be *co-specialized* with the innovation; that is, they are so specialized that they have little value without the innovation (Teece, 1986). A custom piece of machinery only useful for producing a new product is an example here. In the strategic IT field, Merrill Lynch's CMA Financial Product provided the standard services of a traditional brokerage margin account, automatic sweeps of available funds into high-yielding money market accounts, as well as check and debit card access to funds. Certain components of this product, such as Merrill Lynch's retail presence and money market fund management expertise, were complementary to the CMA product because the innovation allowed Merrill Lynch to utilize these resources in a much larger market.

[4] This section draws primarily from the work of Teece (1986).

If, as assumed for the domain of this discussion, there are low barriers to imitation and first mover effects are negligible, then a good portion of the economic value created by the innovation can be expected to accrue to customers through lower prices. Competition among producers would drive prices down, output would expand, and resources would flow into the industry (or converted for use with the innovative know-how) until equilibrium is restored. In the worst case, producer profitability may be unchanged while customers enjoy at low cost the benefits of the innovation.

However, if something prevents the free flow of key complementary resources into the industry, the prices of those resources will be bid up. Therefore, a portion of the economic benefits from the innovation will be retained by the initial owners of the constrained resources. This windfall capital gain will be realized as supra-normal returns on investment (i.e., competitive advantage) by the resource owner until the resource is sold or, of course, until subsequent events further change the value of resources. Subsequent sale of the resource services to capitalize the increase in resource value; future resource owners will earn only average returns.

How much of the economic value created by an innovation will be realized as increases in resource prices depends on the nature of the complementary resources. If the resource is commodity-like and freely available in competitive supply, it is less likely that an innovation will significantly affect the price of the resource; all firms will face similar costs for these resources, whether they acquire the resource outright or contract for access. On the other hand, if the resource is unique, not easily duplicated, or highly specialized to the innovation, it is more likely that contracting for access will be difficult and that resource owners will be in a position to appropriate some of the benefits from the innovation. It is these latter resources that can be referred to as *strategic complementary resources.*

As a stylized example, consider the introduction of an IT innovation into a mature industry. If this IT innovation increases the scale economies available in the industry, established customer base or market share can be an important complementary resource. Since this resource is constrained, the price of this resource will be bid up considerably.[5] This scenario is being played out in several industries, including financial services and distribution. The increase in the value of the complementary resources reflected by established customer base is reflected in the purchase premiums paid to acquire existing firms. Such premiums can be as much as 50 percent of market value, as in retail banking and drug distribution (Rhodes, 1986). The owners of the acquired small firms appear to be appropriating some of the benefits from the scale-enhancing innovations. Real efficiencies may be

[5] On the other hand, the computers used to implement the IT innovation can also be considered an important complementary resource, but because this resource is effectively not constrained, i.e., computer technology is freely available to all industry participants, the price is likely to remain unchanged.

realized from the acquisition, but a substantial part of these efficiencies must be used to pay off the acquisition premium paid to the previous owner, possibly leaving net profitability little changed. The increase in resource value due to a discontinuity in the strategic resource market will be realized as increased profitabiliy by the resource owner until the resource is sold, at which point the increase in value is capitalized in the purchaser's acquisition price.

Thus we would argue that when the innovator has an initial comparative advantage in the key strategic complementary resources (compared to competitors and potential entrants), he or she is likely to appropriate some of the benefits from the innovation as a windfall increase in the value of those resources. Rapid imitation of the innovation is likely to erode all of the innovator's benefis to customers. Conversely, if the innovator has a comparative disadvantage in the key complementary resources, rapid imitation would lead to other resource owners, possibly competitors, appropriating more of the benefit stream. Just as importantly, the advantage gained from increased resource values is likely to be sustainable because all future competitors will face the higher resource prices.

In analyzing how resource differences influence competitor reactions to an innovation and the resulting strategic outcomes, it is also necessary to look at the effects of the innovation on the values of substitute resources as well as the general costs of organizational change. An innovation can reduce the value of certain strategic resources, possibly rendering obsolete an existing competitive advantage. Moreover, the innovation may necessitate major and costly organizational change as the firm disposes of obsolete resources and acquires new resources. Both of these factors may depress returns on investment in the innovation below those attainable with current strategies, particularly where there are alternative strategies of equal potential; some competitors, therefore, may not want to imitate.

This may have been the case when American Airlines first introduced its travel agent reservation system. Major airlines, such as TWA and Eastern, did not choose to develop such a system, because the system did not contribute to their strategies at the time. These different strategies were equally viable under regulation. It was not until later that deregulation destroyed these separate niches and made travel agent relationships a valuable resource and travel agent systems a strategic necessity. And this belief that the existing strategy is viable, given the cost of imitation, was almost certainly a contributing factor in E. F. Hutton's initial decision not to respond immediately to Merrill Lynch's CMA Financial Product.

While sometimes competitors will not want to imitate, or will be at a disadvantage in imitating, there are situations where the impacts of an innovation are so great that failure to duplicate threatens the viability of competitors. In these situations, the innovation quickly becomes a strategic necessity. It appears that many strategic applications of information technology fall into this class, including ATMs and distribution systems for wholesale drug distribution (Banker and Kauffman, 1988; Clemons, 1989; Clemons and Row, 1988).

The actual timing of competitor responses in a specific situation varies based on many factors, including the magnitude of the benefits generated by the innovation, the distribution of strategic complementary resources, and ease of imitation. Rather than trying to predict actual timing, the important point here is that the relative positions of competitors and potential entrants in the complementary strategic assets are important in determining the outcomes of strategic applications of information technology. In other words, resource differences among firms are of crucial importance when setting strategy. In order to understand which resources are complementary to an IT innovation, we need a history of what IT does.

IT and interactions

In the previous section, we argued that resource positions are important in explaining the division of economic benefits from an innovation. Our thesis is that this division of benefits is important in explaining or predicting what the competitive outcomes are likely to be. To know what resources are complementary to a specific application requires a basic theory of the economies of IT applications: what can IT do? This section suggests that transactions cost economics provides such a basic theory. This approach leads to a focus on IT applications to manage interactions between economic activities. In the next section, we use this theoretical framework to suggest how IT can be used to leverage several types of structural resource differences among firms.

Unlike classical economics, which considers the firm and its production function as the indivisible unit of analysis, transactions cost theory (e.g. Williamson, 1975) focuses on transactions – transfers of goods and services between separate economic activities. Transactions cost economics is useful in explaining the structure of firms and industries in terms of the balance between production economies and transactions costs. Production economies are technical characteristics that allow for more efficient utilization of resources in the production of a good or services. Examples include economies of scale, scope, and specialization.[6] Production economies argue for activities to be organized as separate firms with markets mediating the transactions between them.[7] In some situations, however, contracting

---

[6] The presence of scale economies indicates that average production costs will decrease as production volume increases. The presence of scope economies indicates that average production cost will decrease when multiple products are jointly produced. It has been shown (Teece, 1980) that economies of scope indicate that there are economies of scale in some common factor of production. Specialization economies exist when average costs decrease as productive resources are focused on a narrower range of tasks.

[7] By markets we mean bilateral exchange between independent entities.

problems will be encountered with market exchange, increasing transactions costs. At some point, managing the interaction hierarchically, i.e., within a single firm, becomes more efficient than market organization. Principal sources of transactions cost are the risks associated with non-recoverable or transaction-specific investments and the costs of monitoring the performance of outside agents. An investment is said to be sunk, non-recoverable, or transaction-specific when the resources have little value in any other use. An example could be investment in staff training to operate a certain vendor's computer system. To the extent that one firm or agent makes a non-recoverable investment, that agent has significantly reduced its bargaining power: the difference between the value of the asset in its current (or best use) and its next best allocation is at risk. Often this difference can be appropriated by the other party. That is, the other party can reduce previously agreed-upon payments or performance by an amount up to the difference between best and next best uses without inducing the agent to withdraw the committed resource (Klein, *et al.*, 1978). Of course, in a world of binding contracts and perfect information, contracts can be written to protect against such opportunism. However, contracts are difficult to enforce, and performance is costly to monitor. The risk of appropriation (or related transactions costs to control this risk) increases with the level of transaction-specific capital and the level of uncertainty as to agents' behavior and state of the world.

It has been suggested that many strategic effects of IT applications stem from changing the transactions costs between economic activities (Clemons and Kimbrough, 1986; Malone, *et al.*, 1987). Uncertainty, a key influence on transactions costs, has been defined as 'the difference between the amount of information required to perform the task and the amount of information already possessed by the organization' (Galbraith, 1973, p. 5). Because IT can improve the cost, timing, and quality of information flows and decision processes, it can radically change the transaction economics with far-reaching strategic results. Monitoring costs and, hence, uncertainty can be decreased.

A transactions cost approach leads us to focus on applications that manage interactions between separable productive activities.[8] There are other types of IT applications. For example, IT can become part of the product itself, as in micro-processor systems in stereos or automobiles, or IT can change the technology of a productive activity, as in the case of flexible manufacturing techniques. However, systems to manage interactions describe a significant class of strategic applications. Moreover, many applications that are not primarily oriented toward interactions do, in fact, influence interactions. Again, flexible manufacturing can be an example: to be successful, these

[8] Of course, in practice the unit of analysis of activity – machines, plants, or strategic business units – will depend on the situation under study.

applications must restructure many of the interactions within a firm. Sales, production, and procurement all must be much more tightly integrated under a flexible manufacturing environment than under traditional manufacturing methods.

There are two basic types of interactions that can be affected by IT: vertical interactions and horizontal interactions. *Vertical interactions* involve the flow of goods, services, and information along a single value chain with the output of one process becoming the input of the next.[9] Where this flow is between independent firms, we have the traditional product markets of economics or the strategic resource markets of the resource-based theory. The flow of products from a manufacturer to a retailer is a vertical interaction, as is the flow of market information from the retailer back to the manufacturer. But vertical interactions can also be within a firm, such as interactions between manufacturing and sales in a single organization.

Horizontal interactions, on the other hand, involve coordination of similar or complementary strategic resources, or fixed factors of production, in multiple markets or uses. For example, ATM networks allow sharing of machines among multiple banks. Where this access is within a single firm, it typically involves linkages between different strategic business units.[10] Horizontal interactions between independent organizations are less common, consisting of various cooperative arrangements and their joint ventures. The distinction between horizontal and vertical is made to clarify the economic effects of IT. In practice the distinction may be much less clear. The airline CRS was initially developed to manage the vertical interactions between the airlines and travel agents (and their customers). Subsequently, these systems were expanded to include other travel-related services, such as hotels and rental cars. These relationships are essentially horizontal in that the CRS infrastructure is being shared over multiple lines of business.

We suggest that there are fundamental differences in how IT can be used to manage these different types of interactions and, in particular, the complementary resources needed to exploit the different types of application.

Vertical interactions

Information technology can be used to manage the flow of goods, services, and information between productive activities along a single industry value chain. We call these vertical interactions. Applications to manage vertical

---

[9] The value chain is a common concept in economics and strategy. The idea is that the production of a good or service involves a series of distinct, sequential activities, each of which generates a portion of the economic value of the final product. Several authors have introduced their own versions of the value chain; perhaps the most popular one today is due to Porter (1985).

[10] Hence the term 'horizontal.' Diversification into new industries, i.e., acquiring bundles of resources, is frequently referred to as 'horizontal diversification,' as opposed to 'vertical integration,' or expanding along a single value chain.

interactions have received considerable attention in the IT literature, particularly those applications that manage interactions across organizational boundaries (e.g., Cash and Konsynski, 1985; Clemons and Kimbrough, 1986; Ives and Learmonth, 1984; Johnston and Vitale, 1988; Malone, *et al.*, 1987). What hasn't received much attention is the conditions under which such systems will confer advantage.

IT can reduce the basic transactions costs involved in the vertical flow of goods and services along a value chain. This includes direct savings, such as the costs of searching for suppliers, placing the order, and monitoring the execution, as well as indirect savings, such as reduced inventories and faster reactions times. The system may change the allocation of costs between the buyer and seller and may even change the structure of the interaction, i.e., whether the exchange occurs in a market or within a firm's hierarchy. Malone, *et al.* (1987) have argued that IT can reduce transactions costs to the point where transactions previously performed within a firm will be more efficiently performed in a market. This would lead to vertical de-integration. However, it is not immediately apparent how reducing such costs affects the relative positions of the competitors, particularly if the systems are quickly duplicated.

Horizontal interactions

IT can be used to coordinate strategic resources in similar or complementary activities in different value chains. These horizontal interactions may be intra-organizational. We have found such applications to be significant, and yet they are largely ignored in the IT literature. Just as importantly, many organizations are organized along lines of business, with few procedures in place to identify and exploit such potential interactions among business units; thus, they are probably underemphasized in many organizations.

Horizontal IT applications can exploit scale and scope economies in certain key strategic resources common to several markets or industries in which the firm participates. Inherent scale economies in these resources are often not realized due to the costs of coordinating the resources in different markets. IT can reduce the coordination costs, thus realizing these latent scale economies.[11]

For example, Hewlett Packard (HP), the electronic equipment manufacturing giant, has used IT to coordinate component procurement across its diverse and decentralized US manufacturing operations (Kimbrough, 1988). This system, termed PROMIS for 'PROcurement Management Information System,' automates component procurement, from purchase order generation to inventory disposition, for HP's 55 manu-

[11] Panzar and Willig (1981) have demonstrated that economies of scope implies some common fixed factor of production. Teece (1980) has investigated the critical role of coordination costs in the realization of such scope economies.

facturing divisions. The system has realized considerable benefits stemming from closer vertical coordination with suppliers, such as reduced inventory, reduced buyer time, and improved component quality. Perhaps more importantly, PROMIS enables coordination of component procurement among the decentralized manufacturing divisions while being flexible enough not to compromise the divisions' autonomy and flexibility, which are considered key strategic strengths. This horizontal coordination generates considerable benefits that are not available to smaller players:

- Economies of scale in procurement systems. The fixed development cost of IT for purchasing support can be spread over all divisions, lowering the average cost. Moreover, innovations and enhancements to purchasing procedures can be rapidly diffused throughout the organization using IT.
- Economies of scale, economies of specialization, and load leveling in procuring common components. Centralizing procurement of these components directly reduces costs and allows HP to exploit fully its considerable bargaining power in the component markets.

While the most easily realized economic effects of horizontal IT applications are cost reductions through economies of scale exploited by coordinating similar resources, there are situations where dissimilar, but complementary, resources can be coordinated to increase the value of the resulting activity to customers. Merrill Lynch's CMA product is a classic example of such 'super-additive' value functions, where the value of the combined activity is greater than the sum of the values of individual activities. Merrill Lynch combined functions of a traditional brokerage margin account with those of a checking account, debit card, and money market fund. The resulting product had a higher value to customers than the sum of the functional parts. Moreover, when the super-additive product combines resources not enjoyed by competitors, it will be extremely difficult for competitors to respond. Thus, if the product is demanded by customers and creates competitive advantage, this advantage is likely to be sustainable.

Identifying resources that can be exploited with horizontal IT applications is problematic given the great variety of resources. The framework presented in the next section offers some assistance in this process.

Analyzing resource differences

Previous sections have argued that IT can be used to manage interactions among economic activities and that firms' resource positions are important in explaining the emergence of these applications and their strategic outcomes. This section makes the implications of this more concrete by analyzing the opportunities for strategic IT in the presence of important differences among firms, including differences in vertical integration, diversification, and resource quality or organization.

Differences in vertical integration

Firms can differ in their degree of vertical integration, that is, in the set of productive activities they perform within a particular market or industry value chain. The transactions cost theory reviewed earlier posits that firms expand vertically in the presence of market imperfections that make use of market mechanisms more risky and costly than internal production. By performing more activities within a firm, the business can achieve higher efficiency and integration in vertical linkages, but at the expense of some of the production economies of scale, scope, and specialization that may be available when these activities are performed by a separate firm.

Information systems can exploit efficiencies through increased operational integration among vertically related activities while reducing the transactions costs and risks usually associated with such coordination. In other words, IT may decrease the benefits of vertical integration of ownership by allowing 'virtual' integration: using vertical applications of IT to achieve the benefits of vertical integration while also realizing the production economies available to separate, specialized firms. Firms with shorter value chains will therefore benefit by developing vertical systems that increase the level of operational integration with suppliers or customers. While vertically integrated firms can potentially match the level of operational integration, it is not as easy to match the production economies and flexibility of independent, specialized firms.

This change in the value of vertically integrated operations is clearly demonstrated in the automobile industry. General Motors manufactures more of the components in its automobiles than either Ford or Chrysler, which both outsource over half the value of the materials in their automobiles (Chrysler outsources close to 70 per cent). This captive manufacturing capability (and its assured customer demand) used to be a strategic advantage for GM. Now, as Chrysler and Ford use IT to manage their relationships with suppliers, gaining assured quality, flexibility in service and delivery, and the cost advantage that comes from their suppliers' lower wage scales, GM's advantage has been converted into a disadvantage.[12] This trend of vertical de-integration appears to be continuing in the industry. Saab has recently announced plans to sell some component manufacturing divisions (*AutoNews*, 1989). Clearly, forces other than IT are at work here,

---

[12] This is at least partly acknowledged even by General Motors. Roger Smith, chairman of GM, recently admitted that its degree of vertical integration has ceased to be an advantage. 'What had been an advantage for us turned out to be a semi-disadvantage,' he says (Hampton and Norman, 1987, p. 110.)

including changes in the competitive environment, changing wage scales, and the need to exploit scale advantages or specialization where possible. However, IT has been critical in forging a response to these trends, one that now frequently entails outsourcing to gain these advantages. Without IT to coordinate relationships with suppliers, outsourcing would be a more expensive and less viable strategy.

Another example of such virtual integration is Benetton S.p.A. (Vitale, 1987). Benetton, one of the world's largest garment producers, outsources the vast majority of its knitting, assembly, and finishing through a large network of small subcontractors. Most of these subcontractors work solely for Benetton. Moreover, the vast majority of its retail presence is through franchised stores, which, in 1987, numbered over 4,000 and were located in some 60 countries. IT is very important in coordinating this fragmented value chain. Orders from franchises are electronically entered and sorted by material and production requirements, matching demand with the capacity of the subcontractor network to aid in production scheduling. Goods are automatically tracked through the system from order to delivery to the franchise. The heavy use of outsourcing allows Benetton rapidly to adjust capacity, thereby reducing costs. The IT support of operational integration makes this strategy possible without excessive coordination costs and expensive delays. Moreover, this close operational integration through IT is achieved without owning the various activities.

Benetton is an example of an increasing trend toward outsourcing critical functions. Information technology enables companies to shorten their value chains by outsourcing critical portions of the chain to specialized providers. For example, the value of retail distribution in financial services remains unclear. Some companies like Merrill Lynch consider their distribution systems to be sources of competitive strength. Other competitors are forging strategic alliances to achieve the same results; they argue that in an economic downturn Merrill Lynch's distribution system becomes an enormous fixed cost that will be difficult to cover.

Alternatively, companies can also use IT to achieve shorter value chains by bypassing entirely some activities that their competitors may choose to perform and may consider critical, sometimes turning resources considered essential into competitive disadvantages. For example, brick and morter branch networks have been considered essential for retail banks. It seems clear that branch networks require an enormous expense, both for physical plant and for personnel. It is also clear that this expense was justified in the past because it provided the means by which banks collected funds, and it offered customers convenient access to their deposits. Credit unions, in particular, are now able to offer a comparable level of customer convenience through their participation in shared ATM networks, with virtually none of the expense of a branch network. In fact, we have on one occasion overheard an executive vice president of a major Philadelphia area bank complaining that although he incurred significant expense maintaining dozens of branches (while a credit union had only one) both offered essentially equivalent customer access to deposits through the same ATM network.

Differences in diversification

Another source of difference among firms that can be exploited through IT is their diversification strategy, including the range of markets and industries in which a firm participates as well as its position in those markets. Differences in diversification can be exploited through IT in three ways:

- **Exploiting Scale Advantage in Key Resources.** Opportunities may exist for using IT to coordinate similar resources across business lines. Through increased coordination, IT can improve resource utilization, lowering costs.
- **Exploiting Technology Transfer.** Often skills required in different lines of business are similar. IT can be used to develop and transfer a skill base between lines of business, leveraging a firm's expertise.
- **Exploiting New Uses for Existing Resources.** Different, but complementary, resources or product lines may be combined in ways that create more value for the customer, independent of the impact on costs.

Diversification for scale advantage

A key source of benefits from horizontal interactions is in exploiting scale economies in key resources used in several markets or industries. Hewlett Packard's centralized procurement system, mentioned earlier, is a good example. The system allowed economies of scale and specialization in the purchasing function to be exploited. The centralization of order entry and procurement also played a big role in McKesson Drug Company's dramatic cost reduction over the past 10 years (Clemons and Row, 1988).

As another example, Otis Elevator Company has achieved lower costs and dramatically improved service by centralizing its elevator maintenance operations with its Otisline information system (Stoddard, 1987). Prior to Otisline, Otis, the world leader in elevator sales and service, received calls for elevator service and dispatched service personnel through a highly decentralized network of field offices, ranging in size from one or two people to as many as 100 people. Service performance in terms of number of calls and response time varied greatly among the field offices. By centralizing elevator maintenance information and the dispatching of personnel through Otisline, Otis was able to reduce dispatching costs and improve service response time. Centralization of dispatching reduced costs through economies of scale and load leveling within the dispatching function. Information provided by the system also allowed Otis actively to manage response time, service personnel productivity, and other aspects of elevator maintenance in order to reduce costs and improve service. The system supports marketing in the form of service statistics to back up a guaranteed response time policy. Otisline even affects engineering by pinpointing recurring problems that are indicative of design problems.

In all of these cases, the coordination of similar activities and resources across markets or industries yielded reduced costs for all of the coordinated activities. Moreover, the level of benefits realized is critically linked to the horizontal scope of the firm. For example, Procter & Gamble, the consumer products giant, is using IT to coordinate outbound logistics (ordering and delivery) across product lines. This enables them to offer just-in-time product delivery to major retailers such as Wal-Mart. Manufacturers with more limited product lines are at a distinct cost disadvantage in matching that service.

Diversification and technology transfer

The above examples involve on-going, operational coordination of similar resources among several markets or industries. Exploiting horizontal differences need not involve the tightly integrated operations demanded by centralizing functions. The horizontal interaction may simply be in the form of *technology transfer*. McKesson Corporation is a distributor for several lines of products, among them pharmaceuticals, liquor, veterinary supplies, and office supplies. While these businesses are operationally distinct, their similarity allows McKesson to leverage his expertise, particularly in software development, across all of these businesses.

Diversification and new uses for existing resources

Leveraging advantages in similar resources across markets or industries is not the only way IT can generate differential benefits. Opporunities exist for using IT to combine different but complementary resources or product lines in ways that create more value for customers than simply the sum of the parts. As seen earlier, Merrill Lynch's CMA is an example: by combining functions of a brokerage account, money market fund, and demand deposit account into a single product, Merrill Lynch created additional value and a new product class. Similarly, all the major airline reservation systems expanded relatively early into hotel reservations, rental car reservations, and other travel-related services. This move exploited horizontal interactions among similar resources, i.e., the reservation technology and customer base, but the cost advantage of leveraging similar resources was only part of the benefits. By decreasing the agent's search and transacting costs, the reservation systems also increased the value of the service.

Airline reservation systems offer a more striking opportunity to create super-additive value, not by combining breadth of coverage of product lines as AHS exploited, but by combining and facilitating several different aspects of travel. While reservation systems' offering of air, hotel, and ground travel reduces travel agent search costs, they do little for the traveler. Allegis attempted to combine the different components into an integrated travel service, smoothing and facilitating business travel for the actual traveler and adding significant value. Perhaps a single illustrative example will suffice.

A simple systems flow analysis indicates that rental car customers return their cars, queue up to take care of the paper work, rush madly for their flights while encumbered by heavy luggage, and then queue up again to check in. Allegis sought to integrate Hertz and United Airlines so that customers would queue up once to return their rental cars, check their bags, and receive their United boarding cards; they could then make their way to their flights more readily, without excess baggage, and without the need to check in again at the terminal. This could be expected to produce additional market share both for United and for Hertz. And this could be expected to produce particular loyalty among the prized full-fare business traveler.

Of course, Wall Street's desire for an immediate payoff, together with serious tactical errors on the part of Allegis's chairman, combined to subvert this strategy. It is not yet clear that the strategy was in error: Lufthansa, for example, owns 25 percent of European Avis and tried actively to acquire Hilton International from Allegis. And SAS owns 40 percent of Intercontinental Hotels and seems to be enjoying real benefits from its ability to provide superior ground support for travelers.

While horizontal and vertical systems can be viewed as conceptually distinct, in practice there is considerable overlap. It is frequently the case that horizontal differences are critical in the strategic outcomes of vertical systems. For example, American Hospital Supply's ASAP vertical order-entry system achieved its success largely because AHS had the horizontal scope to provide a full line of products and allow single source shopping. Such a proprietary vertical system would not have been possible for companies with narrower product lines.

Other resource differences

Other resource differences can provide an opportunity for advantage through IT. These include differences in resource quality (e.g., competence in a primary value-adding activity) or resource organization. Generally, strategy differences will not provide opportunities for advantage unless accompanied by significant resource differences; in the absence of such differences, there are few barriers preventing adoption of a superior strategy.

In many cases, an important resource difference is simply scale of operations or market share. For example, vertical systems can provide advantage when they exploit scale advantages. This allows a firm to provide services that are more expensive for competitors than they are for itself. For example, McKesson Drug Company's Economost system uses IT to reduce transactions costs in placing and filling orders as well as providing inventory reports and other management services. Such systems are also provided by all major competitors; however, McKesson's market share advantage makes these services cheaper for McKesson than for smaller competitors (the desire for requisite scale to justify these systems was, of course, an important factor driving industry consolidation) (Clemons and Row, 1988).

A comparative advantage in some activity can also be leveraged horizontally in other markets. For example, by 1982 many major brokerages recognized the need to compete with Merrill Lynch's CMA product and went out for competitive procurement. A surprise winner was Provident National Bank, which possessed critical resource advantages, including expertise in credit card processing, demand deposit, securities custodial, trust management, and even discount brokerage services. It is important to note that Provident was not a better systems integrator than firms such as ADP and EDS, but Provident did already have the systems to integrate! Provident had other, less obvious advantages. Brokerage firms did not view Provident as a potential competitor, able to offer a similar product directly to these firms' customers. And Provident's excellent cost accounting system let it price its initial winning proposal for Shearson at what was known to be a profitable price. Subsequent contracts, with little additional incremental expense due to the scale-intensive nature of the systems, were of course easy for Provident to win, yielding Provident with an extremely profitable business as a third-party provider of processing services for consolidated asset management accounts.

Another example where a resource advantage was effectively leveraged is Barclays de Zoete Wedd's (BZW) TRADE system (Clemons and Weber, 1990). TRADE is an automated order execution system for trading securities in Britain developed by BZW, a leading British securities house. Brokers connected to BZW via TRADE can examine securities prices and execute small and medium-sized trades electronically. In addition to greatly reducing the execution costs of small brokers, the system provides electronic interfaces to settlement systems. BZW has several advantages in key complementary resources that are virtually impossible for any competitor to match. An automatic execution system is of course only useful when it works, and the market maker offering the system can only provide automatic execution for the securities in which it 'makes market.' BZW is a market maker for over 1,800 UK equities and for almost 100 bonds; only one of its competitors comes close, and most cover 800, 600, or even far fewer securities. This scope difference makes a system from BZW far more useful than one from a competitor.

Additionally, BZW has established relationships with brokers and has the largest share of retail order flow. A competitor with less established retail operations would incur essentially the same fixed cost in offering automatic execution and thus far greater per transaction costs; this difference would make a comparable offering prohibitively expensive for competitors. This combination – scope of coverage, scale of operations, and established relationships – is extremely difficult for competitors to match. TRADE was not the first automatic execution system offered in London; its technology is not particularly innovative, and much was obtained from a third-party vendor. Still, it has eclipsed its older competitor and deterred BZW's competitor market makers from launching their own systems. TRADE has significantly increased BZW's share of retail orders while increasing the net contribution of each retail order by about £5 to £7. The combination of greater profitability and increased market share is of course quite attractive, and the advantage BZW enjoys appears to be sustainable because of fundamental resource differences, not because of first mover effects or any technical advantage.

Vertical systems can also be used to by-pass or substitute for activities where a firm has a comparative disadvantage, or where a firm just wants to capture more of the value added. The development of alternative distribution channels is becoming increasingly important in financial services. For example, securities firms acting as underwriters in the issuing of new securities are able to charge a significant fee for their services. Issuers using computerized systems for direct private placement are able to sell their new securities directly to institutional investors for dramatically reduced fees. Morgan Stanley's Capital Link has been successfully used by public utilities to reduce the fees paid on new issues from more than a full percent of face value to 20 basis points.

As another example, American Airlines' SABRE reservation system is now being offered directly to customers through the Prodigy network. While this alternative to the traditional travel agent is currently being offered in partnership with large travel agents such as Rosenbluth Travel, it seems plausible that the objective is to develop an alternative distribution channel that reduces or eliminates the 10 percent commission that must be paid to a travel agent.

Other strategy differences can be exploited with IT when they are accompanied by resource differences. For example, a strategy of 'Design to manufacture' requires close interactions between product development and manufacturing (Rhein, 1986). A strategy focusing on customer service requires close links between sales and the customer (Ives and Learmonth, 1984). As we have claimed above, IT allows firms more cost effectively to increase the coordination and integration of decisions across vertically related activities, thus increasing the responsiveness and flexibility of these vertical links without requiring ownership. In general, we would expect this to reduce the advantage of small, flexible niche players because larger players are able to better capitalize on their scale advantages without the performance penalties usually associated with size.

Conclusions
Summary of principal results

Information systems are vital strategic business tools. However, we have found little evidence that they have conferred competitive advantage in any but a few instances. This should not be surprising. Information technology – equipment, software, services, and personnel – is available to all firms. While these resources may be expensive for small firms, they are seldom prohibitively expensive for major players of comparable size. Later entrants often benefit from the innovator's experience and duplicate the system with newer technology, allowing comparable services to be delivered at lower costs. Even smaller players can often acquire the necessary technology through cooperative arrangements or by outsourcing (Clemons and Knez, 1988; Sager, 1988; 1989).

It is still possible to defend IT-based advantages in the presence of strong first mover effects where customer adoption is rapid, competitor response is relatively slow, and customers face significant switching costs (Clemons and Kimbrough, 1986). This does occur, but it has been far less common than expected.

This article suggests that benefits resulting from an innovative application of information technology can be more readily defended if the system exploits unique resources of the innovating firm so that competitors do not fully benefit from imitation. IT can change the value of key resources by reducing the cost of integrating and coordinating economic activities. This increases the potential production economies, such as scale, scope and specialization, that can be exploited. The benefits will therefore be related to the complementary resources controlled by each participant. These differences are structural in that selling and acquiring resources require interaction with strategic resource markets, which can be difficult and costly, particularly where the resource is unique or of limited availability.

Structural resource differences can take the form of differences in vertical integration, diversification, or resource quality and organization. IT reduces the transaction costs of coordinating vertical interactions, favoring firms that are less vertically integrated (in terms of ownership) and enabling the by-passing or substitution of some activities. Similarly, IT reduces the costs of coordinating similar resources in multiple markets, favoring firms with scale or scope advantages in those resources. And IT can enable the coordination of different but related resources to create new products and services with enhanced value to consumers.

The resource-based theory presented here is significant in that it is grounded in economic theory, increasing its potential for predictive power. Moreover, the theory is supported empirically by a considerable number of case studies (e.g., Clemons and Row, 1988; Clemons and Weber, 1990). Finally, the resource approach holds some significant implications for managers.

Managerial implications

An implication of this approach is that looking at the totality of the firm is important. Horizontal interactions between business units are important, often overlooked opportunities for IT. Planning approaches that examine only individual business units will miss many opportunities for IT. Planning approaches that examine only individual business units will miss many opportunities and may leave the firm exposed to integration strategies of competitors. An awareness of the importance of structural differences can guide the search for oportunities for competitive uses of IT. This is demonstrated by Provident's successful push to become a third-party processor of cash management accounts. Structural differences can also suggest remedial uses of technology to address weaknesses or emerging problems, as was the case with Philadelphia National Bank's development of the MAC network to counter a significant disadvantage in ATMs.

We have focused on resource control by a single firm, but an increasingly important issue is the conditions under which resources can be coordinated across firm boundaries. For example, Allegis initially embarked on a strategy based on integrating travel services from hotels to rental cars to airlines based on wholly owned business units. Although this ownership-based strategy has apparently been rejected, it may ultimately prove possible for its partly owned Covia reservation subsidiary to deliver travelers the same service by contracting with the independent hotel chains and rental car companies.

As suggested by Klein, *et al.* (1978) firms may encounter significant risk when they become dependent upon others for critical resources; in fact, this is often the principal transactions cost, sufficient to drive firms to integrate rather than to rely upon access in the market. Nonetheless, information technology improves coordination across distances and across firm boundaries, making it easier to effectively use resources belonging to others. IT improves monitoring reducing uncertainty in how these resources are being used and making it much less risky to rely upon resources belonging to others. It is still essential that these relationships be mutually beneficial in order to be stable, as much of the literature on joint ventures has shown. When all three are combined – ease of coordination, reduced risk of dependence, and mutual benefits – firms can cooperate in the sharing of critical resources. This sharing of resources, mediated by IT, can be a special case of exploiting structural differences for sustainable advantage. We call this case 'sustainable cooperative advantage' (Clemons, 1991).

Directions for future research

We believe that the resource-based approach is extremely promising in advancing our understanding of the strategic impacts of information technology. Areas for future work include:

- Developing planning methodologies that explicitly consider resources and opportunities for integration.
- Expanding the theory to encompass shifts in firm boundaries and the structure and inter-relationships of industries. This is critical in understanding opportunities for interorganizational cooperation and outsourcing.
- Developing empirical tests for this theoretical approach.

References

Autonews. 'Saab Plans to Sell 3 Car and Truck Component Plants,' September 4, 1989, p. 8.

Banker, R. D. and Kauffman, R. J. 'Strategic Contributions of Information Technology: An Empirical Study of ATM Networks,' *Proceedings of the Ninth International Conference on Information Systems*, Minneapolis, MN, December 1988, pp. 141–150.

Barney, J. B. 'Strategic Factor Markets: Expectations, Luck and Business Strategy,' *Management Science* (32:10), October 1986, pp. 1231–1241.

Cash, J. I. and Konsynski, B. R. 'IS Redraws Competitive Boundaries,' *Harvard Business Review* (63:2), March–April 1985, pp. 134–142.

Clemons, E. K. 'MAC – Philadelphia National Bank's Strategic Venture in Shared ATM Networks,' *Proceedings of the 22nd Hawaii International Conference on System Sciences*, January 1989, pp. 214–222.

Clemons, E. K. 'Corporate Strategies for Information Technology: A Resource-Based Approach,' forthcoming in *Computer*, IEEE Computer Society.

Clemons, E. K. and Kimbrough, S. O. 'Information Systems, Telecommunications, and Their Effects on Industrial Organization,' *Proceedings of the Seventh International Conference on Information Systems*, San Diego, CA, December 1986, pp. 99–108.

Clemons, E. K. and Knez, M. 'Competition and Cooperation in Information Systems Innovation,' *Information & Management* (15:1), August 1988, pp. 25–35.

Clemons, E. K. and Row, M. C. 'Structural Differences Among Firms: A Potential Source of Competitive Advantage in the Application of Information Technology,' *Proceedings of the Eighth International Conference on Information Systems*, Pittsburgh, PA, December 1987, pp. 1–9.

Clemons, E. K. and Row, M. C. 'McKesson Drug Company: A Case Study of Economost,' *Journal of Management Information Systems* (5:1), Summer 1988, pp. 36–50.

Clemons, E. K. and Weber, B. W. 'Making the Technology Investment Decision – Barclays de Zoete Wedd's TRADE System,' *Proceedings of the 23rd Hawaii International Conference on System Sciences*, January 1990, pp. 137–146.

Copeland, D. G. and McKenney, J. L. 'Airline Reservations Systems: Lessons from History,' *MIS Quarterly* (12:3), September 1988, pp. 353–370.

Galbraith, J. R. *Designing Complex Organizations*, Addison Wesley, Boston, MA, 1973.

Hampton, W. J. and Norman, J. R. 'General Motors: What Went Wrong,' *Business Week*, March 16, 1987, pp. 103–110.

Ives, B. and Learmonth, G. P. 'Information Systems as a Competitive Weapon,' *Communications of the ACM* (27:12), December 1984, pp. 1193–1201.

Johnston, H. R. and Vitale, M. R. 'Creating Competitive Advantage with Interorganizational Information Systems,' *MIS Quarterly* (12:2), June 1988, pp. 153–165.

Klein, B., Crawford, R. G., and Alchian, A. A. 'Vertical Integration, Appropriable Rents and the Competitive Contracting Process,' *Journal of Law and Economics* (21:2), October 1978, pp. 297–326.

Malone, T. W., Yates, J., and Benjamin, R. I. 'Electronic Markets and Electronic Hierarchies,' *Communications of the ACM* (30:6), June 1987, pp. 484–497.

Panzar, J. C. and Willig, R. D. 'Economies of Scope,' *AEA Papers and Proceedings* (71:2), May 1981, pp. 268–272.

Penrose, E. T. *Theory of the Growth of the Firm*, Blackwell, Oxford, England, 1959.

Pfeffer, J. and Salancik, G. R. *The External Control of Organizations: A Resource Dependence Perspective*, Harper and Row, New York, NY, 1978.

Porter, M. E. *Competitive Advantage*, The Free Press, New York, NY, 1985.

Porter, M. E. and Millar, V. E. 'How Information Gives You Competitive Advantage,' *Harvard Business Review* (63:4), July-August 1985, pp. 149–160.

Rhein, R. 'New Design Philosophies Improve Costs, Assembly,' *MIS Week*, June 16, 1986, pp. 26, 35.

Rhodes, A. F. (ed). *Mergerstat Review*. W. T. Grimm & Co., Chicago, IL, 1986.

Rubin, P. H. 'The Expansion of Firms,' *Journal of Political Economy* (81:4), July-August 1973, pp. 936–949.

Rumelt, R. P. 'Diversification Strategy and Profitability,' *Strategic Management Journal* (3:4), October-December 1982, pp. 359–369.

Rumelt, R. P. 'Theory, Strategy and Entrepreneurship,' in *The Competitive Challenge*, David Teece (ed.), Ballinger Publishing Co., Cambridge, MA, 1987, pp. 13–157.

Sager, M. T. 'Competitive Information Systems in Australian Retail Banking,' *Information & Management* (15:1), August, 1988, pp. 59–67.

Sager, M. T. 'Competitive Alliances with IT – The Australian Retail Banking Experience,' *Proceedings of the 22nd Hawaii International Conference on System Sciences*, Janary 1989, Kailua Kona, HI, pp. 189–196.

Stoddard, D. 'Otisline,' Harvard Business School Case Services No. 9, 186–304, Harvard University, Boston, MA, April 1987.

Teece, D. 'Economies of Scope and the Scope of the Enterprise,' *Journal of Economic Behavior and Organization* (1:3), September 1980, pp. 223–247.

Teece, D. 'Firm Boundaries, Technological Innovation, and Strategic Management,' in *The Economics of Strategic Planning*, Lacy Glen Thomas (ed.), Lexington Books, Lexington, MA, 1986, p. 187–199.

Teece, D. 'Profiting from Technological Innovation: Implications for Integration, Collaboration, Licensing, and Public Policy,' in *The Competitive Challenge*, David Teece (ed.), Ballinger Publishing Co., Cambridge, MA, 1987, pp. 185–219.

Vitale, M. R. 'The Growing Risks of Information Systems Success,' *MIS Quarterly* (10:4), December 1986, pp. 327–334.

Vitale, M. R. 'Benetton S.p.A.: Industrial Fashion,' Harvard Business School Case Services No. 9-188-003, Harvard University, Boston, MA, August 1987.

Williamson, O. *Markets and Hierarchies: Analysis and Antitrust Implications*, The Free Press, New York, NY, 1975.

Winkler, M. and Miller, M. 'Merrill Lynch Let Competitors Use Bond Price System,' *Wall Street Journal*, October 17, 1988, p. B1.

9 Globalization and information management strategies

J. Karimi and B. R. Konsynski

1 Introduction

Recently, the globalization of competition has become the rule rather than the exception for a number of industries [39]. To compete effectively, at home or globally, firms often must coordinate their activities on a worldwide basis. Although many global firms have an explicit global business strategy, few have a corresponding strategy for managing information technology internationally. Many firms have information interchange protocols across their multinational organizational structures, but few have global information technology architectures. A global information management strategy is needed as a result of (1) *industry globalization*: the growing globalization trend in many industries and the associated reliance on information technologies for coordination and operation, and (2) *national competitive posture*: the aggregation of separate domestic strategies in individual countries that may contend with coordination. While Procter and Gamble contends with the need to address more effectively its global market in the branded packaged goods industry, Singapore requires improved coordination and control of trade documentation in order to compete more effectively in the cross-industry trade environment that is vital to the economic health of that nation. Each approach recognizes the growing information intensity in their expanding markets. Each in turn must meet the challenges brought about by the need for cross-cultural and cross-industry cooperation.

Globalization trends demand an evaluation of the skills portfolio that organizations require in order to participate effectively in their changing markets. Porter [41] suggests that coordination among increasingly complex networks of activities dispersed worldwide is becoming a prime source of competitive advantage: global strategies frequently involve coordination with coalition partners as well as among a firm's own subsidiaries. The benefits associated with globalization of industries are not tied to countries' policies and practice. Rather, they are associated with how the activities in the industry value chain are performed by the firm's worldwide systems. These systems involve partnerships [31] with independent entities that involve information and management process interchange across legal organization boundaries, as well as across national boundaries.

For a global firm, the coordination concerns involve an analysis of how similar or linked activities are performed in different countries. Coordination [31] involves the management of the exchange of information, goods, expertise, technology, and finances. Many business functions play a role in such coordination – logistics, order fulfillment, financial, etc. Coordination involves sharing and use, by different facilities, of information about the activities within the firm's value chain [30]. In global industries, these skills permit a firm to (1) be flexible in responding to competitors in different countries and markets, (2) respond in one country (or region) to a change in another, (3) scan markets around the world, (4) transfer knowledge between units in different countries, (5) reduce costs, (6) enhance effectiveness, and (7) preserve diversity in final products and in production location. The innovations in information technology (IT) in the past two decades have greatly reduced coordination costs by reducing both the time and cost of communicating information. Market and product innovation often involves coordination and partnership across a diverse set of organizational and geographically dispersed entities. Several studies [26, 27, 38, 42] suggest ways in which companies/nations achieve competitive advantage through innovation.

Organizations must begin to manage the evolution of a global IT architecture that forms an infrastructure for the coordination needs of a global management team. The country-centered, multinational firm will give way to truly global organizations that will carry little national identity [49, 50]. It is a major challenge to general management to build and manage the technical infrastructure that supports a unique global enterprise culture. This chapter deals with issues that arise in the evolution of a global business strategy and its alignment with the evolving global IT strategy.

Below we present issues related to the radical changes taking place in both the global business environment and the IT environment, with changes in one area driving changes in the other. Section 2 describes changes taking place in the global business environment as a result of globalization. It highlights elements from previous research findings on the effects of globalization on the organizational strategies/structures and coordination/control strategies. Section 3 deals with the information technology dimension and addresses the issue of development of a global information systems (GIS) management strategy. The section emphasizes the need for 'alignment' of business and technological evolution as a result of the radical changes in the global business environment and technology.

Section 4 summarizes and presents other challenges to senior managers that are emerging in the global business environment.

2 Globalization and changes in the business environment

Since World War II, a number of factors have changed the manner of competition in the global business community. The particular catalyst for globalization and for evolving patterns of international competition varies among industries. Among the causative factors are increased similarity in available infrastructure, distribution channels, and marketing approaches among countries, as well as a fluid global capital market that allows large flows of funds between countries. Additional causes include falling political and tariff barriers, a growing number of regional economic pacts that facilitate trade relations, and the increasing impact of the technological revolution in restructuring and integrating industries. Manufacturing issues associated with flexibility, labor cost differentials, and other factors also play a role in these market trends.

Table 1 Global business environment – strategy/structure and coordination control

Business strategy structure	Strategic management processes	Tactical business processes	Coordination and control processes
multinational/ decentralized– federation	informal HQ-subsidiary relationships; strategic decisions are decentralized	mainly financial flows; capital out and dividends back	socialization; careful recruitment, develop- ment, and acculturation of key decision makers
global/ centralized federation	tight central control of decisions, resources and information	one-way flows of goods, resources and information	centralization; substan- tive decision making by senior management
international/ coordinated– federation	formal management planning and control systems allow tighter HQ–subsidiary linkages	assets, resources, responsibilities decentralized but controlled from HQ	formalization; formal systems, policies and standards to guide choice
transnational/ integrated– network	complex process of coor- dination and cooperation in an environment of shared decision making	large flows of tech- nology, finances, people, and informa- tion among inter- dependent units	co-opting; the entire portfolio of coor- dinating and control mechanisms
interorganiza- tional/coordinated federation of business groups	share activities and gain competitive advantage by lowering costs and raising differentiation	vertical disaggregation of functions	formalization; multiple and flexible coordination and control functions

Widespread globalization is also evident in a number of industries that were once largely separate domestic industries, such as software, telecommunications, and services [9, 32, 40]. Recently, the political changes in the Soviet Union and the Eastern European countries, plus the evolution of the European Common Market toward a single European market without national borders or barriers by 1992 [13], also have led to growing international competition. Other factors are changing the economic dynamics in the Pacific Rim area, with changes in Hong Kong, Japan, China and Taiwan, Korea, Singapore, and the reentry of certain nations to the global economic community (e.g., Vietnam).

Previous research indicates that significant changes have taken place in organizational strategies/structure during the 1980s because of ever-increasing global competition and growth in the communications and information-processing industry. Researchers in international business have pointed out that the structure of a global firm's value chain is the key to its strategy: its fit with the environmental requirements that determine economic performance [3, 15, 37, 40]. Another study found that, in successful global firms, organization structure and strategy are matched by selecting the most efficient or lowest cost structure that satisfies the information-processing requirements inherent in the strategy [12]. That is, the firm's strategy and its information-processing requirements must be in alignment with the firm's organizational structure and information-processing capabilities. To understand changes in organizational designs for global forms, these changes are highlighted in relation to the changes in strategies.

2.1 Evolution of the global firm's strategy/structure

Global strategy is defined by Porter [40] as strategy from which 'a firm seeks to gain competitive advantage from its international presence through either a concentrated configuration of activities, or coordinating among dispersed activities, or both.' Configuration involves the location(s) in the world where each activity in the value chain is performed, it characterizes the organizational structure of a global firm. A global firm faces a number of options in both configuration and coordination for each activity in the value chain. As implied by these definitions, there is no one pattern of international competition, neither is there one type of global strategy.

Bartlett [3, 4] suggests that for a global firm value-chain activities are pulled together by two environmental forces: (1) national differentiation, i.e., diversity in individual country-markets; and (2) global integration, i.e., coordination among activities in various countries. For global firms, forces for integration and national differentiation can vary depending on their global strategies. Table 1 shows the evolution of the global firms' strategy/structure and their coordination/control strategies as a result of globalization of competition. The vocabulary of Bartlett [4] and Porter [40] will be further used in our framework.

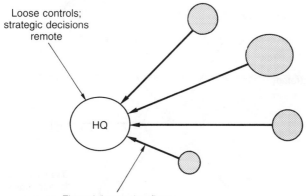

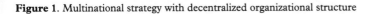

Figure 1. Multinational strategy with decentralized organizational structure

Under a *multinational* strategy, a firm might differentiate its products to meet local needs to respond to diverse interests. In such an approach, the firm might delegate considerable operating independence and strategic freedom to its foreign subsidaries. Under this *decentralized* organizational structure, highly autonomous national companies are often managed as a portfolio of offshore investments rather than as a single international business. A subsidiary is focused on its local market. Coordination and control are achieved primarily through personal relationships between top corporate management and subsidiary managers than by written rules, procedures, or a formal organizational structure. Strategic decisions are decentralized and top management is involved mainly in monitoring the results of foreign operations. Figure 1 presents this organizational strategy/structure.

This model was the classic strategy/structure adopted by most European-based companies expanding before World War II. Examples include Unilever in branded packaged products, Phillips in consumer electronics, and ITT in telecommunications switching. However, much changed for European companies in the 1970s with the reduction of certain tariff barriers by the EEC and with the entrance of both American and Japanese firms into local markets.

In the machine lubricant industry, automotive motor oil tends toward a multinational competitive environment. Countries have different driving standards and regulations and regional weather conditions. Domestic firms tend to emerge as leaders (for example, Quaker State and Pennzoil in the United States). At the same time, multinationals with country subsidies (such as Castrol, UK) become leaders in regional markets. In the lodging industry, many segments are multinational as a result of the fact that a

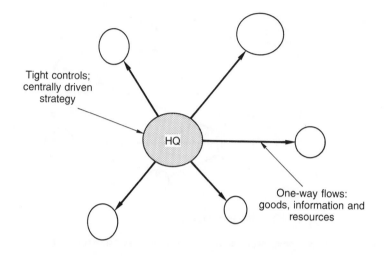

Figure 2. Global strategy with centralized organizational structure

majority of activities in the value chain are strongly tied to buyer location. Further, differences associated with national and regional preferences and lifestyle lead to few benefits from global coordination.

Under a pure *global* strategy, a firm may seek competitive advantage by capitalizing on the economies associated with standardized product design, global-scale manufacturing, and a centralized control of world-wide operation. The key parts of a firm's value-chain activities (typically product design or manufacturing) are geographically concentrated. They are either retained at the center, or they are centrally controlled. Under this *centralized* organizational structure, there are primarily one-way flows of goods, information, and resources from headquarters to subsidiaries; key strategic decisions for worldwide operations are made centrally by senior management. Figure 2 depicts this organizational strategy/structure.

This export-based strategy was/is typical in Japanese-based companies in the postwar years. They typically require highly coordinated activities among subsidiaries. Examples include KAO in branded packaged products, Matsushita in consumer electronics, NEC in telecommunications switching, and Toyota in the automobile industry. Toyota started by capitalizing on a tightly controlled operation that emphasized worldwide export of fairly standardized automobile models from global-scale plants in Toyota City, Japan. Lately, because of growing protectionist sentiments and lower factory costs in less-developed countries, Toyota (among others) has found it necessary to establish production sites in less-developed countries in order to sustain its competitive edge. The marine engine lubricant industry is a global industry that requires a global strategy. Ships move freely around the world and require that brand oil be available wherever they put into port. Brand reputations thus become global issues. Successful marine engine lubricant competitors (such as Shell, Exxon, and British Petroleum) are good examples of global enterprises.

In the area of business-oriented luxury hotels, competitors differ from the majority of hotel accommodations and the competition is more global. Global competitors such as Hilton, Marriott, and Sheraton have a wide range of dispersed properties that employ common brand names, common format, common service standards, and worldwide reservation systems to gain marketing advantage in serving the highly mobile business travelers. Expectations of global standards for service and quality are high.

Under an *international strategy*, a firm transfers knowledge and expertise to overseas environments that are less advanced in technology and market development. Local subsidiaries are often free to adapt new strategies, products, processes, and/or ideas. Under this *coordinated federation* organizational structure, the subsidiaries' dependence on the parent company for new processes and ideas requires a great deal more coordination and control by headquarters than under a classic multinational strategy. Figure 3 depicts this organizational strategy/ structure.

This strategy/structure defines the managerial culture of many US-based companies. Examples include Procter and Gamble in branded packaged products, General Electric in consumer electronics, and Ericsson in telecommunications switching. These companies have a reputation for professional management that implies a willingness to delegate responsibility while retaining overall control through sophisticated systems and specialist corporate staffs. But, under this structure, international subsidiaries are more

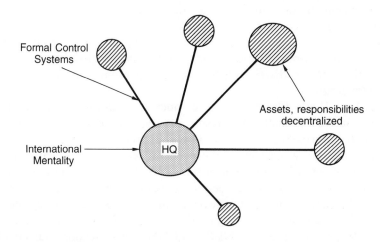

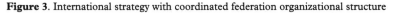

Figure 3. International strategy with coordinated federation organizational structure

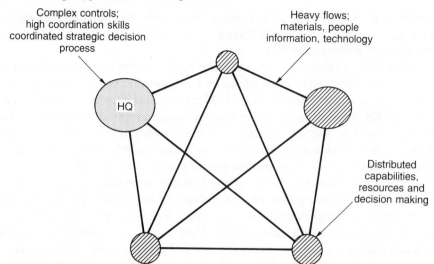

Complex controls;
high coordination skills
coordinated strategic decision
process

Heavy flows;
materials, people
information, technology

Distributed
capabilities,
resources and
decision making

Figure 4. Transnational strategy with integrated-network organizational structure

dependent on the transfer of knowledge and information than are subsidiaries under a multinational strategy; the parent company makes a greater use of formal systems and controls in its relations with subsidiaries.

Under a *transnational* strategy, a firm coordinates a number of national operations while retaining the ability to respond to national interests and preferences. National subsidiaries are no longer viewed as the implementors of centrally-developed strategies. Each, however, is viewed as a source of ideas, capabilities, and knowledge that can be beneficial to the company as a whole. It is not unusual for companies to coordinate product development, marketing approaches, and overall competitive strategy across interdependent national units. Under this *integrated network* organizational structure, top managers are responsible for: (1) coordinating the development of strategic objectives and operating policies, (2) coordinating logistics among operating divisions, and (3) coordinating the flow of information among divisions [3]. Figure 4 presents this organizational strategy/structure.

During the 1980s, forces of global competition required global firms to be more responsive nationally. As a result, the transnational strategies are being adopted by increasing numbers of global firms [3]. This adoption is becoming necessary because of the need for worldwide coordination and integration of activities upstream in the value chain (e.g., inbound logistics, operations) and because of the need for a greater degree of national differentiation and responsiveness at the downstream end (e.g., marketing, sales, and services). For example, adoption of a transnational mode allowed companies such as Procter and Gamble, NEC, and Unilever to respond effectively to the new and complex demands of their international business environments.

They were able to replace exports with local manufacture and to develop more locally differentiated products [3, 9]. In contrast, the inability to develop a similar organizational capability is seen by some to be a factor contributing to the strategic and competitive difficulties faced by companies such as ITT, GE, and KAO.

Special situations relate to another form of the *coordinated federation* organizational structure, *interorganizational* design, which is a particular form of the organizational framework represented in Figure 4. An interorganizational design consists of two or more organizations that have chosen to cooperate by combining their strengths to overcome individual weaknesses [51]. There are two modes of interorganizational design: equity and non-equity collaboration. *Equity collaborations* are seen in joint ventures, minority equity investments, and franchises. *Non-equity collaborations* are seen in forms of licensing arrangements, marketing and distribution agreements, and interorganizational systems [2, 21, 30, 31]. For example, in the airline industry, achieving the economies of scale in developing and managing a large-scale reservation system are now beyond the capacities of the medium-sized airlines. In Europe, two major coalitions have been created, the Amadeus Coalition and the Galileo Coalition. Software for Amadeus is built around System One, the computer reservation system for Continental and Eastern. Galileo makes use of United's software. Even the largest carriers have acknowledged their inability to manage a large-scale reservation system by themselves; they have joined coalitions [31].

Another highly visible example that demonstrates the notion of regional or national coordination in order to compete in a global market is the paper industry of Finland. The 19 Finnish paper companies comprise a $3 billion industry that is heavily dependent on exports. Recently they determined that, to compete effectively in that service-oriented business, they must provide online electronic data interchange (EDI) interfaces with key customers and their sales offices. The Finnpap organization combined the efforts of the mill owners to develop an information system that reaches around the globe. The initial budget estimate of $40 million for five years has grown to an annual commitment of $10 million for the foreseeable future. None of the individual companies in the Finnish paper industry had the size, skills, and/or financial strength to create and deliver the world-class services necessary to compete against the large American, Canadian, and other global competitors. A regional cooperation was needed among the competitors in order to compete in the global market.

There has been a virtual explosion in the use of interorganizational designs for both global and domestic firms as a result of increased global competition during the 1980s. In 1983 alone, the number of domestic joint ventures announced in communications and information systems products and services industries exceeded the sum of all previously announced joint ventures in those sectors [17]. Research suggests that interorganizational designs can lead to (1) 'vertical disaggregation' of functions (e.g., marketing, distribution) typically conducted within the boundaries of a single organization performed independently by the organizations within the network, (2) the use of 'brokers,' or structure-independent organizations, to link together the different organizational units into 'business groups' for performance of specific tasks, and (3) the substitution of 'full disclosure information systems' in traditional organization for lengthy trust-building processes based on experience [36].

2.2 Evolution of the global firm's coordination control strategies

Strategic control is considered to be the key element for the 'integration' of a firm's value-chain activities; it is defined as 'the extent of influence that a head office has over a subsidiary concerning decisions that affect subsidiary strategy' [10]. Previous research found that, as resources such as capital, technology, and management become vested in the subsidiaries, head offices cannot continue to rely on control over these resources as means of influencing subsidiary strategy [1, 10, 44]. The nature of strategic control by the head office over its subsidiaries shifts with time; there is a need for new forms of administrative control mechanisms such as those offered through improved information management strategies.

In a study of nine large worldwide companies and by interviewing 236 managers both in corporate headquarters and in a number of different national subsidiaries, Bartlett and Ghoshal [4] found that many companies had reached a coordination crisis by 1980. New competitive pressures were requiring the global firms to develop multiple strategic capabilities, even as other environment forces led them to reconfigure their historical organization structures. Many familiar means of coordination (e.g., socialization, centralization, and formalization – shown in Table 1) characteristically proved inadequate to this new challenge.

The study further reports that European companies began to see the power and simplicity of more centralized coordination of subsidiaries. The Japanese increasingly adopted more formal systems, routines, and policies to supplement their traditional time-consuming, case-by-case negotiations. American managers took new interest in shaping and managing the previously ignored informal processes and value systems in their firms. The study also found that the challenge for many global firms was not to find the organizational structure that provided the best fit with their global strategies, but to build and manage the appropriate decision-making processes that can respond to multiple changing environmental demands. Furthermore, because of evolving global strategies from multinational to transnational, decision making is no longer concentrated at corporate headquarters. Today's global firm must be able to carry a great deal of complex information to diverse locations in its integrated network of operations.

As we have seen, research on international business suggests that globalization has caused a change in the coordination/control needs of global firms. As a result, new organizational designs are created to meet new organizational coordination needs and to deal with increased organizational complexity and size. The traditional organizational designs [18, 29] such as functional, multidivisional, and matrix forms, are largely inappropriate for today's global firms.

Research further suggests that different organizational strategies/structures are necessary across products or businesses with diverse (global) environment demands. In response, there have been two relatively new trends in organizational strategies: (1) a shift from a multinational strategy with decentralized organizational structures to a transnational strategy and globally integrated networks of operations, and (2) a rapid proliferation of interorganizational designs and structurally independent organizational units and business groups.

In short, the success in global competition depends largely on (1) a proper fit between an organization's business strategy and its structure, (2) an organization's ability to adapt its structure in order to balance the environmental forces of national differentiation and global integration for its value-chain activities, and (3) the manner of coordination/control of the organization's value-chain activities. As presented above, the globalization of competition and the evolving business environment suggest that the success of today's global firms' business and its coordination/control strategies may be linked to a global information management strategy. In the following section, the roles and characteristics of global information systems (GIS) and their differences with traditional distributed data-processing systems are discussed. A global information system management strategy is proposed. The need for 'alignment' of the organization's business strategy/structure with its information system management strategy is emphasized as part of this strategy.

3 Global information systems

Due to the dramatic changes in IT, and the increased skills in organizations to deploy and exploit those advances, there are an increasing number of applications of IT by global firms in both service and manufacturing industries. The earliest were in international banking, airline, and credit authorization. However, during the 1980s, due to rapid improvements in communication and IT, more and more activities of global firms were coordinated using information systems. At the same time, patterns in the economies of IT development are changing [19, 22, 38]. The existence or near completion of public national data networks and of public or quasi-public regional and international networks in virtually all developed (and a few developing) countries has resulted in rapid growth in data-service industries, e.g., data processing, software, information storage and retrieval, and telecommunications services [26, 46].

Today global firms not only rely on data-service industries and IT to speed up message transmission (e.g., for ordering, marketing, distribution, and invoicing), but also to improve the management of corporate systems by: (1) improving corporate functions such as financial control, strategic planning, and inventory control, and (2) changing the manner in which global firms actually engage in production (e.g., in manufacturing, R&D, design and engineering, CAD/CAM/CAE) [46]. Therefore, more and more of global firms' mechanisms for planning, control and coordination, and reporting depend on information technology. According to the head of information systems at the $35 billion chemical giant, information systems will either be a facilitator or an inhibitor of globalization during the 1990s [35].

A *global information system* (GIS) is a distributed data-processing system that crosses national boundaries [7]. There are a number of differences between domestic distributed systems [25] and GISs. Because GISs cross national boundaries, unlike domestic distributed systems, they are exposed to wide variations in business environments, availability of resources, and technological and regulatory environments. These are explained briefly below.

Business Environment. From the perspective of the home-base country, there are differences in language, culure, nationality, and professional management disciplines among subsidiary organizations. Due to differences in local management philosophy, business/technology planning responsibilities are often fragmented rather than focused in one budgetary area. Business/technology planning, monitoring, and control and coordination functions are often difficult and require unique management skills [24].

Infrastructure. The predictability and stability of available infrastructure in a given country are major issues when making the country a hub for a global firm. 'It is a fact of life that some countries are tougher to do business in than others' [8]. Regional economic dependence on particular industry and cross-industry infrastructure may be informative. Singapore [26] has provided, through TradeNet, a platform for fast, efficient trade document processing. Hong Kong [27], on the other hand, is still dealing with its unique position as the gateway to the People's Republic of China, and its historic 'free port' policies in developing its TradeLink platform. Lufthansa, Japan Airlines, Cathay Pacific, and other airlines are trying to pool their global IT infrastructure in order to deliver a global logistics system. At the same time, global banks are exploring the influence their IT architectures have on the portfolio of instruments they can offer on a global basis [37].

Resource availability can vary due to import restrictions or to lack of local vendor support. Since few vendors provide worldwide service, many firms are limited in choice of vendors in a single project, because of operational risk. Finally, availability of telecommunications equipment/technology (e.g., LAN, private microwave, fiber optic, satellite earth stations, switching devices, and other technologies) varies among countries and geographic regions.

Regulatory Environments. Changes in government, economy, and social policy can lead to critical changes in the telecommunications regulations that pose serious constraints on the operation of GLSs. The price and availability of service, and cross-border data-flow restrictions vary widely from one country to another.

The PTT (post, telephone, and telegraph) in most countries sets prices based on volume of traffic rather than based on fixed-cost leased facilities. By doing so, the PTT increases its own revenues and, at the same time, prevents global firms from exploiting economies of scale. The nature of the internal infrastucture systems may also influence the interest and ability to leverage regulation [38, 49, 50].

There are regulations restricting usage of leased lines or import of hardware/software for GISs. These affect the GIS options possible in different countries: restrictions on connections between leased lines and public telephone networks, the use of dial-up data transmission, and the use of electronic mail systems for communications. It is not unusual for some companies to build their own 'phone company' in order to reduce dependence on government-run organizations [8]. Hardware/software import policies also make local information processing uneconomical in some countries. For example, both Canada and Brazil have high duties on imported hardware, and there are software import valuation policies in France, Saudi Arabia, and Israel [6].

Transborder data flow (TBDF) regulations, in part, govern the content of international data flows [5]. Examples are requirements to process certain kinds of data and to maintain certain business records locally, and the fact that some countries don't mind data being 'transmitted in' but oppose interactive applications in which data are 'transmitted out.' Although the major reasons for regulating the content of TBDF are privacy protection and economic and national security concerns, these regulations can adversely affect the economies of GSs by forcing global firms to decentralize their operations, increase operating costs, and/or prohibit certain applications.

Standards. International, national, and industry standards play a key role in permitting global firms to 'leverage' their systems development investment as much as possible. Telecommunication standards vary widely from one country to another concerning the technical details of connecting equipment and agreements on formats and procedures. However, the conversion of the world's telecommunications facilities into an integrated digital network (IDN) is well underway, and most observers agree that a worldwide integrated digital network and the integrated services digital network (ISDN) will soon become a reality (34, 48]. The challenge is not a problem of technology – the necessary technology already exists. Integration depends on creating the necessary standards and getting all countries to agree.

Telecommunications standards are set by various domestic governments or international agencies, and by major equipment vendors (e.g., IBM's System Network Architecture (SNA), Wang's Wangnet, Digital Equipment's DecNet, etc). There are also standards set by groups of firms within the same industry, such as SWIFT (Society for Worldwide International Funds Transfer) for international funds transfers and cash management, EDI (Electronic Data Interchange) for formatted business transactions such as purchase orders between companies (ANSI, EDIFACT, etc) [16], and SQL (Structured Query Language) as a common form of interface for coordinating data across many databases.

3.1   Global information management strategy

Table 2 shows the alternative information systems management strategy/structure as a result of the evolution in global business environment and technology. New information technologies are allowing closer integration of adjacent steps on the value-added chain through the development of electronic markets and electronic hierarchies [33]. As that study reports, the overall effect of technology is the change of coordination mechanisms. This will result in an increase in the proportion of economic activities coordinated by markets rather than by hierarchies. This also supports and explains change in the global firm's strategies from multinational, global strategies to international (interorganizational), transnational strategies.

Table 2   Alignment of global and information management strategies

Business strategy/structure	Coordination control strategy	Coordination control mechanisms	IS strategy structure
multinational decentralized–federation	socialization	*hierarchies;* managerial decisions determine the flow of materials and services	decentralization/ standalone databases and processes
global/ centralized–federation	centralization		centralization/ centralized databases and processes
international and and interorganiza-tional/coordinated federation	formalization	*markets;* market forces determine the flow of materials and services	IOS/linked databases and processes
transnational integrated network	co-opting		integrated architecture/ shared databases and processes

The task of managing across corporate boundaries has much in common with that of managing across national borders. Managing strategic partnership, coalitions, and alliances has forced managers to shift their thinking from the traditional task of controlling a hierarchy to managing a network [11, 31, 43]. As discussed earlier, managers in transnational organizations must gather, exchange, and process large volumes of information; formal strategies/structure cannot support such huge information-processing needs. Because of the widespread distribution of organizational units and the relative infrequency of direct contacts among those in disparate units in a transnational firm, top management has a better opportunity to shape relationships among managers simply by being able to influence the nature and frequency of contacts by using a proper information system management strategy.

The strategy should contain the senior management policy on corporate information systems architecture (ISA). Corporate ISA (1) provides a guide for systems development, (2) facilitates the integration and data sharing among applications, and (3) supports development of integrated, corporate systems that are based on a data resource with corporate-wide accessibility [19]. Corporate ISA for a global firm is a high-level map of the information and technology requirements of a firm as a whole; it is composed of network, data, and application and technology architectures. In the international environment, the network and data architectures are generally considered to be the key enabling technologies because they are the highway systems for a wide range of traffic [24].

A new GIS management strategy needs to address organizational structural issues related to coordination and configuration of value-chain activities, by proper ISA design. The key components of a GIS management strategy are (1) a centralized and/or coordinated business/technology strategy on establishing data communications architecture and standards, (2) a centralized and/or coordinated data management strategy for creation of corporate databases, and (3) alignment of global business and GIS management strategy. These are explained below.

3.1.1 Network management strategy and architecture

Network architecure describes where applications are executed, where databases are located, and what communications links are needed among locations. It also sets standards ensuring that all other ISA components are interrelated and working together. The architecture is important in providing standards for interconnecting very different systems instead of requiring commonality of systems. At present, the potential for network architecture is determined more often by vendors than by general industry or organizational standards [24].

Architecture. Research on international business points out that the structure of a global firm's value chain is the key to its strategy; its fit with environmental requirements derives economic performance. However, the environments of GISs are external to their global firms and thus cannot be controlled. Services provided by GISs must be globally coordinated, integrated, standardized, and tailored to accommodate national differences and individual national markets.

Deciding on appropriate network architecture is a leading management and technology issue. Research in the global banking industry found that an international bank providing a wide range of global electronic wholesale banking services has some automated systems that need to be globally standardized (e.g., global balance reporting system), while others (e.g., global letter of credit system) need to be tailored to individual countries' markets [37]. The research also suggests that appropriate structure for GISs may vary for different product and service portfolios: uniform centralization/decentralization of strategy/structure may not be appropriate for all GIS applications. Further, the research found that international banks cannot expect to optimize the structure of environmentally diverse information systems with a symmetrical approach to GIS architecture, since any such approach may set limits on the product and service portfolios called for by the bank's global business strategy. An asymmetrical approach, structuring each system to suit the environmental needs of the service delivered, although more complex, can significantly improve international banks' operational performance. Such an approach may, however, significantly increase coordination costs.

Standards. Use of standards is an important strategic move for most companies, since many of today's companies limit the number of intercompany formats they support. With the success in the development and adoption of global standards, in particular in narrow areas (e.g., EDIFACT), it is much harder to make standards mistakes than was possible several years ago. By using standards, companies can broaden their choice of trading partners in the future. Absence of uniform data and communications standards in international, national, and industry environments means that no single product can address more than a fraction of the hardware and communications protocols scattered throughout a firm.

Standards are often set by government rules and regulations, major computers and communications vendors, and/or cooperative arrangements within an industry. Regardless of how the standards are set, they are critical to the operations of GISs. Because standards are the key to connectivity of a set of heterogeneous systems, explicit senior management policy on standards is important to promote adoption and compliance. There should be one central policy regarding key technologies/standards (e.g., EDI, SQL). This policy should include a management agenda for understanding both standards and the standard-setting process within industry, national, and international environments [23]. Such a central policy accomplishes several objectives, reducing cost, avoiding vendor viability, achieving economies of scale, reducing potential interface problems, and facilitiating transborder data flow. Therefore, decisions about the components of network architectures and standards require a move toward centralized, corporate management coordination and control. However, decisions regarding adding traffic need decentralized planning; they require conformity by IS managers to data communications standards.

3.1.2 Data management strategy and architecture

Data architecture concerns the arrangement of databases within an organization. Although every organization that keeps data has a data architecture, in most organizations it is the result of evolution of application databases in its various departments and not the result of a well-planned data management strategy [14, 45]. Data management problems are amplified for large global firms with diverse product families. For a global firm with congested data highways, the problems of getting the right data in the right amount to the right people at the right time multiply as global markets emerge [8].

Lack of a centralized information management strategy often causes corporate entities (e.g., customers and products) to have multiple attributes, coding schemes, and values across databases (14). This makes linkages or data sharing among value activities difficult at best; establishing linkages requires excessive time and human resources; costs and performance of other data-related activities within the value chain are affected. These factors make important performance and correlation data unavailable to top management for decision making, thereby creating important obstacles to the firm's competitive position and its future competitive advantage.

Strategy/Architecture. To increase coordination among a global firm's value-chain activites, its data architecture should be designed based on an integrated data management strategy. This strategy should mandate creation of a set of *corporate databases* derived from the firm's value-chain activities. A recent study has pointed out the significance of a firm's value-chain activities in deploying IT strategically [20]; however, no specific information management strategy is proposed.

Corporate data is used by more than one functional area within the value-chain activities. In contrast, department data is often used mainly by departments within the functional area that comprises a value-chain activity. Corporate data is used by departments across functions.

Corporate databases should be based on business entities involved in value-chain activities rather than around individual applications. A firm must define (1) appropriate measures of performance for each value activity (e.g., sales volume by market by period). (2) corporate entities by which the performance is measured (e.g., product, package type). (3) relationships among the entities defined, (4) entities' value sets, coding schemes, and attributes, (5) corporate databases derived from the entities, and (6) relationships among the corporate databases. For example, for a direct value-adding activity such as marketing and sales within a firm's value chain, the corporate databases may include: advertisement, brand, market, promotion, sales.

Given this data management strategy, corporate databases are defined independent of applications; they are accessible by all potential users. This data management strategy allows a firm's senior management to (1) integrate and coordinate information with the value-adding and support activities within the value chain, (2) identify significant trends in performance data, and (3) compare local activities to activities in other comparable locations.

This data management strategy creates an important advantage for a global firm, because activities used for the firm's strategic business planning are used to define the corporate databases. The critical establishment of linkage between strategic business planning and strategic information systems planning is possible when this stategy is used, because the activities that create value for the firm customers also create data the firm needs to operate. However, the strategy does not imply that all application databases should be replaced by corporate databases. Application databases should remain (directly or indirectly) as long as the applications exist; but there should be a disciplined flow of data among corporate, functional, and application databases.

3.1.3 Alignment of global business and GIS management strategy: a plan for action

One challenge facing management today is the necessity for the organization to align its business strategy/structure to its information systems management/development strategy. A proper design of critical linkages among a firm's value-chain activities results in an effective business design involving information technology and an improved coordination with coalition partners, as well as among a firm's own subsidiaries. Previous research has emphasized the benefits of establishing proper linkages between business-strategic planning and technology-strategic planning for an organization [22, 28]. Among these are proper strategic positioning of an organization, improvements in organizational effectiveness, efficiency and performance, and full exploitation of information technology investment.

Establishing the necessary alignment requires the involvement of and cooperation with both the senior business planner and the senior IS technology manager. This results in a new set of responsibilities and skills for both. For the senior business planner, new sets of responsibilities include (1) formal integration of the strategic business plan with the strategic IS plan, (2) examination of the business needs associated with a centralized and/or coordinated network, technology, and data management strategy, (3) review of the network architecture as a key enabling technology for the firm's competitive strategy and assessment of the impact of network alternatives on business strategy, (4) awareness of key technologies/standards and standard-setting processes at the industry, national, and international levels, (5) championing the rapidly expanding use of industry, national, and international standards.

For the senior information technology manager, new and critical responsibilities include (1) awareness of the firm's business challenges in the changing global environment and involvement in shaping the firm's leverage of information technology in its global business strategy, (2) preparing a systems development environment that recognizes the long-term company-wide perspective in a multi-regional and multi-cultural environment, (3) planning the development of the application portfolio on the basis of the firm's current business and its global strategic posture in the future, (4) making the 'business purpose' of the strategic systems development projects clear in a global business context, (5) selecting and recommending key technologies/standards for linking systems across geographic and cultural boundaries, (6) setting automation of linkages among the internal/external activities within the firm's value chain as goals and selling them to others, (7) designing corporate databases derived from the firm's value-chain activities, accounting for business cultural differences, and (8) facilitating corporate restructuring through the provision of flexibility in business services.

4 Summary and conclusions

Changes in technologies and market structures have shifted competition from national to a global scope. This has resulted in the need for new organizational strategies/structures. Traditional organizational designs are not appropriate for the new strategies, because they evolved in response to different competitive pressures. New organizational structures need to achieve both flexibility and coordination among the firm's diverse activities in the new international markets.

Globalization trends have resulted in a variety of organizational designs that have created both business and information management challenges. A global information systems (GIS) management strategy is required.

The key components of a GIS management strategy should include: (1) a centralized and/or coordinated business/technology strategy on establishing data communications infrastructure, architecture, and standards, (2) a centralized and/or coordinated data management strategy for design of corporate databases, and (3) alignment of global business and GIS management strategy. Such a GIS management strategy is appropriate today because it facilitates coordination among a firm's value-chain activities and among business units, and because it provides the firm with the flexibility and coordination necessary to deal effectively with changes in technologies and market structures. It also aligns information systems management strategy with corporate business strategy as it provides a foundation for designing information systems architecture (ISA).

In addition to the global enterprise's competitive posture, globalization also refers to the competitive posture of nations and city-states [26, 27]. The issues related to coordination and control in the global enterprise also invest the nation/state to review the alignment of its cross-industry competitive posture [31, 42]. It is incumbent on governments to seek appropriate levels of intervention in the business practices of the state that influence the state's competitive position in the global business community.

The challenges to general managers in the emerging global economic environment extend beyond the IT infrastructure. At the same time, with the information intensity in the markets (products, services, and channel systems) and the information intensity associated with coordination across geographic, cultural, and organizational barriers, global general managers will rely increasingly on information technologies to support their management processes. The proper alignment of the evolving global information management strategy and the global organizational strategy will be important to the positioning of the global firm in the global economic community.

References

1 Baliga, B. R., and Jaeger, A. M. Multinational corporations, control systems and delegation issues. *Journal of International Business Studies* 15, 2 (Fall 1984), 25–40.
2 Barrett, S., and Konsynski, B. Interorganizational information sharing systems. *MIS Quarterly*, special issue (1982), 93–105.
3 Bartlett, C. A., and Ghoshal, S. Organizing for worldwide effectiveness: the transnational solution. *California Management Review*, 31, 1 (1988), 1–21.
4 Bartlett, C. A., and Ghoshal, S. *Managing across Borders: The Transnational Solution.* Boston: Harvard Business School Press, 1989.
5 Basche, J. Regulating international data transmission: the impact on managing international business. Research report no. 852 from the Conference Board. New York, 1983.
6 *Business Week.* Special report on telecommunications: the global battle (October 1983).
7 Buss, M. Managing international information systems. *Harvard Business Review*, special series (1980).
8 Carlyle, R. E. Managing IS at multinationals. *Datamation* (March 1, 1988), 54–66.
9 Chandler, A. D. The evolution of modern global competition. In [39], 405–488.
10 Doz, Y. L., and Prahalad, C. K. Headquarters influence and strategic control in MNCs. *Sloan Management Review* (Fall 1981), 15–29.
11 Eccles, R. G., and Crane, D. B. Managing through networks in investment banking. *California Management Review*, 30 (Fall 1987), 176–195.
12 Engelhoff. W. Strategy and structure in multinational corporations: an information processing approach. *Administrative Science Quarterly*, 27, 3 (1982), 435–458.
13 Frenke, K. A. The European community and information technology. *Communications of the ACM* (special section the EC '92), 33, 4 (1990), 404–412.
14 Goodhue, D. L.; Quillard, J. A.; and Rockart, J. F. Managing the data resource: a contingency perspective. *MIS Quarterly*, 12, 3 (September 1988), 372–391.
15 Ghoshal, S., and Noria, N. International differentiation within multinational corporations. *Strategic Management Journal*, 10, 4 (July/August 1989), 323–337.
16 Hansen, J. V., and Hill, N. C. Control and audit of electronic data interchange. *MIS Quarterly*, 13, 4 (December 1989), 403–413.

17 Harrigan K. R. *Strategies for Joint Ventures.* Lexington, MA: 1985.

18 Huber, G. P. The nature and design of post industrial organization. *Management Science,* 30 (1984), 928–951.

19 Iramon, W. H. *Information Systems Architecture.* Englewood Cliffs, NJ: Prentce-Hall, 1986.

20 Johnston, H. R., and Carrico, S. R. Developing capabilities to use information strategically. *MIS Quarterly,* 12, 1 (March 1988), 36–48.

21 Johnston, H. R., and Vitale, M. Creating competitive advantage with interorganizational information systems. *MIS Quarterly,* 12, 2 (June 1988), 152–165.

22 Karimi, J. Strategic planning for information systems: requirements and information engineering methods. *Journal of Management Information Systems,* 4, 4 (Spring 1988), 5–24.

23 Keen, P. G. An international perspective on managing information technologies. ICIT Briefing Paper no. 4101, 1987.

24 Keen, P. G. *Competing in Time: Using Telecommunications for Competitive Advantage.* Cambridge, MA: Ballinger Publishing Co., 1988.

25 King, J. Centralized vs. decentralized options. *Computing Surveys* (December 1983).

26 King, J., and Konsynski, B. Singapore TradeNet: a tale of one city. N1-191-009, Harvard Business School, 1990.

27 King, J., and Konsynski, B. Hong Kong TradeLink: news from the second city. N1-191-026. Harvard Business School, 1990.

28 King, W. R. Strategic planning for IS: the state of practice and research. *MIS Quarterly,* 9, 2 (June 1985), Editor's comment, vi–vii.

29 Knight, K. Matrix organization: a review. *Journal of Management Studies,* 13 (1976), 111–130.

30 Konsynski, B., and Warbelow, A. Cooperating to compete: modeling interorganizational interchange, Harvard Business School working paper 90-002, 1989.

31 Konsynski, B., and McFarlan, W. Information partnerships – shared data, shared scale. *Harvard Business Review* (September/October 1990), 114–120.

32 Lu, M., and Farrell, C. Software development: an international perspective. *The Journal of Systems and Software,* 9 (1989), 305–309.

33 Malone, T. W.; Yates, J.; and Benjamin, R. I. Electronic markets and electronic hierarchies. *Communications of the ACM,* 30, 6 (June 1987), 484–497.

34 Martin, J., and Leben, J. *Principles of Data Communications.* Englewood Cliffs, NJ: Prentice-Hall, 1988.

35 Mead, T. The IS innovator at DuPont. *Datamation* (April 15, 1990), 61–68.

36 Miles, R. E., and Snow, C. C. Organizations: new concepts for new forms. *California Management Review,* 28 (1986), 62–73.

37 Mookerjee, A. S. Global Electronic Wholesale Banking Delivery System Structure. PhD thesis, Harvard University, 1988.

38 O'Callaghan, R., and Konsynski, B. Banco Santander: el banco en casa, 9-189-185, Harvard Business School, 1989.

39 Porter, M. E. *Competition in Global Industries.* Cambridge, MA: Harvard Business School Press, 1986.

40 Porter, M. E. Competition in global industries: a conceptual framework. In [39], 15–59.

41 Porter, M. E. From competitive advantage to corporate strategy. *Harvard Business Review* (May/June 1987), 43–59.

42 Porter, M. E. The competitive advantage of nations. *Harvard Business Review* (March/April 1990), 73–92.

43 Powell, W. Hybrid organizational arrangements. *California Management Review,* 30 (Fall 1987), 67–87.

44 Prahalad, C. K., and Doz, Y. L. An approach to strategic control in MNCs. *Sloan Management Review* (Summer 1981), 5–13.

45 Romero, V. Data Architecture: The Newsletter for Corporate Data Planners and Designers, 1,1 (September/October 1988).

46 Sauvant, K. International transactions in services: the politics of transborder data flows. *The Atwater Series on World Information Economy*, 1. Boulder: Westview Press, 1986.
47 Selig, G. J. A framework for multinational information systems planning. *Information and Management*, 5 (June 1982), 95–115.
48 Stallings, W. *ISDN: An Introduction.* New York: Macmillan, 1989.
49 Warbelow, A.; Kokuryo, J.; and Konsynski, B. Aucnet: TV auction network system. 9-190-001, Harvard Business School, 1989, p. 19.
50 Warbelow, A.; Fjeldstad, O.; and Konsynski, B. Bankenes Betalings-Sentral A/S: the Norwegian bank giro. N9-191-037, Harvard Business School, 1990, p. 17.
51 Zammuto, R. *Organization Design: Structure, Strategy, and Environment.* The Dryden Press, forthcoming.

10 Information technology and business process redesign

T. H. Davenport and J. E. Short

At the turn of the century, Frederick Taylor revolutionized the workplace with his ideas on work organization, task decomposition, and job measurement. Taylor's basic aim was to increase organizational productivity by applying to human labor the same engineering principles that had proven so successful in solving the technical problems in the work environment. The same approaches that had transformed mechanical activity could also be used to structure jobs performed by people. Taylor came to symbolize the practical realizations in industry that we now call industrial engineering (IE), or the scientific school of management.[1] In fact, though work design remains a contemporary IE concern, no subsequent concept or tool has rivaled the power of Taylor's mechanizing vision.

As we enter the 1990s, however, two newer tools are transforming organizations to the degree that Taylorism once did. These are *information technology* – the capabilities offered by computers, software applications, and telecommunications – and *business process redesign* – the analysis and design of work flows and processes within and between organizations. Working together, these tools have the potential to create a new type of industrial engineering, changing the way the discipline is practiced and the skills necessary to practice it.

This chapter explores the relationship between information technology (IT) and business process redesign (BPR). We report on research conducted at MIT, Harvard, and several consulting organizations on nineteen companies, including detailed studies of five firms engaged in substantial process redesign. After defining business processes, we extract from the experience of the companies studied a generic five-step approach to redesigning processes with IT. We then define the major types of processes, along with the primary role of IT in each type of process. Finally, we consider management issues that arise when IT is used to redesign business processes.

IT in business process redesign

The importance of both information technology and business process redesign is well known to industrial engineers, albeit as largely separate tools for use in specific, limited environments.[2] IT is used in industrial engineering as an analysis and modeling tool, and IEs have often taken the lead in applying information technology to manufacturing environments. Well-known uses of IT in manufacturing include process modeling, production scheduling and control, materials management information systems, and logistics. In most cases where IT has been used to redesign work, the redesign has most likely been in the manufacturing function, and industrial engineers are the most likely individuals to have carried it out.

IEs have begun to analyze work activities in non-manufacturing environments, but their penetration into offices has been far less than in factories. IT has certainly penetrated the office and services environments – in 1987 *Business Week* reported that almost 40 percent of all US capital spending went to information systems, some $97 billion a year – but IT has been used in most cases to hasten office work rather than to transform it.[3] With few exceptions, IT's role in the redesign of non-manufacturing work has been disappointing; few firms have achieved major productiviy gains.[4] Aggregate productivity figures for the United States have shown no increase since 1973.[5]

Given the growing dominance of service industries and office work in the Western economies, this type of work is as much in need of analysis and redesign as the manufacturing environments to which IT has already been applied. Many firms have found that this analysis requires taking a broader view of both IT and business activity, and of the relationships between them. Information technology should be viewed as more than an automating or mechanizing force; it can fundamentally reshape the way business is done. Business activities should be viewed as more than a collection of individual or even functional tasks; they should be broken down into processes that can be designed for maximum effectiveness, in both manufacturing and service environments.

Our research suggests that IT can be more than a useful tool in business process redesign. In leading edge practice, information technology and BPR have a recursive relationship, as Figure 1 illustrates. Each is the key to thinking about the other. Thinking about information technology should be in terms of how it supports new or redesigned business processes, rather than business functions or other organizational entities. And business processes and process improvements should be considered in terms of the capabilities information technology can provide. *We refer to this broadened, recursive view of IT and BPR as the new industrial engineering.*

Taylor could focus on workplace rationalization and individual task efficiency because he confronted a largely stable business environment;

How can IT support business processes?

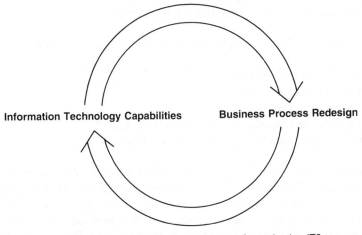

Information Technology Capabilities   Business Process Redesign

How can business processes be transformed using IT?

Figure 1. The recursive relationship between IT capabilities and business process redesign

today's corporations do not have the luxury of such stability.[6] Individual tasks and jobs change faster than they can be redesigned. Today, responsibility for an outome is more often spread over a group, rather than assigned to an individual as in the past. Companies increasingly find it necessary to develop more flexible, team-oriented, coordinative, and communication-based work capability. In short, rather than maximizing the performance of particular individuals or business functions, companies must maximize interdependent activities within and across the entire organization. Such business processes are a new approach to coordinating across the firm; information technology's promise – and perhaps its ultimate impact – is to be the most powerful tool in the twentieth century for reducing the costs of this coordination.[7]

What are business processes?

We define business processes as a set of logically related tasks performed to achieve a defined business outcome. This definition is similar to Pall's: 'The logical organization of people, materials, energy, equipment, and procedures into work activities designed to produce a specified end result (work product).'[8]

A set of processes forms a business system – the way in which a business unit, or a collection of units, carries out its business. Processes have two important characteristics:

● They have customers; that is, processes have defined business outcomes, and there are recipients of the outcomes. Customers may be either internal or external to the firm.

- They cross organizational boundaries, that is, they normally occur across or between organizational subunits. Processes are generally independent of formal organizational structure.

Common examples of processes meeting these criteria include:

- developing a new product;
- ordering goods from a supplier;
- creating a marketing plan;
- processing and paying an insurance claim; and
- writing a proposal for a government contract.

Ordering goods from a supplier, for example, typically involves multiple organizations and functions. The end user, purchasing, receiving, accounts payable, etc., and the supplier organization are all participants. The user could be viewed as the process's customer. The process outcome could be either the creation of the order, or, perhaps more usefully, the actual receipt of the goods by the user.

Our examples so far are of large-scale processes that affect whole organizations or groups. There are more detailed processes that meet the definitional criteria above. These might include installing a windshield in an automobile factory, or completing a monthly departmental expense report. IT-driven process redesign can be applied to these processes, but the implications of redesigning them may be important only in the aggregate. In many of the firms studied, analyzing processes in great detail was highly appropriate for some purposes, for example, the detailed design of an information system or data model to support a specific work process. However, the firms that were truly beginning to redesign their business functions took a broader view of processes.

A brief history of process thinking

Process thinking has become widespread in recent years, due largely to the quality movement. Industrial engineers and others who wish to improve the quality of operations are urged to look at an entire process, rather than a particular task or business function. At IBM, for example, 'process management will be the principal IBM quality focus in the coming years.'[9] But process discussions in the quality movement's literature rarely mention information technology. Rather, the focus is usually on improving process control systems in a manufacturing context; when IT is discussed, it is in the context of factory floor automation. Recent IE literature also borders on process thinking when advocating cross-functional analysis,[10] although, as we will discuss, cross-functional processes are only one possible type of process.

Other than quality-oriented manufacturing process redesign, most processes in major corporations have not been subject to rigorous analysis and redesign. Indeed, many of our current processes result from a series of ad hoc decisions made by functional units, with little attention to effectiveness across the entire process. Many processes have never even been measured. In one manufacturing company studied, for example, no one had ever analyzed the elapsed time from a customer's order to delivery. Each department (sales, credit checking, shipping, and so on) felt that it had optimized its own performance, but in fact the overall process was quite lengthy and unwieldy.

Even fewer business processes have been analyzed with the capabilities of IT in mind. Most business processes were developed before modern computers and communications even existed. When technology has been applied, it is usually to automate or speed up isolated components of an existing process. This creates communication problems within processes and impediments to process redesign and enhancement. For example, in a second manufacturing firm studied, the procurement process involved a vendor database, a materials management planning system, and accounts payable and receivable systems, all running on different hardware platforms with different data structures. Again, each organizational subunit within the process had optimized its own IT application, but no single subunit had looked at (or was responsible for) the entire process. We believe the problems this firm experienced are very common.

Redesigning business processes with IT: five steps

Assuming that a company has decided its processes are inefficient or ineffective, and therefore in need of redesign, how should it proceed? This is a straightforward activity, but five major steps are involved: develop the business vision and process objectives, identify the processes to be redesigned, understand and measure the existing process, identify IT levers, and design and build a prototype of the new process (see Figure 2). We observed most or all of these steps being performed in companies that were succeeding with BPR. Each step is described in greater detail below.

Develop business vision and process objectives

In the past, process redesign was typically intended simply to 'rationalize' the process, in other words, to eliminate obvious bottlenecks and inefficiencies. It did not involve any particular business vision or context. This was the approach of the 'work simplification' aspect of industrial engineering, an important legacy of Taylorism. An example of the rationalization approach appears in a 1961 'Reference Note on Work Simplification' from the

Harvard Business School:

> A good manager asks himself *why* things are done as they are, extending his inquiry to every aspect of the job and surroundings in which it is performed, from the flow of paper work to the daily functioning of his subordinates. . . . He is expected to supply the stimulus and show that job improvement or simplification of work is not only important but also is based on commonsense questioning aimed at uncovering the easiest, most economical way of performing a job.[11]

Our research suggests strongly that rationalization is not an end in itself, and is thus insufficient as a process redesign objective. Furthermore, rationalization of highly decomposed tasks may lead to a less efficient overall process. Instead of task rationalization, redesign of entire processes should be undertaken with a specific business vision and related objectives in mind.

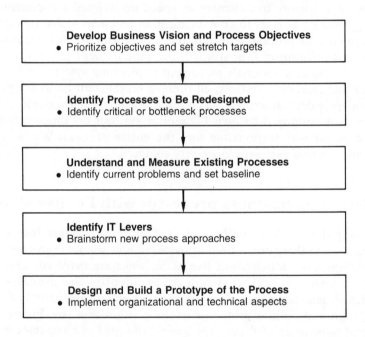

Figure 2. Five steps in process redesign

In most successful redesign examples we studied, the company's senior management had developed a broad strategic vision into which the process redesign activity fits.[12] At Xerox, for example, this vision involved taking the perspective of the customer and developing systems rather than stand-alone products; both required cross-functional integration. At Westinghouse, the vision consisted largely of improving product quality. Ford's involved adopting the best practices of Japanese automobile manufacturers, including those of Mazda, of which it is a partial owner.

Each of these visions implied specific objectives for process redesign. The most likely objectives are the following:

● **Cost Reduction.** This objective was implicit in the 'rationalization' approach. Cost is an important redesign objective in combination with others, but insufficient in itself. Excessive attention to cost reduction results in tradeoffs that are usually unacceptable to process stakeholders. While optimizing on other objectives seems to bring costs into line, optimizing on cost rarely brings about other objectives.

● **Time Reduction.** Time reduction has been only a secondary objective of traditional industrial engineering. Increasing numbers of companies, however, are beginning to compete on the basis of time.[13] Processes, as we have defined them, are the ideal unit for a focused time reduction analysis. One common approach to cutting time from product design is to make the steps begin simultaneously, rather than sequentially, using IT to coordinate design directions among the various functional participants. This approach has been taken in the design of computers, telephone equipment, automobiles, and copiers (by Digital Equipment, AT&T Bell Labs, Ford, and Xerox, respectively).

● **Output Quality.** All processes have outputs, be they physical – such as in manufacturing a tangible product – or informational – such as in adding data to a customer file. Output quality is frequently the focus of process improvement in manufacturing environments; it is just as important in service industries. The specific measure of output quality may be uniformity, variability, or freedom from defects; this should be defined by the customer of the process.

● **Quality of Worklife (QWL)/Learning/Empowerment.** IT can lead either to greater empowerment of individuals, or to greater control over their output. Zuboff points out that IT-intensive processes are often simply automated, and that the 'informating' or learning potential of IT in processes is often ignored.[14] Moreover, Schein notes that organizations often do not provide a supportive context for individuals to introduce or innovate with IT.[15] Of course, it is rarely possible to optimize all objectives simultaneously, and in most firms, the strongest pressures are to produce tangible benefits. Yet managers who ignore this dimension risk failure of redesigned processes for organizational and motivational factors.

Some firms have been able to achieve multiple objectives in redesigning processes with IT. American Express, for example, set out to improve the cost, time, and quality of its credit authorization process by embedding the knowledge of its best authorizers in an 'Authorizer's Assistant' expert system. This successful redesign led to a $7 million annual reduction in costs due to credit losses, a 25 percent reduction in the average time for each authorization, and a 30 percent reduction in improper credit denials.

Finally, all firms found it was important to set specific objectives, even to the point of quantification. Though it is difficult to know how much improvement is possible in advance of a redesign, 'reach should exceed grasp.' Setting goals that will stretch the organization will also provide inspiration and stimulate creative thinking. For example, a company might decide to reduce the time to bring new products to market by 80 percent. In the accounts payable process at Ford, the 'stretch' goal was to eliminate invoices – to pay suppliers upon receipt of their products or services. This goal has been achieved with help from an information system to confirm expected deliveries at the loading dock. As a result, Ford has eliminated three-quarters of the jobs in accounts payable.

Identify processes to be redesigned

Most organizations could benefit from IT-enabled redesign of critical (if not *all*) business processes. However, the amount of effort involved creates practical limitations. Even when total redesign was the ultimate objective, the companies we studied selected a few key processes for initial efforts. Moreover, when there was insufficient commitment to total redesign, a few successful examples of IT-enhanced processes became a powerful selling tool.

The means by which processes to be redesigned are identified and prioritized is a key issue. This is often difficult because most managers do not think about their business operations in terms of processes. There are two major approaches. The *exhaustive* approach attempts to identify all processes within an organization and then prioritize them in order of redesign urgency. The *high-impact* approach attempts to identify only the most important processes or those most in conflict with the business vision and process objectves.

The exhaustive approach is often associated with 'information engineering' (developed by James Martin in the early 1980s), in which an organizaton's use of data dictates the processes to be redesigned.[16] For example, one information engineering method, employed at several divisions of Xerox, involves identifying business activities and the data they require using a data-activity matrix. The clusters of data activity interactions in the cells of the matrix are the organization's major business processes. Once processes are identified, Xerox managers prioritize them in the order in which new IT applications support should be provided. Although process identification in some Xerox divisions has taken as little as three months, many companies find this approach very time consuming.

The alternative is to focus quickly on high-impact processes. Most organizations have some sense of which business areas or processes are most crucial to their success, and those most 'broken' or inconsistent with the business vision. If not, these can normally be identified using senior management workshops, or through extensive interviewing.[17] At IBM, the salesforce was surveyed to determine the relative importance of various customer support processes; the generation of special bids emerged as the highest priority and was the first process to be redesigned.

Companies that employed the high-impact approach generally considered it sufficient. Companies taking the exhaustive approach, on the other hand, have not had the resources to address all the identified processes; why identify them if they cannot be addressed? As a rough rule of thumb, most companies we studied were unable to redesign and support more than ten to fifteen major processes per year (i.e., one to three per major business unit); there was simply not enough management attention to do more. And some organizations have abandoned the exhaustive approach.[18]

Whichever approach is used, companies have found it useful to classify each redesigned process in terms of beginning and end points, interfaces, and organization units (functions or departments) involved, particularly including the customer unit. Thinking in these terms usually broadens the perceived scope of the process. For example, a sales manager may be aware that there are inefficiencies in customer order entry. A skilled process consultant might decide that the whole process – negotiating, receiving, and fulfilling orders – needs to be redesigned. Whether the problem is broken down into three processes or viewed as one is not important; expanding the *scope* of the process analysis is the key issue.

High-impact should also have owners.[19] In virtually all the process redesigns we studied, an important step was getting owners to buy in to both the idea and the scope of process redesign at a early stage. In several companies, managers felt that the process owner's job should be either above the level of the functions and units involved, or, if on the same level, that the owner should be willing – and able – to change the status quo. The difficulty, however, is that some processes only come together at the CEO level. In this situation, the CEO should designate a senior manager as owner and invest him or her with full authority. Processes that are fully contained within a single function or department can normally be owned by the manager of that area.

Understand and measure existing processes

There are two primary reasons for understanding and measuring processes before redesigning them. First, problems must be understood so that they are not repeated. Second, accurate measurement can serve as a baseline for future improvements. If the objective is to cut time and cost, the time and cost consumed by the untouched process must be measured accurately. Westinghouse Productivity and Quality Center consultants found that simply graphing the incremental cost and time consumed by process tasks can often suggest initial areas for redesign. These graphs look like 'step functions' showing the incremental contribution of each major task.

This step can easily be overemphasized, however. In several firms, the 'stretch' goal was less to eliminate problems or bottlenecks than to create radical improvements. Designers should be informed by past process problems and errors, but they should work with a clean slate. Similarly, the process should not be measured for measurement's sake. only the specific objectives of the redesign should be measured. As with the high-impact process identification approach, an 80–20 philosophy is usually appropriate.

Identify IT levers

Until recently, even the most sophisticated industrial engineering approaches did not consider IT capabilities until after a process had been designed. The conventional wisdom in IT usage has always been to first determine the business requirements of a function, process or other business entity, and then to develop a system. The problem is that an awareness of IT capabilities can – and should – influence process design. Knowing that product development teams can exchange computer-aided designs over large distances, for example, might affect the structure of a product development process. The role of IT in a process should be considered in the early stages of its redesign.[20]

Several firms accomplished this using brainstorming sessions, with the process redesign objectives and existing process measures in hand. It was also useful to have a list of IT's generic capabilities in improving business processes. In the broadest sense, *all* of IT's capabilities involve improving coordination and information access across organizational units, thereby allowing for more effective management of task interdependence. More specifically, however, it is useful to think about IT capabilities and their organizational impacts in eight different ways (see Table 1).

There are undoubtedly other important IT capabilities that can reshape processes. Organizations may want to develop their own lists of capabilities that are specific to the types of processes they employ. The point is twofold: IT is so powerful a tool that it deserves its own step in process redesign, and IT can actually create new process design options, rather than simply support them.

Design and build a prototype of the process

For most firms, the final step is to design the process. This is usually done by the same team that performed the previous steps, getting input from constituencies and using brainstorming workshops. A key point is that the actual design is not the end of the process. Rather, it should be viewed as a prototype, with successive iterations expected and managed. Key factors and tactics to consider in process design and prototype creation include using IT as a design tool, understanding generic design criteria, and creating organizational prototypes.

Table 1 IT capabilities and their organizational impacts

Capability	Organizational impact benefit
Transactional	IT can transform unstructured processes into routinized transactions
Geographical	IT can transfer information with rapidity and ease across large distances, making processes independent of geography
Automational	IT can replace or reduce human labor in a process
Analytical	IT can bring complex analytical methods to bear on a process
Informational	IT can bring vast amounts of detailed information into a process
Sequential	IT can enable changes in the sequence of tasks in a process, often allowing multiple tasks to be worked on simultaneously
Knowledge Management	IT allows the capture and dissemination of kowledge and expertise to improve the process
Tracking	IT allows the detailed tracking of task status, inputs, and outputs
Disintermediation	IT can be used to connect two parties within a process that would otherwise communicate through an intermediary (internal or external)

- **IT as a Design Tool.** Designing a business process is largely a matter of diligence and creativity. Emerging IT technologies, however, are beginning to facilitate the 'process' of process design. Some computer-aided systems engineering (CASE) products are designed primarily to draw process models. The ability to draw models rapidly and make changes suggested by process owners speeds redesign and facilitiates owner buy-in. Some CASE products can actually generate computer code for the information systems application that will support a modeled business process. Several Xerox divisions, for example, are moving directly from process modeling to automated generation of computer code for high-priority processes. They report improved productivity and high user satisfaction with the resulting systems. A further benefit is that when the business process changes, the IS organization can rapidly modify the affected system. Use of code generation products generally presumes that process designers will use the exhaustive approach to process identification.
- **Generic Design Criteria.** Companies used various criteria for evaluating alternative designs. Most important, of course, is the likelihood that a design will satisfy the chosen design objectives. Others mentioned in interviews included the simplicity of the design, the lack of buffers or intermediaries, the degree of control by a single individual or department (or an effective, decentralized coordinative mechanism), the balance of process resources, and the generalization of process tasks (so that they can be performed by more than one person).
- **Organizational Prototypes.** Mutual Benefit Life's (MBL) redesign of its individual life insurance underwriting process illustrates a final, important point about process design. At MBL, underwriting a life

insurance policy involved 40 steps with over 100 people in 12 functional areas and 80 separate jobs. To streamline this lengthy and complex process, MBL undertook a pilot project with the goal of improving productivity by 40 percent. To integrate the process, MBL created a new role, the case manager. This role was designed to perform and coordinate all underwriting tasks centrally, utilizing a workstation-based company. After a brief start-up period, the firm learned that two additional roles were necessary on some underwriting cases: specialists such as lawyers or medical directors in knowledge-intensive fields, and clerical assistance. With the new role and redesigned process, senior managers at MBL are confident of reaching the 40 percent goal in a few months. This example illustrates the value of creating organizational prototypes in IT-driven process redesign.

Creating prototypes of IT applications has already gained widespread acceptance. Advocates argue that building a prototype of an IT change usually achieves results faster than conventional 'life cycle' development, and, more important, that the result is much more likely to satisfy the customer. Building prototypes of business process changes and organizational redesign initiates can yield similar benefits.[21] The implications of this extention are that process designs, after agreement by owners and stakeholders, would be implemented on a pilot basis (perhaps in parallel with existing processes), examined regularly for problems and objective achievement, and modified as necessary. As the process approached final acceptance, it would be phased into full implementation.

Defining process types

The five steps described above are sufficiently general to apply to most organizations and processes. Yet the specifics of redesign vary considerably according to the type of process under examination. Different types require different levels of management attention and ownership, need different forms of IT support, and have different business consequences. In this section, we present three different dimensions within which processes vary.

Understanding and classifying the different types of processes are important because an organization can appear to be a seamless web of interconnected processes. With various process *types* in mind, a manager can begin to isolate particular processes for analysis and redesign, including activities that, without process thinking, might otherwise be overlooked.

Three major dimensions can be used to define processes (see Figure 3). These are the organizational entities or subunits involved in the process, the type of objects manipulated, and the type of activities taking place. We describe each dimension and resulting process type below.

Process Dimension and Type	Typical Example	Typical IT Role
Entities		
Interorganizational	Order from a supplier	Lower transaction costs; eliminate intermediaries
Interfunctional	Develop a new product	Work across geography; greater simultaneity
Interpersonal	Approve a bank loan	Role and task integration
Objects		
Physical	Manufacture a product	Increased outcome flexibility; process control
Informational	Create a proposal	Routinizing complex decisions
Activities		
Operational	Fill a customer order	Reduce time and costs; increase output quality
Managerial	Develop a budget	Improve analysis; increase participation

Figure 3. Types of processes

Defining process entities

Processes take place between types of organizational entities. Each type has different implications for IT benefits.

Interorganizational processes are those taking place between two or more business organizations. Increasingly, companies are concerned with coordinating activities that extend into the next (or previous) company along the value-added chain.[22] Several U.S. retail, apparel, and textile companies, for example, have linked their business processes to speed up reordering of apparel. When Dillard's (department store) inventory of a particular pants style falls below a specified level, Haggar (apparel manufacturer) is notified electronically. If Haggar does not have the cloth to manufacture the pants, Burlington Industries (textile manufacturer) is notified electronically. As this example of electronic data interchange (EDI) illustrates, information techology is the major vehicle by which this interorganizational linkage is executed.

For most companies, simple market relationships are the most common source of interorganizational processes. All the tasks involved in a selling-buying transaction form a critical process for sellers, and an increasingly important one for buyers seeking higher quality, cost efficiency, and responsiveness. Yet much of the focus has been on a simple transaction level, rather than on an interorganizational business process level. Again, how EDI is used illustrates this point.

Buyers and sellers have used EDI largely to speed up routine purchasing transactions, such as invoices or bills of materials. Few companies have attempted to redesign the broader procurement process – from the awareness that a product is needed, to the development of approved vendor lists, or even to the delivery and use of the purchased product. In the future, sellers will need to look at all buyer processes in which their products are involved.

Moreover, many firms will need to help the buyer improve those processes. Du Pont's concept of 'effectiveness in use' as the major criterion of customer satisfaction is one leading approach to measuring the effectiveness of interorganizational processes. Du Pont is motivated not simply to sell a product, but to link its internal processes for creating value in a product, to its customer's processes for using the product. This concept led Du Pont to furnish EDI-provided Material Safety Data Sheets along with the chemicals it sells to its customers to ensure their safe use.

Westinghouse used an interorganizational process approach in dealing with Portland General Electric (PGE), a major customer of power generation equipment. PGE managers called upon Westinghouse's Productivity and Quality Center, a national leader in process improvement, to help them implement EDI, but the Westinghouse team asked if it could analyze the entire process by which PGE procured equipment from Westinghouse and other suppliers. They found that, while implementing EDI could yield efficiencies on the order of 10 percent, changing the overall procurement process, including using EDI and bypassing the purchasing department altogether for most routine purchase orders, could lead to much greater savings. In one case, the time to execute a standard purchase order, for example, could be reduced from fifteen days to half a day; the cost could be reduced from almost $90 to $10.

A second major type of business process is *inter-functional*. These processes exist within the organization, but cross several functional or divisional boundaries. Interfunctional processes achieve major operational objectives, such as new product realization, asset management, or production scheduling. Most management processes – for example, planning budgeting, and human resource management – are interfunctional.

Many manufacturing companies that focused on quality improvement found that producing quality products and services required addressing difficult interfunctional issues. Yet most firms have never even listed their key interfunctional processes, let alone analyzed or redesigned them, with or without the aid of IT.

Two companies that recently analyzed their key interfunctional business processes are Baxter Healthcare Corporation and US Sprint Communications Company. Baxter's 1985 merger with American Hospital Supply provided the context for a major analysis of key business strategies, and the alignment of the IT infrastructure with those strategies.[23] As part of a seven-month IT planning effort, the company defined twenty-nine major interfunctional processes and analyzed the current and future role of IT in supporting them. For example, in the distribution area, the company identified order entry, inventory, warehouse management, purchasing, transportation, and equipment tracking as key processes. The success of this IT planning effort led Baxter to incorporate the process definition approach into its annual corporate planning process.

At US Spring, well-publicized problems with the customer billing system prompted the company's IT function to develop a model of information flows for the entire business as part of a comprehensive systems improvement program. This model defined the critical information and key interfunctional processes necessary to run the business. Sprint is now assigning ownership to key processes and continuing to identify improvements – and ways to measure them – in each process. The systems improvement program raised the IT organization's composite internal quality index by more than 50 percent in one year.[24]

A major problem in redesigning interfunctional processes is that most information systems of the past were built to automate specific functional areas or parts of functions. Few third-party application software packages have been developed to support a full business process. Very few organizations have modeled existing interfunctional processes or redesigned them, and companies will run into substantial problems in building interfunctional systems without such models.

Interpersonal processes involve tasks within and across small work groups, typically within a function or department. Examples include a commercial loan group approving a loan, or an airline flight crew preparing for takeoff. This type of process is becoming more important as companies shift to self-managing teams as the lowest unit of organization. Information technology is increasingly capable of supporting interpersonal processes; hardware and communications companies have developed new networking-oriented products, and software companies have begun to flesh out the concept of 'groupware' (e.g., local area network-based mail, conferencing, and brainstorming tools).[25]

Several companies, including GM's Electronic Data Systems (EDS), are exploring tools to facilitate the effectiveness of meetings and small group interactions. At EDS, the primary focus is on enhancing the interpersonal processes involved in automobile product development. The company's Center for Machine Intelligence has developed a computer-supported meeting room, and is studying its implications for group decision making and cooperative work.[26]

We should point out that IT can make it possible for employees scattered around the world to work as a team. As an example, Ford now creates new car designs using teams that have members in Europe, Central America, and the United States. Because Ford has standardized computer-aided design systems and created common data structures for the design process, engineers can share complex three-dimensional designs across the Atlantic. Similarly, a small team at Digital Equipment used the company's electronic mail and conferencing capabilities to build the core of a new systems integration business. The team was scattered around the United States and Europe and only rarely met in person.

Defining process objects

Processes can also be categorized by the types of objects manipulated. The two primary object types are physical and informational. In physical object processes, real, tangible things are either created or manipulated; manufacturing is the obvious example. Informational object processes create or manipulate information. Processes for making a decision, preparing a marketing plan, or designing a new product are examples.

Many processes involve the combination of physical and informational objects. Indeed, adding information to a physical object as it moves through a process is a common way of adding value. Most logistical activities, for example, combine the movement of physical objects with the manipulation of information concerning their whereabouts. Success in the logistics industry is often dependent on the close integration of physical and informational outcomes; both UPS and Federal Express, for example, track package movement closely.

The potential for using IT to improve physical processes is well known. It allows greater flexibility and variety of outcomes, more precise control of the process itself, reductions in throughput time, and elimination of human labor. These benefits have been pursued for the past three decades. Still, manufacturing process flows are often the result of historical circumstance and should usually be redesigned before further automation is applied. This is particularly true in low volume, job shop manufacturing environments.[27] Redesigners of physical processes should also consider the role of IT in providing information to improve processes: Shoshana Zuboff has described this 'informating' effect in detail for the paper industry.[28]

Strangely, the proportion of informational processes already transformed by IT is probably lower than that of physical processes. True, legions of clerks have become unemployed because of computers. But the majority of information processes to which IT has been applied are those involving high volume and low complexity. Now that these processes are well known even if not fully conquered, the emphasis needs to shift to processes that incorporate semistructured and unstructured tasks and are performed by high-skill knowledge workers. Relevant IT capabilities include the storage and retrieval of unstructured and multimedia information, the capturing and routinizing of decision logic, and the application of far-flung and complex data resources. A computer vendor's advertising videotape, for example, illustrates how artificial intelligence and 'hypertext', or mixed-media databases, combine to lead a manager through the process of developing a departmental budget. The IT capabilities in the video are available today, but they are rarely applied to such information-intensive yet unstructured processes.

Defining process activities

Our examples of business processes have involved two types of activities: operational and managerial. Operational processes involve the day-to-day carrying out of the organization's basic business purpose. Managerial processes help to control, plan, or provide resources for operational processes. Past uses of IT to improve processes, limited as they are, have been largely operational. We will therefore focus almost entirely on managerial processes in this section.[29]

Applying IT to management *tasks* is not a new idea. The potential of decision support systems, executive support systems, and other managerial tools has been discussed for over twenty years. We believe, however, that the benefits have not been realized because of the absence of systematic process thinking. Few companies have rigorously analyzed managerial activities as processes subject to redesign. Even the notion of managerial activities involving defined outcomes (a central aspect of our definition of business processes) is somewhat foreign. How would such managerial processes as deciding on an acquisition or developing the agenda for the quarterly board meeting be improved if they were treated as processes – in other words, measured, brainstormed, and redesigned with IT capabilities?

The generic capabilities of IT for reshaping management processes include improving analytic accuracy, enabling broader management participation across wider geographical boundaries, generating feedback on actions taken (the managerial version of 'informating' a process), and streamlining the time and resources a specific process consumes. Texas Instruments and Xerox's corporate headquarters provide excellent examples.

Texas Instruments has developed an expert system to facilitate the capital budgeting process. Managers in a fast-growing and capital-intensive TI divisions were concerned that the time and experience necessary to prepare capital budget request packages would become an obstacle to the division's growth. The packages were very complex and time consuming, and few employees had the requisite knowledge to complete them accurately. The expert system was developed by two industrial engineers with expertise in both the technology and the budget process.

TI's system has radically improved the capital budget request process. Requests prepared with the system require far less time than the manual approach and conform better to the company's guidelines. One experienced

IT-driven process redesign at Rank Xerox UK

Rank Xerox U.K. (RXUK), a national operating company of Xerox Corporation, has undertaken the most comprehensive IT-driven process redesign we have studied. The process was led by David O'Brien, the division's managing director, who arrived at the company in 1985. O'Brien quickly came to two realizations: first, the company needed to focus on marketing 'office systems' in addition to its traditional reprographics products; and second, the company's strong functional culture and inefficient business processes would greatly inhibit its growth. He began to see his own organization as a place to test integrated office systems that support integrated business processes; if successful, he could use RXUK as a model for customers.

The company began to redesign its business in 1987. In a series of offsite meetings, the senior management team reappraised its external environment and mission, then identified the key busness processes needed if the company was to achieve its mission. The group began to restructure the organization around cross-functional processes, identifying high-level objectives and creating task forces to define information and other resource requirements for each process. It created career systems revolving around facilitation skills and cross-functional management, rather than hierarchical authority. O'Brien decided to keep a somewhat functional formal structure, because functional skills would still be needed in a process organization and because the level of organizational change might have been too great with a wholly new structure.

The level of change was still very high. Several senior managers departed because they could not or would not manage in the new environment. Two new cross-functional senior positions, called 'facilitating directors,' were created, one for organizational and business development, the other for process management, information systems, and quality. O'Brien took great advantage of the honeymoon period accorded to new CEOs, but managing the change still required intense personal attention:

> Of course, this new thinking was in sharp contrast to some of the skills and attitudes of the company. We were introducing a change in management philosophy in a company that, in many ways, was very skillful and effective, but in a different product-market environment. We faced all the issues of attitudinal change and retraining that any such change implies. We were moving to a much more integrated view of the world and had to encourage a major shift in many patterns of the exising culture. This meant a very hard, tough program of selling the new ideas within the organization as well as an extensive and personal effort to get the new messages and thinking to our potential customers.*

As the key processes were identified and their objectives determined, the company began to think about how information technology (its own and from other providers) could enable and support the processes. The facilitating director of processes and systems, Paul Chapman, decided that the firm needed a new approach to developing information systems around processes. His organization used the information engineering approach discussed earlier and worked with an external consultant to refine and confirm process identification. They uncovered 18 'macro' business processes (e.g., logistics) and 145 'micro' processes (e.g., fleet management).

The senior management team reconvened to prioritize the identified processes and decided that seven macro processes had particular importance: customer order life cycle, customer satisfaction, installed equipment management, integrated planning, logistics, financial management, and personnel management. It selected personnel management as the first process to be redesigned because this was viewed as relatively easy to attack and because personnel systems were crucial in tracking the development of new skills. The personnel system has now been successfully redesigned, using automated code generation capabilities, in substantially less time than if normal methods had been used.

RXUK's financial situation began to improve as it redesigned its business processes. The company emerged from a long period of stagnation into a period of 20 percent revenue growth. Jobs not directly involved with customer contact were reduced from 1,100 to 800. Order delivery time was, on average, reduced from thirty-three days to six days. Though many other market factors were changing during this time. O'Brien credits the process redesign for much of the improvement.

Other Xerox divisions heard of RXUK's success with process redesign and began efforts of their own. Xerox's U.S. product development and marketing divisions now have major cross-functional teams performing process redesign. Paul Chapman has been loaned to Xerox corporate headquarters, where he is heading a cross-functional team looking at corporate business processes. Commitment to IT-driven process redesign by Xerox senior corporate management is also growing.

---

* David O'Brien, quote in B. Denning and B. Taylor, 'Rank Xerox UK, Office Systems Strategy (C): Developing the Systems Strategy.' (Henley on Thames, England: Henley – The Management College case study, September 1988). Other Rank Xerox U.K. information comes from personal interviews.

employee reported a reduction in package preparation time from nine hours to forty minutes; of the first fifty packages prepared with the system, only three did not conform to guidelines, compared to an average of ten using a manual approach.[30]

At Xerox Corporation headquarters, IT has been used to improve the review of division strategic plans. Prior to the development of the company's Executive Information System (EIS), the planning process was somewhat haphazard; each division prepared its planning documents in a different format and furnished different types of information to corporate headquarters. Plans often came in too late for the corporate management committee to review them before the quarterly or annual review meeting. The EIS was developed to include standard information formats and user friendly graphical interface enabling fast comprehension. Divisional plans are now developed on the EIS and delivered instantaneously over Xerox's network to all corporate management committee members. These members can now read and discuss the plans beforehand and can move directly to decisions at the review meetings. The workstations are even used in the meetings themselves, allowing revisions to be made and agreed upon before adjournment. As one manager put it, '. . . [the system] lets us communicate at higher speed and in greater depth.'[31]

Management issues in IT-enabled redesign

Companies have found that once a process has been redesigned, several key issues remain. These include the management role in redesigned activity, implications for organization structure, new skill requirements, creating a function to perform IT-enabled BPR, the proper direction for the IT infrastructure, and the need for continuous process improvement. We discuss each below.

Management roles

Perhaps the greatest difficulty in IT-driven redesign is getting and keeping management commitment. Because processes cut across various parts of the organization, a process redesign effort driven by a single business function or unit will probably encounter resistance from other parts of the organization. Both high-level and broad support for change are necessary.

To perform the five redesign steps described above, several companies created a cross-functional task force headed by a senior executive. These task forces included representatives from key staff and line groups likely to be affected by the changes, including IT and human resources. It was particularly important that the customer of the process be represented on the team, even when the customer was external. The team composition was ideal if some members had some record of process or operations innovation involving IT.

As the redesign teams selected processes and developed objectives, they needed to work closely with the managers and staff of the affected units. Managing process change is similar to managing other types of change, except that its cross-functional nature increases the number of stake-holders, thereby increasing the complexity of the effort.

It was also important to have strong, visible commitment from senior management. Employees throughout the organization needed to understand that redesign was critical, that differences of opinion would be resolved in favor of the customer of a process, and that IT would play an important role. In many cases, the CEO communicated any structural implications of the redesign effort.

An example of the importance of the CEO's role is found at GUS Home Shopping, the largest home shopping company in Europe. GUS undertook a $90 million project to redesign its logistical processes with IT. Redesign objectives involved both cost and time to be able to sell a product within five minutes of its arrival on the loading dock, and to be able to deliver a product to the customer's door at an average cost of sixty cents. The company's managing director commented on his role in meeting these objectives:

> To change our business to the degree we have [done] demands integration. How involved should the managing director get in designing computer systems? My view is totally, because he's the one who can integrate across the entire organization.[32]

Process redesign and organizational structure

A second key issue is the relationship between process orientation and organizational structure. Certainly someone must be in charge of implementing a process change, and of managing the redesigned process thereafter. But process responsibilities are likely to cut across existing organizational structures. How can process organization and traditional functional organization be reconciled?

One possible solution is to create a new organization structure along process lines, in effect abandoning altogether other structural dimensions, such as function, product, or geography. This approach presents risks, however; as business needs change, new processes will be created that cut across the previous process-based organization. This does not mean that a process-based structure cannot be useful, but only that it will have to be changed frequently.

While no firm we studied has converted wholly to a process-based structure, a few organizations have moved in this direction. For example, Apple Computer recently moved away from a functional structure to what executives describe as an IT-orientated, process-based, customer satisfaction-driven structure called 'New ENTERPRISE.' The company relishes its lack of formal hierarchy. Apple managers describe their roles as highly diffuse, and team and project based.

A more conservative approach would be to create a matrix of functional and process responsibilities. However, because of the cross-functional nature of most processes, the functional manager who should have responsibility for a given process is not always easy to identify. The company may also wish to avoid traditional thinking in assigning process responsibilities. For example, it may be wiser to give responsibility for redesigning supplies acquisition to a manager who uses those supplies (i.e., the customer of the process), rather than to the head of purchasing.

New skill requirements

For process management to succeed, managers must develop facilitation and influence skills. Traditional sources of authority may be of little use when process changes cut across organizational units. Managers will find themselves trying to change the behavior of employees who do not work for them. In these cases, they must learn to persuade rather than to instruct, to convince rather than to dictate. Of course, these recommendations are consistent with many other organizational maxims of the past several years; they just happen to be useful in process management as well.[33]

Several organizations that are moving toward IT-driven process management are conducting programs intended to develop facilitation skills. These programs encourage less reliance on hierarchy, more cross-functional communication and cooperation, and more decision making by middle- and lower-level managers. Such a program at American Airlines is being used to build an organizational infrastructure at the same time a new IT infrastructure is being built.

An ongoing organization

Organizations that redesign key processes must oversee continuing redesign and organizational 'tuning,' as well as ensure that information systems support process flows. In most companies, the appropriate analytical skills are most likely to be found in the IT function. However, these individuals will also require a high degree of interpersonal skills to be successful as the 'new industrial engineers.' The ideal group would represent multiple functional areas, for example, information systems, industrial engineering, quality, process control, finance, and human resources.

There are already some examples of such process change groups. Silicon Graphics has created a specific process consulting group for ongoing process management; it is headed by a director-level manager. At United Parcel Service, process redesign is traditionally concentrated in the industrial engineering function. The UPS group is incorporating IT skills in the IE function at a rapid rate, and creating task forces with IT and IE representation for process redesign projects. Federal Express has gone even further, renaming its IE organization the 'Strategic Integrated Systems

Group,' placing it within the Information Systems function, and giving it responsibility for designing and implementing major IT-driven business changes.

Process redesign and the IT organization

Just as information technology is a powerful force in redesigning business processes, process thinking has important implications for the IT organization and for the technology infrastructure it builds. Though few IT groups have the power and influence to spearhead process redesign, they can play several important roles. First of all, the IT group may need to play a behind-the-scenes advocacy role, convincing senior management of the power offered by information technology and process redesign. Second, as demand builds for process redesign expertise, the IT group can begin to incorporate the IE orientated skills of process measurement, analysis, and redesign, perhaps merging with the IE function if there is one. It can also develop an approach or methodology for IT-enabled redesign, perhaps using the five steps described above as a starting point.

What must the information systems function do technologically to prepare for process redesign? IT professionals must recognize that they will have to build most systems needed to support (or enable) processes, rather than buy them from software package vendors, because most application packages are designed with particular functions in mind. IT professionals will need to build robust technology platforms on which process-specific applications can be quickly constructed. This implies a standardized architecture with extensive communications capability between computing nodes, and the development of shared databases. However, like the organizational strategies for process management described above, these are appropriate technology strategies for most companies, whether or not they are redesigning processes with IT.

Continuous process improvement

The concept of process improvement, which developed in the quality movement, requires first that the existing process be stabilized. It then becomes predictable, and its capabilities become accessible to analysis and improvement.[34] Continuous process improvement occurs when the cycle of stabilizing, assessing, and improving a given process becomes institutionalized.

IT-enabled business process redesign must generally be dynamic. Those responsible for a process should constantly investigate whether new information technologies make it possible to carry out a process in new ways. IT is continuing to evolve, and forthcoming technologies will have a substantial impact on the processes of the next decade. The IT infrastructure must be robust enough to support the new application appropriate to a particular process.

Summary

We believe that the industrial engineers of the future, regardless of their formal title or the organizational unit that employs them, will focus increasingly on IT-enabled redesign of business process. We have only begun to explore the implications and implementation of this concept, and only a few companies have ventured into the area. Many companies that have used IT to redesign particular business processes have done so without any conscious approach or philosophy. In short, the actual experience base with IT-enabled process redesign is limited.

Yet managing by customer-driven processes that cross organizational boundaries is an intuitively appealing idea that has worked well in the companies that have experimented with it. And few would question that information technology is a powerful tool for reshaping business processes. The individuals and companies that can master redesigning processes around IT will be well equipped to suceed in the new decade – and the new century.

References

1   L. Gulick, 'Notes on the Theory of Organization,' in L. Gulick and L. Urwick, eds., *Papers on the Science of Administration* (New York: Institute of Public Administration, 1937), p. 9.
2   S. Sakamoto, 'Process Design Concept: A New Approach to IE,' *Industrial Engineering*, March 1989, p. 31.
3   'Office Automation: Making It Pay Off.' *Business Week*, 12 October 1987, pp 134–46. For an alternative perspective, see R. E. Kraut, ed., *Technology and the Transformation of White-Collar Work* (Hillsdale, New Jersey: Lawrence Erlbaum Associates, 1987).
4   G. W. Loveman, 'An Assessment of the Productivity Impact of Information Technologies' (Cambridge, Massachusetts: MIT Sloan School of Management, Management in the 1990s. Working Paper 90s: 88-054, July 1988). Loveman studied microeconomic data from manufacturing firms to estimate econometrically the productivity impact of IT in the late 1970s and early 1980s. In finding no significant positive productivity impact from IT, he argues that his findings in manufacturing raise serious questions about impacts in nonmanufacturing firms as well. Baily and Chakrabarti (1988) studied white-collar productivity and IT as one part of a broader inquiry into poor productivity growth. They found no evidence of significant productivity gain. See M. N. Baily and A. Chakrabarti, *Innovation and the Productivity Criss* (Washington, D. C.: Brookings Institution, 1988).
5   Loveman (1988); Baily and Chakrabarti (1988). See also L. C. Thurow, 'Toward a High-Wage, High-Productivity Service Sector' (Washington, D. C.: Economic Policy Institute, 1989).
6   Robert Horton, who became chairman and chief executive of British Petroleum in March 1990, argues that his major concern in setting BP's course in the next decade is 'managing surprise.' Horton's belief is that the external business environment is so unpredictable that surprise, rather than managed change, is inevitable. See R. Horton, 'Future Challenges to Management,' *MIT Management*, Winter 1989, pp. 3–6.
7   T. Malone, 'What is Coordination Theory?' (Cambridge, Massachusetts: MIT Sloan School of Management, Center for Coordination Science, Working Paper No. 2051-88, February 1988); K. Crowston and T. Malone, 'Information Technology and Work Organization' (Cambridge, Massachusetts: MIT Sloan School of Management, Center for Information Systems Research, Working Paper No. 165, December 1987).
8   G. A. Pall, *Quality Process Management* (Englewood Cliffs, New Jersey: Prentice-Hall,

1987). Our definition also complements that of Schein, who focuses on human processes in organizations – e.g., building and maintaining groups, group problem solving and decision making, leading and influencing, etc. See E. H. Schein, *Process Consultation: Its Role in Organization Development.* Vol. 1, 2nd ed. (Reading, Massachusetts: Addison-Wesley, 1988).

9   E. J. Kane, 'IBM's Total Quality Improvement System' (Purchase. New York IBM Corporation, unpublished manuscript), p. 5.

10   See, for example, M. F. Morris and G. W. Vining, 'The IE's Future Role in Improving Knowledge Worker Productivity,' *Industrial Engineering,* July 1987, p. 28.

11   'Reference Note on Work Simplification' (Boston: Harvard Business School, HBS Case Services #9-609-0601961, 1961).

12   The relationship between business vision and IT has been explored by several researchers under the auspices of the MIT Sloan School's five-year 'Management in the 1990s' research program. An overview volume is scheduled for publication by Oxford University Press in August 1990.

13   See, for example, G. Stalk, Jr., 'Time – The Next Source of Strategic Advantage,' *Harvard Business Review,* July-August 1988, pp. 41–51.

14   S. Zuboff, *In the Age of the Smart Machine* (New York: Basic Books, 1988).

15   E. H. Schein, 'Innovative Cultures and Organizations' (Cambridge, Massachusetts: MIT Sloan School of Management, Management in the 1990s, Working Paper 90s: 88-064, November 1988).

16   Information engineering and other redesign approaches based on data modeling are necessarily limited in scope. More than data is exchanged in many process relationships. Note too that many companies have used information engineering methods *without* a specific process orientation.

17   Examples of IT planning approaches where high-impact objectives and/or goals are defined include critical success factors (CSFs) and business systems planning (BSP). See J. F. Rockart, 'Chief Executives Define Their Own Data Needs,' *Harvard Business Review.* March–April 1979, pp. 81–93; and IBM, *Information Systems Planning Guide,* 3rd ed. (Business Systems Planning Report No. GE20-05527-2, July 1981).

18   D. Goodhue, J. Quillard, and J. Rockart, 'Managing the Data Resource: A Contingency Perspective' (Cambridge, Massachusetts: MIT Sloan School of Management, Center for Information Systems Research, Working Paper No. 150, January 1987).

19   J. F. Rockart, 'The Line Takes the Leadership – IS Management in a Wired Society,' *Sloan Management Review,* Summer, 1988, pp. 57–64.

20   J. C. Henderson and N. Venkatraman, 'Strategic Alignment: A Process Model for Integrating Information Technology and Business Strategies' (Cambridge, Massachusetts: MIT Sloan School of Management, Center for Information Systems Research, Working Paper No. 196, October 1989).

21   Dorothy Leonard-Barton introduced the concept of organizational prototyping with regard to the implementation of new information technologies. See D. Leonard-Barton. 'The Case for Integrative Innovation: An Expert System at Digital,' *Sloan Management Review.* Fall 1987, pp. 7-19

22   R. Johnston and P. R. Lawrence. 'Beyond Vertical Integration – The Rise of the Value-Adding Partnership,' *Harvard Business Review,* July-August 1988, pp. 94–101. See also N. Venkatraman. 'IT-Induced Business Reconfiguration: The New Strategic Management Challenge' (Cambridge, Massachusetts: Paper presented at the annual conference of the MIT Center for Information Systems. Research, June 1989).

23   T. J. Main and J. E. Short, 'Managing the Merger: Building Partnership through IT Planning at the New Baxter,' *Management Information Systems Quarterly.* December 1989. pp. 469-486.

24   C. R. Hall, M. E. Friesen, and J. E. Short. 'The Turnaround at US Sprint: The Role of Improved Partnership between Business and Information Management,' in progress.

25   R. R. Johansen, *Groupware: Computer Support for Business Teams* (New York: The Free

Press, 1988). Also see C. V. Bullen and R. R. Johansen, 'Groupware: A Key to Managing Business Teams?' (Cambridge, Massachusetts: MIT Sloan School of Management, Center for Information Systems Research, Working Paper No. 169, May 1988).

26   See L. M. Applegate, 'The Center for Machine Intelligence Computer Support for Cooperative Work' (Boston: Harvard Business School Case Study No. 189–135, 1988, rev. 1989).

27   J. E. Ashton and F. X. Cook, 'Time to Reform Job Shop Manufacturing,' *Harvard Business Review*, March-April 198, pp. 106–111.

28   See cases on 'Tiger Creek,' 'Piney Wood,' and 'Cedar Bluff' in S. Zuboff (1988); other industries discussed by Zuboff primarily involve informational processes.

29   One might consider managerial processes synonymous with informational processes. Certainly the vast majority of managerial processes, such as budgeting, planning, and human resource development, involve informational objects. Yet it is important to remember that informational processes can be either operational or managerial, so we believe that this separate dimension of process types is warranted.

30   A case study describes the process and the creation of the expert system. See 'Texas Instruments Capital Investment Expert System' (Boston: Harvard Business School Case Study No. 188-050, 1988).

31   Some aspects of this process improvement are described in L. M. Applegate and C. S. Osborne. 'Xerox Corporation Executive Support Systems' (Boston Harvard Business School Case Study No. 189-134, 1988, rev. 1989).

32   R.H. C. Pugh, address to McKinsey & Co information technology practice leaders, Munich, Germany, June 1989.

33   See, for example, A. R. Cohen and D. L. Bradford, 'Influence without Authority. The Use of Alliances. Reciprocity, and Exchange to Accomplish Work,' *Organizational Dynamics*, Winter 1989, pp 4–17.

34   See G. A. Pall (1987).

Part Three
Some Further Management Considerations

In Parts One and Two we have covered some of the major issues associated with the planning, introduction and utilization of information technology in business as we move towards the next millennium. Part One gave us a view of the developments in business applications of information technology and a vision of the future. Major issues confronting management were also identified in general terms. A key feature of the latter involved the strategic opportunities that are available through modern information technology, and this was the focus of Part Two. A key lesson to be learnt from Part Two is the need for careful planning to take account not only of these opportunities but to integrate this kind of thinking into the on-going business management strategy process. The latter includes: business strategy formation and implementation; business process redesign; and the management of change issues associated with this and the introduction of new technologies.

Part Three is designed to pick up on some of the general themes identified in Part One and to investigate these in greater depth. Questions relating to how to best organize one's information services, how to encourage, yet control the development of systems in business units rather than rely solely on centralized developments, and how to deal with the vexed question of evaluating information technology investments are all dealt with in this final section of the book. We also look at the political dimension of information ownership within organizations and the implications this has for implementing computer-based information systems. In addition, picking up on the inter-organizational and global aspects of information systems strategy introduced in Part Two, we consider issues associated with organizational interdependence and the impact that cultural differences might have on information management.

As indicated in the introductions to Parts One and Two, there have been a number of surveys conducted since the early 1980s which attempt to identify the critical issues faced by executives in managing information systems in their organization (e.g. Brancheau and Wetherbe, 1987; Galliers, et al., Niederman, et al., 1991: Parker and Idundun, 1988). It may be surprising to some, but it has consistently been the case that the major concerns relate to organizational and strategic issues rather than technological ones – and these are the views of IT executives remember.

Table 1 provides a summary of the major concerns expressed by North American and British IT executives since 1986. Clearly, there are some differences in perspectives between the two groups and some movement in terms of the rankings of the issues over time but generally speaking, a reasonably clear pattern emerges, with the major concerns being about ensuring that information technology investments meet business needs; that the organization of the information systems function is in line with organizational imperatives, and that information systems/technology is *understood* by business colleagues.

Table 1   A comparison of the key information systems management issues as perceived by US and UK IT executives

Issue	*Rank*			
	USA		*UK*	
	1986	1989	1987	1992
Information architecture	8	1	NR	6
Data resource management	7	2	9	2
Strategic IS planning	1	3	3	2
IS human resources	12	4	6	14
Organizational learning re IS/IT; education of senior management	3	5	4	7
Technology infrastructure	NR	6	NR	20
IS organizational alignment	5	7	1	13
Competitive advantage from IS/IT	2	8	2	5
Quality of software development	13	9	10	4
Telecommunication systems	11	10	8	12
IS's role and contribution	4	11	NR	10
Electronic data interchange	14	12	NR	22
Distributed systems	NR	12	NR	15
Business process redesign	NR	NR	NR	1

Source: Galliers *et al.*, (1994); Niederman *et al.*, (1991)

There are a number of problems associated with this kind of survey research. First, as identified in the introduction to Part Two, it is often not clear what is meant precisely by the term *key* issue. Figure 4, page 122 is helpful in this regard. In addition, respondents to such surveys may turn out not to be a representative sample, although given the large sample sizes in each of the above exercises and corroborative evidence from elsewhere (e.g. Broadbent *et al.*, 1992; Craumer *et al.*, 1992; Watson and Brancheau, 1991), we can be reasonably certain that these results are representative of commonly-held views on the matter.

We shall now look at some of these issues in greater depth in the context of the seven chapters that go to make up Part Three.

Chapter 11, by Edwards and colleagues at Oxford's Institute of Information Management, looks at the question of the organization of the information systems function. Further reading on this topic can be found in La Belle and Nyce (1987).

Over the years there has been considerable debate about whether the information systems function should be centralized or decentralized (see, for example, Ein-Dor and Segev, 1980; Kalogeras, 1977; Robson, 1994, pp. 223-264). The argument for the former position rests on the presumed cost savings and efficiency of centralization, with corporate systems being developed by technically competent people; the argument for the latter rests on the presumed greater relevance and effectiveness of systems developed in business units, by people who know their business.

It has been generally accepted for some time that the information systems function's structure should mirror that of the organization as a whole (e.g. Seib, 1978). Having said that, some have predicted its disappearance as a separate entity altogether (e.g. Dearden, 1987), given, for example, the increasing power and ease of use of the technology and an increasingly knowledgeable and skilled end-user computing community (see also Chapter 13). Others, more recently, have advocated a move to third party provision of information systems services, commonly described as *outsourcing* (see Chapter 12). The conclusion drawn in Chapter 11, however, is that organizations should adopt a *federal* approach – a combination of centralized, corporate support services and systems, and of decentralized systems development in business units, focusing on strategic opportunities associated with particular products and services.

It is because of this on-going debate and concern for their future that issues such as the information systems function's role and contribution appears high on the agenda of IT Directors, as shown in Table 1 above.

As indicated previously, outsourcing is the focus of Chapter 12. In it Loh and Venkatraman report on research into what is seen by many as a particularly recent phenomenon, although those of us who can remember the very early days of commercial computing will recall many companies being reliant on bureaux services for their business data processing! And even in its current varieties, the outsourcing phenomenon has been with us throughout the 1980s (Reponen, 1993).

The research that forms the basis of Chapter 12 provides us with some useful information on the determinants of the outsourcing decision. It seems, as one might have expected, that considerations of cost and the perception of IT performance in-house both have considerable influence on the decision to outsource. Concern over high IT budgets and the perception of limited positive impact, in business terms, of IT investments both presage the decision to outsource.

Over the years, the phenomenon of end-user computing has also been a concern for executives and very much on the strategic information management agenda. Chapter 13 deals with this phenomenon, by attempting to identify the key determinants of successful end-user computing. Cheney, Mann and Amoroso provide some very useful insights into this aspect of information management, both from a theoretical and practical perspective. For example, they illustrate the range of forms of end-user computing, review previous research on the topic, and pin-point key organizational factors that lead to success. The desired outcome from their analysis should be either 'the abandonment of a doomed [end-user computing facility] or the design of a controlled environment within which the [facility] may flourish' (Cheney *et al.*, 1986, p. 77).

One of the reasons why there is so much debate about who should be responsible for information systems developments and who should benefit from its provision relates to the old maxim 'information is power'. Land and Kennedy-McGregor (1987) remind us that information comes in a variety of types. Their taxonomy suggests that information may be:

- *descriptive* of the real (*sic*) world, i.e. data that, once assimilatated, provides a picture or snapshot of the real world;
- *probablistic*, in the sense that is often the case that we cannot always know for certain what is actually going on in the real world, but we may be able to infer what is going on from sample data, such as in forecasting future events;
- *explanatory/evaluative*, since decision makers may well not only need to know the *facts* of the matter but also the *explanations* that gave rise to these facts;
- *unexpected*, in terms of the *source* of the information or *unanticipated* as being relevant at first sight; this often causes problems for systems developers, who are often heard complaining that users 'change their minds' about their information needs;
- *propaganda*, in that rather than being objective and verifiable, much information is used to shape attitudes, beliefs, actions and decisions.

It is in line with the last information type – propaganda – in particular that Chapter 14 is included. As indicated above, we often hear that 'information is power' and it is because of this that many resist the sharing of information in organizations. The author of Chapter 14, Markus, introduces us to three basic theories as to the causes of such resistance, with a view to aiding the information systems *implementation* process. We forget such lessons at our peril when investing in IT and managing the systems implementation process!

Chapter 15, by Tricker, focuses our attention on the cross-cultural issues of information usage and the development of information systems. Much of the literature on strategic information

244 *Strategic Information Management*

management has an English-speaking bias. In an era when we are increasingly involved in transnational and even global inter-relationships in business, it is clearly essential that we incorporate cultural issues onto our management agenda. Tricker takes up this theme by providing a synopsis of the characteristics and culture of Chinese business methods as a basis for investigating the cultural aspects of information. While the Chinese culture is but one example, this chapter provides much food for thought in introducing a cultural dimension to information systems development.

That aspect of the argument for including the previous chapter in this book concerned with the increasing interdependence of organizations is a theme taken up in Chapter 16. Rockart and Short investigate the question of the organizational impact of IT and conclude it is precisely in the area of enabling organizational interdependence that IT has its most important role. The authors review IT's major impacts *within* organizations, i.e. its ability to change stuctures, roles and processes; its ability to foster teamwork, flatter organizations and effect greater integration across otherwise quite disparate functions and businesses. Having done so, they focus their attention on an organization's *value-chain* and demonstrate the opportunities IT provides for organizational interdependence – interorganisational systems in the terminology of Cash (1985) – and it is this analysis that results in the identification of a management agenda for the 1990s which focuses attention on such strategic alliances and the need to manage the flow of information between the alliance's organizational partners.

As we have seen from Table 1, one of the major concerns of IT directors relates to demonstrating the worth of IT investments – survival is the strongest instinct in the jungle! Clearly, however, this concern is shared by non-IT executives in companies (e.g. Grindley, 1992). We bring the book to a close by focusing attention on this important topic. Willcocks reviews both the *problems* associated with evaluating and managing IT investments, and the *techniques* commonly used by companies in undertaking such evaluations. His analysis pinpoints the limitations of our current practice and provides a way forward for improving IT evaluation.

References

Brancheau, J. C. and Wetherbe, J. C. (1987). Key issues in information systems management. *MIS Quarterly*, 11(1), March.

Broadbent, M., Hansell, A., Dampney, C. N. G. and Butler, C. (1992). Information systems management: the key issues for 1992. *Australasian SHARE/GUIDE Ltd Conference*, Sydney, 31 August–2 September 1992.

Cash, Jr, J. I. (1985). Interorganizational systems: an information society opportunity or threat? *The Information Society*, 3(3). Also in E. K. Somogyi and R. D. Galliers (eds.) (1987), Towards *Strategic Information Systems*, Abacus Press, Cambridge, Mass., pp. 200–220.

Cheney, P. H. Mann, R. I. and Amoroso, D. L. (1986). Organizational factors affecting the success of end-user computing. *Journal of Management Information Systems*, 3(1), Summer, pp. 63–80.

Craumer, M. A. Buday, R. S. Waite, T. J. and Walseman, S.M. (1992). *Critical Issues of Information Systems Management for 1992*, CSC Index, Cambridge, Mass., February.

Dearden, J. (1987) The withering away of the IS organization. *Sloan Management Review*, Summer.

Ein-Dor, P. and Segev, E. (1980). Organizational arrangements for MIS units. *Information and Management*, 3, pp. 19–26.

Galliers, R. D. (ed.) (1992). *Information Systems Research: Issues, Methods and Practical Guidelines*, Blackwell Scientific, Oxford.

Galliers, R. D. Merali, Y and Spearing, L (1994). Coping with information technology? How British executives perceive the key information systems management issues in the mid-1990s. *Journal of Information Technology*, 9(1), March.

Grindley, K. (1992). *Information Technology Review 1992/93*, Price Waterhouse, London.

Kalogeras, C. M. (1977). Centralized vs. local DP organization. *Journal of Systems Management,* **28**, March, pp. 28–31.

La Belle and Nyce, H. E. (1987). Whither the IT organization? *Sloan Management Review,* Summer.

Land, F. F and Kennedy-McGregor (1987). Information and information systems: concepts and perspectives. In R. D. Galliers (ed.) (1987) *Information Analysis: Selected Readings,* Addison-Wesley, Sydney.

Niederman, F. Brancheau, J. C. and Wetherbe, J. C. (1991). Information systems management issues for the 1990s. *MIS Quarterly,* **15**(4), December, pp. 474–500.

Parker, T and Idundun, M. (1988). Managing information systems in 1987: the top issues for IS managers in the UK. *Journal of Information Technology,* **4**(1), March, pp. 34–42.

Reponen, T. (1993). Outsourcing or insourcing. *Proceedings: Fourteenth International Conference on Information Systems,* Orlando, Florida, 5–8 December.

Robson, W. (1994). *Strategic Management and Information Systems: An Integrated Approach,* Pitman Publishing, London.

Seib, R (1978). DP facilities structure should look like your organization. *Journal of Systems Management,* **29**, October, pp. 26–27.

Watson, R. T. and Brancheau, J. C. (1991). Key issues in information systems management, **20**, pp. 213–223. Also in R. D. Galliers (ed.) (1992). *op cit.,* pp. 112–131.

11 Any way out of the labyrinth for managing information systems?

B. R. Edwards, M. J. Earl and D. F. Feeny

To judge by the behaviour of many complex organizations, management approaches towards structuring the information systems (IS) function look to be uncertain, diverse and sometimes downright contradictory. Quite different organizational arrangements for IS can be found not only between similar businesses in the same sector, but across different parts of the same business.

'Complex organizations' exist in both the government and private sectors. They are large (over say one billion dollars in annual revenues), diversified and divisionalized into partly autonomous entities, often into strategic business units (SBUs).

Corporations of that sort are common in the Western world, indeed they are commoner than unitary companies at that size. In them the IS organizational issue is very frequently seen to be problematic, commonly demonstrated by controversy and dramatic change. Our experience over many years, and in recent research, shows that the problems exist in patterns, and that there is a small number of general solutions, and that there is a preferred one.

Here are sketches of three frustrated senior executives who could all be from the same corporation. We suggest that they speak for very many of their peers; indeed they are composite portraits made from a number we know.

● An Information Systems (IS) Director in the coporate headquarters of a large multi-divisional group finds that some divisions are simply bypassing corporate IS. They are installing small and not so small systems of various hues. Meanwhile corporate IS is struggling to deliver new application function from a headcount-limited development resource, and the approved application backlog grows. Moreover the heavy costs of running all the services of a corporate data centre make his charge-out rates look extravagant, and the performance of his department suspect.

- A Divisional Chief Executive needs new IS capabilities simply to stay in his present markets, let alone enhance competitive potential. Customers are insisting on electronic exchange of orders and invoices and products support material is being demanded in electronic form. Corporate IS apparently cannot deliver in the needed timeframe, yet would like to veto divisional initiatives to go-it-alone for fear of generating inconsistencies and of duplicating costs. There is controversy about what represents the lowest real total cost.

- The President is being pressed on all sides with the message that IS should be the key strategic enabler for the business, but all he sees is a mess and all he hears is grumbles. His instincts are generally to let divisions behave like true strategic business units (SBUs), having accountability for business performance, and as much autonomy as he can responsibly devolve. Yet he is told that in IS matters, uniquely, there is a need for a corporate approach to 'architectures' and 'infrastructure', in order to achieve corporate coherence and synergy.

It would almost seem as though the complex, multidivisional business stands at a disadvantage compared with simpler businesses in the matter of managing IT. And where does this leave government sector organizations which are almost always complex?

In those caricatures the issues appear to include:

- *Authority for application decisions* – who decides whether a particular application proposal is justified and what priority it should have when there is contention?
- *Technical policy and support structure* – how much need is there for an overall technical structure and for efforts in pursuit of potential corporate synergies?
- *Centralization versus decentralization* – what should be the overall distribution of IS responsibilities and resources between corporate and business unit managements?

None of these are new; but all are becoming more pressing as IS becomes all-pervasive, more demanding of resource and attention and more 'mutual' both within and between businesses. We have been working with businesss for many years as they have attempted to resolve these conflicts.

We believe from recent research that it is possible to describe quite a small number of approaches to IS arrangement and to comment on the prospects for their success. (A research study was conducted by the authors in fourteen complex organizations headquartered in Europe and North America. A detailed research instrument was applied through interviews with IS Directors, user managers and IS sponsors.)

The first stage of getting control of something is to find words to describe it

It is worth describing the model approaches for IS arrangements. We use 'arrangements' to cover far more than simple organization structure. As will be seen, the models describe where powers reside, how investment and other decisions are made and reviewed, what the missions of various IS groups are, and what management controls are appropriate.

Five types can be described; we have studied all of them. In some very widespread organizations more than one model is present. Three of them are *centralized*, but differ profoundly in their goals and management dynamics. One is decentralized and one is a compromise.

Let's describe the models and illustrate typical arguments in their favour.

Corporate service (centralized)

IS is a unified function reporting to corporate management. There may be distributed equipment, but it is under the operational control of central IS. If business units have people whose focus is systems they are intended to be spokespeople for users, and negotiators with central IS. The service disposes of tens of hundreds of millions of dollars annually and employs hundreds or thousands of people.

The centralized corporate service is justified through features like:

- Economies of scale.
- Critical mass of skills.
- Opportunity for a corporate systems approach.
- Priorities adjudicated at corporate level.
- 'Data is a corporate resource.'
- The professionalism possible in a really large IS organization.

Internal Bureau (centralized)

This possesses the characteristics of the corporate service but is managed as a profit centre rather than a functional cost centre. It has many of the characteristics of a wholly-owned business subsidiary including targets for profitability, return on investment and cash flow. There will commonly be account managers aligned with nominated business units, and services and applications may be considered as a portfolio of 'products'. Any external business arises accidentally, for example through continuing to service a small business which has been divested.

Justification for the internal bureau has included the following in addition to those of the central corporate service:

- Demonstration of financial probity.
- Comparability with external data servicers.

- Motivation for staff in the bureau.
- More responsiveness to divisions, owing to a 'market-led' business culture.
- Prevalence of a profit centre management control system in the corporation at large.
- Ability to pioneer or prototype new technology through a managed R&D programme which is funded out of operating profits.

Business venture (centralized)

This is like the internal bureau, but it has in addition an explicit mission to seek revenue by offering IS services outside the group. (This could be limited – one unit we know has an objective of 10 per cent external revenue – or unconstrained). Indications that this is the mode would be the existence of published tariffs, marketing literature, dedicated external salesmen, and products which are for external offering only.

Justification beyond the arguments for an internal bureau include:

- Enhanced economies of scale, because of even higher capacity becoming justified and further mileage being extracted from assets.
- Motivational value for professionals and managers in the bureau.
- Demonstrable competitiveness of costs and services to sceptical group users.
- Ability to use group businesses to prototype and develop generalized external offerings.
- Conforming to a corporate direction towards diversification, in this case towards information services.
- Opportunity to learn 'new tricks' from other external businesses.
- Enhanced power and business leverage due to greater size.

Decentralized

By contrast to the three above cases, IS is a distributed function. Each business unit contains its own IS capability under its own control, or elects to employ commercial data servicers. There is no central IS unit or responsibility except for the support of corporate headquarters' functions such as consolidating financial returns. Corporate management review the units' capital and budget submissions for IS only to the extent required for general financial planning and control purposes. A new computer is therefore treated like a new stamping press of similar cost.

Justification for delegating all IS authority and planning includes:

- Full consistency with principles of SBU accountability and autonomy.
- Least impediment to SBU's initiatives for radical IS exploitation.
- No impediment to acquisition or divestment of businesses.
- No addition to the deadweight of corporate staffs.

Federal

IS is a partly distributed function, with business units containing and controlling some IS capability. There is, in addition, some central IS presence which has responsibility for defined aspects of policy and architecture across the organization. There is often central provision of some common or shared services, which may or may not be coincident with the central IS policy unit. The name of this model deliberately borrows from political vocabulary because the idea of Federal 'powers reserved' is balanced against delegated 'SBU rights'.

The justification for this compromise has included:

- Helping to distinguish responsibility for strategy (*what* IS is to contribute) from policy (*how* IS is to be done).
- Allowing for fast local decisions on applications and priorities while, preserving corporate mediation on selected issues e.g. security, common systems, vendor selection and procurement practices.
- Providing a corporate framework for selected corporate provision e.g. networks, data etc.

Earlier we said that in some complex corporations more than one model might be working. In one case which is worth illustrating, every one is present!

> One British-based multinational corporation operated IS at the highest level on a *federal* basis, with a distinct unit having oversight of the worldwide IS policies. There still exists a substantial *internal bureau*, which is the successor to a *corporate service* unit that once served all headquarters functions. That bureau is now accepting business targets which in effect redefine it as an *external bureau*. One major international division within the corporation once operated towards its national business units in a way closest to *decentralized*, but it is now exerting extended control of a truly *federal* nature. There was until recently, one division whose business was to be an *external bureau*.

When we discuss those five models with either IS executives or general business executives, they are able readily to identify their own situation with one or more of them. *There are seldom boundary difficulties.*

It seems extraordinary that as we enter the fourth decade of business computing, there still exists such a diversity of management approaches to IS. Is any one preferred; is there any evidence of differential performance?

But a plague on all your houses!

When we described the five models for the positioning of IS people and powers, we offered a justification for each. There might be said to be little to choose between such well-defined cases, until we look at the downside, or the dangers implicit in each. Here are some criticisms which we have heard of each, sometimes expressed with considerable emotion – particularly by non-IS managers.

Corporate service

This is commonly perceived as:

- Inaccessible.
- Arrogant in its pursuit of technological objectives, and belief that it possessed superior understanding of the dynamics of the business.
- Unresponsive to SBU needs and priorities.
- Profligate in its spending, and greedy and unfair in its recharging of costs.
- Resistant to modern technology's opportunity e.g. distributed systems, user-controlled development.

Internal bureau

Shows possibly all the above, but is in addition:

- Biased in its advice, because of its perceived preference to sell its own services even when they might not offer the optimal solution.
- Reluctant to invest in progressive enhancement of installed systems.
- Bureaucratic and dominated by administration.
- More concerned about its bottom line than about serving the users in the SBUs and therefore shy about investment.

Business venture

Shows the above problems and in addition experiences:

- Incompatibility between mission of serving the group's businesses and mission of growing external revenue.
- Diversion of key, skilled people to development and selling of new services to external customers.
- Holding 'our' needed solution back while generalizing it to create a marketable common solution or package.
- Being content to use revenue from group SBUs as cash flow to nourish exciting external ventures.
- Conflict between the desire to maintain competitive edge through an exclusive application, and the desire to offer it profitably to the industry sector.

Decentralized

Without restraints, it is believed you will get:

- Incompatible systems and technology, cutting off emerging potential for common or shared systems.
- Some SBUs simply doing computing badly.
- Security exposures.
- Incompatible IS and IT constraining the business from reorganization.
- Limited leverage on IT suppliers, owing to diversity; lack of single customer image.
- Opportunity for 'awakened' SBUs to persist in systems darkness until their industry overtakes them.

Federal

Although this was offered as a constructive compromise, sceptics ask these sorts of questions:

- Who writes the rules and defines the boundaries?
- How can a group-wide IS policy be supported by business line management who don't understand the terminology or appreciate its significance?
- How can it be promulgated by corporate IS people who have no power?
- What happens when the group acquires a new company?
- How do you fund the overheads involved in writing and mediating IS policies?

What that says is that no model is ideal, and that you could screw up just as well with any of them. We saw poor results coming from every one of those models. What, then, are the indicators to nudge a preference one way or another? Basically there are two:

1 Making IS arrangements consistent with the way the business works and is organised.
2 Having regard to the history and traditions of IS in the organisation.

Our shorthand jargon for these is:

'Host organization characteristics', and:
'IS heritage'.

Indicators – or decision rules – in practice

The first indicator says that on a centralized-decentralized spectrum it makes little sense to position IS differently from all the other main business activities. Arrangements for IS should follow the characteristics of the host organization. Applying this decision rule requires a lot of sensitivity and honesty about the real nature of the business, and of how it is changing.

We have seen a number of organizations where a clear move away from one of the three centralized models towards some devolution was in progress. In every case this has been consistent with the degree of decentralization that the rest of the business possessed or was aspiring to. We have also seen one case where a major business in the process of recentralizing had taken he decision to recentralize IS. (We have been struck by the high proportion of businesses in which major refocusing and reorganization at corporate level has been in process, or a feature of recent history. A common concern is to focus better on the 'core business', or as one group put it, 'decluttering the business'.)

The second indicator, IS heritage, or 'where are we coming from?' should, however, be seen as a modifier to the decision rule just stated. In one British metal products corporation it was perceived that the centralized IS organization was a clear misfit with the decentralized management of what were very diverse businesses. The decision was taken to abolish the central IS resource, dispersing part to the larger business units, and instructing smaller units to seek support from local data servicers.

Although the devolution was to be mediated by a newly-created corporate IS consultancy unit, the process was a relative disaster. IS staff declined to move; the businesses were in no way ready to assume responsibility; and there was no tradition of a corporate unit being able to manage a policy across the SBUs. The group's IS remained in frozen immobility, with considerable personal misery, for some time.

A solution which took proper account of 'IS heritage' would have respected the momentum and culture of the existing IS arrangements, sought out where they were really wanting, and ameliorated them. Sudden and sweeping changes in direction of IS arrangement seem rarely to succeed and are costly in terms of organizational disruption and breaks in service.

By contrast, in another British case a food business with dispersed and disparate product divisions was frustrated by a 'business venture' which was its mandated IS supplier. Divisions felt that they were paying too much for systems that did not keep up to date with business needs and were if anything a constraint on their business.

The solution was not to dismantle the bureau, but to remove its mandate, institute a federal policy with a corporate steward of policies, and promote divisional initiatives. One division after another then developed modern networked distribution systems with a new sense of divisional self-help, yet often voluntarily relying on the bureau for technical and development services. This food business began to benefit from a 'best of both worlds' set of IS arrangements.

So, one reason for compromise arrangements is that any abstract ideal based on organizational type needs to be tempered by consideration for the starting position, how remote that is from the ideal, what is politically and personally acceptable, and what really needs fixing. Another quite different reason for compromise is that few host organizations occupy extreme positions of centralization or decentralization anyway, and thus 180° turns in structuring and controlling IS are likely to substitute one misfit IS organization for another.

The problem of organizing IS has often been posed as a question of choosing between decentralization and centralization. The use of such opposites as labels or metaphors may help in understanding the issues to be faced. However, in practice it encourages constrained thinking, suggests inevitable conflict, and does not fit the variety of organizational contexts to which IS functions have to respond. Above all it might suggest that it is impossible to seek a mix of the benefits of centralization and decentralization. We believe such a balance is quite feasible in many circumstances; the federal solution is the key.

The federal solution is of course one of compromise, and for some people 'compromise' is a dirty word. Where compromise consists of sacrificing every point of principle in pursuit of some consensus, that might be valid. But to compromise by combining strengths seems to us responsible.

The federal model offers strengths that suit many variants of the complex business organization, in particular because it is adaptable. IS competence and resource are usually positioned at corporate level *and* in SBUs or divisions. Consequently IS can respond to new demands and imperatives at either level, without a need to create new organizational entities.

There remains a validity for the centralized corporate service for IS where the business organization, however complex, is being managed in a centralized, integrated fashion. It is necessary to be sensitive to the dangers inherent in this style, which were outlined earlier.

Decentralized IS clearly fits where the host organization truly intends to leave its businesses functionally free. In one financial services conglomerate we recently heard it stated that this was to become the model, and that the only value added by corporate was the maintenance of the group logo and the brand image. But the group must be confident that this will remain a stable intention, because the opportunity for SBUs to develop in different directions can make any later attempt to coordinate very difficult.

What businesses are doing

Attracted by the apparent sense behind the federal model, we looked at the proportion of organizations in our research sample which best fitted that model in 1987 compared with four years before that. In 1987 *eight* out of fourteen were federal, compared with *three* out of fourteen earlier. The three centralized models had all declined; corporate from five to two, bureaux from four to three. In many cases major changes had come about because of growing frustration about efficiency and effectiveness. The three caricatures at the beginning of this article can lead to explosive tensions. In a number of cases the crisis had only been resolved after escalation to group board level.

Those data appear inconclusive about the bureau models, but in fact we believe that the arguments against the two bureau models are particularly powerful. The business managers to whom we spoke expressed great unease about dependence upon a unit whose mission was to itself. We concluded that of four bureaux which had existed in 1983 *none* would remain as the predominant IS presence in their corporations.

We make these predictions: they will detach themselves and become freestanding data servicers; or they will revert to serving in a federal model as a corporate technical resource; or they will persist as a valued niche provider of specialist services. The driving force for these changes will be the unstoppable demand from SBUs – or corporate management – for truly strategic and business integrated systems that simply cannot be developed on a customer-contractor basis.

The predictions for the other models include further slight increase in federal behaviour, and an increase in decentralized cases followed the adoption – or recognition – of truly decentralized business practices. The following table summarizes recent change, and our predictions for the future.

IS organization structure	Number in sample		
	4 years ago	*Now*	*Outlook*
Centralized – corporate service	5	2	1
Internal bureau	3	1	0
Business venture	1	2	0
Federal	3	8	9
Decentralized	2	1	4

Do not imagine, however, that all the federal conditions had come about by conscious decision! In some cases 'federal' is the nearest model to an uneasy de facto distribution of power and activity. Some companies have been relieved to discover that their compromise has a name and can be justified, and have used our language to articulate it better.

If there is one message from our work it is that the federal approach to IS arrangements is rational and responsible, and can be made more effective if it is pursued deliberately and rationally. The following section discusses how it can be pursued.

How are they getting on?

We have discussed five approaches to IS arrangements; the businesses in our sample had been selected to represent all of them. We did not know in choosing them how good they were at applying IS in the business, how far they diverged in aspects other than organization, or whether our data gave indications of good practice.

We believe that our research helps in all those questions. We can show why there is, and will remain, diversity; there are different results, and there is a preferred approach. Taking performance first, we found in our study no evidence of striking differences in *efficiency* of provision of IS services, as measured by cost, quality or reliability. (We are not confident that the same would be found if we explored a population of smaller organizations.) The general level of capability in managing the technical service was consistent and high in both centralized and decentralized units. So we suggest that efficient delivery of information services can be provided however the IS function is organized, provided only that the function is adequately resourced.

However, across the organizations we have studied, we found striking differences in *effectiveness*; that is the acknowledged contribution of IS now, and in the future to significant business needs.

This effectiveness aspect relates particularly to one of the issues identified early in this paper, namely that of 'authority for application decisions'. Now 'authority' sounds like a bureaucratic concept; however, getting application decisions, and getting them rightly resourced, requires a great deal of personal commitment and sense of ownership. What practices foster these characteristics?

Our research has suggested quite strikingly that there are a number of 'preferred' practices. We discovered these by first looking at the effectiveness of IS exploitation in our subject SBUs. This was done by combining views of the actual achievements, the judgements of the business people and the judgements of the IS executives.

The differences were striking and we could rate the cases as high, medium or low on the degree of *integration* between IS and the business which was being achieved: that is, the success at knitting IS applications and services into the fabric of the business. Could we find differences in methods, habits or attitudes between the high integrators and the low? We found seven differences – features which *all* the high integators showed but *none* of the low integrators did. Here they are:

1   The business executives all declared that future exploitation of IT was going to be of truly strategic significance to business performance. An unremarkable comment, until we reflect that none of the low-integrated group so judged. Now, it is impossible to legislate in favour of this being the required view, but it may well have been affected by the following feature.
2   The highly integrated all had a continuing (rather than a once-off) process for educating business managers in IT capabilities and opportunities. The vehicles varied; the resolution to do it did not.
3   In all the highly-integrated cases there was an IS executive in post in the SBU who operated as a key member of the SBU management team. Titles varied and do not matter; acceptance and involvement do.

4   Coupled with that, each 'highly-integrated' SBU had some IS development resource at its disposal and under its direction. This group did not necessarily undertake all development for the SBU, but it was of sufficient size to enable rapid response to changing business circumstances or priorities. The group did not in all cases line report to the SBU. What mattered was the ability of the SBU to determine the goals and priorities of the development group, and the degree of identification of the group with the culture and personalities of the SBU.

5   All 'high' respondents described a process through which IS opportunity and business plans were reviewed integrally. The IS application and service strategy was developed 'top down' from this, reflecting the relationships described in 3 above. This mode of planning was further confirmed by getting respondents to identify themselves with a number of IS planning caricatures.

6   Initiatives to introduce or pilot new technologies were, in the high integration group, SBU dominated. That is not to say that there was no place for corporate technical support or funding; but that the drive and commitment necessary for an effective pilot project have to emanate from SBU management.

7   In the matter of charging for IS services, all the 'high' respondents operated relatively straightforward cost distribution systems, rather than sophisticated pricing mechanisms. Some organizations had, in fact, reverted from the sophistication of advanced price-based charging to cost distribution at a high level, e.g. to SBU only. It had been felt that detailed and subtle pricing had been a distraction and diversion, contributing little.

To summarize that set of evidence, it is clear that SBU ownership of IS strategy and commitment to it is vital. IS strategy is here defined as those things which IS is going to do for the business – as opposed to how IS is to be administered.

Further, it is vital that IS and business management operate in close partnership at SBU level, and feel that jointly they are in control of:

● The IS application strategy and its delivery resource.
● IS pilot projects.

These will be aided if the SBU management team is continually refreshed by information about emerging IS opportunity, and the SBU IS executive is not encumbered by an elaborate financial and charge-out bureaucracy.

Corporate management can set a climate which encourages SBU managements to grasp the initiative in these ways, but it cannot command commitment. In research we found SBUs within the same corporation which lay at opposite ends of the low-high spectrum in terms of IS integration.

What does the federal authority do?

It is useful to identify and distinguish a number of activities which, in a federal set-up, take place at corporate level. In relation to the issues raised at the beginning of the chapter, we are now relating to 'technical policy and support structure'.

1 *Corporate applications* These may be extensive or minimal in size and extent, but there must be provision for defining, operating and maintaining them. This is an area where the nature of the complex organization profoundly affects the approach. For example, some complex organizaions operate with a high degree of integration of business operations, and this integration will be largely enabled through information systems. On the other hand, a conglomerate group run on a portfolio basis will be likely to concentrate only on financial reporting and consolidation as corporate applications. It can be fair to count common systems which are replicated across a number of congruent business units as corporate systems, because it is through the systems that a consistent business image is presented.

2 *Group policy for information systems and technology* This is the set of powers reserved through which the corporate executive maintains its desired level of direction of the IS initiatives and resources throughout the group. Broad topic areas from which these may be developed include the following. These topics were found to be the subject of corporate policy in the majority of the researched organizations:

● Standards about permissible equipment, suppliers, programs, network services etc.
● Standards about how to do things, e.g. defining requirements, implementing solutions, quality and security.
● Personnel and human resources issues (IS careers, skills, job specifications, trade unions).
● Financial arrangements for IS-capital expenditure appraisal, budgeting, chargeout.
● Relationships and negotiations with IT suppliers.
● Developing and propagating common systems.
● Degrees of freedom for SBUs in selecting and using IT, and deciding where to apply it.
● Use of corporate systems, services or resources.

It is important to note that policies of these sorts are and should be predominantly of an enabling nature, and not seen as straitjackets.

3　*Group provided services in information systems and technology*　The extent of this provision is one of the decisions required from group policy. The management and development of group resources are critical areas. Components of group resources we saw in action in our research included:

- Internationally travelling consultants.
- Systems development groups, both for doing common systems and for commissioned divisional systems.
- Data centre operations and related technical planning and support services.
- Industry-specialized R&D pilot e.g. CADCAM, EDI.
- National and international network management.
- Archiving.
- Training and education.
- Support of corporate-wide office automation systems.

The organizational arrangements for these components were varied. Sometimes they co-resided in a single corporate group, sometimes they were separated. Success was related less to structure than to vision, relationships and mutual confidence between SBU and corporate IS entities.

The successful federator

Here we address the third of the issues noted at the beginning – the distribution of responsibilities and resources, or 'centralization versus decentralization'.

What follows is brief, but that does not mean that it is simple in execution. It is folly to imagine that, in a complex corporation, solutions to long-standing problems will be other than complex. Principles, however, can and should be simple and widely understood.

Corporate management, in the name of the Chief Executive, should:

- Proceed from an assumption that some form of federalism is both desirable and feasible.
- Determine not once, but regularly, what topics should lie within the powers reserved to the corporate officers in the IS/IT arena.
- Create (or adapt) and resource a management system to review and propose IS policies.
- Understand, negotiate and ultimately promulgate a set of policies and keep them up to date.
- Articulate and foster the desired extent of SBU ownership of, and accountability for, IS strategies within SBU business plans.

- Review and adapt the extent of provision for corporate systems and technology and articulate its mission.,
- Review, and endorse or constructively criticize, both SBU and headquarters plans and performance in respect of IS.
- Determine the appropriate goals and vehicles for continuing executive enlightenment about IT capability and IS management issues.

Corporate management should not:

- Delegate the definition of either policies or strategies to consultants – although it can be most valuable to consult them.
- Delegate the *determination* of either policies or strategies to IS management at any level – although the IS role in *proposing and negotiating* both cannot be overstated.
- Assume that the appointment of a corporate officer for information at a very high level in the organization absolves general managers from concern about IS; on the contrary, it affords them a peer with whom to argue about it, and a focus for needed staff work, as well as a reporting line for any retained corporate IT resources.
- Relax under an impression that IS/IT is, and will remain, of only peripheral significance in 'our' industry sector; even if this represented a correct assessment in relation to today's IT capability, step advances in IT function or economics over the next decade could transform the opportunity.
- Relax into a feeling that all necessary dispositions for IS policies and strategies have been made, and that corporate management can turn away from those issues to something which addresses 'real' business. The systems which are enabled by information technology are increasingly becoming critical parts of the real business.

Conclusions

We have been surveying the manifold approaches to IS arrangements for years, and we have been amazed at the *diverse* and *contradictory* nature of them. So that we could study them in a systematic way, we defined five model approaches and initially assessed them disinterestedly. The issues that separate them were found to relate to effectiveness in integrating with the business; far less to technical adequacy and efficiency.

So in studying complex organizations we have gained confidence in the stability, and common sense behind the *federal* approach.

The federal approach is not a panacea. Host organization characteristics should be the prime determinant of IS arrangements. So the federal approach will have the best prospects for success in those organizations which plan to maintain certain levels of consistency and planned synergy in the business while devolving much functional management to SBUs. Centralized and decentralized businesses can still sensibly be supported by similarly arranged IS resources, subject to confidence that the business will remain loyal to those extreme styles.

The bureau model is likely to have long-term validity only where the host organization explicitly wishes to make a business of information services, and even then the tendency will be towards separation of group service from outside client service.

We predict, therefore, that the federal solution is the most effective and stable from the complex organizations of today's type.

Finally, creating a federal management is not an overnight event and maintaining it needs continuing effort. It will have the best chances of success where its design is clearly related to the business needs. Above all, the corporate executive must develop a clear vision of why a federal solution is required and how it should work.

The federal solution has the merit that it is best able to cope not only with the typically continuous evolution of host organization design, but also the ongoing experience of IS successes and failures, or 'IS heritage'. The federal approach provides a framework within which complex organizations can work out the most suitable balance of IS arrangements as events unfold – without catastrophic lurches between the extremes of centralization and decentralization.

12 Information technology outsourcing: a cross-sectional analysis

L. Loh and N. Venkatraman

It is a truism that information technology (IT) has transcended its established administrative support function and has moved toward playing a more central role of business operations (see, for instance, [14, 18, 25, 35]). Within this tradition research efforts have focused on the use of IT to *influence* the boundaries of a firm with its suppliers, buyers, and other intermediaries [6, 8, 21]. There is, however, a glaring lack of research emphasis on the role of IT infrastructure as a *component* of the firm boundary itself. In other words, while IT has been considered a critical mechanism of multiorganizational business relationships, the research stream has treated the governance of IT infrastructure as if it were within one single firm's hierarchy. Such an approach fails to recognize the recent trend toward managing a firm's IT infrastructure through a variety of governance mechanisms with other firms.

Under contractual arrangements popularly termed 'outsourcing,' firms are increasingly shifting specific components of their IT infrastructure away from a 'hierarchical' mode toward a 'market' mode of governance. The well-publicized decision by Eastman Kodak to hand over its entire data center to IBM, its microcomputer operations to Businessland, and its telecommunications and data networks to Digital Equipment Corporation and IBM is a classic illustration [43, 45]. Beside this particular case, it appears that IT outsourcing is becoming a serious strategic option for many firms. The Yankee Group estimated that all Fortune 500 firms would evaluate outsourcing, that a fifth of them would sign outsourcing deals during the 1990s, and that the outsourcing market would increase from $29 billion in 1990 to $49.5 billion in 1994 [7].

IT outsourcing can be dependent on several factors across multiple levels. At the level of the economy, the temporal effects of trends and cycles may motivate firms to rationalize the management of the IT infrastructure through arrangements like outsourcing. At an industry level, competitive pressures may induce firms to establish 'partnership-based' relationships with key IT vendors. At the firm level, the quest for competitive advantage may serve as a critical impetus to the IT outsourcing decision. Within the firm, the decision to outsource may be dependent on several managerial factors. For instance, managers may like to build empires by accumulating control over corporate resources [27] such as the IT infrastructure. Further, the association of information with power [17] may inhibit the outsourcing decision.

The practice of IT outsourcing has been extensively documented in the business periodicals, but there is scant attention provided to articulate its determinants. In other words, we know the phenomenon in some detail but we do not fully grasp the set of factors leading to the outsourcing decision. Our objective in this chapter is to develop a research model on the determinants of IT outsourcing. We recognize the complex array of factors discussed above; but as a first attempt at establishing an empirical model, we focus on factors at the *firm level* with appropriate controls for industry sector effects.

Framework of IT outsourcing

Outsourcing can be framed as a 'make-versus-buy' decision facing a firm. In its generic form, it has been studied in several settings, such as the manufacturing of parts in the automobile industry [30, 40], the sales function in the electronic industry [1], the procurement of components or services in the naval shipbuilding industry [23], and the distribution of equipment, components, and supplies across a broad set of industrial firms [16].

Within the IT profession, the term 'outsourcing' is often viewed as a buzz word that is confusing and often misunderstood [44]. We define IT outsourcing as the *significant contribution by external vendors in the physical and/or human resources associated with the entire or specific components of the IT infrastructure in the user organization*. This definition is consistent with the conceptualization of the IT infrastructure in terms of 'the internal organization of people and resources devoted to computer based systems . . . [involving] both the tangible equipment, staff and applications and the intangible organization, methods and policies by which the organization maintains its ability to provide system services' [22, p. 148].

In the context of IT sourcing, vendors may contribute computer assets for the user. Alternatively, the ownership of certain computer assets of the user may be transferred to the vendor. Similarly, vendors may utilize their personnel to provide the required services, or existing staff of the user may be employed by the vendor. In Figure 1 we depict the distinction between outsourcing and insourcing based on the two dimensions central to our definition: (1) the degree of internalization of physical resources by the user, and (2) the degree of internalization of human resources by the user. By internalization, we mean the ownership of the computer assests or the employment of the system personnel. Several modes of the IT infrastructure have been commonly outsourced by firms. These include applications development, data center systems integration, systems design/planning, telecommunications/network, and time sharing. The modes of IT outsourcing vary through the different levels of contribution of physical and human resources by the user and the vendor. We also illustrate in this figure the typical location of each mode of outsourcing in the delinitional framework.

The various modes of IT outsourcing also differ in the domain of influence within the corporation. Domain of influence refers to the extent to which IT is inherent in the business processes as well as the administrative and functional coordination of the organization. For instance, an application development outsourcing arrangement ordinarily affects a specific domain of

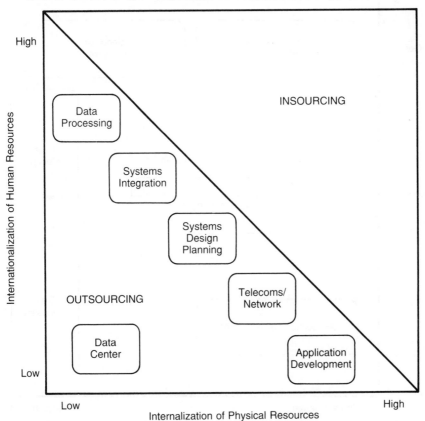

Figure 1. Outsourcing versus insourcing

the firm, while a telecommunications/ network outsourcing arrangement may affect a more general domain of the firm. Further an outsourcing arrangement differs in terms of the contractual mode (i.e. the type of relationship between the user and the vendor as governed by the agreement) for example, a systems design/ planning outsourcing contract may be project based, while a data center operations outsourcing contract may be period based. In Figure 2 we show the characteristics framework and illustrate the various models of IT outsourcing along the two above dimensions.

The research model

In this chapter, we develop a model of the determinants of IT outsourcing, with a particular emphasis on economic constructs from both the business and the IT contexts. Our framework is based on an argument that management should constantly reassess the scope of those activities that

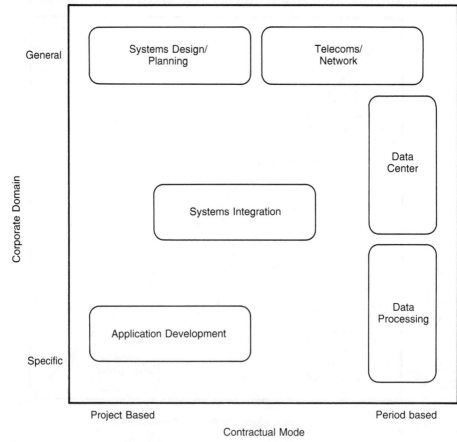

Figure 2. Characteristics of different IT outsourcing modes

should be carried out with a firm's hierarchy and those that are best performed by external partners, including IT vendors. The guiding considerations for such make-versus-buy decisions include: relative cost advantage, and economies of scale and scope. Thus, it is likely that in some cases, an IT vendor may be a more appropriate entity to manage the firm's IT infrastructure than the firm itself. This is because an outsourcing vendor – being a specialist – serves multiple users simultaneously. To the extent that the knowledge, skills, and capacity can be pooled across different customers, there can be benefits of economies of scale, which are otherwise absent when single users perform the same tasks. In addition, the wide variety of IT projects undertaken by the vendors permits the reaping of economies of scope. The lower costs attributable to the vendor also arise from the enhanced IT competence and experience, both of which are absolutely crucial in managing the IT infrastructure in the complex and rapidly changing information era.

We follow Henderson and Venkatraman's [12] model on aligning business and IT domains to derive the specific constructs of the research model. Thus, business and IT strategies are viewed as involving the dimensions competence and governance. Further, we posit that IT governance (specifically, outsourcing) is dependent on the structural characteristics of the user organization, especially business competence, business governance, and IT competence. We elaborate our rationale below.

Business competence

Business cost structure

A well-accepted axiom in the strategy and economics literature is that a firm's business cost structure (the entire spectrum of costs directly associated with the actual production and coordination of the firm's product line) is a significant source of business competence given its role in explaining business profitability (see for instance [32]). Thus, firms try to produce their output below the average cost and are constantly under pressure in a competitive marketplace to reduce the relative cost of business operations. Given the ubiquitous nature of IT, which pervades the entire process of transforming inputs into outputs [33], the costs associated with a particular IT governance include the direct technology cost and indirect cost of supporting the *administration* of the enterprise. Thus, a firm in a situation of high relative cost will seriously consider the available options to reduce its business cost structure, including reassessing the positioning of its IT infrastructure within the scope of the firm's hierarchy.

Therefore we hypothesize that a firm's business cost structure is a crucial determinant of IT outsourcing:

Hypothesis 1: The firm's business cost structure will be positively related to the degree of IT outsourcing.

Business performance

Another component of business competence is reflected by the level of business performance. As noted in a trade periodical: 'Reduced profits . . . are causing management to look everywhere to increase margins' [9, p. 89]. Under conditions of poor business performance, firms often seek to streamline their operations, including selling off or redeploying assets [10]. The traditional view of IT operations as an investment center or a service center is rapidly giving way to an emergent notion of a profit center. Thus, the IT infrastructure is no longer off limits to the management team seeking superior performance. In fact, 'much of what is fanning the fire for . . . outsourcing is that business is having to restructure to remain competitive' [9, p. 90]. When the firm does not perform well vis-à-vis its competition, the need to reevaluate the traditional governance modes of all its major spheres of operations, including the IT arena becomes even greater. We thus seek to test:

Hypothesis 2: The firm's business performance will be negatively related to the degree of IT outsourcing.

Business governance

Financial leverage

The need to reduce reliance on debt financing has been one of the key impetus to outsource the IT infrastructure. Indeed, as widely cited among practitioners, increased debt 'has been a major reason for cutting costs in the IS area, thus supporting the use of outsourcing' [9, p. 90]. Within the context of an imperfect corporate financing environment (see [28]), financial leverage can result in problems relating to financial distress or bankruptcy [3] as well as agency [15]. Further, the cost of equity capital increases with financial leverage [13].

Debt and equity have been argued to be more than alternative financial instruments: they are different business governance structures [47]. Accordingly, it is posited that the choice between debt and equity depends on the characteristics of the assets in which the funds are used. Debt governance is more appropriate for financing redeployable assets, while equity governance is more suitable for nonredeployable assets. Due to the complex and customized nature of systems, application and staff, the degree of redeployability of an installed IT infrastructure may be limited. Thus, debt governance is not the optimal form of business governance. A high level of debt hence results in a need to reduce the non-redeployable assets which then gives use to a greater level of IT outsourcing. Thus we test:

Hypothesis 3: The firm's financial leverage will be positively related to the degree of IT outsourcing.

IT competence

IT cost structure

Investment in IT has recently escalated, and its importance is nowhere less evident than in its dramatic increase from $55 billion to $190 billion in the company in tact. IT accounts for about half of most large firms' capital expenditures [18]. Due to the enormous outlay associated with the IT infrastructure, firms have found it necessary to adopt a better cost control approach to IT. In line with this notion, IT must be treated as a capital investment and not just an overhead of the firm. Firms have been plagued by the astronomic rise of IT expenditure in many specific IT areas that are necessary to run the business. For instance, in the area of application development a critical problem has been the control of the cost of internally conceived software [11]. Consequently, corporations are rationalizing their capital outlay on IT. Where possible drastic restructuring of the traditional inhouse mode of IT governance is undertaken to trim the high cost of IT infrastructure. As Weizer and Associates [42] put it, 'Outsourcing can free capital tied up in data center hardware and save operating costs.'

An extremely attractive option available to firms is to outsource the IT infrastructure to value-added vendors who are more efficient in terms of managing and operating the IT. In three often cited early cases of IT outsourcing, American Standard reportedly saved $2 million per year for its financial and payroll operation. Copperweld cut its systems budget from $8 million to $4 million, and Foodmakers slashed its data processing costs by 17 percent [36]. Other recent cases are Wabco and American Ultramar, which trimmed their annual processing costs from $8 million to $3 million and from $3 million to $1.5 million respectively [46]. We thus seek to verify.

Hypothesis 4: The firm's IT cost structure will be positively relative to the degree of IT outsourcing.

IT performance

With the elevation of the role of IT from the 'backroom' to the monthly of business operations, firms are making IT directly accountable for its direct contribution to the overall corporate profitability. The profit-oriented posture imposed on the IT infrastructure puts intense pressure on the technology to result in tangible economic returns. With the escalating level of IT investments needed to support business in the contemporary marketplace, there is a need to reconfigure the IT infrastructure in ways that make it possible to ascertain the benefits in a clear manner [38]. As IT expenditure has risen rapidly over the last decade [41], it is not surprising that managers are more stringent than ever before in assessing the productivity of their IT infrastructure. Thus, when economic profits fall in

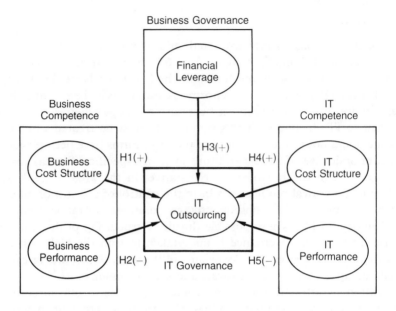

Figure 3. The research framework

relation to IT investments, management faces an immense need to reevaluate the role of IT. As efficiency of organizing is tied intimately to the mode of governance, it is natural that there is a greater shift from the usual inhouse management to external involvement. Indeed, it has been the view within the practicing and consulting IT communities that 'outsourcing is a key strategy that enable [companies to] . . . improve return on equity' [31]. Therefore, we test:

> *Hypothesis 5: The firm's IT performance will be negatively related to the degree of IT outsourcing.*

Figure 3 is a schematic representation of the research model with the five hypotheses.

Methods

Sampler

We began with a sample from the list of companies in a study of 200 major U.S. corporations carried out by G2 Research, Inc., which provided data on their level of IT outsourcing [24]. We also required that the level of total IT expenditure be available for operationalizing some of our independent constructs. Data availability across these two variables limited our study sample to fifty-seven firms (see the appendix for the list of companies). We collected corresponding data on the independent constructs pertaining to back firms in our sample for the fiscal year 1989 from Standard and Poor's Compustat II and Lotus' CD/Corporate on CD-ROM.[1] Thus, our data represents the use of both primary and secondary sources. During discussions with the managers of G2 Research, we ascertained that the data on outsourcing expenditure are an integral part of their professional service to their clients. Our overall assessment is that their method of data collection and verification meets the standards of our research purposes. Further, the integrity of the secondary data sources for the independent constructs is widely accepted within accounting, economics, and finance research.

Operationalization

We need to operationalize four key constructs. For the degree of outsourcing (Y), we developed a ratio of IT outsourcing expenditure to total assets for each firm so that the level of IT outsourcing is normalized by firm size. The business cost structure (X_1), was computed as the sum of the cost of goods sold and the selling, general and administrative expenses, divided by net sales and total assets.[2] Business performance (X_2), was captured by return of assets and earnings per share (fully diluted and excluding extraordinary items), representing the economic efficiency of the entire business as measured by its assets or equity. For financing leverage (X_3), we took the ratios of long-term debt as well as of total liabilities with shareholder equity.

Operationalization of constructs in the IT context is more difficult given the paucity of prior research. The metric used to evaluate the effectiveness of IT has evolved from code analytic (1970-78), through design analytic (1978-84) and function analysis (1984-90), to the current business directed (1990-present) measures [37]. In short, the criteria used are shifting from metrics that focus on IT output to those that focus on the economic outcomes of IT activities. Further, it has been argued that the economic benefit of information systems can be best evaluated by measurements pertaining to the company's entire IT expenditure level, as opposed to the economic benefits derived from individual systems [4]. Thus, for IT cost structure (X_4), we used the ratio of IT expenditure with both gross plant, property, and equipment (i.e., before depreciation) and net plant, property, and equipment (i.e., after depreciation) which is analogous to the extent to which the physical infrastructure of the firm is represented by the IT infrastructure. IT performance (X_5), was measured by net income and sales divided by IT expenditure, which corresponds to the economic efficiency of the IT assets.

In addition, we specified two control variables, one for business size (X_6) and another for industry (X_7). The size variables included net sales and total assets, while binary dummy variables were formed for service and industrial sectors.

Analysis

Due to the possibility of multicollinearity among our independent measures, we performed a factor analysis using the principal components method and a varimax rotation to discern the factor pattern inherent in the data structure. This procedure ensures that the independent constructs used for our subsequent regression are orthogonal. We obtained the corresponding scores associated with a prespecified set of the four factors for the business context and two factors for the IT context. In our multiple regression, we used the ratio of IT outsourcing expenditure to total assets as the dependent variable and the set of factor scores for the business and the IT contexts and the industry sector dummy variable as the independent variables. The econometric specification for our analysis is as follows:

$$(1)\ Y = \beta_0 + \beta_1 X_1 + \beta_2 X_2 + \beta_3 X_3 + \beta_4 X_4 + \beta_5 X_5 + \beta_6 X6_6 + \beta_7 X_7 + \epsilon$$

where ϵ represents the random error.

Results

Descriptive statistics and factor structure

Table 1 summarizes the means and standard deviations for all the individual indicators, while Table 2 provides the matrix of zero-order correlations. In Table 3, we depict the results of factor analysis for the business and IT contexts. With a varimax rotation, four factors in the business context can be interpreted: (1) business performance; (2) business cost structure; (3) business size; and (4) financing leverage. Two factors extracted for the IT context can be interpreted as: (1) IT cost structure, and (2) IT performance.

Test of hypotheses

The results of estimating equation (1) are shown in Table 4. The overall model has an F-value of 2.10 ($p<0.06$), and explains about 24 percent of the variance, which is acceptable for an exploratory research and a limited number of independent variables. In the business context, we accept H1 since the coefficient for business cost structure is significant at the 0.05 level with the expected sign. In the IT context, we accept H4 and H5 since the coefficients for IT cost structure and IT performance are significant at the 0.1 and 0.05 levels, respectively. In contrast, the other two hypotheses (H2 and H3) relating to business performance and financial leverage in the business context are not supported. Further, the two control variables did not emerge as significant.

Table 1 Means and standard deviations

Description	Variable	Mean	Std Dev
Outsourcing Expenditure Total Assets	OSTA	0.002578	0.004085
Cost of Goods Sold+Selling, General & Administrative Expenses Sales	CSSA	0.8336	0.1555
Cost of Goods Sold+Selling, General & Administrative Expenses Total Assets	CSTA	0.6754	0.6706
Long Term Debt Shareholders Equity	LDSE	0.4783	1.989
Total Liabilities/Shareholders Equity	TLSF	5.138	7.005
Return on Assets	REOA	0.02667	0.06765
Earnings per Share ($)	EAPS	3.089	5.257
IT Expenditure Gross Plant, Property & Equipment	ITGP	0.1355	0.1748
IT Expenditure, Net Plant, Property & Equipment	ITNP	0.1522	0.1738
Net Income IT Expenditure	NIIT	2.385	7.298
Sales/IT Expenditure	SAIT	56.91	14.81
Total Assets ($ million)	ASSE	21000	26300
Sales ($ million)	SALE	9405	9877
Service Sector	SERV	0.5965	0.4950
Industrial Sector	INDU	0.4035	0.4950

Discussion

The empirical results provide general support for our research model. First, H1 was accepted, which suggests that the business cost structure is the actual determinant of IT outsourcing. A high level business cost structure may motivate a firm to review its overall cost structure reflected in its costs of physical infrastructure (such as plant and equipment), including its IT infrastructure. Such restructuring may signal to the capital markets the strong commitment of corporate management to improve its business efficiency. Further, as IT pervades the entire value chain of the business, the adoption of IT outsourcing may result in a superior control of the business through the 'variable costing' of IT outsourcing, as opposed to the traditional 'fixed costing' of inhouse governance.

Second, H4, which posited a positive relationship between IT cost structure and outsourcing, was empirically supported. As noted in a trade periodical, 'Outsourcing is being seriously considered in more and more organizations as a potential solution to rising IS [information systems] costs' [9, p. 89]. To compete effectively in the modern information era, complex and costly systems are required to support and propel a corporation in its quest for competitive advantage. In particular, the key compelling force driving companies to outsource is cost savings: 'In some cases, outsourcing vendors have promised to reduce annual IS outlays by 50%, although 15% to 30% savings are more common' [7, p. 47]. Thus, our empirical finding is

Table 2 Correlation matrix

	OSTA	CSSA	CSTA	LDSE	TLSE	REOA	EAPS	ITGP	ITNP	NIIT	SAIT	ASSE	SALE	SERV
CSSA	0.1671													
CSTA	0.2845 (**)	0.4582 (***)												
LDSE	0.0386	-0.0573	-0.0228											
TLSE	-0.1599	-0.2055	-0.430 (***)	0.5079 (***)										
REOA	-0.0828	-0.0949	-0.0347	-0.1775	-0.2447 (*)									
EAPS	-0.0411	0.0603	-0.0056	-0.0934	-0.2148	0.7390 (***)								
ITGP	-0.0120	-0.2361 (*)	-0.3156	0.0802 (**)	0.5963	-0.1010 (***)	-0.0616							
ITNP	0.0200	-0.2058	-0.2709 (**)	0.0829	0.5603 (***)	-0.0861	-0.0228	0.9809 (***)						
NIIT	-0.2769 (**)	-0.1571	-1767	-0.1108	-0.1450	0.8184 (***)	0.6449 (***)	0.0846	0.0831					
SAIT	-0.0978	0.1827	0.5067 (***)	0.0196	-0.2291 (*)	-0.1375	-0.0497	-0.2089	-0.2307 (*)	0.0966				
ASSE	-0.1586	-0.3132 (**)	-0.3759 (***)	0.1348	0.4799 (***)	-0.0474	0.0605	0.2603 (*)	0.2279 (*)	0.0132	-0.1607			
SALE	0.0888	-0.0163	0.0740	0.1069	-0.0586	0.1549	0.2548 (*)	-0.1814	-0.164	0.0581	0.1088	0.6031 (***)		
SERV	-0.2845 (**)	-0.2993 (**)	-0.3162 (**)	0.1664	0.4547 (***)	-0.0161	0.0473	0.2725 (*)	0.2499 (*)	0.1724 -	0.0220 (***)	0.345 (***)	-0.0211	
INDU	0.2845 (**)	0.2992 (**)	0.3162 (**)	-0.1664 (***)	-0.4547 (***)	0.0161	-0.0473	-0.2725 (**)	-0.2499 (*)	-0.1724	0.0220	0.0211 (***)	0.0211	-1.0000 (***)

Note: See Table 1 for a description of the variables. (***), (**), and (*) denote two-tailed significance at 0.01, 0.05, and 0.10 levels respectively.

Table 3 Factor analysis results

3(a) Factor structure for business context

	Factor 1 (Business Performance)	Factor 2 (Business Cost Structure)	Factor 3 (Business Size)	Factor 4 (Financial Leverage)
Eigenvalue	2.3561	1.9860	1.3070	0.9965
Cum. Prop. of Var. Explained	0.2945	0.5428	0.7062	0.8308
Variables		Rotated Factor Pattern		
CCSA	-0.0287	*0.7909*	-0.0645	0.0187
CSTA	-0.0191	*0.8611*	-0.0194	-0.1233
LDSE	-0.0270	0.0981	0.0513	*0.9172*
TLSE	-0.2323	-0.4195	0.1128	*0.7561*
REOA	*0.9257*	-0.0861	0.0009	-0.1503
EAPS	*0.9257*	0.0474	0.1319	-0.0324
ASSE	-0.0586	-0.4225	*0.8217*	0.2159
SALE	0.1780	0.1413	*0.9321*	-0.0132

3(b) Factor structure for IT context

	Factor 1 (IT Cost Structure)	Factor 2 (IT Performance)
Eigenvalue	2.0782	1.0822
Cum. Prop. of Var. Explained	0.5196	0.7902
Variables	Rotated Factor Pattern	
ITGP	*0.9788*	-0.0241
ITNP	*0.9814*	-0.0380
NIIT	0.2032	*0.8246*
SAIT	-0.3246	*0.6409*

Note: See Table 1 for a description of the variables.

consistent with the prevailing view regarding the need to rationalize the IT cost structure in order to stay competitive in the market.

Third, H5, which specified a negative between IT performance and outsourcing, was also empirically supported. Low economic returns on IT investment appear to affect the propensity of firms to outsource more of their IT infrastructure to vendors. The present dilemma facing many IT executives appears to be a justification of investing in an IT infrastructure based on its productivity. Although there are several possible metrics to gauge the performance of IT such as reliability, quality, timeliness, and the like, our results suggest that economic measures are valid indices to evaluate the productivity of IT in terms of the adoption of an efficient mode of IT governance.

Table 4 Multiple regression results

	OLS Estimate	Standard Deviation	Significance
Constant	0.003217	0.000902	(***)
Business Cost Structure (X₁)	0.001498	0.000637	(**)
Business Performance (X₂)	0.000548	0.000623	
Financial Leverage (X₃)	-0.000313	0.000579	
IT Cost Structure (X₄)	0.000806	0.000621	(*)
IT Performance (X₅)	-0.001520	0.000655	(**)
Business Size (X₆)	0.000255	0.000543	
Service Sector (X₇)	-0001017	0.001251	
Model Fit	F=2.10	R2=0.24	

Note (***), (**), and (*) denote one-tailed significance at 0.01, 0.05, and 0.10 levels respectively.

Fourth, we did not find empirical support for H2 – which specified a negative relationship between business performance and outsourcing and H3 – which specified a positive relationship between financial leverage and outsourcing. The general implication from these two results is that business performance and financial leverage may be too far removed in terms of influencing the level of IT outsourcing directly. Although we specified direct effects, which were not empirically supported, we urge that future research consider indirect effects (for example, through business and/or IT cost structures) or moderator effects.

Finally, both business size and industry sector as control variables did not emerge as significant determinants. The implication is that our results are generally robust and valid across firms differing in sizes (within the spectrum covered by the sample) as well as industry versus service categorization.

Toward a comprehensive model of IT governance

While we have provided some empirical support for a set of conventional wisdom regarding IT outsourcing in this paper, we recognize the limited scope of our model. We suggest a set of directions for refining this line of inquiry in the future. As we move away from the consideration of a firm-level focus using a neoclassical economic perspective, we identify three avenues of future research: (a) an organizational economic model of IT outsourcing; (b) a diffusion process model of IT outsourcing; and (c) an organizational process model of IT outsourcing.

An organizational economic model of IT outsourcing

Research in the general arena of make-versus-buy (including outsourcing) has been anchored within an organizational economic perspective [2], especially transaction cost theory (for a review, see [48]). In addition, agency theory with particular emphasis on constructs such as goal alignment, incentive payment, and monitoring [15] has the potential to provide insights on the governance of IT outsourcing. Moreover, it may be appropriate to reflect refinements such as the articulation of bargaining and influence costs [26] in the governance of IT infrastructure. For instance, constructs relevant to bargaining costs may involve coordination failure and information acquisition/asymmetry, and those related to influence costs may include exchange facilitation and competition foreclosure. While the present dataset did not allow us to operationalize constructs from an organizational economic perspective, a research design involving primary data from organizational informants would allow us to better understand and predict not only the degree of IT outsourcing (as done in the present study), but also the mode of outsourcing (see Figures 1 and 2). We are in the midst of such a study.

A diffusion process model of IT outsourcing

In this chapter, we have developed a 'variance' model [29] for explaining IT outsourcing. We can adopt the view that an IT outsourcing arrangement constitutes an administrative innovation [19, 39]. Such an argument is based on the emergent departure of many firms from an established hierarchical mode of governing the IT infrastructure toward a market mode. Outsourcing fundamentally transforms the traditional requirements of managing IT from those rooted on an adversarial, 'arms-length' approach to those structured on a cooperative 'partnership-based' relationship. Using a macro-organizational level of analysis, the diffusion model will specifically examine the underlying force that motivates firms to adopt IT outsourcing. With this approach we can analyze whether the diffusion of IT outsourcing can be explained by imitative behavior. The findings are interesting in view of the prominence of the Kodak-IBM outsourcing contract which purportedly encouraged many other firms to consider such a governance option seriously [34]. We are currently pursuing this diffusion-of-innovation study of IT outsourcing.

An organizational process model of IT outsourcing

Another complementary extension would be to focus on the organizational routines underlying the management of this IT mode of governance by developing an organizational process model. Such a research initiative would go a long way in enhancing our understanding of the new phenomenon in the marketplace. The process model may incorporate new structures (e.g., shared authority, responsibility, property rights, and risk-bearing), management processes (e.g., allocation and coordination of resources, performance assessment, and joint planning), and managerial roles (e.g., liaison, decision making, and leadership) that are required to derive the benefits from this mechanism effectively.

Conclusion

Based on data from large US corporations, we empirically identified a set of important determinants – reflecting both IT and business contexts – of IT outsourcing. Thus, we offer the first empirical assessment of a set of widely held assertions and beliefs as to why firms outsource their IT infrastructure. We have also identified some important directions for extending this line of inquiry – reflecting an organizational economic view, a diffusion-of-innovation view, and an organizational process view.We hope that our attempt at empirically testing this emergent phenomenon will stimulate others to look at this important strategic challenge facing firms from a rigorous theoretical perspective. Such research initiatives will allow us not only to better understand this complex phenomenon, but also to derive useful management prescriptions grounded on systematic theory-based research.

Notes

1 The final sample size is 55 due to missing data in Compustat and CD/ Corporate. Our sample comprises a rough split between industrial and service firms (about 40-60). The selection is limited by the availability of data across multiple sources. It is possible that the primary data regarding IT expenditures may have been skewed, since our sources surveyed only large corporate users of IT (e.g., firms within the Fortune 500 and Fortune Service 500 categories). In our sample, the level of IT expenditures as a percentage of revenue is 1.8 percent. This is compared with another survey [20] that obtained figures for ten different industries, ranging from 0.9 percent to 4.2 percent. Although the set of companies used is not a random sample of the entire population of firms in the economy, we believe that our choice of data sources allows us to include a sample that is representative of the set of major users of IT (i.e., large firms).

2 It is necessary to sum these two 'costs' as the accounting treatment is not consistent for industrial and service firms in the sample.

References

1   Anderson, E. The saleperson as outside agent or employee: a transaction cost analysis. *Marketing Science*, 4, 3 (1985), 234-253.
2   Barney, J. B., and Ouchi, W. G., eds. *Organizational Economics*. San Francisco: Jossey-Bass, 1986.
3   Baxter, N. Leverage, Risk of ruin and the cost of capital. *Journal of Finance*, 22, 3 (1967), 395-403.

4   Bender, D. H. Financial impact of information processing. *Journal of Management Information Systems*, 3, 2 (1986), 22-110.
5   Buzzell, R. D., and Gale, B. T. *The PIMS Principles*. New York: Free Press, 1987.
6   Cash, J.I., and Konsynski, B. IS redraws competitive boundaries. *Harvard Business Review*, 63, 2 (March-April 1985), 134-142.
7   Eckerson, W. Changing user needs driving outsourcing. *Network World*, July 2, 1990, pp. 1, 47.
8   Gurbaxani, V., and Whang, S. The impact of information systems on organizations and markets. *Communications of the ACM*, 34, 1 (January 1991), 59-73.
9   Hammersmith, A. G. Slaying the IS dragon with outsourcery. *Computerworld*, September 18, 1989, pp. 89-93.
10   Harrigan, K. R. *Strategies for Declining Businesses*. Lexington, MA: Lexington Books, 1980.
11   Helms, G. L., and Weiss, I. R. The cost of internally developed applications: analysis of problems and cost control methods. *Journal of Management Information Systems*, 3, 2 (1986), 5-32.
12   Henderson, J., and Venkatraman, N. Strategic alignment: a model for organizational transformation through information technology, In T. Kochan and M. Useem, eds., *Transforming Organizations*. New York: Oxford University Press, 1992.
13   Hsia, C.C. Coherence of the modern theories of finance. *Financial Review*, 16, 1 (1981), 59-82.
14   Ives, B., and Learnmonth, G. P. The information system as a competitive weapon. *Communications of the ACM*, 27, 12 (December 1984), 1193-1201.
15   Jensen, M., and Meckling, W. H. Theory of the firm: managerial behaviour, agency costs, and ownership structure. *Journal of Financial Economics*, 3, 3 (1976), 305-360.
16   John, G., and Weitz, B. A. Forward integration into distribution: an empirical test of transaction cost analysis. *Journal of Law, Economics, and Organization*, 4, 2 (1988), 337-355.
17   Kanter, R. M Power failure in management circuits. *Harvard Business Review*, 57, 4 (July-August 1979), 65-75.
18   Keen, P. G. W. *Shaping the Future: Business Design through Information Technology*. Boston: Harvard Business School Press, 1991.
19   Loh, L., and Venkatraman, N. Information technology outsourcing as an administrative innovation: imitative behaviour as an explanation of the diffusion pattern. MIT Sloan School of Management Working Paper, December 1991.
20   Maglitta, J., and Sullivan-Trainor, M. L. Do the right thing(s). *Computerworld*. September 30, 1991, section 2, pp. 6-12.
21   Malone, T. W.; Yates, J.; and Benjamin, R. I. Electronic markets and electronic hierarchies. *Communications of the ACM*, 30, 6 (June 1987), 484-497.
22   Markus, M. 1. *Systems in Organizations*. Marshfield, MA: Pitman, 1984.
23   Masten, S. E.; Meehan, J. W.; and Snyder, E. A. The costs of organization. *Journal of Law, Economics and Organization*, 7, 1 (1991), 1-25.
24   McCormick, J. J. Outsourcing action. *Information Week*, September 10, 1990, pp. 84-92.
25   McFarlan, F. W. Information technology changes the way you compete. *Harvard Business Review*, 62, 3 (May-June 1984), 98-103.
26   Milgrom, P., and Roberts, D. J. Bargaining costs, influence costs, and the organization of economic activity. In J. Alte and K. Shepsle, eds., *Perspectives on Positive Political Economy*. Cambridge: Cambridge University Press, 1990.
27   Mintzberg, H. *Power In and Around Organizations*. Englewood Cliffs, NJ: Prentice Hall, 1983.
28   Modigliani, F., and Miller, M. Corporate income taxes and the cost of capital: a correction. *American Economic Review*, 53, 3 (1963), 433- 443.
29   Mohr, L. *Explaining Organizational Behavior*. San Francisco: Jossey-Bass, 1982.
30   Monteverde, K., and Teece, D. Supplier switching costs and vertical integration in the

automobile industry. *Bell Journal of Economics*, 13, 1 (1982), 206-213.

31   Oltman, J. R. 21st century outsourcing. *Computerworld* April 16, 1990, pp. 77-79.

32   Porter, M.E. *Competitive Strategy*. New York: Free Press, 1980.

33   Porter, M. E., and Millar, V. E. How information gives you competitive advantage. *Harvard Business Review*, 63, 4 (July-August 1985), 149-160.

34   Radding, A. The dollars and sense of outsourcing: the ride is no bargain if you can't steer. *Computerworld*, January 8, 1990, pp. 67- 72.

35   Rockart, J. F., and Scott Morton, M. S. Implications of changes in information technology for corporate strategy. *Interfaces*, 14, 1 (1984), 84-95.

36   Rothfeder, J. More companies are chucking their computers. *Business Week*, June 19, 1989, pp. 72-74.

37   Rubin, H. Measure for measure. *Computerworld*, April 15, 1991, pp. 77-78.

38   Strassmann, P. A. *The Business Value of Computers*. New Canaan, CT: The Information Economics Press, 1990.

39   Teece, D. The diffusion of an administrative innovation. *Management Science*, 26, 5 (1980), 464-470.

40   Walker, G., and Weber, D. A transaction cost approach to make-or-buy decisions. *Administrative Science Quarterly*, 29, 3 (1984, 373- 391.

41   Weill, P., and Olson, M. H. Managing investment in information technology: mini-case examples and implications. *MIS Quarterly*, 13, 1 (1989), 3-17.

42   Weizer, N., and Associates. *The Arthur D. Little Forecast on Information Technology and Productivity; Making the Integrated Enterprise Work*. New York: John Wiley, 1991.

43   Wilder, C. Kodak hands processing over to IBM. *Computerworld*, July 31, 1989, pp. 1, 6.

44   Wilder, C. Outsourcing: fad or fantastic? *Computerworld*, December 25/January 1, 1989-90, p. 8.

45   Wilder, C. DEC, IBM play ball in Kodak deal. *Computerworld*, January 15, 1990, p. 8.

46   Wilder, C. Outsourcing: from fad to respectability. *Computerworld*, June 11, 1990, pp. 1, 122.

47   Williamson, O.E. Corporate finance and corporate governance. *Journal of Finance*, 43, 3 (1988), 567-591.

48   Williamson, O. E. Transaction cost economics. In R. Schmalensee and R. D. Willig, eds., *Handbook of Industrial Organization*. Amsterdam: North-Holland, 1989.

Appendix: List of companies in the sample

Aetna Life and Casualty Co
Air Products and Chemicals
Amax Inc
Armco Inc
Ashland Oil Inc
Atlantic Richfield Co
Bank of Boston Corp
Bankamerica Corp
Baxter International Inc
Champion International Corp
Chrysler Corp
Consolidated Rail Corp
Continental Bank Corp
Control Data Corp
Corning Inc
CSX Corp
Dow Chemical Co

Harrier Inc
Homefed Corp
Illinois Power Co
Ingersoll Rand Co
Keycorp
Lincoln National Corp
Mack TRUCKS Inc
Manufacturers Hanover Corp
NCR Corp
Norfolk Southern Corp
PNC Financial Corp
Quantum Chemical Corp
Reynolds Metals Co
Rockwell International Corp
Rohm and Haas Co
SCECorp
Security Pacific Corp

E I Du Pont De Nemours and Co
Duke Power Co
Eastman Kodak Co
Entergy Corp
First Bank System Inc
Fleming Cos Inc
Geico Corp
General Dynamics Corp
General Electric Co
General Re Corp
Great Western Financial Corp
GTE Corp

Sun Co Inc
Texaco Inc
Textron Inc
Travelers Corp
UAL Corp
Union Carbide Corp
Unisys Corp
United Technologies Corp
US Air Group Inc
Valley National Corp
Westinghouse Electric Corp

13 Organizational factors affecting the success of end-user computing

P. H. Cheney, R. I. Mann and D. L. Amoroso

Introduction

Although end-user computing (EUC) is still in its early stages, signs of rapid growth are evident. Companies studied by Rockart and Flannery [53] experienced annual EUC growth rates of 50 to 90%, while their traditional data processing systems were growing at a much smaller annual rate of 5 to 15%. Benjamin [8] has predicted that by 1990 EUC will absorb as much as 75% of the corporate computer resource. Edelman [22] estimated that at least ten cents out of every revenue dollar is spent on the management of information, a far cry from the traditional management information systems (MIS) rule of thumb which places the MIS budget at 1% of sales. Edelman goes on to state that at RCA traditional data processing accounts for 10% of the MIS budget, administrative systems for 20%, and the white-collar labor contingent for 70%.

The increasing proliferation of EUC is obvious from the above evidence. If the concomitant problems in the areas of security, integrity, documentation, and accountability are not addressed quickly, we may see management imposing drastic cutbacks on the organizational use of EUC. Confusion, inefficiency, and a perceived or real lack of productivity may force management into constraining what we believe to be a major force in the management of the information resource through the end of this century. For these reasons the identification of variables that may affect the success of end-user computing facilities (EUCF) within an organization is extremely important.

Nolan and Wetherbe [48] presented a research model which viewed MIS as an open system which transforms data, requests for information, and organizational resources into information within the *context of an organization*. Similarly, Ives, Hamiltion, and Davis [34] classified existing MIS research and generated illustrative hypotheses using a research model which described the interactions between three classes of variables: *the environment, the process,* and *the information system*. These researchers, among others [9, 14, 23, 27, 28, 32], recognize the importance of organizational characteristics as a potential influence on MIS success. This chapter attempts to identify organizational variables affecting the success or failure of EUC within an organization. Propositions relating the variables to EUC success are presented and supported by logical arguments and previous research findings.

The source of data for this chapter was a survey of the academic and trade literature. Only recently have EUC issues appeared in the literature with any regularity. Most of these publications contained conceptualizations about end-user computing based on practical experience; a smaller number represented empirical studies. To the extent that conceptualizations are based on experience, they are a valid source of data in an environment in which empirical data are in short supply. We will attempt to segregate conceptual and empirical findings whenever possible.

The literature review yielded a list of organizational context variables as well as data and opinions concerning those variables. Few of the concepts and opinions have as yet been tested; thus, the results of this investigation are presented as a series of propositions that represent the dominant positions on the issues examined. The propositions are not intended to be formal hypotheses; rather, they are stated as general research questions which will require more extensive empirical investigation.

Our view of organizational end-user computing

We take a very broad view of EUC and basically adopt the Rockart and Flannery [53] categorization of end users. They defined six distinct types of end users within organizations.

- nonprogramming end users who access data through predeveloped menu-driven software packages;
- command level end users who generate unique reports for their own purposes, usually with simple query languages;
- end-user programmers who utilize command and procedural languages to access, manipulate, and process data for their personal information needs:
- functional support personnel who produce end-user software for managers within their functional area;
- end-user computing support personnel who develop application and/or decision support software within an information center environment.

● data processing (DP) programmers who accumulate knowledge concerning relevant hardware, software, communications, and management that will facilitate end-user computing within the organization.

The dependent variable for our propositions is end-user computing success. Previous literature has suggested several measures for information systems success. These include user information satisfaction, system utilization, decision effectiveness, organizational performance (e.g., return on investment, profitability), and the application of computer-based information systems to the major problems of the organization [35]. Critical success factors, if identifiable, have also been cited as a measure of information systems success [52].

We assume that an end user will utilize EUC facilities only when they

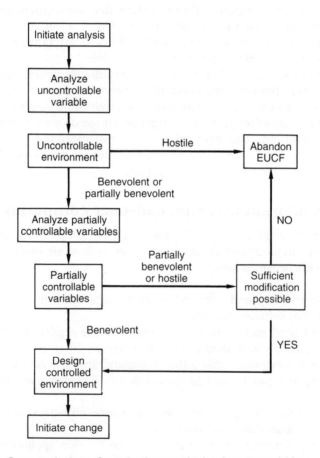

Figure 1. Conceptual scheme for evaluating organizational context variables

meet at least some of the criteria cited above. Unless use is mandatory, information systems are used extensively only when they are perceived to be of value to the end user. We, among others, believe that *utilization* is highly correlated with the other surrogate measures of MIS and EUC success [43, 51, 57, 58]. Organizational performance and decision effectiveness are difficult measures to use due to the numerous intervening environmental variables that tend to influence them.

Several instruments have been developed and validated to measure user information satisfaction [2, 6, 22, 36]; therefore, end-user information satisfaction and system utilization statistics provide readily available surrogate measures for EUCF success. If other criteria cited above are tractable, they should be used as well.

A conceptual scheme

Ein-Dor and Segev [24] suggest a useful conceptual scheme for relating organizational context variables and MIS success. That scheme, which we adopt here, categorizes independent variables as uncontrollable, partially controllable, or fully controllable. The classification permits a stepwise analysis of the organizational context variables as they relate to EUC success, making the scheme useful for evaluating either existing or planned end-user computing facilities (see Figure 1).

The uncontrollable variables are those whose status is given with respect to the EUCF. They are uncontrollable because the information systems executive responsible for the EUCF has little or no control over the factors or because the time frame for change is longer than can be tolerated. The variables in this group are the task technology variables and the organizational time frame. If analysis of the uncontrollable variables reveals a totally hostile environment, there is no point in continuing the operation of an existing EUCF or planning for the establishment of such facilities.

If the uncontrollable variables appear to be partially or wholly benevolent, then the partially controllable variables should be analyzed. The partially controllable variables are those in which change in the desired direction can be induced within an acceptable period of time. The variables in this group include the existing systems development backlog and the psychological climate (management attitudes toward EUC.) The fully controllable variables are those that are totally under the control of management. They include the rank of the executive responsible for EUC, end-user training, and corporate end-user computing policies.

In order to establish the feasibility of using these variables, suggestions for operationalizing them are provided in Table 1. Interactions between variables are possible. All of the variables interact with EUC success, the dependent variable. In some cases there may be a feedback relationship where EUC success affects specific variables. This indicates that those

Table 1   Suggested operational measures for EUC variables

Variable	Operational measure
Uncontrollable	
1 Task technology variables	
a management activities	strategic planning executives; management control executives; operational control managers (classify by organizational chart and position title)
b task structuredness	classify as unstructured; semistructured and structured via the task's description
c task repetitiveness	how frequently is the task performed
d task interdependence	classify the task as independent; pooled interdependent or sequential interdependent via its description
2 Organizational time frame	planning horizon; rate of technological change within the industry
Partially controllable	
3 Psychological climate	attitudes toward EUC; expectations about EUC
4 Systems development backlog	mean number of months to begin a software development project once it is approved
Fully controllable	
5 End-user computing (EUC) training	variety (tutorials, consultants, documentation, formal classes, programmed instruction, computer-assisted instruction (CAI), help command, external assistance) and availability of training
6 Rank of EUC executive	number of levels below CIO (Chief Information Officer)
7 EUC policies	existence and quality of EUC policy manuals

variables and EUC success are mutually dependent. Psychological climate and the systems development backlog in particular are affected by, and in turn impact, EUC success.

Propositions: suggestions for research

The following propositions represent suggestions for future research in the area of end-user computing. Each of the variables and the interactions between them is discussed, and previous research in the area is cited. Table 2 summarizes the references and the propositions to which they relate. Each reference is categorized as an empirical study (E), a survey study (S), a case study (C), or a theoretical argument (T).

Table 2   Proposition-related references

Reference number	Author(s)	Background	1	2	3	4	5	6	7	8	9	10	11	12
1	Adams, 1975		E								E			
2	Ahituv, 1980	T												
3	Alexander, 1980							T						
4	Alloway, Quillard, 1983					E				E	E			
5	Argyris, 1971								T					
6	Bailey, Pearson, 1983	E												
7	Barkin, Dickson, 1977						E							
8	Benjamin, 1982	T					T		T		T			
9	Bennett, 1976	C			C	C								
10	Benson, 1983	E				E			E					
11	Brady, 1967									T				
12	Canning, 1981									T				
13	Carlson, Grace, Sutton, 1977					C								
14	Cheney, 1984	E												
15	Cheney, Dickson, 1982						E				E			
16	Culnan, 1983			E	E									
17	Davis, Olson, 1985											S/E		
18	Dearden, 1972							T						
19	DeBrabander, Edstrom, 1977						E							
20	Dickson et al,. 1984									S				
21	Dickson, Simmons, 1970		S											
22	Edelman, 1981	T												
23	Edstrom, 1977	E						E						
24	Ein-Dor, Segev, 1978	T					T							
25	Ein-Dor, Segev, 1982										E			
26	Franz, Killingsworth, 1982							E						
27	Gallagher, 1974	E		E										
28	Gingras, McLean, 1982	E		E										
29	Ginzberg, 1978							C						
30	Guthrie, 1974												S	
31	Hammond, 1974		T					T						
32	Heany, 1972	T/C												
33	Henderson, Treacy, 1984	S												S
34	Ives, Hamilton, Davis, 1980	T												
35	Ives, Olson, 1984	S												
36	Ives, Olson, Barudi, 1983	E												
37	Jenkins, 1977								E					
38	Johnson, 1984								C					
39	Lefkovits, 1979	T												
40	Lucas, 1973				S		S			S			S	

Table 2   (continued)

Reference number	Author(s)	Back-ground	1	2	3	4	5	6	7	8	9	10	11	12
												Proposition number		
41	Lucas, 1975		E			E				E				
42	MacIntosh, Daft. 1978				E	E								
43	Maish, 1979	E												
44	Manley, 1975												T	
45	Mann, Watson, 1984					T								
46	McCartney, 1983					T								
47	McLean, 1979			E			E			E				
48	Nolan, Wetherbe, 1980	T												
49	Reimann, Waren, 1985	E												
50	Rivard, Huff, 1984												E	
51	Robey, 1979	E												
52	Rockart, 1979	T												
53	Rockart, Flannery, 1983	E				E							E	E
54	Rockart, Treacy, 1982										S/C			
55	Schonberger, 1980		S	S										
56	Sprague, Carlson, 1982									T/S				
57	Swanson, 1976	S												
58	Swanson, 1978	T												
59	Wegner, 1971										E			

S = survey
E = empirical research
T = theoretical
C = case

Uncontrollable variables

Task Technology

Proposition 1. *The higher the level of management activity being supported, the more likely the success of an EUCF.*

End-user computing can be considered as the ultimate user involvement in IS development. Several authors [1, 27, 28, 41] have found a positive relationship between the perceived value of information systems and managerial position. Gingras and McLean [28] noted that managerial level is positively related to the amount and quality of system use. In addition Dickson and Simmons [21] noted that, the higher the managerial level, the less resistance to change is encountered. Schonberger [55] states that greater user involvement is needed at higher management levels due to the decision-oriented nature of the computer applications at the strategic planning level. Because top management recognizes the importance and value of information systems, they are less resistant to change and they recognize that their involvement is necessary if decision support applications are to be successful. As a result they will be more involved with and concerned about the success of the EUCF. Although we suspect that the upper levels of management may have neither the time nor the inclination to develop their own software, they will in many cases interact closely with their support staff in order to acquire and use the EUCF to meet their needs [1, 21, 27, 28]. To the extent that these needs are satisfied, the likelihood of a successful EUCF is enhanced.

Proposition 2. *The more structured the tasks being performed by the end-user, the more likely the success of the* EUCF.

Although this proposition may appear to contradict the former, we are positing each independently of the others. Given the level of management activity, the more structured the task, the easier the development process. Hence the greater likelihood of success.

Several authors [16, 31, 42] have noted that additional tools, procedures, and techniques are necessary when developing systems to support unstructured task situations. The information needs of end users are much more difficult to identify and specifically define in unstructured situations [16, 31, 40, 42, 55]. Culnan [16] also states that, the more unstructured the task, the more sophisticated the needed mode of access.

Proposition 3. *The more repetitive the task being supported, the more likely the success of the* EUCF.

Although task repetitiveness does not appear to have any consistent relationship with user involvement in the development of a decision support system [45], some authors believe that it is unlikely that end users will often develop software to support ad hoc, one-time tasks [4, 13]. Others [10, 6, 53] contradict this point. The more repetitive the task, the clearer the frame of reference and the easier it is for the end user to formulate procedures to solve problems [13]. Even though there is no complete agreement on this point, we believe it requires further investigation. Information reporting, data base management, office automation, and institutionalized decision support systems represent the tasks most easily supported by end-user computing facilities [9, 10, 42].

Proposition 4. *The more interdependent the tasks being supported, the more likely the success of an* EUCF.

Some evidence exists [9, 15] that higher levels of task interdependence enourage higher levels of user involvement. Tasks that are highly interrelated have less well defined information needs initially and tend to evolve over time. Traditional systems development methodologies demand the specification of clearly defined requirements prior to system design. These requirements imply that interdependent tasks may be better supported as end-user-developed systems. Several authors [8, 13] have noted that different users develop different problem-solving approaches. The approaches used by problem solvers depend upon the needed integration across organizational areas. Barkin and Dickson [7] state that the relationship of tasks to other tasks can positively affect information systems utilization. Others [19, 40, 41, 42] state that strategic planners require a higher level of integration than the management and operational control management groups.

Organizational time frame

Proposition 5. *The shorter the organizational time frame, the greater the likelihood of* EUC *success.*

Ein-Dor and Segev [24] proposed that, the shorter the organizational time frame, the greater the likelihood of MIS failure. This would be likely because traditional systems development is a time-consuming process, whereas setting up an EUCF would take a shorter time. If the time frame for the development process is longer than the time frame of the organizational need, the traditional systems development approach is not capable of solving the organization's information problems. McLean [47] states the systems development task can be transferred to the user subject to consideration of the organizational time frame, maintenance problems, and the scope and orientation of the applications developed. The overall organizational time frame is composed of a combination of individual time horizons. The shorter the time horizon, the more satisfied the user is with the EUCF, primarily because it is the only way such persons can get the systems they need [24, 31, 47]. Users have become impatient with the systems development backlog and the long development times once their projects are finally begun. EUC facilities, with their relatively short development time frames, are particularly useful in these situations, thus enhancing the likelihood of their success [47].

Partially controllable variables

Psychological climate

Proposition 6. *The more realistic the expectations of top management, information systems professionals, and end users, the greater the likelihood of* EUC *success.*

Every organization develops its own psychological climate with respect to EUC just as it does with every other aspect of MIS. This climate is established by the members of the organization including top management, information systems professionals, and end users.

Unrealistic expectations may be self-induced or they may be fostered by experts. In the unrealistically high direction, end users expect more from the EUCF than is reasonable. Management has often perceived that computer hardware and software products have been oversold. The products, in many cases, never performed as effectively as the salesperson had promised.

Alternatively, sources of low expectations concerning EUC are the less than satisfactory EUC experiences of other organizations. The impact of horror stories has, in the case of MIS, deterred organizations from adopting specific systems or technologies [3, 18, 23, 29]. If the system is adopted, managers often refrain from making any significant demands on the new system or they may not participate in the design, development, or implementation of the system. The lack of confidence and user involvement in the development process are indications of unrealistic user expectations. Unrealistic expectations (low or high) inhibit EUC success.

Franz and Killingsworth [26] noted that the users with the most training and experience will have formed expectations about an information system which are closer in line with those of the analysts and designers of the system. In these situations expectations tend to be more realistic.

Systems development backlog

Proposition 7. *The larger the existing systems development backlog of projects, the greater the likelihood of* EUCF *success.*

It is estimated that the formal systems development backlog in most organizations is three to four years [10]. These large backlogs stem primarily from the shortage of systems development personnel. A common user complaint is that there are not enough analysts and programmers to keep up with the demand for new systems. There are several alternative solutions to this problem including: (1) making analysts and programmers more productive, (2) increasing the utilization of software packages, and (3) transferring the development function from the systems staff to end users [5]. The latter alternative is appropriate when end users can do the task satisfactorily and have an adequate EUCF for applications development.

Another important systems development backlog consists of the applications that end users fail to propose formally because costs of these projects are difficult to justify and because the existing formal backlog is already so large that even if the project were approved it would be years before development could begin. This 'invisible backlog' is reputed to be 4 to 5 years in length at most organizations and is in addition to the known formal backlog [4, 11]. Alloway and Quillard [4] state that this 'invisible backlog' is 784% greater for managerial support systems than for transaction processing systems. They also state that the actual backlog may be overstated if it includes projects which have not as yet been formally approved. Obviously, the larger these two backlogs (i.e., formal and invisible), the greater the propensity for establishing an EUCF. Once the system is established, the probability of the EUCF succeeding should also be enhanced.

Fully controllable variables

EUC training

Proposition 8. *The availability of end-user training is positively related to the success of the* EUCF.

Educational program development has received attention in the MIS literature for over two decades beginning with Brady's 1967 study, which suggested that lack of education is a major reason for the lack of MIS utilization [11]. A more recent study of the key information system issues for the 1980s ranked 'user education' as the sixth most important issue [20]. A number of researchers have included the education of end users as a component in their research frameworks (35, 40, 48]. Lucas [41] notes that 'the older and less educated member of the organization is most likely to resist a computer based system.' Sprague and Carlson [56] suggest several different educational techniques including tutorials (one student-one instructor); professional development seminars; programmed instruction; computer-assisted instruction; resident experts; and 'help' components in software packages. Education is a major activity of the traditional MIS systems development process. It is also a major type of support provided by information centers [12, 38]. Additional research into the most effective forms of end-user education is needed.

Rank of the responsible executive

Proposition 9. The likelihood of a successful EUCF *declines rapidly, the lower the rank of the executive responsible for the* EUCF.

Experience, supported by the findings of several studies, suggests that the likelihood of MIS success, including the success of EUC, declines rapidly, the lower the rank of the executive to whom the EUC or MIS chief reports. In the case of overall MIS activities the chief information officer (CIO) must be no more than two levels removed from the chief executive office (CEO) [15, 17]. As EUC becomes more important, we believe the same argument holds on a different scale. The domain of the CIO used to be primarily in data processing. Today he/she is often responsible for office automation; data, voice, and image communication; and decision support, as well as the traditional data processing function [1]. Alloway and Quillard [4] state that the management of the information systems resource should occur at the very highest management levels if the MIS function is to be successful. Ein-Dor and Segev [25] found a significant correlation between the rank of the MIS director and MIS success. In our opinion it is imperative that the director of the EUCF report directly to the CIO if the maximum benefits from the facility are to be achieved [1, 57].

Corporate policies

Proposition 10. The establishment of corporate policies covering the creation and operation of the EUCF *will increase the likelihood of* EUCF *success.*

It is not sufficient to merely build and support systems; these projects must meet overall organizational objectives and sustain a level of quality and completeness that is appropriate to the organizational unit and decision activity [17]. In the traditional development of information systems, the analyst provides an independent review of the information requirements and systems design specifications. The analyst also provides an organizational mechanism for enforcing appropriate standards and practices in the areas of testing, documentation, programming controls, operating controls, audit trails, and interfaces with other systems [17, 53]. These same controls are needed when end users develop, maintain, and use their own systems. Benjamin [8] was among the first to recognize that the rapid growth in end-user computing will cause information systems management to develop policy and control mechanisms for the management of the EUCF. He states that the traditional policy and control methods may not work in this area and new ones will have to be developed.

Interactions between variables

EUC success and psychological climate

Proposition 11. EUC *success and psychological climate are mutually dependent.*

Attitudes and expectations play an important role in establishing the psychological climate in an organization before the installation of MIS, whether it is developed by MIS professionals or by end users [23, 30]. Once a system has been installed, the pyschological climate is also affected by the end users' experiences with it. End-user attitudes are substantially affected. Lucas and others have found that the quality of the system determines the attitudes towards it [40, 44]. Good experiences with the EUCF and EUC systems generate favorable attitudes and encourage continued widespread use of the EUCF.

Successful MIS efforts have been linked in several studies to a favorable psychological climate [44, 50], but little study has been done relative to EUC activity. Research in this area promises to add greatly to our understanding of EUC successes and failures and the ability of management to establish a favorable EUC organizational environment.

EUC success and systems development backlog

Proposition 12. EUC *success and the systems development backlog are mutually dependent.*

The lack of enough analysts and programmers has been a principal reason for establishing corporate EUCFs. As the EUCF successfully designs, develops, operates, and maintains new systems this will reduce the existing systems development backlog. However, if the EUC systems do not work it will increase the systems development backlog [33, 53].

Remarks

We have attempted to identify a set of organizational factors potentially affecting the success or failure of end-user computing in an organization. In doing so we have adopted a conceptual scheme within which these variables might be analyzed by management. The desired outcome from the analysis is either the abandonment of a doomed EUCF or the design of a controlled environment within which the EUCF may flourish.

In addition, we have advanced a set of propositions for research. Neither the set of organizational variables nor the set of propositions is expected to be complete. We encourage researchers to expand our set of variables and propositions, as well as to conduct empirical studies on the research questions raised by this chapter.

References

1 Adams, C. R. How management users view information systems. *Decision Sciences*, 6 (1975), 337–345.

2 Ahituv, N. A systematic approach toward assessing the value of an information system. *Management Information Systems Quarterly*, 4, 4 (December 1980), 61–75.

3 Alexander, T. Computers can't solve everything. *Fortune*, 80, 5.

4 Alloway, R.M., and Quillard, J. A. User managers' systems needs. *Management Information Systems Quarterly*, 7, 2 (June 1983), 27–43.

5 Argyris, C. Management information systems: the challenge to rationality and emotionality. *Management Science*, 17, 6 (February 1971), 275–292.

6 Bailey, J. E., and Pearson, S. W. Development of a tool for measuring and analyzing computer user satisfaction. *Management Science*, 29, 5 (May 1983), 530–545.

7 Barkin, S. R., and Dickson, G. W. An investigation of information system utilization. *Information and Management*, 1 (1977), 35–45.

8 Benjamin, R. I. Information technology in the 1990s: a long range planning scenario. *Management Information Systems Quarterly*, 6, 2 (June 1982), 11–31.

9 Bennett, J. Integrated users and decision support systems. *Proceedings of the 6th and 7th Annual Conferences of the Society for Management Information Systems* (1976), 77–86.

10 Benson, D. H. A field study of end user computing: findings and issues. *Management Information Systems Quarterly*, 7, 4 (December 1983), 35–45.

11 Brady, R. H. Computers in top-level decision making. *Harvard Business Review* (July–August 1967), 67–76.

12 Canning, R. G. Supporting end-user programming. *EDP Analyzer*, 19, 6 (June 1981).

13 Carlson, E. D.; Grace, B. F.; and Sutton, J. A. Case studies of end user requirements for interactive problem solving systems. *Management Information Systems Quarterly*. 1, 1 (March 1977), 51–63.

14 Cheney, P. H. Effects of individual characteristics, organizational factors and task characteristics on computer programmer productivity and job satisfaction. *Information and Management* (July 1984), 209- 214.

15 Cheney, P. H., and Dickson, G. B. Organizational characteristics and information systems: an exploratory investigation. *Academy of Management Journal*, 25, 1 (March 1982), 170–184.

16 Culnan, M. J. Chauffeured versus end user access to commercial databases: the effects of task and individual differences. *Management Information Systems Quarterly*, 7, 1 (March 1983); 55–68.

17 Davis, G. B., and Olson, M. H. *Management Information Systems: Conceptual Foundations, Structure, and Development.* 2nd ed. New York: McGraw Hill, 1985.

18 Dearden, J. MIS is a mirage. *Harvard Business Review*, 50, 1 (January–February 1972), 90–99.

19 DeBrabander, B., and Edstrom, A. Successful information system development projects. *Management Science*, 24, 2 (October 1977), 191–199.

20 Dickson, G. W.; Leitheiser, R. L.; Wetherbe, J. C.; and Nechis, M. Key information systems issues for the 1980's. *Management Information Systems Quarterly*, 8, 3, 135–162.

21 Dickson, G. W., and Simmons, J. K. The behavioral side of MIS. *Business Horizons* (August 1970), 59–71.

22 Edelman, F. Managers, computing systems, and productivity. *Management Information Systems Quarterly*, 5, 3 (1981), 1–19.

23 Edstrom, A. User influence and the success of MIS projects. *Human Relations*, 30 (1977).

24 Ein-Dor, P., and Segev, E. Organizational context and the success of management information systems. *Management Science*, 24, 10 (June 1978), 1064–1077.

25 Ein-Dor, P., and Segev, E. Organizational context and MIS structure: some empirical evidence. *Management Information Systems Quarterly* (September 1982), 55–68.

26 Franz, C. R., and Killingsworth, B. A comparison of user and analyst perceptions of the user involvement process. *Proceedings of the 14th Annual Meeting of the American Institute for Decision Sciences* (1982), 186–188.

27 Gallagher, C. A. Perceptions of the value of a management information system. *Academy of Management Journal*, 17, 1 (March 1974), 46–55.

28 Gingras, L., and McLean, E. R. Designers and users of information systems: a study in differing profiles. *Proceedings of the 3rd International Conference on Information Systems* (1982), 169–182.

29 Ginzberg, M. J. Steps towards a more effective implementation of MS and MIS. *Interfaces*, 8, 3 (May 1978), 57–63.

30 Guthrie, A. Attitudes of user managers toward management of information systems. *Management Informatics*, 3, 5 (1974).

31 Hammond, J., The roles of the manager and management scientist in successful implementation. *Sloan Management Review*, 15, 2 (Winter 1974), 1–24.

32 Heany, D. F. Education the critical link in getting managers to use information systems. *Interfaces*, 2, 3 (May 1972), 1–7.

33 Henderson, J. C., and Treacy, Michael E. Managing end user computing. CISR Working Paper No. 114, Cambridge, MA, MIT Center for Information Systems Research, May 1984.

34 Ives, B.; Hamilton, S.; and Davis, G. B. A framework for research in computer-based management information systems. *Management Science* (September 1980), 910–934.

35 Ives, B., and Olson, M. User involvement and MIS success: a review of research. *Management Science*, 30, 5 (1984), 586–603.

36 Ives, B.; Olson, M.; and Baroudi, S. The measurement of user information satisfaction. *Communications of the ACM*, 26, 10 (October 1983), 785–793.

37 Jenkins, A. M. An investigation of some management information systems design variables and decision making performance: a simulation experiment. Unpublished Ph.D. Thesis, University of Minnesota, Minneapolis, 1977.

38 Johnson, J. W. The infocenter experience. *Datamation*, 30, 1 (January 1984), 137–142.

39 Lefkovits, H. C. A status report on the activities of Codasyl End User Facilities Committee (EUFC). *Information and Management*, 2 (1979), 137–163.

40 Lucas, H. C., Jr. A descriptive model of information systems in the context of the organization. *Proceedings of the Wharton Conference on Research on Computers in Organizations* (1973). In *Data Base*, 5, 2 (1973). 27–36.

41 Lucas, H. C. Performance and use of information systems. *Management Science*, 21, 8 (April 1975), 908–919.

42 MacIntosh, N. B, and Daft, R. L. User department technology and information design. *Information and Management*, 1, 3 (1978), 123–131.

43 Maish, A. M. A user's behavior toward his MIS. *Management Information Systems Quarterly*, 3, 1 (March 1979), 39–52.

44 Manley, J. Implementation attitudes: a model and a measurement methodology. Chapter 8 in Schultz, Randall T., and Slevin, Dennis P., eds. *Implementing Operations Research/Management Science*. New York: American Elsevier, 1975.

45 Mann, R. I., and Watson, H. J. A contingency model for user involvement in DSS development. *Management Information Systems Quarterly*, 8, 1 (March 1984), 27–38.

46 McCartney, L. The new info centers. *Datamation*, 29, 7 (July 1983), 30–46.

47 McLean, E. R. End users as application developers. *Management Information Systems Quarterly*, 3, 4 (December 1979), 37–46.

48 Nolan, R. L., and Wetherbe, J. C. Toward a comprehensive framework for MIS research. *Management Information Systems Quarterly*, 4, 2 (June 1980), 1–9.

49 Reimann, B. C., and Waren, A. D. User-oriented criteria for the selection of DSS software. *Communications of the ACM*, 28, 2 (February 1985), 166–179.

50 Rivard, S., and Huff, S. L. User developed applications: evaluations of success from the DP department perspective. *Management Information Systems Quarterly*, 8, 1 (March 1984), 39–50.

51 Robey, D. User attitudes and management information system use. *Academy of Management Journal*, 22, 3 (1979), 527–538.

52 Rockart, J. F. Critical success factors. *Harvard Business Review* (March–April 1979). 81–91.

53 Rockart, J. F., and Flannery, L. S. The management of end user computing *Communications of the ACM*, 26, 10 (October 1983), 776–784.

54 Rockart, J. F., and Treacy, M. E. The CEO goes online. *Harvard Business Review* (January–February 1982), 82-88.

55 Schonberger, R. J. MIS design: a contingency approach. *Management Information Systems Quarterly*, 4, 1 (March 1980), 13–20.

56 Sprague, R. H., Jr., and Carlson, E. D. *Building Effective Decision Support Systems*. Englewood Cliffs, N. J.: Prentice-Hall, 1982.

57 Swanson, E. B. Measuring user attitudes in MIS research: a review. *Omega*, 10, 2 (1976), 157–165.

58 Swanson, E. B. A note on interpersonal information systems use. *Information and Management*, 1, 6 (1978), 287–294.

59 Wegner, P. Education related to the use of computers in organizations. *Communications of the ACM*, 14, 9 (September 1971), 573–588.

14 Power, politics and MIS implementation

M. L. Markus

Introduction

No one knows how many computer-based applications, designed at great cost of time and money, are abandoned or expensively overhauled because they were unenthusiastically received by their intended users. Most people who have worked with information systems encounter at least mild resistance by those who are designated to input data or use the output to improve the way they do their jobs.

Many explanations have been advanced to account for people's resistance to change in general, to technological change in particular, and most specifically to management information systems (MIS) implementation efforts. Some of these explanations are informal rules of thumb that practitioners rely on in the heat of action; others are purportedly based on social scientific theories or research findings. Some are said to apply in every situation; others are contingent upon a variety of prevailing conditions. Some are mental models that form the basis for actions but are rarely articulated or explicitly examined for consistency and completeness; others are more formal models with clearly spelled-out connections. Familiar comments regarding resistance are:

1. To avoid resistance, get top management and obtain user involvement in the design process [16];
2. Technically sound systems are less likely to be resisted than those with frequent downtime and poor response time [1];
3. Users resist systems that are not 'user friendly' (assertions by EDP equipment vendors);
4. All other things being equal, people will resist change (received wisdom);
5. People will resist an application when the costs outweigh the benefits (received wisdom).

Explanations of resistance are important because, however informal or implicit, they guide the behavior and influence the actions taken by managers and systems analysts concerned with implementing computer-based applications. The premise of this chapter is that better theories of resistance will lead to better implementation strategies and, hopefully, to better outcomes for the organizations in which the computer applications are installed. This suggests the need to examine commonly used explanations and the assumptions underlying them in some detail.

Critical examination of implementors' theories regarding the causes of resistance is a process that, according to at least one view of resistance (cost versus benefits), implementors themselves may be expected to resist. Such examination is hard work, and the examiner runs the risk of discovering (a) that his or her mental models are just fine, in which case the effort appears wasted, or (b) that the explanations need changing, which is uncomfortable and requires more hard work. In addition, it is not likely that the commonly held heuristics mentioned earlier (e.g. top management support) can be very far from wrong: in the first place, there is some academic research to support each one of them, and second, many analysts and managers have found that the heuristics have prevented them from making blunders in everyday situations. Consequently, many readers may decide that the uncertain benefits of examining their personal models of resistance are outweighed by the costs of doing so. This chapter is written either for those who compute the costs and benefits differently or for those whose behavior is describable by a different explanation of resistance to change.

The argument of the chapter follows this format: Three basic theories of resistance are presented and contrasted in terms of their underlying assumptions about information systems, organizations, and resistance itself. Several bases for evaluating the theories are enumerated, including the applicability of basic assumptions, the accuracy of predictions drawn from theories, and the utility for implementors of the strategies and prescriptions derived from the theories. The chapter then proceeds to evaluate the theories using logic and the limited data of a single case. The chapter concludes with recommendations for implementors.

Types of theories

Kling [13] has provided a very helpful starting point for examining theories of resistance. He identified six distinct theoretical perspectives: Rational, Structural, Human Relations, Interactionist, Organizational Politics, and Class Politics. Kling shows how these perspectives differ on a variety of dimensions, such as their view of technology and of the social setting into which it is introduced, their key organizing concepts, their ideologies of the workplace and of 'good' technology, and their implied theories of the dynamics of technical diffusion. For ease of comparison, he groups the first three perspectives into the category of Systems Rationalism and the latter three into Segmented Institutionalism.

This chapter builds upon Kling's work by exploring different theoretical perspectives as they relate to one small aspect of computing in organizational life – the introduction and implementation of computer-based information systems, and the human resistance that so often accompanies them. Since this chapter emphasizes the perspectives from the viewpoint of their implications for action, that is, for the implementation strategies of managers and systems analysts, rather than of their theoretical differences *per se*, this chapter may group Kling's perspectives differently while liberally drawing on his insights.

Three theories

An implementor trying to decide what to do about resistance of individuals or organizational subunits may hold one of three divergent theories about why that resistance occurred. First, the person or subunit may be believed to have resisted because of factors internal to the person or group. These factors may be common to all persons and groups or unique to the one being examined. Examples of explanations compatible with this theory are: people resist all change; people with analytic cognitive styles accept systems, while intuitive thinkers resist them.

Second, the person or group may be believed to have resisted because of factors inherent in the application or system being implemented. Examples of compatible explanations are people resist technically deficient systems, systems that are not ergonomically designed, and systems that are not user friendly. A fair amount of research has been done to support the contention that technical and human factors problems are associated with resistance and system failure. For example, Ginzberg [6] reviewed much of the (then) existing literature on OR/MS/MIS research and noted that several studies identified technical problems as a factor related to system failure (over 100 factors were mentioned at least once in the studies reviewed). Alter [1] studied 56 systems and reported that technical problems were related to implementation problems in several cases.

These two theories are clearly divergent, because the first assumes that a person's (group's) behavior is determined internally, and the second assumes that behavior is determined externally by the environment or by technology. Nevertheless, implementors often implicitly hold both theories simultaneously, believing that behavior is determined both from within and from without. An example of such a compound theory is: there is always a tendency for people to resist systems, but, other things being equal, they are less likely to resist ones that are well designed.

The third theory holds that people or groups resist systems because of an interaction between characteristics related to the people and characteristics related to the system. This theory is difficult to define, but easier to describe. The theory is not the same as a simultaneous belief in the two previously mentioned theories. The operant word in the definition is 'interaction.' Examples of explanations derived from the interaction theory are: systems that centralize control over data are resisted in organizations with decentralized authority structures, systems that alter the balance of power in organizations will be resisted by those who lose power and accepted by those who gain it, and resistance arises from the interaction of technical design features of systems with the social context in which the systems are used.

Several distinct variations of the interaction theory can be identified. One, which may be called the sociotechnical variant, focuses on the distribution of responsibility for organizational tasks across various roles and on the work-related communication and coordination around this division of labor. New information systems may prescribe a division of roles and responsibilities at variance with existing ones; they may structure patterns of interaction that are at odds with the prevailing organizational culture. In this light, systems can be viewed as a vehicle for creating organizational change. The greater the implied change, the more likely the resistance. Similar articulations of a variant of the interaction theory can be found in Keen [9], Ginzberg [7]. and Kling [13].

It should be noted that this explanation identifies neither the system nor the organizational setting as the cause of resistance, but their interaction. The system-determined theory would predict that a given system be accepted or resisted in every setting because of its design features. The interaction theory can explain different outcomes for the same system in difficult settings. Similarly, the people-determined theory would predict the rejection of all systems in a setting in which any one system is resisted. The interaction theory can explain different responses by the same group of users to different settings. Compared with a concatenated people-plus-system-determined theory, the interaction theory allows for more precise explanation and predictions of resistance.

A second variant of the interaction theory can be called the political version. There, resistance is explained as a product of the interaction of system design features with the intraorganizational distribution of power, defined either objectively, in terms of horizontal or vertical power dimensions, or subjectively, in terms of symbolism. The appendix provides additional details on the political variant of the interaction theory and compares it briefly with other variants. The case analysis given in this chapter employs the political variant exclusively.

How are we to evaluate these theories? This is a difficult thing to do, if for no other reason than that there are several ways to do it, each of which may yield different results. Scientists are generally agreed that theories cannot be tested directly, which in our case means that it is impossible to say without doubt that people resist computer applications because of internal factors, external factors, or interaction effects. But the basic assumptions underlying the theories can be examined and compared with facts in the 'real world,' predictions derived from theories can be tested against observed occurrences, and the implications for action derived from theories can be tested for their usefulness to implementors. This last test may be conducted independently of the first two, and implementors may prefer this. Because this chapter assumes that good implementation strategies derive from good theories, we attempt to address all three types of evaluations.

Basic assumptions of the theories

In order to perform the first type of evaluation, it is necessary to identify the assumptions that underlie the theories. Kling's list of theoretical perspectives yields two that are especially relevant for comparing theories of resistance with computer-based applications: assumptions about the nature of technology (in this case, information systems) and assumptions about the nature of the setting in which the applications are introduced. A third assumption can be added – beliefs about the nature of resistance. The first two dimensions, the people-determined and system-determined theories of resistance, are similar and easily contrasted with the interaction theory.

Assumptions about information systems

Information systems can be described and categorized in many ways: by type of processing technology – interactive or batch: by type of data (numbers, text, graphics, audio, video); by degree of centralization, distribution, or decentralization. One analytic scheme that proves especially fruitful for examining resistance is that of system 'purpose,' which refers to the intentions of system designers. Purpose is a tricky thing to pin down, because systems can be viewed from many angles, and users may describe a system's purpose differently than designers. Rather than haggle about whose view is right, one can infer system purpose from system design features and other clues to the designer's goals, values, and intentions.

Generally speaking, system purposes can be lumped into two classes, depending upon whether the purposes are consistent with the Rational Theory of Management. Very briefly summarized, the Rational Theory of Management holds that organizations have goals and that they behave in ways that are consistent with achieving these goals. For many businesses, a major goal is to achieve a specified profit subject to certain constraints. System purposes that are consistent with the Rational Theory are: to rationalize work (achieve predictable outputs with consistent units of input – a goal of many operational systems), to enhance managerial decision-making and planning, to control and motivate the performance of employees toward agreed-upon goals, and to improve communication and coordination among people in the organization or between the organization and aspects of its environment (customers, suppliers, competitors, etc.).

Without denying the existence of these Rational purposes for systems, some researchers and theoreticians have pointed out that other purposes of systems can be identified. Kling [10] and Markus and Pfeffer [19] have described systems whose purpose is to appear as though they were intended to rationalize work or to improve decision-making without having any real impact on organizational procedures or outcomes. Systems with this purpose can be useful in attracting outside funding or in discouraging external intervention. Another non-Rational purpose of systems is to change the balance of power inside a firm. The system described later in this chapter can be argued to have had the purpose of creating a power shift among organizational subunits, although great pains were taken to make the system appear as if the only motivations for it were Rational ones. Still another non-Rational purpose is to gain control over or reduce dependence on members of a different occupational group. Noble [22] has described particular designs of numerically controlled machine tools whose purpose, he argues, was for managers to wrest control over production from the hands of shop floor machinists. These purposes are not consistent with the Rational Theory, and hence are called non-Rational; there is considerable evidence to suggest that at least some systems are partly, if not totally, intended to achieve non-Rational purposes [12, 13].

Assumptions about organizational contexts of use

The organizations in which information systems are used can be described by

Structure: functional, divisional, matrix, centralized, decentralized:
Culture: power-oriented, cooperative, Theory Z;
Employment contracts: professional, bureaucratic, semiprofessional.

For purposes of understanding resistance, it is most useful to describe organizations in terms of the degree to which the people and subunits affected by the proposed information system are believed to have congruent goals and values or divergent ones.

The view of organizations that most frequently coexists with the Rational Theory of Management and with beliefs in the Rational purposes of information systems is that all organizational members share common goals for the organization and that, generally speaking, they will collaborate to achieve these objectives. In contrast, the non-Rational view assumes that different individuals or subgroups in the organization have different objectives depending upon their location in the hierarchy and that, in general, they can be expected to try to achieve these local goals rather than global organizational goals whenever differences exist. Some empirical work has described the existence of competing intraorganizational goal systems (Dalton [5] and Crozier [4] are classics), and analysts of the 'class politics' persuasion take chronic conflicts of interest between workers and managers as an article of faith [3]. Thus, there is reason to believe that, at least in some

organizations at certain times, there are situations that do not conform to the Rational perspective.

Assumptions about the nature of resistance

Quite apart from one's view of the cause of resistance, people can hold different assumptions about the nature of resistance and the role it plays in organizations. As used in this chapter, resistance is defined as behaviors intended to prevent the implementation or use of a system or to prevent system designers from achieving their objectives. However, careful inspection of the trade press and even some MIS scientific literature will reveal that the term is also applied to behaviors that may not have these intentions. For example, the label 'resistance' is frequently applied to all cases of nonuse of a system, even when nonuse may reflect ignorance of the system's existence, inadequate training in system operation, or personal fear of the computer. This author would make the following distinction: where one individual's use of a system is not critical to the operation of a system, that individual's choice not to use the system cannot be considered resistance. Data entry is a use critical to the operation of a system; use of a decision support system to evaluate a stock portfolio by one analyst in a department of 20 is not. Resistance is easiest to identify when a person engages in behavior that may result in the disruption or removal of a system that is interdependently used by others as well as by that person.

Social scientists are justifiably leery of any concept that requires an attribution of intention, for two reasons. First, behaviors can be observed, but intentions cannot. Second, the act of attributing intention often indicates more about the person doing the attributing than about the person to whom the intention is attributed. In other words, many people who identify a behavior as resistance are really saying, 'they are not doing things the way I want them to.' This implies that resistance is a relative rather than an absolute behavior. It can only be defined in the context of two or more parties, each with desires and intentions. Party A intends to introduce a change of certain design; party B intends to prevent this from happening. Consequently, resistance can only be believed to be bad or undesirable if the intentions of the designer or implementor are accepted as good or desirable.

In the people-determined and the system-determined theories of resistance, the objectives and intentions of designers and implementors are never identified or analyzed. The implicit assumptions are either that designers' objectives are good, or that, whether good or bad, the intended users of a system do or should accept these objectives. Consequently, both of these theories tend to regard resistance as a negative result, which must be avoided or overcome.

In contrast, the interaction theory does not examine resistance out of the context of designer intentions. The interests and intentions of both users and designers are identified and compared. When these interests are very similar, resistance rarely occurs. As the difference between their interests widens, the possibility of resistance increases. Resistance is viewed as neither good nor bad, unless you align yourself with the interests of either party. Resistance can be destructive, because it generates conflict and ill-will and consumes time and attention. But resistance can also be functional for organizations, by preventing the installation of systems whose use might have on-going negative consequences (e.g. stress, turnover, reduced performance).

Table 1 Theories of resistance: underlying assumptions

	People-determined	*System-determined*	*Interaction theory*
Cause of resistance	Factors internal to people and groups	System factors such as technical excellence and ergonomics	Interaction of system and context of use
	Cognitive style Personality traits Human nature	Lack of user-friendliness Poor human factors Inadequate technical design or implementation	*Sociotechnical variant:* Interaction of system with division labor *Political variant:* Interaction of system with distribution of intra-organizational power
Assumptions about purposes of information systems	Purposes of systems are consistent with Rational Theory of Management, can be excluded from further consideration	Purposes of systems are consistent with Rational Theory of Management, can be excluded from further consideration	*Sociotechnical variant:* Systems may have the purpose to change organizational culture, not just workflow
			Political variant: Systems may be intended to change the balance of power
Assumptions about organizations	Organizational goals shared by all participants	Organizational goals shared by all participants	*Sociotechnical variant:* Goals conditioned by history
			Political variant: Goals differ by organizational location; conflict is endemic
Assumptions about resistance	Resistance is attribute of the intended system user; undesirable behavior	Resistance is attribute of the intended system user; undesirable behavior	Resistance is a product of the setting, users, and designers; neither desirable nor undesirable

Table 1 summarizes the underlying assumptions about information systems, organizations, and resistance for each of the three theories. One basis for evaluating the theories is the degree to which data from real-world cases can be found to be consistent with the assumptions of the theories. If the assumptions are shown to be unrealistic or inoperative in natural settings, the theories may be rejected on this account. One case study from the author's research is presented to illustrate the application of the theories and to serve as a basis for preliminary evaluation.

Background of the FIS Case Study

The methodology employed in this case research study was historical reconstruction of the initiation, design process, design content, installation, and use of information systems in large manufacturing firms [18]. Sources of data included interviews with over 30 designers and users of the systems and documentary evidence about the systems and the organizations. The documentary evidence included corporate annual reports (spanning in the case of a financial information system (FIS), 15 years from 1964 to 1979), organizational charts, systems training manuals and design documents, and internal correspondence about the systems. Our account is organized as follows. The system is briefly described. Then the context of system use is examined to see whether the three theories apply. First, are there differences between resistors and nonresistors? Second, are there technical problems with the system? Third, what is the political context of system use? Subsequently, we evaluate the theories in the light of case data.

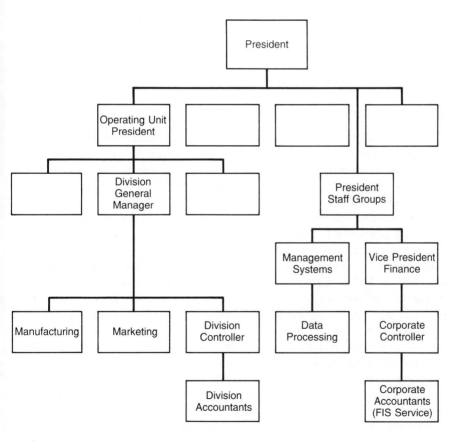

Figure 1. Golden Triangle Corporation, 1978

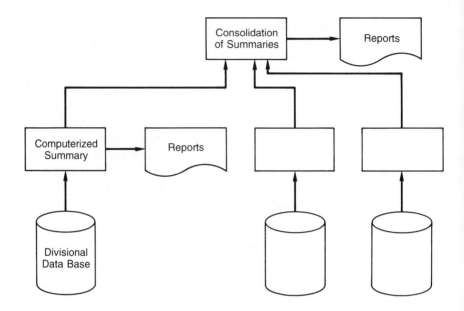

Figure 2. FIS purchased package design

The FIS system

A financial information system collects and summarizes financial data for the
Golden Triangle Corporation (GTC) (see Figure 1). The inputs to the
system are transactions involving revenues and expenditures, assets and
liabilities. The outputs are monthly profit and loss statements for each
division and for the Corporation as a whole; balance sheets are produced by
the system. The information managed by FIS is primarily used for external
reporting purposes (to the SEC), although profit and loss information is
relevant to managerial decision-making.

Obviously, financial reports was not a new function at GTC, but FIS,
installed in 1975, incorporated some innovative features. Prior to FIS,
divisional accountants collected and stored transaction data however they
saw fit, but reported summary data to corporate accountants in a
standardized format (see Figure 2). With FIS, divisional accountants entered
their transactions into the system (identified and retrievable by a 24-digit
account code) which specified the type of transaction (asset-office furniture,
expense-travel) and place of origin (group, division, plant). FIS
automatically summarized these data into reports for corporate accountants
and for the relevant division (see Figure 3).

The idea for FIS originated in the corporate accounting department
around 1971. A task force was formed to evaluate the need for such a system

and to estimate its costs and benefits. This task force was composed entirely of people from within the corporate accounting group, some of whom had considerable data processing experience.

In 1972, after the necessary investigations and approvals, the task force arranged for the purchase of a financial accounting package from a software vendor (much to the chagrin of GTC's internal data processing department who would have preferred to build it themselves). The package purchased was designed so that it mirrored almost exactly the way in which financial accounting was then performed at GTC (see Figure 2), except that formerly manual databases were computerized, inconsistent summarization procedures were standardized, and consolidation was automated. Nevertheless, the FIS task force decided to modify the package, ostensibly to make use of modern database management techniques. In the process of modification, however, which took over $2^1/_2$ years, the design team also replaced separate divisional databases with a single corporate database (see Figure 3).

The task force members did not solicit information from divisional accountants about the design of FIS until 1974, when it was time to set up the database. Divisions were, however, invited to attend presentations describing the need of FIS and the benefits to be derived from it. Implementation of the system was to be done in phases. FIS task force

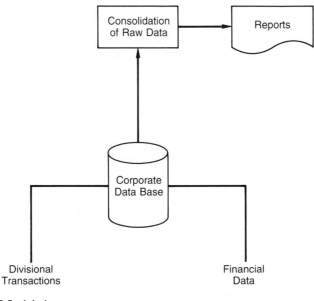

Figure 3. FIS final design

members had decided to solicit a volunteer for the first division to 'go up' on FIS. After the initial division had found it workable, the other divisions would be required to use it. FIS was meant to be *the* corporate financial system.

Resistance to FIS

The largest division of GTC volunteered to pioneer FIS in January 1975. In October 1975, an accountant from this division wrote a memo complaining that

> . . . Except for providing more detailed information, the FIS system has not been beneficial to us.

In response to complaints from this person and other individuals in several divisions, a study team was created to explore problems related to 'system inefficiency.' The study team met for several months and made technical recommendations to the data processing department. These changes proceeded slowly, and were set back in early 1977, when the data processing project leader quit.

In the meantime, other divisions had started up on the new system; all major divisions were using FIS by the end of 1975. This was surprising in light of the problems experienced by the initial FIS-using division, especially since participation in the system was supposed to be voluntary. Many accountants on the central corporate staff later pointed to this fact with pride as evidence of the success of FIS, but one person explained the incongruity as follows:

> Participation was voluntary on the surface, but there was a hidden inducement to participate. Those who wanted to wait to join FIS could do so, but they had to provide the same information manually. This would have been quite burdensome. So it really wasn't all that voluntary.

There is evidence that later divisonal users were no happier about the new system than the original division. One division kept on using its old accounting methods after it started using FIS, even though this required twice the effort. There were frequent discrepancies between the two sets of books, and the staff of this division claimed that its system (thick manual ledger books!) was accurate and that FIS was at fault. The staff of this 'recalcitrant' division persisted in this behavior for two years, until a member of the corporate accounting staff actually carried the old ledgers away. Some divisional accountants also admitted to slight 'data fudging' to circumvent the technical and human factors problems with the system.

> If it turned out that an account we needed had not already been defined to FIS, rather than wait for the special account creation run, we might change the plant code, just to get the data in. After all, we knew what the numbers really were!

At the same time, corporate accountants, who used the system for corporate consolidation, were delighted with it. FIS automatically performed tedious tasks of calculation and reporting that they had formerly done by hand. In addition, FIS provided several totally unanticipated benefits for them, such as automated tax accounting. Corporate accountants could not account for the resistance of the divisions' staff members. They bitterly denounced the 'troublemakers.' One said:

> I can't understand why the divisions don't like FIS. There are so many benefits.

But the divisional accounting staff apparently did not perceive these benefits, even after substantial experience with FIS. Here is an excerpt from another memo written by the accountant who first complained about the system in October 1975. This memo is dated August 1977.

> After being on FIS for several months, I expressed the opinion that the system was basically of little benefit. After two years and seven months, my opinion has not changed. Even worse, it seems to have become a system that is running people rather than people utilizing the system.

When this author visited GTC, well over one year after that memo was written, many divisional accountants reported that they were still very unhappy with FIS.

Differences between resistors and nonresistors

From the preceding description, it can be seen that those who could be said by their behavior to resist FIS were divisional accountants; those who accepted it and liked it were corporate accountants. According to the people-determined theory of resistance, resistors and acceptors should differ psychologically or cognitively in some significant way. In fact, several corporate accountants interviewed in 1979 subscribed to this notion; their stated explanation for the resistance was the personality characteristics of the resistors, who were 'troublemakers.' Although this author did not administer any psychological tests, there are some factors that lend credibility to the hypothesis that differences between the groups accounted for the resistance.

First, corporate accountants performed tasks that can be described as financial accounting.' They dealt wth historical data, largely for purposes of external reporting. In contrast, divisional accountants, who reported to divisional general managers, can be described as 'managerial accountants.' They saw their role as one of providing future- and profit-oriented information to managers. Second, prior to 1975, there was little mobility between corporate and divisional accounting groups. Mobility would probably have encouraged more homogeneity in outlook; lack of it undoubtedly led to greater differences in outlook.

These differences, however, are not the inherent cognitive style differences usually studied by information systems theorists [26]. Rather, they are cognitive differences derived from status and functional location within a firm's hierarchy and division of labor.

Technical problems with FIS

According to the system-determined theory, resistance can be traced to human factors and technical design features. Evidence can be found in the FIS case to support the reasonableness of this contention.

Part of the reason for the complaints of early FIS users can be found in a series of technical and human factors problems with the system. The database management system chosen for this application did not work well with the computer's operating system, and there was insufficient main storage to meet the applications requirements. Consequently, downtime was frequent and reports were often late. At the same time, the schedule of monthly closings were not relaxed to accommodate the problems. In addition, the data entry procedures were cumbersome. For example, FIS represents accounts with 24-digit account codes; the systems it replaced had 8-digit codes. New accounts had to be created almost daily, but to do so required a special computer run. In the special run, once weekly, the new account had to be related to the other accounts in the hierarchy. This was not quite as difficult as might be inferred from the 1024 possible accounts, but the rules for doing it were difficult to learn and not documented in a user manual. Transactions were entered into the system daily; those intended for an as-yet-undefined account wound up in a suspense account. Given the weekly periodicity of the account creation run, the suspense accounts often grew to staggering amounts.

Political context of FIS at GTC

According to the interaction theory, resistance can be attributed to an interaction between the design features of the system and features of its organization and social context of use. One aspect of this context is the intraorganizational politics and power dynamics between corporate and division accountants. Sufficient data exist in the FIS case to provide a basis for the plausibility of the interaction theory.

GTC is a major chemical and energy products manufacturing concern, with sales from its international operations exceeding $3 billion. It is currently decentralized into a staff group that includes corporate accounting and four operating groups with relative autonomy over marketing strategy and investment decisions for their product lines (see Figure 1). Within each operating group are several divisions, headed by general managers with only a 'dotted line relationship' to the corporate accounting group, whose role is to provide 'broad policy guidelines.'

This organizational stucture dated back to about 1968. In 1967, Golden Chemical Company had merged with two energy product concerns to form

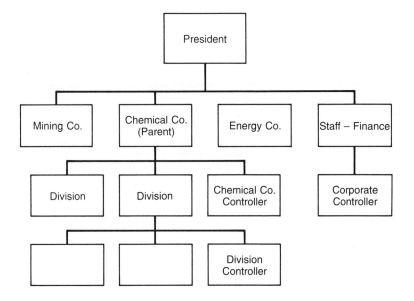

Figure 4. Golden Triangle Corporation, 1968

GTC. In the restructuring the old parent company was subjugated to a new corporate entity. This subjugation was reflected in the creation of a new staff group, corporation accounting, interposed between corporate management (which was disproportionately staffed with non-chemical Company people) and the Chemical Divisions (see Figure 4). A Chemical Company manager (Howard) was chosen to head the corporate controller's office. Whether by accident or by design is unknown, but Howard was the rival of the head controller for the Chemical Company divisions (Spade). (Spade had hired Howard many years before.) Respondents described the relationship between the two men as 'strained at best,' especially during 1972–1973, about the time that FIS was initiated and designed.

Howard found himself in an unenviable position. He had before him the task of creating an important and influential staff group where none had previously existed. Furthermore, a charter called for him to provide broad policy guidelines to all divisional accounting units, but he had no authority over them other than dotted-line relationships. Finally, because of his bad relationship with the Chemical Company controller, Howard was uncertain whether he had an accurate picture of reality: all data came to him through Spade.

> Corporate accountants felt the divisions were lying to them. And maybe there was some withholding of data on our side.
>
> *Divisional Accountant*

Howard felt that the divisions were doing things behind his back, and that he needed a better way of ferreting out how the knaves were doing in the trenches. A large part of the reason for initiating FIS was to provide this information.

Corporation Accountant

All three theories, then, appear at least plausible in the context of FIS since some data can be found to support their basic assumptions. It remains to demonstrate how well predictions drawn from each theory account for subsequent events in the case.

Predictions derived from the three theories

The people-determined theory leads to the prediction that replacing individual resistors or coopting them by allowing them to suggest improvements to the system might reduce or eliminate resistance. The system-determined theory predicts that if the technical features and human factors of a resisted system are changed, then resistance will disappear. The political variant of the interaction theory argues that neither of these changes will have much effect on the intensity of resistance if the resistance was generated by patterned interactions among competing groups. These predictions are summarized in Table 2.

Actual evidence from the FIS case supports the political variant of the interaction theory and gives no support to the other two. The test of a single case is not a strong proof, nor is it so intended here. But it can be a useful illustration. Consequently, the reader is invited to try out any version of the interaction theory on any familiar situation to test its ability to account for

Table 2 Theories of resistance: predictions

	People-determined	System-determined	Interaction theory (political variant)
Facts needed in real-world case for theory to be applicable	System is resisted, resistors differ from nonresistors on certain personal dimensions	System is resisted, system has technical problems	System is resisted, resistance occurs in the context of political struggles
Predictions derived from theories	Change the people involved, resistance will dissappear	Fix technical problems, resistance will disappear	Changing individuals and/or fixing technical features will have little effect on resistance
	Job rotation among resistors and nonresistors	Improve system efficiency Improve data entry	Resistance will persist in spite of time, rotation and technical improvements. Interaction theory can explain other relevant organizational phenonema in addition to resistance

events. However, our exposition of the case does not stop with demonstrating the utility of the interaction theory in accounting for events; we now show the assumptions of the interaction theory to be useful in helping an implementor to predict, to gather data, to explain resistance, and to develop strategies for implementation.

Changing the people

The people-determined theory predicts, among other things, that if some acceptors were moved into positions occupied by the resistors, resistance among divisional accountants would diminish or vanish. While hardly a scientific test of this prediction, such an event did take place accidentally within GTC.

After 1975, GTC encouraged more mobility among corporate and divisional accountants for career development purposes. Under this policy, one of the corporate accountants who had participated in the design of FIS in the original design task force became the controller in one of the divisions. According to one informant, this accountant rapidly became convinced of the problems with FIS (at least as seen by divisional accountants) and became an active and critical member of the second efficiency task force formed in December 1977 to improve FIS.

Further, while it surely does not conclusively refute the people-determined theory, behavioral evidence and interview reports show that resistance continued. It persisted in 1979, four years after the introduction to FIS. Evidence to support this statement will be given shortly.

Fixing technical problems

The system-determined theory predicts that fixing technical problems eliminates resistance. The second FIS efficiency task force was formed in December 1977, composed of several 'resistors' (divisional accountants) in addition to data processing specialists. This task force made technical recommendations similar to those of the first task force, but also speculated about whether FIS should be scrapped and replaced. Before it could complete its deliberations on the latter issue, the second task force was disbanded in March 1978.

This date coincided with the completion of the technical recommendations from the two task forces. The Data Processing Department had purchased and installed a larger computer with a more powerful operating system. This technical change improved the efficiency of FIS. In addition, the processing mode of the system had been changed from a batch to a transaction (on-line) basis; together, these changes reduced downtime to an acceptable level. Changes were made to the method of data entry, from remote batch to on-line, and the method of creating new accounts was simplified.

In spite of all these improvements in technical features and human factors, divisional resistance to FIS did not disappear. In fact, when data were collected for this study, about one year after the last of these changes was installed, informants in the divisions still spoke resentfully of FIS. Many felt strongly that the system should be replaced because FIS was inadequate as a tool for managerial accounting, even though it (now) functioned adequately as a tool for performing financial accounting. (Managerial accounting was the chief concern of divisional accountants.) Corporate accountants, however, maintained that FIS was more than adequate for managerial accounting (not their specialty), and they were increasingly pressuring divisional accountants to use FIS for this additional purpose.

Organizational politics

The interaction theory predicts that neither changing people (by removing them, by educating them, or by attempting to coerce them), nor changing technical features of the system will reduce resistance as long as the conditions which gave rise to it persist. Resistance-generating conditions are mismatches between the patterns of interaction prescribed by a system and the patterns that already exist in the setting into which the system is introduced. According to the political version of the interaction theory (see the appendix), the existing political setting can be identified as follows.

Corporate accounting had little formal organizational power and no independent information on which to base its attempts to develop and administer broad policy guidelines. An obvious solution to this problem was to develop a system by means of which the necessary information would flow directly to Corporate Accounting without the intermediate step of manipulation by the divisions. This is precisely what FIS did, as can be seen in Figures 2 and 3.

The way in which FIS was designed implied a major gain of power for corporate accountants relative to their prior position vis à vis the divisional accountants. Prior to FIS, divisional accountants summarized raw data on the transactions in their divisions and sent the summaries to the corporate accountants for consolidation. Divisions retained control of their own data and exercised substantial discretion in summarizing it. This allowed them to 'account for' unusual situations before reports reached corporate accountants or divisional general managers. After FIS, however, all financial transactions were collected into a single database under the control of corporate accountants. The divisional accountants still had to enter data, but they no longer 'owned' it. FIS automatically performed the divisional summaries that both divisional and corporate accountants received. At any time, corporate accountants had the ability to 'look into' the database and analyze divisional performance.

Corporate accountants designed and used FIS to create a substantial change in the distribution of, or access to, financial data, a valued resource.

It is not surprising that those who gained access (corporate accountants) were pleased with the system and that those who lost control (divisional accountants) resisted it by writing angry memos, maintaining parallel systems, engaging in behavior that jeopardized the integrity of the database, and participating in a task force with the public objective of eliminating FIS and replacing it with another system.

Given the details of the design of FIS, it is likely that divisional accountants would have resisted it even if the loss of power implied for the divisions had been accidental. But there is some evidence that the corporate accountants acted deliberately in their design of the new financial accounting system. First, as mentioned above, they had sufficient motive to try to shift the power balance. Second, they clearly felt powerless in their dealings with the divisions. They staffed the FIS project team without any representatives from the divisions, who might voice objections to its design details. This group selected a package, which conformed in overall design principles to the existing information flows at GTC, and modified it deliberately[1] into a design that would alter the power balance between the two groups. Furthermore, some observers with GTC were willing to ascribe the motivation behind FIS to political reasons. For example, the man who was Data Processing Manager in 1975 (long since gone to another company when interviewed in 1979) said,

> FIS was definitely established for political reasons . . . Howard wanted to take over the whole world . . . Therein started the wars between the Chemical Company and Corporate.

A design for FIS that entailed a power loss for one group and a power gain for the other could be expected to strongly affect power dynamics between the groups. Once the resistance of the divisional accountants is understood in this way, it is common sense as well as derivation from theory to hypothesize that changing human factors and even replacing a few key actors would do little to resolve the resistance. In fact, changing them did not eliminate the resistance.

Utility of the interaction theory to implementors

At this point, the superiority of the political variant of the interaction theory has been established based upon the ability of predictions drawn from it to account for the resistance to a system in one case. Rather than stop at this point, the case example can be extended a bit further to show what additional facts and data can be uncovered and explained by an analyst who

---

[1] The modification was optional, not mandatory, since the package was quite operational as purchased. The modification required a negotiated agreement with the vendor and was originally estimated to take six months to complete. (It actually took over two years). To proceed in this way was, therefore, a deliberate decision on the part of the project team.

uses this theory. These additional facts and data may be useful in designing an implementation effort. In the case of FIS, there are two additional relevant 'events': a reorganization of accounting within GTC that occurred in mid-1975, shortly after the start-up of FIS, and the on-going (in 1979) debate about what (else) should be done to or done about FIS.

In 1974, Spade retired. In the next year, his old position as Chemical Company Controller was first moved under the direct line control of corporate accounting and then eliminated the following year (see Figure 5). Similar changes were not made in the Energy Group of GTC. A member of the corporate controller's staff cited this as an example of what FIS was intended to accomplish:

> If (the corporate reorganization in 1975 which eliminated Spade's job as Chemical Company Controller) had occurred several years previously, FIS might never have been instigated. The reorganization eliminated much of the need for FIS.
>
> *Corporate Accountant*

It may seem as though FIS caused this structural change. But it is probably more accurate to view the reorganization as an outgrowth of the same political situation that created the 'need' for FIS. The political variant of the interaction theory, then, helps an analyst understand this event and to explain the resistance it generated.

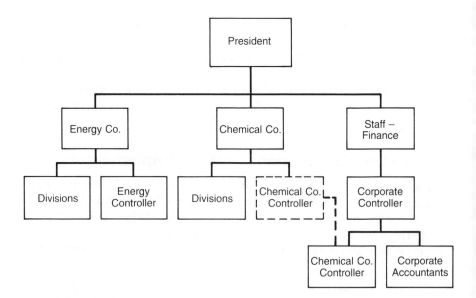

Figure 5. Golden Triangle Corporation, 1975

The political variant of the interaction theory also helps an analyst understand the dynamics of the intraorganization debate about FIS, which continued long after technical problems with the system were fixed. As interviews in 1979 disclosed, resistance to FIS had not disappeared but had changed its form: no longer were the divisions protesting the technical problems with the system (now solved); they were complaining that the corporate accountants were insisting they use FIS for tasks for which the system was inappropriate, namely, managerial accounting.

An administrator reporting to the President of one of GTC's operating groups summarized the feelings of many divisional accountants when he said:

> I think it's about time they realized that FIS is really an operational tool. It just can't do everything.

In this remark, he summarized the view that FIS had been grudgingly accepted by divisional accountants as a tool for performing financial accounting (balance sheets, taxes, and corporate consolidations), but that it was still being resisted as a managerial accounting tool. Divisional accountants argued strenuously that FIS was not useful for managerial accounting.

> FIS does not provide us with the data we need to prepare profit center reports. To prepare profit center reports we must maintain a separate system, the PGP system . . . They tell us we can use FIS for profit center reports! That's garbage! You could do it, but I've already told you how you have to enter data into FIS. To get a profit center report, you'd have to enter each transaction by commodity code. There are a thousand commodity codes. This would be a horrendous job. Besides, PGP is our product gross profit report. We've had this system unchanged for almost ten years . . . Naturally, the profit figures from this and FIS should reconcile, but they never do, so we have to make the necessary adjustments . . .

But an analysis of interview notes, internal memos, and task forces minutes, covering the period from 1975 to 1979, indicates that the difficulty of using FIS was only a secondary complaint; proposed changes in the way managerial accounting would be done was the real issue, one that no amount of technical fixing would solve. Further, this real issue was one of potential loss of power for divisional (managerial) accountants. Consider the following evidence.

First, an early memo about FIS (outlining a presentation to GTC's top management) explained 'the direction we are heading' in the design of FIS. This direction represented a major shift in the way GTC did managerial accounting that is, reporting to management about profit performance on specific products as opposed to the manipulation of aggregated historical data. The intended shift in direction is clear in this excerpt from a 1972 memo:

> The last item of deficiencies that we list is the inability to analyze results on a total variance basis by business unit or corporate wide. By that, we mean a lack of sales information by principal product and the lack of product line profitability. What was the volume of a given product? What was its price for a given period? What did that product

contribute at the gross profit level? To me, the guts of our operation is what we do on a product line basis. In addition, we do not report on a given plant profitability. We feel that all this type of information as was indicated, should all be part of a Financial Information System and available to management when needed.

Thus, corporate accountants had intended from the very beginning that FIS be used for managerial accounting not just, as its name implies, for financial accounting.

Second, corporate accountants did not immediately reveal these intentions to the divisions. When the staff in the divisions first heard about it they were surprised. In an October 1975 memo complaining about FIS, the divisional writer noted:

I think we have to take a good look at what we have right now and improve it before we take *any additional tasks* proposed for the FIS system.

The 'additional tasks proposed' referred to product profit (managerial) accounting.

Third, corporate accountants were quite well aware that the divisions did not see eye to eye with them on the issue of managerial accounting. The second FIS task force was created, it will be recalled, in December 1977 in response to another angry memo written by the accountant in the first FIS-using division. Responding to that memo, a highly placed corporate accountant referred to the heart of the resistance issue in this memo written in August 1977:

I must say that I am not surprised that your attitude toward the FIS system has not changed . . . That same attitude is shared by the entire financial [sic] staff of your division, and hence, FIS will never be accepted nor will it be utilized fully as an analysis tool by your division.

'Analysis tool' here means a tool to be used in the analysis of managerial-oriented profit data. (Note the use of the term 'financial' to refer to the duties of divisional accountants.)

Finally, the divisional accountants themselves were quite explicit in distinguishing between operational and ease of use problems and use of the system for managerial accounting purposes. When the second task force was formed, it was partly 'to improve things from a public relations point of view as well as from a technical point of view,' according to one corporate accountant. But the divisional members of the committee did not intend to settle for symbolic gestures. 'It was never really stated as such but one question we were looking at was: should we look for a new system?' Task force minutes in December 1977 confirm this:

During the sessions we have had thus far, one complex question already surfaced: is the system capable of being any more than a giant book keeping system, e.g. can it ever effectively serve divisional needs for budgeting, reporting, allocations, etc? Therefore, we see two related issues we will attempt to offer recommendations on: (1) ways to deal with problems so the system can be counted on to operate effectively during month-end over the short-term, and (2) what, if anything, must be done to assure us that, for the long-term, we will have a system usable as more than a consolidator.

Since the task force was disbanded before they could tackle the second question, we will never know what they decided, but interview data suggests that the divisions remained very negative both toward FIS and toward the corporate accountants' proposed 'additional' uses for it.

Here is the situation in summary. From the perspective of the divisional accountants, financial accounting is the legitimate domain of corporate accountants. A system intended primarily for financial accounting would have no real impact on the divisions, provided, of course, that it was reasonably easy to use. The FIS sytem was not easy to use, but it was also not just a financial accounting system. It was intended to encroach upon the legitimate domain of the divisional accountants, that is, managerial accounting. Divisional accountants would resist the use of FIS for managerial accounting even if it were easy to use, and, in fact, their resistance continued beyond March 1978

Who won? Did the corporate accountants succeed in their attempt to alter the balance of power between themselves and the divisions? The answer is not altogether clear. The corporate accountants did succeed in having the second task force disbanded (the axe man was the Vice-President of Finance) in March 1978, after the technical problems had been solved but before the committee could decide to replace FIS. The divisional accountants succeeded in redressing the more egregious faults of FIS, but failed in having it removed. In all likelihood, the net result was something of a draw: the corporate accountants had better information than before, an important power advantage in their dealings with the divisions, but not quite the total victory they had wished; the divisional accountants had regrouped and entrenched themselves to prevent any further losses.

Implications of the theories for implementation

The preceding analysis may have convinced an implementor that the interaction theory, at least in its political variation, has superior explanatory and predictive power. But the true test of the theories for the implementor will lie in their implications for implementation. Interaction theories are distinctly different from the people-determined, the system-determined, and the people-plus-system-determined views of resistance in their implications for action. An implementor holding the people-determined theory of resistance, for example, would find certain tactics appropriate. Among these are: carefully selecting the people who will use a new system or allowing users to self-select after careful explanations about the system; training and educating users to change their cognitive styles or attitudes about computing; getting users to participate in the design process so that they will feel more committed to the outcome; gaining support of the users' bosses who will encourage or demand compliance of recalcitrant users: changing organizational structures or reward systems to conform to the features of the system.

An implementor who believes that systems determine people's behaviour will consider some different tactics and some of the same tactics for different reasons. Among these are: modifying packages to conform to the ways people think, work, or do business; training system designers to improve technical efficiency, ergonomic excellence, and a smooth man-machine interface; involving users in the design process so that the design is better than that which would have been developed without user input.

Implementors who hold both people- and system-determined theories simultaneously will pick and choose among the tactics. To these people, user participation in design is the most desirable tactic, because it is consistent with both theories, albeit for different reasons. In the face of prolonged or intense resistance, however, they are often forced to choose between changing people or organizational structures and modifying the systems; and in the process. they reveal their theory of last resort.

Implementors who hold the interaction theory of resistance find that no tactics are useful in every situation. User participation in the design process, for example, is clearly contraindicated in cases where powerful authorities have decided that a specific change, unpopular with users, will take place (see Markus [17]). In such situations, users are likely to resent strongly a tactic that is meant to make them feel as though they have some say in the matter, when they obviously do not.

One major implication of the interaction theory is that computer-based systems alone cannot accomplish the task of radical organizational change. If radical change is desired, a thorough analysis of the existing situation should be conducted to identify factors that will facilitate or hinder the change. Examples of such factors can be inappropriate reporting relationships among individuals or groups, incentive schemes that do not reward the desired behavior or punish undesired behavior, unclear allocation of responsibility for certain tasks. Changes in these areas should be made before a system is implemented, and the system should be designed to be consistent with the revised organizational procedures. In cases like this, the organizational changes may generate resistance, but once they have been implemented, a system that supports them is unlikely to be the target of resistance itself.

Another implication of the interaction theory is that the specific designs of systems are in part a product of the relationships between users and designers. In the case of FIS, the designers were also systems users, as opposed to systems professionals. But similar cases of resistance have occurred where design objectives and specifics have been set by supposedly

Table 3 Theories of resistance: recommendations for implementation

People-determined	*System-determined*	*Interaction theory*
Educate users (training)	Educate designers (better technology)	Fix organizing problem before introducing systems
Coerce users (edicts, policies)	Improve human factors	Restructure incentives for users
Persuade users	Modify packages to conform to organizational procedures	Restructure relationships between users and designers
User participation (to obtain commitment)	User participation (to obtain better design)	User participation is not always appropriate

'neutral' parties such as operations researchers and systems analysts. According to the interaction theory, no designers are ever completely neutral. Consequently, a great deal of thought and attention should be given to the tasks of structuring the relationships between users and designers and of developing methodologies for designing and implementing systems. For example, many organizations with centralized computing facilities have deliberately decentralized systems development to improve relationships between users and designers.

The most important implication of the interaction theory is that the best prescriptions for an implementation strategy and for the specific design content of a system will follow from a thorough diagnosis of the organizational setting in which the system will be used. At present, system builders are using methods such as structured systems analysis which allow them to describe and analyze only the technical features of a setting which is to be automated. To design systems that will not be resisted or to devise ways to modify resisted systems, this technical systems analysis must be augmented with a social or political analysis of the sort performed for FIS. Table 3 summarizes these conclusions.

Conclusion

The final evaluation of the interaction theory (in whatever variation) is to show how it is useful to the implementor of systems. The theory leads to a model of organizational analysis and diagnosis that can be used to design systems that do not generate resistance or to devise strategies to deal with settings in which resistance has already occurred.

In the case of FIS, an analysis of this sort could have been performed prior to the system analysis and development effort to identify where resistance was likely to occur. Given the facts presented in this chapter, the analyst would probably have concluded that divisional accountants would certainly resist design features such as (a) the ability of the corporate accountants to retrieve and analyze raw (unsummarized) data, and (b) the necessity to do profit analysis at a level of aggregation that was meaningless to them. Knowing this and his/her own motives, the analyst could decide upon a course of action that may have included:

1 Altering the design of the system in ways that would be more palatable to divisional accountants;
2 Sacrificing some of the corporate accountants' objectives for the system;
3 Allowing divisional accountants to participate in selected aspects or all aspects of the system design process;
4 Buying acceptance of the system by giving divisional accountants some other concessions valued by them;
5 Touting the system from the start as the ultimate 'managerial accounting information system';
6 Terminating the proposed project.

Once FIS was designed and resistance already apparent, an analysis could have been performed to determine precisely why the resistance occurred and what could be done about it. This analysis would also be useful in helping plan future system implementations involving one or more of the parties affected by the original system. In the case of FIS, one would conclude that for corporate accountants to persist in pressing their view of managerial accounting is probably organizational folly. Furthermore, relations between the two groups are now badly strained. Successful future implementations of financial systems will necessitate either improving these relationships or providing solutions to problems perceived by the divisional accounting group.

The interaction theory has the apparent disadvantage of providing no universal, noncontingent advice to systems analysts and management implementors of systems. But it is more useful than other theories for predicting resistance and for generating varied and creative strategies that will help both to prevent it and to deal with it when it arises. Two observations on the use of the theory are in order.

First, one key to the successful use of the interaction theory is that the implementor consider himself or herself as one of the parties in the analysis. Self-examination of interests, motives, payoffs, and power bases will lend much to the implementor's ability to understand other people's reactions to the systems the implementor is designing and installing.

Second, the analyst should recognize that the goal of the exercise is not to 'overcome' resistance, but to avoid it, if possible, and to confront it constructively, if not. In some cases, this indicates that the implementor may have to lose the battle and sacrifice a pet system project in order to win the war. Resistance is not a problem to be solved so that a system can be installed as intended: it is a useful clue to what went wrong and how the situation can be righted. If the implementor can divorce the need to see a system up and working from the need to achieve a particular result, many more degrees of freedom exist. In conclusion, although the process is difficult and time-consuming, the results produced from the application of the interaction theory of resistance are often substantially better than those produced from the application of the universal heuristics derived from other theories.

Appendix. Details of the political variation of the interaction theory

Several variations of interaction theories are possible; the basic constraint is the notion that resistance is caused by an interaction between organization and system. The specific organizational concepts an analyst uses may vary. The set used in this chapter are concepts of intraorganizational power and politics. Other sets of concepts are also consistent with the interaction theory. One example involves concepts of organizational learning and change (see Keen [9], Ginzberg [7], and Kling [13] for details).

The primary assumption of the political variant of the interaction theory is that information systems frequently embody a distribution of intraorganizational power among the key actors affected by its design. Intraorganizational power is an attribute of individuals or subgroups, such as departments, within the organization; it can be defined as the ability to get one's way in the face of opposition or resistance to those desires [25]. There are a number of ways by which an individual or subgroup can come to have power in an organization, including personal characteristics, such as being an expert or being charismatic, but position in the formal structure of the organization often provides greater access to specific power resources and the legitimacy required to use them. Pfeffer [25] describes the major determinants of power, dependence of others on the power holder, ability of the power holder to provide resources, ability of the power holder to cope with uncertainty and irreplaceability, and ability to affect a decision-making process. All of these determinants of power are relevant to an understanding of MIS implementation, but the most frequently cited is ability to cope with uncertainty.[2] The raison d'etre of MIS is to provide managers with useful information, presumably so that they can cope better with variances arising from their production technologies and from the external units that supply inputs to and distribute outputs from the core technology.

The information required to cope effectively with uncertainty is distributed throughout organizations in a nonrandom way; some people/ groups have more access to this than others, and this gives them power. Many

[2] The ways in which information systems affect the organizational balance of power either through their symbolic aspects or through their effect on the decision process is described in detail in Markus and Pfeffer [19].

management information systems are designed in ways that redistribute non-randomly the information required to cope with uncertainty; thus an MIS can alter bases of power. For example, a relatively stable balance of power will develop in the relationships between the purchasing, engineering, operations, and production control departments in any manufacturing organization. Sometimes engineering will call the shots, sometimes manufacturing. The introduction of a new logistics system may funnel all key information through the production control department, thus giving them an unaccustomed power edge in their dealings with other groups. The result might be a permanent redistribution in the balance of intraorganizational power[3] unless something happens to prevent it. The sufficiently powerful 'something' is resistance by those parties who stand to lose in the reallocation of power.

The political variant makes some precise predictions about where resistance is likely to occur around the implementation of information systems. Power, as it has been defined here, is a valuable resource. People and organizational subunits may differ in the extent to which they actively seek to gain power, but it is unlikely that they will voluntarily give it up. When the introduction of a computerized information system specifies a distribution of power which represents a loss to certain participants, these participants are likely to resist the system. Conversely, when the distribution of power implied in the design of an information system represents a gain in power to participants, these participants are likely to engage in behavior that might signify acceptance of it: frequent use and/or positive statements about the system. In general, one would not expect people who are disadvantaged in their power position by a system to accept it (gracefully), nor would one expect people who gain power to resist.

Testing these propositions might involve comparing distributions of power bases before a system is installed with the distributions implied in a system's design, that is, identifying the winners and losers if the system were to be used exactly as designed. Clearly, however there are some problems with this procedure. Necessary conditions for resistance (acceptance) in the hypotheses as stated are that people perceive the system to represent a power loss (gain) and that people's behavior adequately represents their feelings. In some cases, people may misperceive the loss (gain) they receive as a result of the system. In other cases, people may feel it is not to their advantage to engage in behaviors that could be labeled resistance: criticizing the system, avoiding it, trying to bring out changes [25]. Most of these factors argue that, of the people or subunits who lose power in an objective comparison of new system with former conditions, only some of these are likely to resist, or to resist with any strength. Strength of resistance would appear to be strongly related to size of the loss and its perceived importance.

---

[3] Such redistributions have been documented by Kling [11], Hedberg et al. [8]; research on this topic has been reviewed by Bariff and Galbraith [2].

Some of the specific conditions in the design of an MIS that will spell objective losses or gains in power can be spelled out. It is important to note that a single system can represent a power loss for several individuals or subunits, and at the same time, a power gain for several others. Access to information is probably less important as a basis of power than is the ability to control access to information or to define what information will be kept and manipulated in what ways [10, 14, 23, 24]. When a system centralizes control over data, the individual or subunit who gains the control is likely to accept the system readily, while those units losing control are likely to resist, even if they receive access to larger amounts of data in return. Similarly decentralization of control over data is likely to be resisted by the formerly controlling unit and to be accepted by units gaining control.

If control over data (whether centralized or local) has prevented certain groups from obtaining needed or desired access to it, distribution of data, even unaccompanied by control over it, will provide those receiving it with significant power gains. Their dependence on the controlling group will be reduced, since they will have an alternative source of data. They are likely to accept a system which accomplishes this distribution. On the other hand, those whose data monopoly is threatened in the process are likely to resist. Distribution of data that makes the performance of a subunit more visible, hence subject to control attempts by other units, is likely to be resisted by the group whose performance is exposed [15] and accepted by those who would like to influence the others' performance.

The strength of resistance is also likely to be affected by the organizational position of the person or subunit to whom one loses power. If the 'winner' is located in a vertically superior position in the hierarchy, resistance is much less likely than if the winner is a peer. Formal authority relationships tend to make power differences between superiors and subordinates more legitimate than similar differences among groups at the same horizontal level in the organization.

At this point, the philosophical stance of the political variant toward resistance should be clear. Resistance is neither good nor bad in and of itself; whether or not it is so labeled usually depends on the vested interests of the person or group doing the labeling. Resistance can be an important, even organizationally healthy, phenomenon by signaling that an information system is altering the balance of power in ways that might cause major organizational dysfunctions. The political variant assumes that systems have no inevitable impacts on the organizations which employ them: ultimately, impacts will depend upon the choices made by people about how to use them. Some of these choices are exercised in the design process; others are expressed in the form of resistance, when previously unforeseen consequences that negatively affect a legitimate group of users come to light. Noble [22] makes a similar point about the impact of technological change generally. Specifically, people can alter management information systems as they use them and thus prevent the realization of implied power distributions by sabotaging the system, providing inaccurate data, not using the system at all, keeping other sets of records, circumventing the intent of the system while obeying the letter, and many other ways. Mechanic [20] describes some of the bases of power available even to people very low in the organizational hierarchy that could give the ability to affect the final outcomes of an MIS, and Strauss [27] describes other tactics that have been used laterally between horizontally related subunits.

The degree of resistance generated by the introduction of a computerized information system is seen, then, in the political variant as a variable intervening between the degree of change in the intraorganization balance of power designed into a system and the degree of power shift actually realized in the organization. Obviously, resistance is not the only factor that could intervene here. Systems in practice rarely match perfectly the intentions of designers, partly because of imperfections in the translation and partly because use contributes to learning about how the system ought to have been designed in the first place. Even more important is the degree to which powerful organizational actors, who may directly benefit from others' loss in power and who may actually intend such loss, are motivated to try to overcome the resistance. The preexisting balance of power and the relative adeptness of various groups at the use of political tactics for avoiding and

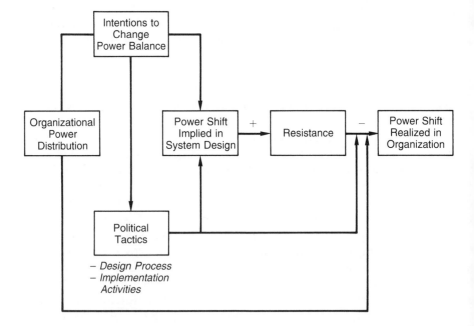

Figure 6. The political perspective

overcoming resistance will largely affect the net outcome for the organization. These considerations are summarized diagrammatically in Figure 6.

The fact that the political version of the interaction theory is only one of several raises the question, when is the political variant more likely than others to be appropriate for understanding MIS implementation? Pfeffer [25] has discussed the circumstances under which organizational decision-making is likely to be accompanied by politics. While the process of designing information systems is not the same as organizational decision-making, it is probably a special case; at least, some of the decision-making processes reported by Mintzberg et al. [21] bear a strong resemblance to the front-half of the information system life cycle. This implies that the political variant is most appropriate when conditions likely to produce political decision-making obtain: when there is disagreement about organizational goals and values: when uncertainty exists about the means required to produce the desired objectives; when resources are scarce; when the decisions are important [25].

Translating these factors into the information systems context suggests that the political variant is the most appropriate analytical framework when organizational participants disagree about the nature of the problem that a system is proposed to solve, when there exists uncertainty about whether a particular proposed system will solve the problem, and when the power bases allocated are highly valued and in short supply. These conditions are most likely to be met when the information system cuts horizontally across several diverse organizational subunits and has many different types of users. Thus the political variant may be more relevant to understanding the implementation of integrated operational information systems, whereas some other perspective, such as one based on concepts of organizational learning may apply better to single-user decision support systems. However, although the political variant may not be most appropriate for every case, it considerably enhances the ability to explain and predict events surrounding the introduction of management information systems into complex organizations.

References

1 Alter S. L. A study of computer aided decision-making in organizations. Unpublished doctoral dissertation. Massachusetts Institute of Technology. Cambridge, Mass., 1975.
2 Bariff, M. L., and Galbraith, J. R. Intraorganizational power considerations for designing information systems. *Accounting Organizations and Society 3* (1978), 15-27.
3 Braverman. H. *Labor and Monopoly Capital*. Monthly Review Press. New York, 1974.
4 Crozier. M. *The Bureaucratic Phenomenon*, Univ. Chicago Press, Chicago, 1964.
5 Dalton, M. *Men Who Manage*. Wiley, New York, 1959.
6 Ginzberg, M. J. A detailed look at implementation research. Rept. CISR-4. Center for Information Systems Research, Massachusetts Institute of Technology, Cambridge, 1974.
7 Ginzberg, M. J. Implementation as a process of change: A framework and empirical study. Rept. CISR-13, Center for Information Systems Research, Massachusetts Institute of Technology, Cambridge, 1975.

8   Hedberg, B., Edstrom, A., Muller W., and Wilpert, S. B. The impact of computer technology on organizational power structures. In E. Grochla and N. Szypersk (Eds.), *Information Systems and Organization Structure*, New York, 1975, pp. 131–148.

9   Keen, P. G. W. Information systems and organizational change. Rept. CISR-46. Center for Information Systems Research, Massachusetts Institute of Technology, Cambridge, 1980.

10   Kling R. Automated information systems as social resources in policy making. *Proceedings of the Association for Computing Machinery*, 1978, pp. 666–74.

11   Kling R. Automated welfare client tracking and service integration: The political economy of computing, *Comm. ACM* (June 1978), 484–493.

12   Kling, R. Defining the boundaries of computing in complex organizations: A Behavioural approach. Working Paper, Univ. California, Irvine, 1982.

13   Kling R. Social analyses of computing: Theoretical perspectives in recent imperial research. *Comput Surv.* 12,1 (1980), 61–110.

14   Landon, K. C. *Computers and Bureaucratic Reform*. Wiley, New York, 1974.

15   Lawler, E. and Rhode, J. G. *Information and Control in Organizations*. Goodyear, Palisades, Calif. 1976.

16   Lucas. H. *Why Information Systems Fail*. Columbia Univ. Press, New York, 1975.

17   Markus, M. L., Implementation politics – Top management support and user involvement. *Systems, Objectives, Solutions* (1981). 203–215.

18   Markus M. I., Understanding information systems use in organizations: A theoretical explanation. Unpublished doctoral dissertation. Case Western Reserve Univ., Cleveland, Ohio, 1979.

19   Markus. M. L. and Pfeffer. J. Power and the design and implementation of accounting and control systems. *Accounting, Organizations and Society*. In press.

20   Mechanic. D. Sources of power of lower participants in complex organization. *Administrative Sci. Quart.* (Dec. 1962), 349–364.

21   Mintzberg H., Raisinghani, D., AND Theoret. A. The structure of 'unstructured' decision processes. *Administrative Sci Quart.* 21. 246– 275.

22   Noble, D. F. Social choice in machine design: The case of automatically controlled machine tools, and a challenge for labor. *Monthly Rev.* (1979).

23   Pettigrew. A. M. Information control as a power resource. *Sociology* (May 1972), 187–204.

24   Pfeffer. J. *Organizational Design*. AHM Publ. Corp. Arlington Heights. Ill., 1978.

25   Pfeffer, J. *Power in Organization*. Pitman Publ. Co., Marshfield Mass., 1981.

26   Robey, D., and Taggart, W. Measuring managers' minds: The assessment of style in human information processing. *Acad. Manag Rev. 6* (3) 1981.

27   Strauss, G. Tactics of lateral relationship: The purchasing agent. In Kolb et al. (Eds.), *Organizational Psychology: A Book of Readings*, 2nd ed., Prentice-Hall, Englewood Cliffs, N. J. 1974.

15 Information resource management – a cross-cultural perspective

R. I. Tricker

1 Introduction

Conventional cliche's about information resource management flow easily from the pen:

Information is modern managements' key resource.

Information management has become a crucial function.

With information technology we are changing organizational intelligence.

This is the information age and the information economy.

Yet in the cascade of cliches we are in danger of drowning an underlying truth: we have not yet adequately defined information.

Boland (5) captures the issue when he writes:

A problem that has plagued research on information systems since the very beginning . . . is the elusive nature of information itself, and the way we as researchers have failed to address the essence of information in our work.

This dilemma is not only an important theoretical issue: there are fundamental practical implications.

Individuals, searching for meaning in a message, seek the information value to them in a stream of data. If we do not understand this process of transformation, if we cannot explain how data becomes information, how can we design effective Information Systems (IS) or Decision Support Systems (DSS)?

This chapter looks at the concept of information from a cultural perspective and points the significance of cultural dimensions for IS design.

2 Derivation and central arguments

This chapter is derived from ongoing work in the University of Hong Kong. For some years, researchers have been studying various aspects of the business management methods of the 'overseas Chinese' (that is Chinese business operating outside the confines of the People's Republic of China, in places such as Taiwan, Singapore and Hong Kong).

Many of these studies have involved cross-cultural comparisons with Western management practices, attitudes, and expectations.

A synopsis of these research findings is the foundation of our consideration of the relevance of cultural issues in effecting information needs, and of the implications of the cultural context for information system design.

The central argument is that Chinese and Western perceptions of business differ. Consequently the information perceived by decision-makers differs; and so must the need for data to inform. In other words, information is culturally influenced: perceptions are culturally determined. In the vernacular – 'what one believes affects what one sees.' Even the data we choose to capture, store, and retrieve is not value-free; our paradigms determine the patterns we preserve – and those we choose to ignore.

The implications are both theoretical and practical.

At the level of theoretical insights, a culture-dependent view highlights the nature of information. Data is not information. There is a process of transformation involved, one which includes the subject in a cultural milieu.

More practically it becomes apparent that IS design is not culturally independent. To date, the development of DSS has tended to be rooted in Western assumptions, values, and ideologies. There is a need to add a cultural dimension where perceptions differ among users.

3 The cultural context

The development of IS can be considered in three contexts: technological, language, and organizational (20). This chapter does not address the technological ways or means by which data streams are delivered, nor the organizational effect or setting in which they are delivered: the perspective is on the way data streams become information for a given recipient.

Various schools of thought and bodies of knowledge have contributions to make in this field:

● the study of cognitive processes, the schemata and styles of thinking (12, 28, 14).
● the study of language, linguistics, symbiotics and semantics (8, 30, 34).
● the behavioural, Skinnerian response view (2, 15).
● the pragmatic, experimental body of knowledge (4, 7).

The perspective adopted here is that of the cultural setting in which messages pass and information is obtained.

The origins of the study of culture are found in anthropology. Cultural anthropology has a rich literature in the field study of the behaviour, customs, ceremonies, artefacts, ways of life, norms, language, and beliefs of native (often primitive) societies.

From such studies, inductive explanations of the effects of culture on individual behaviour have been derived. The apparently non-rational behaviour of people, their customary actions and reactions, are as important to anthropological insights as behaviour that might be perceived as rational.

Boddewyn (3) usefully summarises the findings of cultural anthropology:

'The now-prevailing explanation of the effect of the culture on the individual emphasizes:

1 *Primary groups* as transmitters of the norms. Such groups constitute the immediate milieu within which the individual operates; for example, the relatives or the co-workers who help the individual perceive the environment and ascribe meaning to it.
2 *Language* as the essential vehicle of such social transmission.
3 *Roles* as prescribed behavior or socially expected plans of action for individuals in various situations.
4 *Status* as the various positions that constitute the structure of a group – quite apart from the individuals who occupy these positions.'

The apparent relevance of the viewpoints to the study of information processes is complicated by the different elements.

Redding (26) provides a helpful ordering:

Culture may be seen as operating at three levels and the tree may be seen as interdependent. The base layer is that of the mental world and culture may be said to be more significantly explained in terms of that level, than any other. It is the world of values, of ideals about what is appropriate. It is the perception by the individual of 'the rules of the game' and it is this perception which largely governs behaviour, keeps a society intact and makes it distinct from others. [This is the level of relevance appropriate here'.] Connected to the mental level is the social level which contains the elements of interpersonal behaviour, group identity, basic social forms and patterns . . . The third level is that of institutions and the society as a whole, and it would cover such elements as forms of organization, legal and political systems and economic institutions.

He further suggests that differences exist between Chinese and Western patterns of cognition. Non-Westernised Chinese thinking can be characterised as intuitive, moving from experience via contemplation to understanding, without the abstraction and hypothesis/theory building of Western 'techno-scientific' experience. As a result they are pragmatic but likely to seek conformity to precedence (25, 24).

For the purpose of this study we shall attempt to strike a middle path, adopting Martin's (22) definition:

> (culture is) . . . the shared beliefs, the ideologies and the norms that influence organizational action taking.

Our model of the information process is shown in *Figure 1*; it recognizes:

> an agent (the recipient of the data and the user of the information) who acquires information (and understanding, knowledge) about a given situation state of affairs, set of phenomena), within a cultural context.

It is the cultural context (C) which is the additional dimension, not typically depicted in models of the information process.

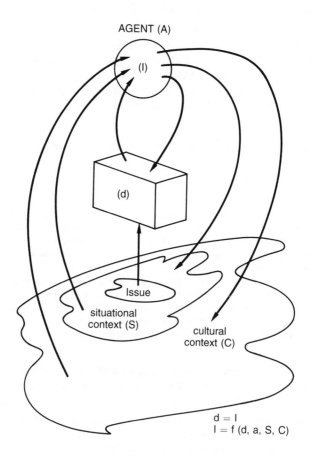

Figure 1.

The agents' information is acquired through a two stage transformation. First, the IS monitors the elements in the situation under surveillance and captures relevant data, transferring and storing them for retrieval. Second the agent is present with, or searches for, the data relevant to his perception of a need to know, thus acquiring information.

The transformation processes may be iterative and the agent's acquisition of understanding a learning process.

We focus on the cultural impact on information acquisition. We use studies of Chinese business and Western cultures to emphasise the importance of the cultural dimension in understanding information processes.

4 The significance of overseas Chinese enterprise

Over the past 100 years or so, there has been a series of movements of people from mainland China to countries around the world. Sometimes the exodus was driven by economic need, e.g., to provide labour for nineteenth century plantations or American construction projects, and sometimes by political turmoil, such as the Shanghai and Southern China refugees around 1950 fleeing from Communist rule.

Consequently there are significant communities of overseas Chinese around the world. Often they retain many of their cultural ties, are not assimilated with the host nation, maintain links with family in China (sometimes remitting money regularly); often they engage in trade and business.

The countries in East Asia that have principally received the influx have been Taiwan (16M Chinese), Hong Kong (5M) (representing 98% of the population) and Singapore (2M).

The economic growth rates of these countries in recent years have been dramatic. Only Japan and South Korea have growth rates that compare. This has led Kahn (13) to offer what have been termed 'the post-Confucian hypothesis'. Noting that Japan, Korea, and the overseas Chinese communities share a common cultural ancestry, dating back to Confucius, he suggested a causal link. Many countries, such as those in Latin America and Africa, which had a similar position on Gross Domestic Product in 1950, have been left far behind in the economic growth stakes; implying that there are lessons to be learned from the impact of a common philosophical ancestry.

5 Characteristics of Chinese firms and cross-cultural comparisons

The characteristics of Chinese firms are now reviewed, for convenience, under five major categories.

But before proceeding, it is worthwhile to challenge any existing shibboleths in the readers' preconceptions with a quotation from a China scholar:

> the route that leads to an understanding of China and the Chinese: those who take it must abandon their preconceptions and be willing to listen with an open mind.

Why? Because Chinese culture has developed in isolation from the West for thousands of years. It possesses a different system of co-ordinates as well as a different scale of values. Many visitors to China find this perplexing, if not downright perverse.

> Chinese history lacks many of the ideas that have helped to shape the Western world. The Chinese have no abstract notion of transcendence or intrinsic goodness, nor have they evolved our strict conception of property. They have taken no interest in metaphysics, logic, and epistemology. They have developed as little thought to the concepts of space and time as to that of freedom, whether in the philosophical sense or in the realm of practical politics. It has never spontaneously occurred to them to count votes and accept majority decisions. Their thoughts have centred all the more on humanity, civilization, and education, on human relationships, on social obligations (not rights), and on the functions of government – in short, on many of the problems that currently beset our own society (32).

6 Family centred firms

The family is the traditional context of the overseas Chinese enterprise. The head of the family fulfils the dominant owner-manager role. Close relatives are employed in key positions. More distant relatives can join in when needed, and long serving employees may acquire an 'honorary membership' of the family circle. The boundaries between business and family are not clear, as they might be in a modern Western company (29, 16, 1, 10).

> In the event, Overseas Chinese organizations are virtually all family businesses, and even the largest of them, having appeared to go public, have rarely become professionally managed bureaucracies of the Western kind, and commonly still display heavy family influence, if not absolute dominance (27).

The family-centric view of the enterprise extends into the business environment. 'Overseas contacts are usually based on uncles and cousins living overseas. Business contacts are friends, and virtually all business is based on personal contacts (18).'

The family-business networks are not held together by formal organization structures or well articulated performance measures but by informal obligation networks.

Social stability and socialisation based on the family unit, promoting sobriety, education, the acquisition of skills, and a sense of responsibility to contribute in tasks, job and other obligations is a primary trait of post-Confucian ideology.

The significance of this family-centric culture goes much deeper than the outward signs of social behaviour: it is inherent in the Chinese view of self. The Chinese person perceives himself inseparable from his networks. He is a being only in-so-far as he connects (11).

> It is perhaps not unreasonable to say that in the West we see the family as an institution which exists to provide an environment in which the individual can be conveniently raised and trained to go out into the world as a full member of society . . . But the emphasis in the traditional Chinese situation was reversed – it was not the family which existed in order to support the individual, but the individual who existed to continue the family (1).

Western thought recognises the primacy of the individual.

> Since the 13th century . . . England has been inhabited by a people whose social, economic and legal system was in essence different, not only from that of peoples in Asia or Eastern Europe, but also in all probability from the Celtic and Continental countries of the same period (31).

Recognition of rights of the individual, enshrined in Magna Carta, the approach to personal ownership of property, and power based on such ownership, suggest that ideas in England had been evolving, emphasising the individual for nearly a thousand years.

> When Jefferson wrote, 'We hold those truths to be sacred and undeniable: that all men are created equal and independent, that from that equal creation they demand rights inherent and inalienable', he was putting into words a view of the individual and society which had its roots in thirteenth-century England or earlier (21).

The Anglo-Saxon concept of the individual is deep-rooted, and needs to be contrasted with the even older Chinese view of man. The English word 'man' with all its overtones of separateness, free-will and individualism does not overlap in meaning with the Chinese word *yan* with all its overtones of connectedness and reciprocal relations.

7 Public funding in family businesses

> Typically overseas Chinese family businesses are small. In Hong Kong, for example, in the manufacturing sector, there are over 45,000 enterprises with fewer than 100 employees whilst less than 150 firms have more than 500 employees, accounting for some 10% of the total workforce in the sector.
>
> [Hong Kong Monthly Digest of Statistics, June 1987]

However, despite their family-capitalism, many of the more successful family enterprises in Hong Kong have created public companies, obtained a Stock Market quotation and attracted funds from individual and institutional investors.

Typically, in inviting outside equity participation, the Chinese-run family business in Hong Kong offers a minority stake in a public company within the network of family firms. Control of this public company is maintained within the family by:

1   Direct investment in the equity by other family companies,
2   Direct investment in the equity by individual family members,
3   Cross holdings with related companies outside the family group,
4   Cross directorships with related companies,
5   Transactions creating an element of control with related parties.

One might legitimately wonder why anyone would invest, as a minority outside shareholder, in such a family firm.

The answer may lie in the attitude of the (largely) Chinese investor. It appears that the appreciation of the nature of a public company is not widespread, nor are there significant expectations of disclosure, regulation, or independent supervision. Rather the investor equates the public company, in which he can buy a share, with the family group of which it is part. The investment is not so much in the specific public company as in the reputation of the owner-entrepreneur, the network of family businesses, and the future good-fortunes of that family.

The cross-cultural contrast with Anglo-American expectation of disclosure and regulation for the protection of investors is rooted in the concept of the joint-stock, limited liability company, which, it should be remembered, is an outgrowth of mid-nineteenth century Western ideologies.

8   Centralised decision taking

Power and prestige in the Chinese business lie with the owner-manager. Responsibility for day to day activities of production and operation may be delegated to managers, but with frequent rearrangements and what would be considered interference in delegated responsibilities by Western executives. Responsibility for financial and personnel matters typically remains with the owner.

> Unlike their more bureaucratic Western counterparts, with extensive reliance on formal rules and written procedures, Chinese managers rely on highly centralised finance and budget decision-making, and on personnel practices which enhance trust and control (6).

Managers have little power or prestige in the Chinese organisational model (23). The owners' image is stamped throughout the enterprise.

In the Chinese culture there is a ready acceptance of authority and the essental rightness of hierarchy. The father of the family is respected and his sons will follow his direction. It is quite normal, for example, for a son who has been highly successful in business abroad, to return at his father's bidding to contribute to the family enterprise. Such an occurence would be much less likely in a Western setting, where individuals expect independence once they 'leave home'.

With the Chinese respect for authority comes a natural acceptance of hierarchy. By contrast, the Western mind has a preference for egalitarianism, reflecting the individual-centred perception.

> The Chinese devoutly believe that a large gap should exist between the entrepreneur-owner and the manager. They see this as a strong incentive to their young people to become entrepreneurs (19).

The contrast between Eastern and Western tolerance of societal power-distance (i.e., the degree of acceptance of social hierarchy) is strikingly shown in the important study by Hofstede (9). In a vast cross-cultural study of over 50,000 people in business organizations, he was able to demonstrate dramatically the different attitudes to power distance and to individualism (see *figure 2*).

Those cultures in the upper right quadrant tolerate large power distances and are low on their view of the significance of the individual as against the collectivity. Notice that all the countries with significant overseas Chinese communities are in this quadrant.

The bottom right quadrant has cultures that also tolerate high power-distance, but which put a higher ranking on the individual. The European Roman-Catholic countries are in this quadrant.

The bottom left quadrant captures those cultures in which toleration of high power-distance is at its least and which rate the individual highly. The other European countries are in this quadrant.

Notice that Great Britain, the USA, Canada, Australia and New Zealand form a special group. They are dramatically differentiated from the rest of the world; and dramatically opposite to the Chinese group.

9 Paternalistic management style

In Chinese organisations there is:

> an admiration for the owner who seems to be in control, who orchestrates everything, who defines the rules and regulations, without being subject to them (19).

Loyalty is expected from the employee, matched by a paternalistic concern, often rooted in economic dependence. Little, if any, effort is made to provide management training; partly because of the low level of authority given to managers, and party to reduce the risk of investing in someone who thereupon leaves to set up a business in competition.

> Recruitment decisions in Chinese firms emphasise trustworthiness and loyalty to a far greater degree than in Western firms. Well known is the tendency to hire kinsmen or closely trusted persons for top level positions, rather than to search more widely for person of the best qualifications . . .(6).

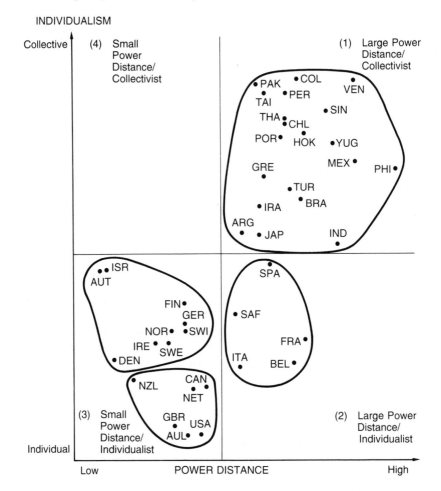

Figure 2. The position of the 40 Countries on Power Distance and Individualism. *Source:* Hofstede, Geert, Motivation, Leadership, and Organization: Do American Theories Apply Abroad?, Organizational Dynamics (Summer 1980) pp. 42–63. *Copyright:* G. Hofstede; reproduced with permission.

Key to figure:

AUT Austria	FRA France	ARG Argentina	PAK Pakistan
DEN Denmark	ITA Italy	BRA Brazil	PER Peru
FIN Finland	SAF South Africa	CHL Chile	PHI Philippines
GER Germany	SPA Spain	COL Columbia	POR Portugal
IRE Ireland		GRE Greece	SIN Singapore
ISR Israel	AUL Australia	HOK Hong Kong	TAI Taiwan
NOR Norway	CAN Canada	IND India	THA Thailand
SWE Sweden	GBR Great Britain	IRA Iran	TUR Turkey
SWI Switzerland	NET Netherlands	JAP Japan	VEN Venezuela
NZL New Zealand	MEX Mexico	YUG Yugoslavia	
BEL Belgium	USA United States of America		

In a society whose social fabric is dependent on networks of relationship, social harmony is likely to be a prerequisite.

A great deal of ritual behaviour takes place in the Chinese organization in an effort to maintain the social harmony which is so highly prized (27). By contrast Western society is likely to emphasise the 'tough-minded, open and frank' discussion in its business dealings. Prepared to risk confrontation for the sake of clarity and to move towards a unequivocal outcome, the Western manager avoids the ambiguity and lack of directness needed in East. His Chinese counterpart would have to employ far more subtlety in the exchange, to avoid putting anyone in the position of risking 'loss of face'.

The concept of face provides a useful insight into the Chinese perception of self in society, and the importance of preserving one's standing.

Loyalty to other members of one's group is the society's most outstanding value and this loyalty requires that friends and relatives go to extreme lengths to honour their obligations to each other. The disloyal person is a person without face . . .(33)

10 Intuitive strategy formulation

The underlying perception of buiness in the Chinese mind is as series of ad hoc deals, a succession of contracts or ventures rather than a dominant strategy to provide a product and create a market. There is a close parallel to the attitude of a trader.

Consequently Chinese manufacturing companies in Hong Kong are often dependent on a handful of customers for whom they manufacture-to-order. There is seldom a research and development function, a marketing function, or expenditure on product or market development.

. . . the special nature of the Chinese management system which is orientated more to deals and resulting streams of cash flow than to balance-sheet accountability and systematic long-term control (27).

There is an element of intuition and hunch, a reliance on good fortune and superstition (accompanied by a toughminded business bargaining stance), which is less apparent in the Western strategic planner who relies, at least overtly, on more analysis and quantitative planning.

It is interesting that both the Confucian and the Protestant perspective produced a work ethic that encourages diligence, the acquisition of skills, thrift, sobriety, and a commitment to hard work. Though the driving forces were quite different (the one to serve the family, the other to achieve rewards thereafter), the effects on individual behaviour were similar.

However the pursuit of wealth, which is a striking feature of the overseas Chinese, their entrepreneurial motivation, and the drive to acquire material success may be better explained by the uncertainties of life within a host society, and memories of recent refugee status (17).

11   Cultural constructs in the search for meaning

The evidence, drawn from cross-cultural studies of Chinese and Western management practices, has now been presented. What inferences might be drawn from this material? In what ways might culturally influenced perceptions affect the transformation of data into meaningful information for a user?

It is postulated that the significant differences between Chinese and Western cultural underpinnings will affect a decision-making agent's interpretation of data received. Examples occur in the recognition of business entity boundaries and purposes, also in the individual's roles and responsibilities.

(a) *Different conceptions of boundaries*

Although the Western educated and influenced decision maker readily perceives the formal boundaries of any company, appreciating the structure of the incorporated limited liability company, they may not so readily appreciate that these boundaries are culturally defined. The joint stock company is an outgrowth of Victorian ideology. The separation of a corporate entity from its owners is a Western concept. The Chinese educated and influenced decision maker, in receipt of similar data stimuli but perceiving the company as business enmeshed in a set of family links and obligations, would obtain a quite different mental image; i.e., strikingly different information.

Evidence to support this contention is found in the actions of Chinese owner-managers in taking decisions about financial matters between various parts of their group of family firms; these decisions are not rational to Western-thinking managers.

(b) *Different perceptions of purpose*

In the Western mind, a business can have a variety of purposes in its own right; e.g., to fulfil a long-term product and market strategy, to provide employment, or to satisfy its shareholders. However, if the business is an integral part of the family activities and fortunes, the notion that a business has purposes, goals, strategies in its own right is not meaningful.

Such differences are fundamental to the message interpreted from a set of data about the business. The 'failure' of the Chinese entrepreneur to develop a cohesive long-term strategy, their lack of detailed analysis, and reliance on intuition and short term reactions, sometimes criticised by Western educated commentators, can be explained by reference to the alternative Chinese view.

Thus we have sought to show that the process through which an agent obtains information of value from a stream of data is influenced by cultural considerations.

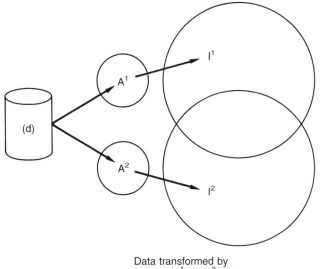

Data transformed by
Agents (A^1) & (A^2) into
Information (I^1) & (I^2)

Figure 3.

Of course, to create a dichotomy suggesting that the Western and the Chinese cultural backgrounds would produce two quite different sets of information from given data is naive. Many elements appear common to both. Chinese agents are influenced by Western education and cultural experiences, and vice versa. A more meaningful description is of two overlapping sets of meaning (*Figure 3*). But it is in the differences within the Venn diagram that the interest lies.

12 Conclusions and implications

Two broad conclusions seem to flow from these arguments:

1 that the transformation process by which an Agent acquires information (as in fig. 1) is culturally significant, and may be culturally dependent.
2 that cultural factors have a part to play in IS Research and Information Resource Management – certainly where there are international, cross-cultural dimensions – and possibly within a nation state where corporate cultures differ.

The traditional paradigms of IS study are rooted in Anglo-Saxon, Western thought. Few system scientists with Western education and Western cultural orientations appreciate that what seem to be absolutes (beliefs about the

importance of the individual, about the right to knowledge, about responsibilities to disclose, about freedoms of expression etc.) are not absolutes at all,
but are culturally derived. In other words, they are based on a view of the
world conditioned by two or three thousand years of Judao/Christian belief.
But alternative systems of belief, thought and culture have also evolved.

What are the implications?

Firstly, an obvious and practical matter is that such cultural differences
and their effects on information processes, need to be recognised – for
example, if one is responsible for Information Resource Management across
cultural boundaries, as in a multi-national company operating in different
countries; and probably even between subsidiaries or divisions, in a single
country, where there are significantly different cultural dimensions.

Secondly, at a more conceptual level another set of implications arise:

(a) Methodologies for DSS, Information Centres, Knowledge-based system
etc. will need to include a cultural dimension if they are to be effective in
multi-cultural circumstances.

(b) Also information resource management has wider boundaries and
responsibilities than many have thus far recognised. The balance
between order and freedom in an organization or in a society is relevant.

We live in a culturally dependent world: the processes through which man
becomes informed about his world, able to interact with it, to control it, are
culturally determined; just as are the processes of information and the
methods by which we seek to manage the information resource.

And there is also a fascinating corollary to the principal argument in this
paper, that to understand infomation, one needs to recognise the cultural
dimension.

Language is a primary feature in distinguishing cultures. We who design
information systems and are managing information, are, in that process,
influencing and changing cultures.

In the Olympian days of old this was a responsibility reserved for the gods:
but if mythology is to be believed the gods had a lot of fun in the process!

References

1   Baker, H. R. D., *Chinese family and kinship*, Macmillan, 1979.
2   Baniff, M. and M. J. Ginzberg, MIS and the behavioural sciences, *Database* 13.1, 1982.
3   Boddewyn, Jean, The cultural approach to business behavior, in: McGuire, J. W.,
    Interdisciplinary studies in business behaviour, South-Western Publishing Co., 1962.
4   Boland, R. J., Control, causality and information system requirements, *Accounting,
    organisation and society*, 4, 5, Pergamon, 1979.
5   Boland, Richard J., Jr., The information of information systems, in Boland and Hirscheim,
    Critical issues in information systems research, Wiley, 1987.
6   Deyo, F. C., Chinese management practices and work commitment in comparative
    perspective. In: L.A.P. Gosling and L.Y.C. Lim (eds.), *The Chinese in Southeast Asia*: Vol
    11, Identity, culture and polities, Maruzen Asia, 1983.

7 Earl, M. J. and A. G. Hopwood, From management information to information management, *The Information Systems Environment:* Lucas, Land and Lincoln (eds.), North Holland, 1980.

8 Hayakawa, S. I., *Language in thought and action.* Harcourt, Brace and World, 1963.

9 Hofstede, G., *Culture's consequences*, Sage Publication, 1980.

10 Hsu, F.L.K., *Americans and Chinese: passage to differences*, University Press of Hawaii, 1981.

11 Hsu, F.L.K., Psychosocial homeostasis and Jon – conceptual tools for advance in psychological anthropology, *American Anthropologist* 73, 1971.

12 Johnson, P. E., The expert mind, in: *Beyond productivity – IS for organizational effectiveness.* Bemelmans (ed). North Holland, 1984.

13 Kahn, H., *World development: 1979 and beyond.* Croom-Helm, 1979.

14 Keen, P. and M. Scott-Morton, *Decision support systems – an organizational perspective*, Addison-Wesley, 1978.

15 Kendall, K. E. and C. Kriebel, Contributions of the Management Science to MIS, *Data Base* 13.1, 1982.

16 Lai, P. W. H., *Nepotism and management in Hong Kong.* Unpublished Dip MS dissertation, University of Hong Kong, 1978.

17 Lau, S. K., *Society and politics in Hong Kong*, Chinese University Press, 1982.

18 Leeming, F., *Street studies in Hong Kong*, Oxford University Press (Hong Kong), 1977.

19 Limlingan, V., *The Chinese walkabout: a case study in entrepreneurial education*, Asian Institute of Management, Manila, 1983.

20 Lyytinen, Kalle, A taxonomic perspective of information systems development, in: Boland and Hirscheim, *Critical issues in information system research*, Wiley, 1987.

21 Macfarlane, Alan, *The origins of English individualism*, Blackwell, 1978.

22 Martin, J., Stories and scripts in organizational settings, in: Hastorf, A. and A. Isem (eds.), *Cognitive social psychology*, Elsevier North-Holland, 1982.

23 MDC, *Case Study of Hong Kong banking company*, unpublished action research report, Management Development Centre of Hong Kong, 1986.

24 Nakamura. H., *Ways of thinking of Eastern Peoples*, University Press of Hawaii, 1964.

25 Northrop, F.S.C., *The meeting of East and West*, Macmillan, 1946.

26 Redding, S. G., *Western and Chinese modes of reasoning – their implications for engineering management*, Hong Kong Engineer, March 1982, Hong Kong Institute of Engineering paper, 14 April, 1982.

27 Redding, S.G. and G. Wong, The psychology of Chinese organizational behaviour, in: M. H. Bond (ed.), *The psychology of Chinese people*, Oxford University Press (Hong Kong), 1986.

28 Shneiderman, B., *Software psychology*, Winthrop, 1981.

29 Silin, R., *Leadership and values*, Harvard University Press, 1976.

30 Stamper, R., Semantics, in: Boland and Hirscheim, *Critical issues in information systems research*, Wiley, 1987.

31 Trevelyan, G. M., *English social history*, Penguin, 1944.

32 Wickert, Erwin, *The Middle Kingdom – inside China today*, (Translated by J. Maxwell Brownjohn), Harvill Press, 1983 and Pan Books, 1984. Original: Deutsche Vorlags-Anstalt, 1981.

33 Wilson, R. W., *Learning to be Chinese: the political socialization of children in Taiwan*, MIT Press, 1970.

34 Wittgenstein, L., *Philosophical Investigations*, Blackwell, 1974.

16 Information technology in the 1990s: managing organizational interdependence

J. F. Rockart and J. E. Short

For the past two decades, the question of what impact information technology (IT) will have on business organizations has continued to puzzle academics and practitioners alike. Indeed, in an era when the business press has widely disseminated the idea that IT is changing the way businesses operate and the way they relate to customers and suppliers, the question of technology's impact on the organization itself has gained renewed urgency.

The literature suggests four major classes of impact. First, there is the view that technology changes many facets of the organization's *internal structure*, affecting roles, power, and hierarchy. A second body of literature focuses on the emergence of *team-based*, problem-focused, often-changing work groups, supported by electronic communications, as the primary organizationl form.

Third, there is the view that organizations today are '*disintegrating*' – their borders punctured by the steadily decreasing costs of eletronic interconnection among firms, suppliers, and customers. Companies, it is believed, will gradually shift to more market-based organizational forms, with specialized firms taking over many functions formerly performed within the hierarchical firm.

Finally, a fourth view of organizational change arises from a technical perspective. Here, it is argued that today's improved communications capability and data accessibility will lead to *systems integration* within the business. This, in turn, will lead to vastly improved group communications and, more important, the integration of business processes across traditional functional, product, or geographic lines.

While each of these four 'IT impact' perspectives offers important insights, there are significant and unresolved questions about each. To shed additional light on this issue, the Center for Information Systems Research (CISR) at the MIT Sloan School of Management recently conducted a fourteen-month study of sixteen major companies. Emerging from this study is the strong belief that the current 'IT impacts' picture is incomplete. There is clear evidence for a fifth viewpoint that draws on and expands these perspectives, providing a more integrated, managerial view with important implications for today's executives.

We will argue here that information technology provides a new approach to one of management's oldest organizational problems: that of effectively *managing interdependence.* Our fundamental thesis is that a firm's ability to continuously improve the effectiveness of managing interdependence is the critical element in reponding to new and pressing competitive forces. Unlike in previous eras, managerial strategies based on optimizing operations *within* functional departments, product lines, or geographical organizations simply will not be adequate in the future.

By 'effective management of interdependence,' we mean a firm's ability to achieve concurrence of effort along multiple dimensions of the organization.[1] Companies have historically been divided into subunits along several dimensions such as functional departments, product lines, and geographic units. It has long been understood that the activities in each of these dimensions, and in each of the subunits *within* these dimensions (e.g., branch offices, manufacturing locations), are far from independent. Many approaches have been devised to manage this evident interdependence. Each approach has the goal of producing the concurrence of effort necessary to allow the organization to compete effectively in the marketplace. Information technology has now been added to these approaches – and it is in this role that it will have its major impact on the firm.

Competitive forces driving the need to manage interdependence

The need to effectively coordinate the activities of individual organizational subunits is vastly greater in 1989 than it was even a few years ago. Competitive pressures are now forcing almost all major firms to become global in scope, to decrease time to market, and to redouble their efforts to manage risk, service, and cost on a truly international scale (see Figure 1).

● **Globalization.** In a world linked by international communication networks and television, global competition stresses the firm's ability to innovate, to capture global levels of manufacturing efficiency, and to understand international marketing and the diversity of the world's markets. All require increasing knowledge and coordination of the firm's operations throughout geographically dispersed subunits.

● **Time to Market.** Black & Decker now brings new products to market in half the time it took before 1985. Xerox and Ford have claimed similar improvements in key product lines. 'Time to market' refers to the firm's ability to develop new products quickly and to deliver existing products effectively. In either case, compressing time to market requires increased integration of effort among functional departments such as design, engineering, manufacturing, purchasing, distribution, and service.

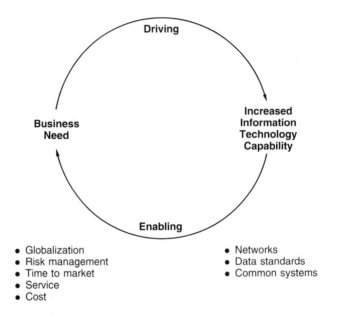

Figure 1 . What is pushing the need to manage interdependence?

● **Risk Management**. Market volatility and competitive pressures can easily overwhelm a firm's ability to track and manage its risk. In one highly publicized incident, Merrill Lynch lost more than $250 million when it failed to adequately oversee an employee trading a complex form of mortgage backed securities.[2] Whatever the industry, the globalization of markets and global market volatility increase the need for effective risk management across once independently managed operations.

● **Service**. 'The excellent companies really are close to their customers,' Peters and Waterman wrote in *The Search for Excellence*. 'Other companies talk about it; the excellent companies do it.'[3] Of course, service is based not only on the effectiveness of a single repair person, but also on management's ability to have organization-wide knowledge of customer's and equipment's status and problems.

● **Cost**. For nearly all organizations, cost reduction is always a concern. In industries where foreign competitors are becoming dominant, reductions in workforce are an increasing reality.

In sum, global competition, risk, service, and cost today require firms to tightly couple their core internal and external business processes. As firms begin to draw these processes together, slack resources (e.g., inventory, redundant personnel) are being reduced.

It is here that information technology plays a major role. Vastly improved communications capability and more cost-effective computer hardware and software enable the 'wiring' together of individuals and suborganizations within the single firm, and of firms to each other. It is this multifunctional, multilevel, multiorganizational, coordinative aspect of current technology that provides managers with a new approach to managing interdependence effectively.

Technology's major impacts on the organization

Several decades of work have produced conflicting perspectives on technology's impacts on the organization. Here we briefly review the four approaches noted above.

Major changes in managerial structure, roles, and processes

In an early, celebrated article, Leavitt and Whisler argued that information technology would lead to a general restructuring of the organization, ultimately eliminating middle management.[4] In their view, IT moved middle managers out of traditional roles, and allowed top managers to take on an even larger portion of the innovating, planning, and other 'creative' functions required to run the business.

Others were quick to comment on these predictions. Some speculated that IT would lead to greater organizational centralization, greater decentraliation, reduced layers of middle or upper management, greater centralization of managerial power, or, alternatively, decentralization of managerial power.[5] Others developed contingency-based models of organizational impact.[6] While it is clear that IT has affected organizations in many ways, it is also clear that this often conflicting literature has produced very little insight into how managers should plan for IT-enabled role or structural changes within their firms. Three newer perspectives begin to address this issue.

The team as hero

According to this second view, teams and other ad hoc decision-making structures will provide the basis for a permanent organizational form. Reich, for example, argues that a 'collective entrepreneurship', with few middle-level managers and only modest differences between senior managers and junior employees, is developing.[7] Drucker speculates that the symphony orchestra or hospital may be models of future team-based organizations.[8]

The relationship between teams and technology in much of this work appears based on a technical dimension. On the one hand, this view stresses technology's role in enabling geographically dispersed groups to better coordinate their activities through enhanced electronic communications.[9] On the other hand, some authors stress the importance of 'groupware' in facilitating teamwork and through better decision-making aids and project and problem management.[10]

Unfortunately, the team-based literature to date is highly speculative. As a general model of organizational structure, it leaves many questions unanswered. Primary among these are the long-term implications of organizing in a manner that moves primary reporting relationships away from the more usual hierarchical functional, geographic, or product structures. These structures work to immerse employees in pools of 'front line', continually renewed expertise. Team members separated too long from these bases tend to lose this expertise.[11]

Corporate 'disintegration': more markets and less hierarchy

A third perspective argues that today's hierarchical organizations are steadily disintegrating – their borders punctured by the combined effects of electronic communication (greatly increased flows of information), electronic brokerage (technology's ability to connect many different buyers and suppliers instantaneously through a central database), and electronic integration (tighter coupling between interorganizational processes). In this view, the main effect of technology on organizations is not in how tasks are performed (faster, better, cheaper, etc), but rather in how firms organize the flow of goods and services through value-added chains.

There are two major threads to this argument. Malone, Yates, and Benjamin state that new information technologies will allow closer integration of adjacent steps in the value-added chain through the development of electronic markets and electronic hierarchies.[12] Johnston and Lawrence argue that IT-enabled value-adding partnerships (VAPs) are rapidly emerging.[13] Typified by McKesson Corporation's 'Economist' drug distribution service, VAPs are groups of small companies that share information freely and view the whole value-added chain – not just part of it – as one competitive unit.

These proposals, however, are very recent and have only small amounts of sample data to support them. And the opposite case – the case for increased, vertical integration of firms – is also being strongly propounded.[14]

Systems integration: common systems and data architecture

A fourth, more technically oriented view is that business integration is supported by systems and data integration. Here the concept of IT-enabled organizational integration is presented as a natural outgrowth of two IT properties: improved inter-connection and improved shared data accessibility.[15] In this view, 'integration' refers to integration of data, of organizational communications (with emphasis on groups), and of business processes across functional, geographic, or product lines.

The need to manage interdependence

While each of these four approaches offers important insights, there is a need for a fifth perspective that expands these views into a more active managerial framework. Our research suggests that the concept of 'managing interdependence' most clearly reflects what managers *actually do* in today's business organizations.

Managers, of course, oversee innumerable large and small interdependencies. What happens in one function affects another. Although companies maintain 'independent' product lines, success or failure in one product line casts a shadow on the others. Individual specialists are also highly interdependent. Surgeons, for example, cannot operate without nurses, technicians, and anesthetists. And even the simplest of manufacturing processes requires the precise interconnection of hundreds of steps. Other examples:

- Production engineers rely on product designers to design parts that can be easily and quickly fabricated. Conversely, designers depend on product engineers to implement design concepts faithfully.
- Sales representatives for a nationwide or a worldwide company are also interdependent. The same large customer may be served by many sales offices throughout the world. Common discounts, contract terms, and service procedures must be maintained. Feedback can be important.
- Companies themselves rely on other companies to supply parts or services. The current shortage of memory chips, and the resulting shortage of some types of computer hardware, is a good example of intra-company interdependence.

In sum, interdependence is a fact of organizational life. What is different today, however, is the increasing need to manage interdependence, as well as technology's role in providing tools to help meet this need.

How do companies today manage interdependence? Several approaches have been proposed: Mintzberg, for example, argued that firms coordinate work through five basic mechanisms: mutual adjustment, direct supervision, standardization of work process, standardization of work output, and standardization of worker skills.[16] Lawrence and Lorsch found that successful companies differentiated themselves into suborganizations to allow accumulation of expertise and simpler management processes driven by shared goals and objectives.[17] Conversely, these same successful firms adopted integrating mechanisms to coordinate work activity across suborganizations. Lawrence and Lorsch postulated five mechanisms to manage the needed integration: integrative departments, whose primary activity was to coordinate effort among *functional* departments; permanent and/or temporary cross-functional teams; reliance on direct management contact at all levels of the firm; integration through the formal hierarchy; and integration via a 'paper-based system' of information exchange.

Galbraith later expanded the intellectual understanding of managing integration through people-oriented mechanisms.[18] He noted that direct contact, liaison roles, task forces, and teams were used primarily for lateral relations, permitting companies to make more decisions and process more information without overloading hierarchical communication channels. He also introduced the concept of computer-based information systems as a vertical integrator within the firm.

Five examples of managing interdependence

Today, Galbraith's vision of computer-based information systems as a *vertical* integrator appears prescient, if incomplete. Given pressures from the 'drivers' noted earlier, major aspects of information technology (networks,

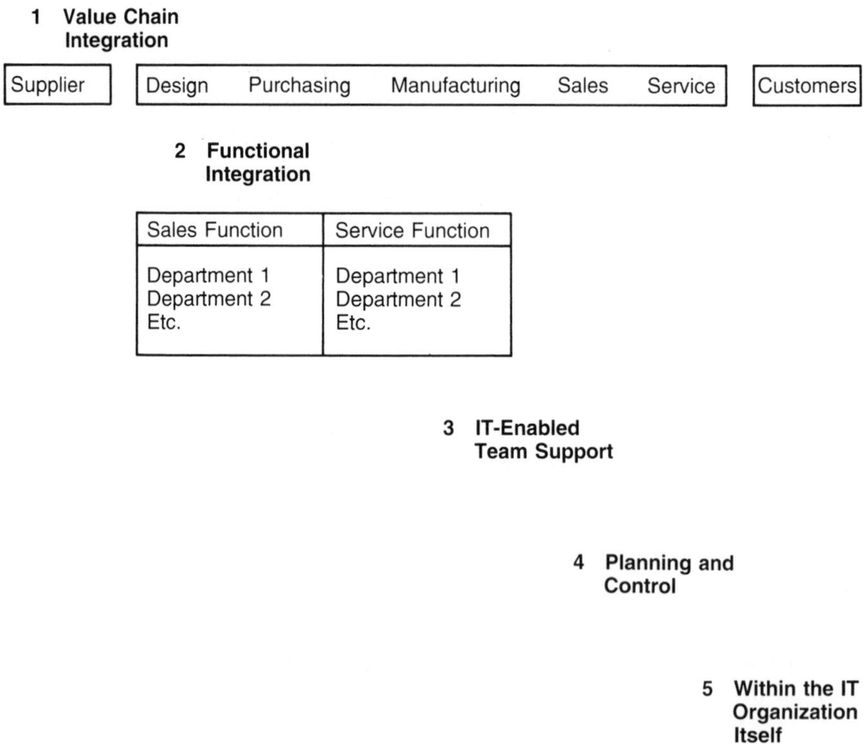

**1 Value Chain
    Integration**

Supplier	Design	Purchasing	Manufacturing	Sales	Service	Customers

**2 Functional
    Integration**

Sales Function	Service Function
Department 1	Department 1
Department 2	Department 2
Etc.	Etc.

**3 IT-Enabled
    Team Support**

**4 Planning and
    Control**

**5 Within the IT
    Organization
    Itself**

Figure 2. Managing interdependence in five organizational contexts

for example; see Figure 1) serve increasingly as mechanisms for both horizontal and vertical integration. In particular, our work has uncovered six organizational contexts where IT-enabled integration efforts strikingly improved a company's ability to manage its functional, product, or geographic subunits. We focus here on five of the six contexts, as illustrated in Figure 2. (A sixth area of interest, interorganizational integration, is well documented in the literature, and can be viewed as carrying intra-organizational integration into the multifirm context.[19])

Value-chain integration

Lawrence and Lorsch noted the use of 'human integrators' to manage concurrence of effort between adjacent functions in the value-added chain (e.g., between manufacturing, distribution, and sales) more than twenty years ago. Today this integration is performed increasingly by using electronic networks, computers, and databases. Firms attempt between-function integration for at least one of three reasons: to increase their capacity to respond quickly and effectively to market forces, to improve the quality of conformance to customer requirements, or to reduce costs.[20]

We have found that successful between-function integration collapses the multistage value-added chain into three major segments: developing new products, delivering products to customers, and managing customer relationships (see Figure 3).[21] In manufacturing companies, for example, it is clear that interdependence revolves around these three macro-organizational activities. In the insurance industry, discussions with five major companies revealed that the same three segments were targets for functional integration.

Turning to the two 'ends' of the modified value-added chain – the product design segment on the one end, and the customer service segment on the other – the effects of technology-enabled integration are clear. To speed *product development*, companies such as Xerox, Lockheed, and Digital are introducing CAD/CAM and other design aids that provide integrated support to product designers, product engineers, materials purchasing, and manufacturing personnel involved in the design-to-production process. This compression has resulted in joint 'buy-in' on new product designs, eliminating a lengthy iterative development process (which occurred because designers did not take the needs and capabilities of other departments into account). Dramatically shortened product development time has been the consequence of this buy-in.

At the *customer service* end of the chain, Otis Elevator, Digital, and Xerox have developed service strategies and new service markets based on electronic networks, an integrated database of customer and service history, and fault signaling that goes directly from the damaged equipment to the supplier's maintenance-monitoring computer. The advantages of Otis's centrally coordinated electronic service system have been well publicized.[22] Perhaps the most important advantage is senior management's ability to view

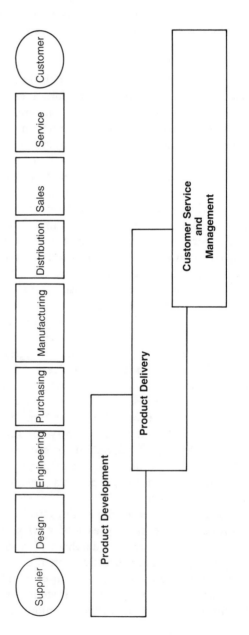

Figure 3. Product development, product delivery and customer service and management: collapsing the value-added chain

the status of maintenance efforts nationwide and to direct sales and service attention where needed. In addition, it is now feasible to provide the company's design, engineering, and manufacturing personnel with direct access to fault data.

In many ways the most interesting stage of the collapsed value chain is *product delivery*, which requires integrating several different information systems: order entry, purchasing, materials resources planning, and distribution management. The critical business issues are to provide customers with information about when orders will be completed, and to forecast and manage outside supplier, product manufacturer, and product distribution processes.

No company has yet accomplished the large-scale integration of functions and systems required to fully manage product delivery. A division of the Norton Company, however, pioneered efforts in this direction in the mid-1980s. Norton initiated a set of major IT projects, ranging from the 'Norton Connection' (a computer-based telecommunications link between the company and its distributors), to a more effective order-processing system, to a series of manufacturing technologies targeted at flexible manufacturing and automated materials control.[23] More recently, Westinghouse initiated a product delivery integration process in several segments of the company. And at General Foods a series of task forces has been charged with developing a similar approach.

Most efforts, however, are more limited in scope. British Petroleum Company's chemical business has developed an integrated order management process spanning thirteen divisions. Baxter Healthcare Corporation is working to enhance its well-known ASAP order entry system to provide customers with full product line visibility to their 125,000-plus products. And a host of manufacturing integration projects have been initiated at Digital Equipment Corporation, Ford Motor, IBM, General Motors, Hewlett-Packard, and Texas Instruments, to name just a few.

Functional integration

Many companies are also recognizing the interdependence of multiple units *within* the same function. This recognition has led to several actions designed to improve coordination across subunits – for example, centralization of functions, central management of geographically separate units, and (in some firms) the development of common systems and/ or standard data definitions to facilitate coordinating organizational units.

At Sun Refining and Marketing Company, for example, senior management identified crude oil trading as one of the most critical business activities in the firm three years ago. At that point Sun's traders were dispersed worldwide, each acting relatively autonomously. Sun began developing a centralized, on-line trading function supported by integrated market information from Reuters and other trade data sources. Today Sun recognizes the importance of its integrated trading funtion in managing risk exposure and in developing effective pricing strategies for the volatile crude market.

At Chemical Bank in New York, foreign exchange trading has become the largest profit generator. To improve management of its worldwide trading operations, Chemical's information technology efforts have ranged from advanced trader workstations to more effective integration of the 'front end' (booking a transaction) with the back office (transaction clearance and settlement). The bank has also improved capital markets auditing through the use of expert systems support.

And finally, while OTISLINE can be viewed as an application enabling integration across stages of the value-added chain, it is also an integrating mechanism within the field maintenance organization itself. Customers with difficult problems can immediately be directed to a specialist, not left to the limited resources of a remote branch office. Frequent trouble from a specific type of elevator can be observed as the pattern develops, and corrective action taken on a nationwide basis. In addition, the quality of telephone responsiveness to anxious customers can be closely monitored.

Similarly, a number of other companies are working aggressively to coordinate the efforts of subunits within a single function, whether it be manufacturing, maintenance, purchasing, sales and marketing, or others. Kodak has developed scheduling of manufacturing plants. Digital is installing common MRP systems throughout all of its manufacturing plants. And so it goes. The business drivers underscoring each of these efforts range from service to cost to time-to-market to global responsiveness – but they all recognize that no single unit in a major function is truly independent.

IT enabled team support

Ken Olsen, Chairman of Digital Equipment Corporation, believes that the ability to bring teams together electronically is one of the most important features of the company's IT capability. Ford Motor has claimed that the 'Team Taurus' approach, much of it IT-enabled, shaved more than a year off the time needed to develop, build, and bring to market the new Taurus/Sable model line. In the future, as Drucker points out, many tasks will be done primarily by teams.[24]

Teamwork, of course, is not a new way to coordinate interdependent ctivities among separate units in an organization. What *is* new is that electronic mail, computer conferencing, and videoconferencing now facilitate this process. Today it is feasible for team members to coordinate asynchronously (across time zones) and geographically (across remote locations) more easily than ever before.

The development and use of computer software to support teams is also moving into an explosive phase. There is a growing body of software labeled 'groupware', a generic name for specialized computer aids designed to support collaborative work groups. As Bullen and Johansen point out, 'Groupware is not a thing. Rather it is a perspective on computing that emphasizes collaboration – rather than individual use.'[25] Several companies, including Xerox, General Motors, Digital, Eastman Kodak, IBM, and AT&T, are experimenting with state-of-the-art meeting and conferencing aids in addition to more 'routine' communications systems such as electronic mail or voice mail systems.

Planning and control

For the past two or three decades, the managerial control process has looked much the same across major companies.[26] Before a new fiscal year begins, an intense planning process culminates with an extended presentation to senior management of each small business unit's (SBU's) proposed activities. Agreed upon plans are then monitored on a monthly basis. Parallel to this formal control process is an informal system of 'keeping in touch', by which senior management assures itself that 'all is going well' in key areas of the business in the interim between formal reports.

Volatility in the business environment, coupled with technology's ability to provide management with efficient communication and information, is radically changing this traditional planning and control scenario. The major issue is how best to use IT for coordination and control of the firm's activities.

At Xerox, Chairman David Kearns and President Paul Allaire have implemented an executive support system that now makes the annual planning and control process a more on-line, team-based, communication- and coordination-based process. The system requires all of Xerox's thirty-four business units to submit their plans over an electronic network in a particular format. Doing this allows the staff to critique the plans more effectively and to reintegrate these plans when looking for factors such as competitive threats across all SBUs, penetration into particular industries by all SBUs, and so forth.

More important, each SBU's plans can be reviewed not only by senior executives and corporate staff but also by other top officers in the firm. Each officer receiving an SBU's plans is encouraged to send corporate headquarters an electronic message raising the issues he or she sees in the plan. The officer may also be asked to attend the review meeting. There is no 'upfront' presentation at this meeting. Only the issues raised by the executives, the staff, or the other officers are discussed.

In short, Allaire's planning and control process is a computer-age process. Through the network, it draws on the entire executive team for input. Understanding of the important issues facing each SBU is deeper and its activities are therefore sometimes subtly, sometimes more precisely, coordinated with those of the other SBUs.

A team-based, network-linked approach to the senior executive job of managing the business is also in evidence at Phillips Petroleum Company's Products and Chemicals Group. There, executive vice president Robert Wallace is linked to his other top nine executives through an executive support system that provides on-line access not only to one another, but also to varying levels of daily sales, refinery, and financial data. External news summaries relevant to the business are entered into the system three times a day. Unlike Allaire, who limits his input to planning and review meetings, Wallace has used the system to take operating command of a few critical decisions for the business. In the volatile petroleum pricing arena, Wallace believes that he and his top executive team can confer with the advantage of data access and can make better pricing decisions than those further down the line. He cites increased profits in the tens of millions as a result of the system.

By far the majority of senior executives today do not use their systems in nearly as dramatic a manner as Allaire and Wallace do.[27] Yet the technology provides the capability for better coordination at the senior management level. It also provides opportunities to move decisions either up or down in the organization. Team decision making is a growing reality, as geographically separated executives can concurrently access and assess data and communicate in 'real-time.' Vertical on-line access to lower levels of data and text, however, violates some established management practices. Yet informal telephone-based systems have always provided some of this information. In an era where management is seen more as a cooperative, coaching activity than as an iron-fisted one, vertical as well as horizontal networking may come of age.

Within the IT organization itself

Line managers and information technology managers are also finding themselves more mutually dependent than ever before. Today, there is a small but rapidly growing number of senior line and staff executives who are taking responsibility for significant strategic projects centered on computer and communication technologies in their companies, divisions, or departments. We have described elsewhere the full extent and importance of 'the line taking the leadership.'[28]

As the line role is growing with regard to innovative systems, the role of the information systems group is becoming more complex, more demanding, and more integrated into the business. Our sample of companies included several firms whose IT planning efforts involved significant degrees of partnership between the line businesses and their IT organizations in designing and implementing new systems.[29] This necessary degree of partnership places four major demands on the IT organization.

First, with regard to systems development, even those systems in which the line is heavily involved require greater competence and skills on the part of the IT organization. The technical design, programming, and operation of business-citical, complex systems present a far greater challenge than do systems of previous eras. Today's integrated, cross-functional product delivery systems require database, project management, telecommunications, and other skills not previously demanded of IT personnel.

Second, today's new systems require the development and implementation of a general and eventually 'seamless,' information technology infrastructure (computers, telecommunications, software, and data). The challenge to IT management is to provide leadership for this vital set of 'roads and highways' in a volatile competitive environment.

Third, there is a need for IT management to help educate line management to its new responsibilities. And fourth, IT executives must educate themselves and their staffs in all significant aspects of the business. Only if this happens will IT personnel be able to knowledgeably assist line management in creating effective, strategy-enhancing systems.

The concomitant demand on line management is twofold: the need to learn enough about the technology to incorporate its capabilities into business plans, and the need to select effective information technology personnel and to work closely with them.

The new managerial agenda: think interdependence

Tomorrow's successful corporations will require increasingly effective management of interdependence. IT-enabled changes in cross-functional integration, in the use of teams, or in within-function integration will force individual managers' agendas to change as well. In short, what managers do now and what they will do in the future is in the process of important change.

Dimensions of change

What areas of emphasis for senior managers stem from the increasing interdependence of organizations? In our view, there are five.

● **Increased Role Complexity**. The typical manager's job is getting harder. One dimension of this difficulty is in the increased pace of organizational change. As companies seek new business opportunities by aggressively defining and executing 'new ways of doing things' – for example, new strategies, new products and services, new customers – managers must adjust more rapidly and frequently to new situations. Similarly, companies must also respond to heightened competitive pressures by improving internal processes. Again, managers must respond quickly to these new situations.

A second dimension of increased role complexity is the manager's need to cope with unclear lines of authority and decision making. As interdependence increases, sharing of tasks, roles, and decision making increases. Managers will be faced with making the difficult calls between what is local to their function and what is global to the business. Moreover, as planning and control systems change, line managers must work more effectively with a wider range of people in the firm.

● **Teamwork**. Teams are real. A vastly increased number of space-and time-spanning, problem-focused, task-oriented teams are becoming the norm. This growth in peer-to-peer (as opposed to hierarchical) activities requires new managerial skills and role definitions.

● **A Changing Measurement Process**. Measurement systems are also changing. Measuring individual, team, or sub-organizational success is difficult in an environment where cooperative work is increasingly necessary. New measurement approaches will have to be devised. A transitional period, during which people will need to adjust both to a changing work mode and to a changing measurement process, will result. As new measurement systems evolve, they will almost surely lag behind the changed organizational reality.

● **A Changing Planning Process**. Information technology is enabling the new planning approaches required to meet new competitive conditions. Our research underscores two major new capabilities. First, better information access and information management allow firms to target what is most critical to the organization. Second, organizations now have the ability to conduct 'real-time', stimulus-driven planning at all levels – in short, to bring key issues to the surface and react to them quickly. The technology provides both the conduit for moving critical data to all relevant decision makers and, more important, the capability to disseminate changes in direction to all parts of the firm.

● **Creating an Effective Information Technology Infrastructure**. People-intensive, integrative mechanisms are limited in what they can accomplish. Accessible, well-defined data and a transparent network are, therefore, the keys to effective integration in the coming years. Developing these resources, however, is not easy. Justifying organization spanning networks whose benefits are uncertain and will occur in the future, and whose costs cannot be atttributed clearly to any specific suborganization, is in part an act of faith. Developing common coding systems and data definitions is a herculean job. This task increases short-term costs for long-term gain – a practice not encouraged by most of today's measurement systems.

References

1 A precise definition of 'interdependence' has generated considerable disagreement among students of organizational behavior. An early and influential view is contained in J. D. Thompson. *Organization in Action. Social Science Bases of Administrative Theory* (New York: McGraw-Hill, 1967).
   Also see critiques of Thompson's work by:
   J. E. McCann and D. L. Ferry. 'An Approach for Assessing and Managing Inter-Unit Interdependence – Note,' *Academy of Management Journal* 4 (1979); and
   B. Victor and R. S. Blackburn, 'Interdependence: An Alternative Conceptualization,' *Academy of Management Journal* 12 (1987): 486–498.

2 'The Big Loss at Merrill Lynch: Why It Was Blindsided,' *Business Week.* 18 May 1987, pp. 112–113.
   See also 'Bankers Trust Restatement Tied to Trading Style.' *New York Times*, 22 July 1988. p. D2.

3 T. J. Peters and R. H. Waterman. Jr., *In Search of Excellence* (New York Harper & Row, 1982). p. 156.

4 H. J. Leavitt and T. L. Whistler, 'Management in the 1980s,' *Harvard Business Review.* November–December 1958, pp. 41–48.

5 For more on organizational centralization, see:
   M. Anshen. 'The Manager and the Black Box,' *Harvard Business Review*, November–December 1960. pp. 85–92;
   T. I. Whistler. *The Impact of Computers on Organizations* (New York Praeger, 1970);
   I. Russaoff Hoos, 'When the Computer Takes over the Office.' *Harvard Business Review*, July–August 1960, pp. 102–112.
   Also see D. Robey, 'Systems and Organizational Structure,' *Communication of the ACM* 24 (1981): 679-687.
   On organizational decentralization; see:
   J. F. Burlingame. 'Information Technology and Decentralization,' *Harvard Business Review*, November–December 1961, pp. 121–126.
   Also see J. L. King, 'Centralized versus Decentralized Computing: Organizational Considerations and Management Options,' *Computing Surveys* 15 (1983): 319–349.
   On reduced layers of middle or upper management, see C. A. Myers, ed., *The Impact of Computers on Management* (Cambridge, MA: MIT Press, 1967), pp. 1–15.
   On greater centralization of managerial power, see:
   A. M. Pettigrew, 'Information Control as a Power Resource,' *Sociology* 6 (1972); 187–204;
   J. Pfeffer, *Power in Organizations* (Marshfield, MA: Pitman, 1981); and
   M. L. Markus and J. Pfeffer, 'Power and the Design and Implementation of Accounting and Control Systems,' *Accounting, Organizations and Society* 8 (1983): 205–218.
   On Decentralization of Managerial Power, See S. R. Klatsky. 'Automation, Size and the Locus of Decision Making: The Cascade Effect,' *Journal of Business* 43 (1970): 141–151.

6 Carroll and Perin argue that what managers and employees *expect* from technology is an important predictor of the consequences observed.
   See J. S. Carroll and C. Perin, 'How Expectations about Microcomputers Influence Their Organizational Consequences' (Cambridge, MA: MIT Sloan School of Management, Management in the 1990s, working paper 90s: 88-044, April 1988).
   Similarly, Invernizzi found that the effectiveness of the process used to introduce technology into the organization strongly influenced its ultimate impact. See E. Ivernizzi, 'Information Technology: From Impact on to Support for Organizational Design' (Cambridge, MA: MIT Sloan School of Management, Management in the 1990s, working paper 90s: 88-057, September 1988).

7 R. B. Reich, 'Entrepreneurship Reconsidered: The Team as Hero,' *Harvard Business Review*, May–June 1987, pp. 77–83.

360 *Strategic Information Management*

8 P. F. Drucker. 'The Coming of the New Organization,' *Harvard Business Review*, January–February 1988, pp. 45–53.
9 M. Hammer and G. E. Mangurian. 'The Changing Value of Communications Technology,' *Sloan Management Review*, Winter 1987. pp. 65–72.
10 C. V. Bullen and R. R. Johansen, 'Groupware: A Key to Managing Business Teams?' (Cambridge, MA: MIT Sloan School of Management, Center for Information Systems Research, working paper No. 169, May 1988).
11 O. Hauptman and T. J. Allen, 'The Influence of Communication Technologies on Organizational Structure: A Conceptual Model for Future Research' (Cambridge, MA: MIT Sloan School of Management, Management in the 1990s, working paper 90s: 87-038, May 1987).
12 T. W. Malone, J. Yates, and R. I. Benjamin, 'Electronic Markets and Electronic Hierarchies,' *Communication of the ACM* 30 (1987): 484– 497.
13 R. Johnston and P. R. Lawrence. 'Beyond Vertical Integration – The Rise of the Value-Adding Partnership,' *Harvard Business Review*, July-August 1988, pp. 9–104.
14 T. Kumpe and P. T. Bolwijn, 'Manufacturing: The New Case for Vertical Integration,' *Harvard Business Review*, March–April 1988, pp. 75–81.
15 R. I. Benjamin and M. S. Scott Morton, 'Information Technology. Integration, and Organizational Change' (Cambridge, MA: MIT Sloan School of Management, Center for Information Systems Research, working paper No. 138. April 1986).
Also see S. Kiesler, 'The Hidden Message in Computer Networks,' *Harvard Business Review*, January–February 1986, pp. 46–60.
16 H. Mintzberg. *The Structuring of Organizations* (Englewood Cliffs, NJ: Prentice-Hall, 1979).
17 P. R. Lawrence and J. W. Lorsch, *Organization and Environment: Managing Differentiation and Integration* (Homewood, Il.: Richard D. Irwin, 1967).
18 J. Galbraith, *Organization Design* (Reading, MA: Addison-Wesley, 1977). Galbraith also introduced the concept of the organization as information processor in this work. He distinguished computer-based, vertical information systems from lateral relations and emphasized the division of organizations into suborganizations because of the need to minimize the cost of communications.
19 S. Barrett and B. R. Konsynski, 'Inter-Organizations Information Sharing Systems,' *MIS Quarterly* 4 (1982): 93–105;
R. I. Benjamin, D. W. DeLong, and M. S. Scott Morton. 'The Realities of Electronic Data Interhange: How Much Competitive Advantage?' (Cambridge, MA: MIT Sloan School of Management, Management in the 1990s, working paper 90s: 87-038, February 1988).
See also N. Venkatraman. 'Changing Patterns of Interfirm Competition and Collaboration' (Cambridge, MA. MIT Sloan School of Management, Management in the 1990s, working paper, forthcoming).
20 On quality process management, see G. A. Pall 'Quality Process Management' (Thornwood, NY. The Quality Improvement Education Center, IBM. 16 February 1988).
21 Although our three collapsed segments in the value chain are integral units, data does flow from one to another. The three segments are also interdependent, but less strongly so than the functions within each segment.
22 'Otis MIS: Going Up,' *Information Week*. 18 May 1987, pp. 32–37.
J. F. Rockart, 'The Lane Takes the Leadership – IS Management in a Wired Society.' *Sloan Management Review*, Summer 1988, pp. 57–64.
W. F. McFarlan. 'How Information Technology is Changing Management Control Systems' (Boston Harvard Business School, Case Note No. 9-187-139, 1987).
23 Rockart (1988).
24 Drucker (1988).
25 Bullen and Johansen (1988).
26 R. N. Anthony. *Planning and Control Systems. A Framework for Analysis* (Boston: Harvard University Press, 1965).

27 J. F. Rockart and D. W. Delong. *Executive Support Systems. The Emergence of Top Management Computer Use* (Homewood, Il. Dow Jones-Irwin, 1988).
28 Rockart (1988).
29 T. J. Main and J. E. Short, 'Managing the Merger Strategic I/S Planning for the New Baxter' (Cambridge, MA. MIT Sloan School of Management, Center for Information Systems Research, working paper No. 178, September 1988).

17 Managing information technology evaluation – techniques and processes

L. Willcocks

As far as I am concerned we could write off our IT expenditure over the last five years to the training budget. (Senior executive, quoted by Earl, 1990).

. . . the area of measurement is the biggest single failure of information systems while it is the single biggest issue in front of our board of directors. I am frustrated by our inability to measure cost and benefit. (Head of IT: AT and T quoted in Coleman and Jamieson, 1991).

Introduction

Information Technology (IT) now represents substantial financial investment. By 1993, UK company expenditure on IT was exceeding £12 billion per year, equivalent to an average of over 1.5% of annual turnover. Public sector IT spend, excluding Ministry of Defence operational equipment, was over £2 billion per year, or 1% of total public expenditure. The size and continuing growth in IT investments, coupled with a recessionary climate and concerns over cost containment from early 1990, have served to place IT issues above the parapet in most organizations, perhaps irretrievably. Understandably, senior managers need to question the returns from such investments and whether the IT route has been and can be, a wise decision.

This is reinforced in those organizations where IT investment has been a high risk, hidden cost process, often producing disappointed expectations. This is a difficult area about which to generalize, but research studies suggest that at least 20% of expenditure is wasted and between 30-40% of IT projects realize no net benefits, however measured (for reviews of research see Willcocks, 1993). The reasons for failure to deliver on IT potential can

An earlier version of this chapter appeared in the *European Management Journal* Vol. 10, No. 2, June, pp. 220 - 229.

be complex. However major barriers, identified by a range of studies, occur in how the IT investment is evaluated and controlled (see for example Grindley, 1991; Kearney, 1990; Wilson, 1991). These barriers are not insurmountable. The purpose of this chapter is to report on recent research and indicate ways forward.

Evaluation: emerging problems

Taking a management perspective, evaluation is about establishing by quantitative and/or qualitative means the worth of IT to the organization. Evaluation brings into play notions of costs, benefits, risk and value. It also implies an organizational process by which these factors are assessed, whether formally or informally.

There are major problems in evaluation. Many organizations find themselves in a Catch 22. For competitive reasons they cannot afford not to invest in IT, but economically they cannot find sufficient justification, and evaluation practice cannot provide enough underpinning, for making the investment. One thing all informed commentators agree on: there are no reliable measures for assessing the impact of IT. At the same time there are a number of common problem areas that can be addressed. Our own research shows the following to be the most common:

- Inappropriate measures
- Budgeting practice conceals full costs
- Understating human and organizational costs
- Understating knock-on costs
- Overstating costs
- Neglecting 'intangible' benefits
- Not fully investigating risk
- Failure to devote evaluation time and effort to a major capital asset
- Failure to take into account time-scale of likely benefits.

This list is by no means exhaustive of the problems faced (a full discussion of these problems and others appears in Willcocks, 1992a). Most occur through neglect, and once identified are relatively easy to rectify. A more fundamental and all too common failure is in not relating IT needs to the information needs of the organization. This relates to the broader issue of strategic alignment.

Strategy and information systems

The *organizational investment climate* has a key bearing on how investment is organized and conducted, and what priorities are assigned to different IT investment proposals. This is affected by:

- the financial health and market position of the organization;
- industry sector pressures;
- the organizational business strategy and direction;
- the management and decision-making culture.

As an example of the second, 1989-90 research by Datasolve showed IT investment priorities in the retail sector focusing mainly on achieving more timely information, in financial services around better quality service to customers, and in manufacturing on more complete information for decision-making. As to decision-making culture, senior management attitude to risk can range from conservative to innovative, their decision-making styles from directive to consensus-driven (Butler Cox, 1990). As one example, conservative consensus-driven management would tend to take a relatively slow, incremental approach, with large-scale IT investment being unlikely. The third factor will be focused on here, that is creating a strategic climate in which IT investments can be related to organizational direction. Shaping the context in which IT evaluation is conducted is a necessary, frequently neglected prelude to then applying appropriate evaluation techniques and approaches. This section focuses on a few valuable pointers and approaches that work in practice to facilitate IT investment decisions that add value to the organization.

Alignment

A fundamental starting point is the need for alignment of business/ organizational needs, what is done with IT, and plans for human resources, organizational structures and processes. The highly publicized 1990 Landmark Study tends to conflate these into alignment of business, organization and IT strategies (Scott Morton, 1991; Walton, 1989). A simpler approach is to suggest that the word 'strategy' should be used only when these different plans are aligned. There is much evidence to suggest that such alignment rarely exists. In a study of 86 UK companies Ernst and Young (1990) found only two aligned. Detailed research also shows lack of alignment to be a common problem in public sector informatization (Willcocks, 1992b). The case of an advertising agency (cited by Willcocks and Mason, 1994) provides a useful illustrative example:

Case: An advertising agency
In the mid-1980s this agency installed accounting and market forecasting systems at a cost of nearly £100,000. There was no real evaluation of the worth of the IT to the business. It was installed largely because one director had seen similar systems running at a competitor. Its existing systems had been perfectly adequate and the market forecasting system ended up being used just to impress clients. At the same time as the

system was being installed the agency sacked over 36 staff and asked its managers not to spend more than £200 a week on expenses. The company was taken over in 1986. Clearly there had been no integrated plan on the business, human resource, organizational and IT fronts. This passed on into its IT evaluation practice. In the end the IT amplifier effect may well have operated. IT was not used to address the core, or indeed any, of the needs of the business. A bad management was made correspondingly worse by the application of IT.

One result of such lack of alignment is that IT evaluation practice tends to become separated from business needs and plans on the one hand, and from organizational realities that can influence IT implementation and subsequent effectiveness on the other. Both need to be included in IT evaluation, and indeed are in the more comprehensive evaluation methods, notably the information economics approach (see below).

Another critical alignment is that between what is done with IT and how that fits with the information needs of the organization. Most management attention has tended to fall on the 'technology' rather than the 'information' element in what is called IT. Hochstrasser and Griffiths (1991) found in their sample no single company with a fully developed and comprehensive strategy on information. Yet it would seem to be difficult to perform a meaningful evaluation of IT investment without some corporate control framework establishing information requirements in relationship to business/organizational goals and purpose, prioritization of information needs and, for example, how cross-corporate information flows need to be managed. An information strategy directs IT investment, and establishes policies and priorities against which investment can be assessed. It may also help to establish that some information needs can be met without the IT vehicle.

IT Strategic Grid

The McFarlan and McKenney (1983) grid is a much-travelled, but useful framework for focusing management attention on the IT evaluation question: where does and will IT give us added value? A variant is shown below in Figure 1.

Cases: Two manufacturing companies

Used by the author with a group of senior managers in a pharmaceutical company, it was found that too much investment had been allowed on turnaround projects. In a period of downturn in business it was recognized that the investment in the previous three years should have been in strategic systems. It was resolved to tighten and refocus IT evaluation practice. In a highly decentralized multinational mainly in the printing/publishing industry, it was found that most of the twenty businesses were investing in factory and support systems. In a recessionary climate competitors were not forcing the issue on other types of system, the company was not strong on IT-know-how, and it was decided that the risk-averse policy on IT evaluation, with strong emphasis on cost justification should continue.

The strategic grid is useful for classifying systems then demonstrating, through discussion, where IT investment has been made and where it should be applied. It can help to demonstrate that IT investments are not being made into core systems, or into business growth or competitiveness. It can also help to indicate that there is room for IT investment in more speculative ventures, given the spread of investment risk across different systems. It may also provoke management into spending more, or less, on IT. One frequent outcome is a demand to reassess which evaluation techniques are more appropriate to different types of system.

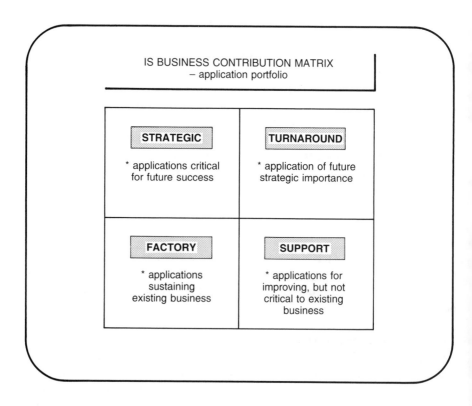

Figure 1. Strategic grid analysis

Value chain

Porter and Millar (1991) have also been useful in establishing the need for value chain analysis. This looks at where value is generated inside the organization, but also in its external relationships, for example with suppliers and customers. Thus the primary activities of a typical manufacturing company may be: inbound logistics, operations, outbound logistics, marketing and sales, and service. Support activities will be: firm infrastructure, human resource management, technology development and procurement. The question here is what can be done to add value within and across these activities? As every value activity has both a physical and an information-processing component, it is clear that the opportunities for value-added IT investment may well be considerable. Value chain analysis helps to focus attention on where these will be.

IT investment mapping

Another method of relating IT investment to organizational/business needs has been developed by Peters (1993). The basic dimensions of the map were arrived at after reviewing the main investment concerns arising on over 50 IT projects. The benefits to the organization appeared as one of the most frequent attributes of the IT investment (see Figure 2).

Thus one dimension of the map is benefits ranging from the more tangible arising from productivity enhancing applications to the less tangible from business expansion applications. Peters also found that the orientation of the investment toward the business was also frequently used in evaluation. He classifies these as *infrastructure* e.g. telecommunications, software/hardware environment; *business operations* e.g. finance and accounts, purchasing, processing orders; and *market influencing* e.g. increasing repeat sales, improving distribution channels. Figure 3 shows the map being used in a hypothetical example to compare current and planned business strategy in terms of investment orientation and benefits required, against current and planned IT investment strategy.

Mapping can reveal gaps and overlaps in these two areas and help senior management to get them more closely aligned. As a further example:

a company with a clearly defined, product-differentiated strategy of innovation would do well to reconsider IT investments which appeared to show undue bias towards a price-differentiated strategy of cost reduction and enhancing productivity.

Multiple methodology

Finally, Earl (1989) wisely opts for a multiple methodology approach to IS strategy formulation. This again helps us in the aim of relating IT investment more closely with the strategic aims and direction of the organization and its key needs. One element here is a *top-down approach*. Thus a critical success

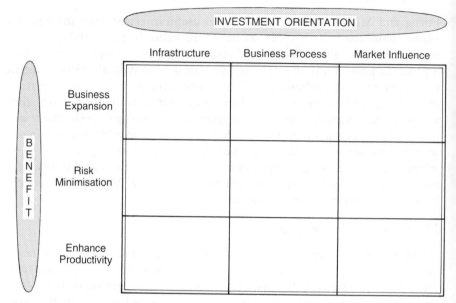

Figure 2. Investment mapping

factors analysis might be used to establish key business objectives, decompose these into critical success factors, then establish the IS needs that will drive these CSFs. A *bottom-up evaluation* would start with an evaluation of current systems. This may reveal gaps in the coverage by systems, for example in the marketing function or in terms of degree of integration of systems across functions. Evaluation may also find gaps in the technical quality of systems and in their business value. This permits decisions on renewing, removing, maintaining or enhancing current sysems. The final leg of Earl's multiple methodology is *'inside-out innovation'*. The purpose here is to 'identify opportunities afforded by IT which may yield competitive advantage or create new strategic options'. The purpose of the whole threefold methodology is, through an internal and external analysis of needs and opportunities, to relate the development of IS applications to business/organizational need and strategy.

Evaluating feasibility: findings

The right 'strategic climate' is a vital prerequisite for evaluating IT projects at their feasibility stage. Here, we find out how organizations go about IT feasibility evaluation and what pointers for improved practice can be gained from the accumulated evidence. The picture is not an encouraging one. Organizations have found it increasingly difficult to justify the costs

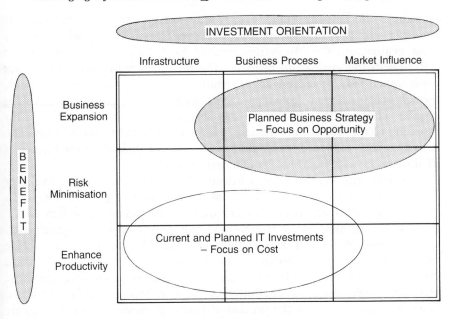

Figure 3. Investment map comparing business and IT plans

surrounding the purchase, development and use of IT. The value of IT/IS investments are more often justified by faith alone, or perhaps what adds up to the same thing, by understating costs and using mainly notional figures for benefit realization (see Farbey et al., 1992; PA Consulting, 1990; Price Waterhouse, 1989; Strassmann, 1990; Willcocks and Lester, 1993).

Willcocks and Lester (1993) looked at 50 organizations drawn from a cross-section of private and public sector manufacturing and services. Subsequently this research was extended into a follow-up interview programme. Some of the consolidated results are recorded in what follows. We found all organizations completing evaluation at the feasibility stage, though there was a fall off in the extent to which evaluation was carried out at later stages. This means that considerable weight falls on getting the feasibility evaluation right. High levels of satisfaction with evaluation methods were recorded. However, these perceptions need to be qualified by the fact that only 8% of organizations measured the impact of the evaluation, that is could tell us whether the IT investment subsequently achieved a higher or lower return than other non-IT investments. Additionally there emerged a range of inadequacies in evaluation practice at the feasiblity stage of projects. The most common are shown in Figure 4.

Senior managers increasingly talk of, and are urged toward, the strategic use of IT. This means doing new things, gaining a competitive edge, and becoming more effective, rather than using IT merely to automate routine operations, do existing things better, and perhaps reduce the headcount. However only 16% of organizations used over four criteria on which to base their evaluation. Cost/benefit was used by 62% as their predominant criterion in the evaluation process. *The survey evidence here suggests that organization may be missing IS opportunities, but also taking on large risks, through utilizing narrow evaluation approaches that do not clarify and assess less tangible inputs and benefits.* There was also little evidence of a concern for assessing risk in any formal manner. However the need to see and evaluate risks and 'soft' hidden costs would seem to be essential, given the history of IT investment as a 'high risk, hidden cost' process.

A sizable minority of organizations (44%) did not include the user department in the evaluation process at the feasibility stage. This cuts off a vital source of information and critique on the degree to which an IT proposal is organizationally feasible and will deliver on user requirements. Only a small minority of organizations accepted IT proposals from a wide variety of groups and individuals. In this respect most ignored the third element in Earl's multiple methodology (see above). Despite the large literature emphasizing consultation with the workforce as a source of ideas, know-how and as part of the process of reducing resistance to change, only 36% of organizations consulted users about evaluation at the feasibility stage, while only 18% consulted unions. While the majority of organizations (80%) evaluated IT investments against organizational objectives, only 22% acted strategically in considering objectives from the bottom to the top, that is evaluated the value of IT projects against all of organization, departmental individual management, and end-user objectives. This again could have consequences for the effectiveness and usability of the resulting systems, and the levels of resistance experienced.

Finally, most organizations endorsed the need to assess the competitive edge implied by an IT project. However, somewhat inconsistently, only 4% considered customer objectives in the evaluation process at the feasibility stage. This finding is interesting in relationship to our analysis that the majority of IT investment in the respondent organizations were directed at achieving internal efficiencies. It may well be that the nature of the evaluation techniques, but also the evaluation *process* adopted, had influential roles to play in this outcome.

Linking strategy and feasibility techniques

Much work has been done to break free from the limitations of the more traditional, finance-based forms of capital investment appraisal. The major concerns seem to be to relate evaluation techniques to the type of IT project, and to develop techniques that relate the IT investment to business/organization value. A further development is in more sophisticated ways of including risk assessment in the evaluation procedures for IT

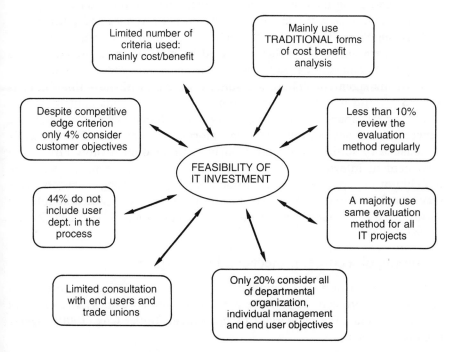

Figure 4. IT evaluation: feasibility findings

investment. *A method of evaluation needs to be reliable, that is consistent in its measurement over time, able to discriminate between good and indifferent investments, able to measure what it purports to measure, and be administratively/organizationally feasible in its application.*

Return on management

Strassman (1990) has done much iconoclastic work in the attempt to modernize IT investment evaluation. He concludes that:

> Many methods for giving advice about computers have one thing in common. They serve as a vehicle to facilitate proposals for additional funding . . . the current techniques ultimately reflect their origins in a technology push from the experts, vendors, consultants, instead of a 'strategy' pull from the profit centre managers.

He has produced the very interesting concept of Return on Management (ROM). ROM is a measure of performance based on the added value to an organization provided by management. Strassman's assumption here is that in the modern organization information costs *are* the costs of managing the enterprise. If ROM is calculated before then after IT is applied to an organization then the IT contribution to the business, so difficult to isolate using more traditional measures, can assessed. ROM is calculated in several stages. First, using the organization's financial results, the total value-added is established. This is the difference between net revenues and payments to external suppliers. The contribution of capital is then separated from that of labour. Operating costs are then deducted from labour value-added to leave management value-added. ROM is management value-added divided by the costs of management. There are some problems with how this figure is arrived at, and whether it really represents what IT has contributed to business performance. For example, there are difficulties in distinguishing between operational and management information. Perhaps ROM is merely a measure in some cases, and a fairly indirect one, of how effectively management information is used. A more serious criticism lies with the usability of the approach and its attractiveness to practising managers. This may be reflected in its lack of use, at least in the UK, as identified in different surveys (see Butler Cox, 1990; Coleman and Jamieson, 1991; Willcocks and Lester, 1993).

Matching objectives, projects and techniques

A major way forward on IT evaluation is to match techniques to objectives and types of projects. A starting point is to allow business strategy and purpose to define the category of IT investment. Butler Cox (1990) suggest five main purposes:

1) surviving and functioning as a business;
2) improving business performance by cost reduction/increasing sales;
3) achieving a competitive leap;
4) enabling the benefits of other IT investments to be realized;
5) being prepared to compete effectively in the future.

The matching IT investments can then be categorised, respectively, as:

1 *Mandatory investments*, for example accounting systems to permit reporting within the organization, regulatory requirements demanding VAT recording systems; competitive pressure making a system obligatory e.g. EPOS amongst large retail outlets.
2 *Investments to improve performance*, for example Allied Dunbar and several UK insurance companies have introduced laptop computers for sales people, partly with the aim of increasing sales.
3 *Competitive edge investments* for example SABRE at American Airlines, and Merrill Lynch's cash management account system in the mid-1980s.
4 *Infrastructure investments*. These are important to make because they give organizations several more degrees of freedom to manoeuvre in the future.

5   *Research investments.* In our sample we found a bank and three
    companies in the computer industry waiving normal capital investment
    criteria on some IT projects, citing their research and learning value.
    The amounts were small and referred to case tools in one case, and
    expert systems in the others.

There seems to be no shortage of such classifications now available. One
of the more simple but useful is the sixfold classification shown in Figure 5.

Once assessed against, and accepted as aligned with required business
purpose, a specific IT investment can be classified, then fitted on to the cost-
benefit map (Figure 5 is meant to be suggestive only). This will assist in
identifying where the evaluation emphasis should fall. For example, an
'efficiency' project could be adequately assessed utilizing traditional financial
investment appraisal approaches; a different emphasis will be required in the
method chosen to assess a 'competitive edge' project. Figure 6 is one view of
the possible spread of appropriateness of some of the evaluation methods
now available.

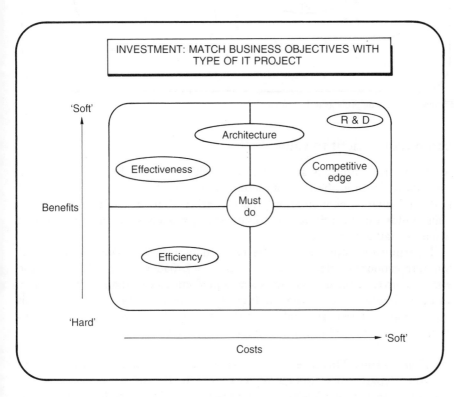

Figure 5. Classifying IT projects

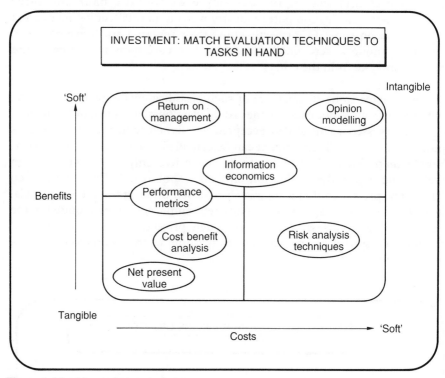

Figure 6. Matching projects to techniques

From cost-benefit to value

A particularly ambitious attempt to deal with many of the problems in IT evaluation – both at the level of methodology and of process – is represented in the information economics approach (Parker, Benson and Trainor, 1988). This builds on the critique of traditional approaches, without jettisoning where the latter may be useful.

Information economics looks beyond benefit to value. Benefit is a 'discrete economic effect'. Value is seen as a broader concept based on the effect IT investment has on the business performance of the enterprise. How value is arrived at is shown in Figure 7. The first stage is building on traditional cost benefit analysis with four highly relevant techniques to establish an enhanced return on investment calculation. These are:

(a) *Value linking*. This assesses IT costs which create additional benefits to other departments through ripple, knock-on effects.
(b) *Value acceleration*. This assesses additional benefits in the form of reduced time-scales for operations.

(c) *Value restructuring.* Techniques are used to measure the benefit of restructing a department, jobs or personnel usage as a result of introducing IT. This technique is particularly helpful where the relationship to performance is obscure or not established. R&D, legal and personnel are examples of departments where this may be usefully applied.

(d) *Innovation valuation.* This considers the value of gaining and sustaining a competitive advantage, while calculating the risks or cost of being a pioneer and of the project failing.

Information economics then enhances the cost-benefit analysis still further through business domain and technology domain assessments. These are shown in Figure 7. Here *strategic match* refers to assessing the degree to which the proposed project corresponds to established goals; *competitive advantage* to assessing the degree to which the proposed project provides an advantage in the marketplace; *management information* to assessing the contribution toward the management need for information on core activities; *competitive response* to assessing the degree of corporate risk associated with not undertaking the project; and *strategic architecture* to measuring the degree to which the proposed project fits into the overall information systems direction.

Case: Truck leasing company

As an example of what happens when such factors and business domain assessment are neglected in the evaluation, Parker *et al.* (1988) point to the case of a large US truck leasing company. Here they found that on a 'hard' ROI analysis IT projects on preventative maintenance, route scheduling and despatching went top of the list. When a business domain assessment was carried out by line managers customer/sales profile system was evaluated as having the largest potential effect on business performance. An important infrastructure project – a Database 2 conversion/installation – also scored highly where previously it was scored bottom of eight project options. Clearly the evaluation technique and process can have a significant business impact where economic resources are finite and prioritization and drop decisions become inevitable.

The other categories in Figure 7 can be briefly described:

- *Organizational risk* – looking at how equipped the organization is to implement the project in terms of personnel, skills and experience.
- *IS infrastructure risk* – assessing how far the entire IS organization needs, and is prepared to support, the project.

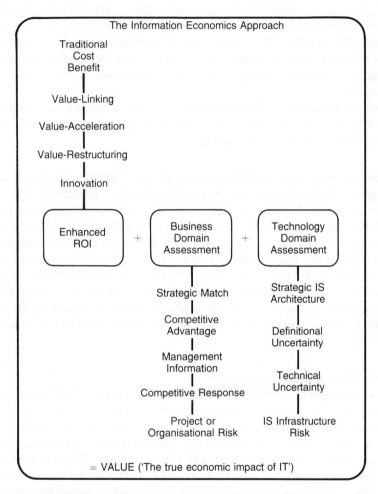

Figure 7. The information economics approach

- *Definitional uncertainty* – assessing the degree to which the requirements and/or the specifications of the project are known. Incidentally, research into more than 130 organizations shows this to be a primary barrier to the effective delivery of IT (Willcocks, 1993). Also assessed are the complexity of the area and the probability of non-routine changes.
- *Technical uncertainty* – evaluating a project's dependence on new or untried technologies.

Information economics provides an impressive array of concepts and techniques for assessing the business value of proposed IT investments. The concern for fitting IT evaluation into a corporate planning process and for bringing both business managers and IS professionals into the assessment process is also very welcome.

Some of the critics of information economics suggest that it may be over-mechanistic if applied to all projects. It can be time-consuming and, may lack credibility with senior management, particularly given the subjective basis of much of the scoring. The latter problem is also inherent in the process of arriving at the weighting of the importance to assign to the different factors before scoring begins. Additionally there are statistical problems with the suggested scoring methods. For example, a scoring range of 1/5 may do little to differentiate between the ROI of two different projects. Moreover, even if a project scores nil on one risk e.g. organizational risk, and in practice this risk may sink the project, the overall assessment by information economics may cancel out the impact of this score and show the IT investment to be a reasonable one. Clearly much depends on careful interpretion of the results, and much of the value for decision-makers and stakeholders may well come from the raised awareness of issues from undergoing the process of evaluation rather than from its statistical outcome. Another problem area may lie in the truncated assessment of organizational risk. Here, for example, there is no explicit assessment of the likelihood of a project to engender resistance to change because of, say, its job reduction or work restructuring implications. This may be compounded by the focus on bringing user managers, but one suspects not lower level users, into the assessment process.

Much of the criticism, however, ignores how adaptable the basic information economics framework can be to particular organizational circumstances and needs. Certainly this has been a finding in trials in organizations as varied as British Airports Authority, a Central Government Department and a major food retailer.

Case: Retail food company

In the final case Ong (1991) investigated a three phase branch stock management system. Some of the findings are instructive. Managers suggested including the measurement of risk associated with interfacing systems and the difficulties in gaining user acceptance of the project. In practice few of the managers could calculate the enhanced ROI because of the large amount of data required and, in a large organization, its spread across different locations. Some felt the evaluation was time-independent; different results could be expected at different times. The assessment of risk needed to be expanded to include not only technical and project risk but also the risk/impact of failure to an organization of its size. In its highly competitive industry any unfavourable venture can have serious knock-on impacts and most firms tend to be risk-conscious, even risk-averse.

Such findings tend to reinforce the view that information economics provides one of the more comprehensive approaches to assessing the potential value to the organization of its IT investments, but that it needs to be tailored, developed, in some cases extended, to meet evaluation needs in different organizatons. Even so, information economics remains a major contribution to advancing modern evaluation practice.

CODA: From development to routine operations

This chapter has focused primarily on the front-end of evaluation practice and how it can be improve. In research on evaluation beyond the feasibility stage of projects, we have found evaluation variously carried on through four main additional stages. Respondent organizations supported the notion of an evaluation learning cycle, with evaluation at each stage feeding into the next to establish a learning spiral across time – useful for controlling a specific project, but also for building organizational know-how on IT and its management (see Figure 8). The full research findings are detailed elsewhere (see Willcocks and Lester, 1993). However, some of the limitations in evaluation techniques and processes discovered are worth commenting on here.

We found only weak linkage between evaluations carried out at different stages. As one example, 80% of organizations had experienced abandoning projects at the development stage due to negative evaluation. The major reasons given were changing organizational or user needs and/or 'gone over budget'. When we reassembled data, abandonment clearly related to underplaying these objectives at the feasibility stage. Furthermore, all organizations abandoning projects because 'over budget' depended heavily on cost-benefit in their earlier feasibility evaluation, thus probably understating development and second-order costs. We found only weak evidence of organizations applying their development stage evaluation, and indeed their experiences at subsequent stages, to improving feasibility evaluation techniques and processes.

Key stakeholers were often excluded from the evaluation process. For example, only 9% of organizations included the user departments/users in development evaluation. At the implementation stage 31% do not include user departments, 52% exclude the IT department, and only 6% consult trade unions. There seemed to be a marked fall-off in attention given to, and the results of, evaluation across later stages. Thus 20% do not carry out evaluation at the post-implementation stage, some claiming there was little point in doing so. Of the 56% who learn from their mistakes at this stage, 25% do so from 'informal evaluation'. At the routine operations stage, only 20% use in their evaluation criteria systems capability, systems availability, organizational needs and departmental needs.

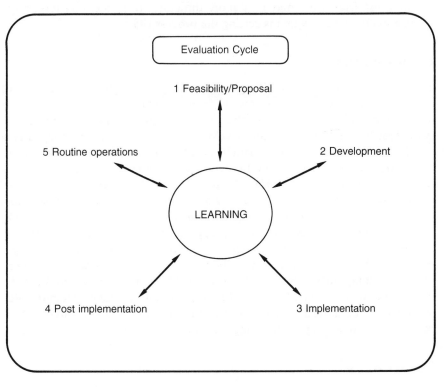

Figure 8. The evaluation cycle

These, together with our detailed findings, suggest a number of guidelines on how evaluation practice can be improved beyond the feasibility stage. At a minimum these include:

1 Linking evaluation across stages and time – this enables 'islands of evaluation' to become integrated and mutually informative, while building into the overall evaluation process possibilities for continuous improvement.

2 Many organizations can usefully reconsider the degree to which key stakeholders are participants in evaluation at all stages.

3 The relative neglect given to assessing the actual against the posited impact of IT, and the fall-off in interest in evaluation at later stages, mean that the effectiveness of feasibility evaluation becomes difficult to assess and difficult to improve. The concept of learning would seem central to evaluation practice but tends to be applied in a fragmented way.

4 The increasing clamour for adequate evaluation techniques is necessary, but may reveal a quick-fix orientation to the problem. It can shift

attention from what may be a more difficult, but in the long term more value-added area, which is getting the process right.

Conclusions

The high expenditure on IT, growing usage that goes to the core of organizational functioning, together with disappointed expectations about its impact have all served to raise the profile of how IT investment can be evaluated. It is not only an underdeveloped, but also an undermanaged area which organizations can increasingly ill-afford to neglect. There are well-established traps that can now be avoided. *Organizations need to shape the context in which effective evaluation practice can be conducted. Traditional techniques cannot be relied upon in themselves to assess the types of technologies and how they are increasingly being applied in organizational settings. A range of modern techniques can be tailored and applied. However, techniques can only complement, not substitute for developing evaluation as a process, and the deeper organizational learning about IT that entails.* Past evaluation practice has been geared to asking questions about the price of IT. Increasingly it produces less than useful answers. The future challenge is to move to the problem of value of IT to the organization, and build techniques and processes that can go some way to answering the resulting questions.

References

Butler Cox Foundation (1990). Getting value from information technology. Research Report 75, June, Butler Cox, London.

Coleman T. and Jamieson, M. (1991). Information systems: evaluating intangible benefits at the feasibility stage of project appraisal. Unpublished MBA thesis, City University Business School, London.

Earl, M. (1989). Management Strategies for Information Technology, Prentice Hall, London.

Earl, M. (1990). Education: The foundation for effective IT strategies. IT and the new manager conference. Computer Weekly/Business Intelligence, June, London.

Ernst and Young, (1990). Strategic Alignment Report: UK Survey, Ernst and Young, London.

Farbey, B., Land, F. and Targett, D. (1992). Evaluating investments in IT. Journal of Information Technology, 7(2), 100-112.

Grindley, K. (1991). Managing IT at Board Level, Pitman, London.

Hochstrasser, B. and Griffiths, C. (1991). Controlling IT Investments: Strategy and Management, Chapman and Hall, London.

Kearney, A. T. (1990). Breaking the Barriers: IT Effectiveness in Great Britain and Ireland, A T Kearney/CIMA, London.

McFarlan, F. nd McKenney, J. (1983). Corporate Information Systems Management: The Issues Facing Senior Executives, Dow Jones Irwin, New York.

Ong, D. (1991). Evaluating IS investments: a case study in applying the information economics approach. Unpublished thesis, City University, London.

PA Consulting Group, (1990). The Impact of the Current Climate on IT – The Survey Report. PA Consulting Group, London.

Parker, M., Benson, R., and Trainor, H. (1988). Information Economics, Prentice Hall, London.

Peters, G. (1993). Evaluating your computer investment strategy. In Willcocks L. (ed.) Information Management: Evaluation of Information Systems Investments, Chapman and Hall, London, pp. 99 – 112.

Porter, M. and Millar, V. (1991). How information gives you competitive advantage. In McGowan, W. Revolution in Real Time: Managing Information Technology in the 1990s, Harvard Business School Pres, Boston, pp. 59-82.

Price Waterhouse (1989). Information Technology Review 1989/90, Price Waterhouse, London.

Scott Morton, M. (ed.) (1991). The Corporation of the 1990s. Oxford University Press, Oxford.

Strassman, P. (1990). The Business Value of Computers. The Information Economics Press, New Canaan.

Walton, R. (1989). Up and Running, Harvard Business School Press, Boston.

Willcocks, L. (1992a). Evaluating information technology investments: research findings and reappraisal. Journal of Information Systems, 2(3), 242-268.

Willocks, L. (1992b). The manager as technologist? In Willcocks, L. and Harrow, J. (eds) Rediscovering Public Services Management, McGraw Hill, London.

Willcocks, L. (ed.) (1993). Information Management: Evaluation of Information Systems Investments, Chapman and Hall, London.

Willcocks, L. and Lester, S. (1993). Evaluation and control of IS investments. OXIIM Research and Discussion Paper 93/5, Templeton College, Oxford.

Willcocks, L. and Mason, D. (1994). Computerising Work: People, Systems Design and Workplace Relations (2nd edition), Alfred Waller Publications, Oxford.

Wilson, T. (1991). Overcoming the barriers to implementation of information systems strategies. Journal of Information Technology, 6(1), 39-44.

Author index

Subject index